THE SCHOOL LEADER IN ACTION

THE SCHOOL LEADER IN ACTION
Discovering the Golden Mean

David L. Cattanach, Ph.D.

TECHNOMIC
PUBLISHING CO., INC.

LANCASTER · BASEL

The School Leader in Action

a **TECHNOMIC** °publication

Published in the Western Hemisphere by
Technomic Publishing Company, Inc.
851 New Holland Avenue, Box 3535
Lancaster, Pennsylvania 17604 U.S.A.

Distributed in the Rest of the World by
Technomic Publishing AG
Missionsstrasse 44
CH-4055 Basel, Switzerland

Printed in the United States of America
10 9 8 7 6 5 4 3 2 1

Main entry under title:
    The School Leader in Action: Discovering the Golden Mean

A Technomic Publishing Company book
Bibliography: p.
Includes index p. 521

Library of Congress Catalog Card No. 95-61925
ISBN No. 1-56676-343-6

*To today's educators, to those yet to come, and to the real hope that
all may find "golden means" for each of the issues
and problems they face, and will face, every day, of every year,
of every decade of their professional lives.
It also remembers educators from earlier eras who dedicated their
careers and themselves to public education and to
American children and youth.*

CONTENTS

AM I READY YET?[1]

Once upon a time, there was a school superintendent.
He had a good digestion and a pleasant disposition too.
He never blew his police whistle at administrative meetings, or wore
sneakers with dragging laces, or walked quietly so no one could hear
him coming.
He never required fire drills in the rain.

His mentor, an old superintendent, said the young fellow should aspire
to sharing his wisdom with others.
He said, "You should write a book, but your attitude needs adjusting,
and you must be ready.
To prepare yourself, study me; I'll show you how it's done."
So he did.

Soon after, the old superintendent called the young one and asked how
he was getting along.
The young superintendent said, "I'm fine, but the principals say I'm
autocratic, am I ready yet?"
His mentor said, no, he wasn't nearly ready yet.

Some time later, the old superintendent again asked his protege how
he was.
The young man said, "The high school principal asked me for help with
an incompetent teacher, and I told her not to bother me with that
because my back hurt, and that she had lipstick on her teeth, am I
ready yet?"

The old superintendent said, no, he wasn't ready yet.
A few years went by, and the younger superintendent said, "I made my
secretary type fourteen drafts of a speech, and the final version was
identical to the first, am I ready yet?"
The older superintendent said, no, he wasn't ready yet.

[1]With apologies to Ogden Nash for my educational parody of "The Strange Case of the Ambitious Caddy" from *I'm a Stranger Here Myself*, Boston: Little, Brown and Company, 1938, pp. 159–161.

Still later, the younger superintendent said, "I criticized each principal's goals for the year, and told those who typed them to do them over again by hand and those who wrote in longhand to have them typed, and when they turned them in again I said obscenities twice to each, am I ready yet?
The older superintendent said, no, he wasn't ready yet.

Some years after, the now middle-aged superintendent said, "I turned on the air conditioner in the central office while it snowed outside and swore at everyone who called me on the phone, am I ready yet?"
The now ancient superintendent said, no, he wasn't ready yet.

Not long thereafter, the still middle-aged superintendent said, "I slept through three board of education meetings this month, insulted three town officials, and ignored seven parent phone calls, am I ready yet?"
His still ancient mentor said, no, not quite.

A bit later, the now late middle-aged superintendent said, "I bet a teacher ten dollars that her principal would have a nervous breakdown within the year, and I told the principal of the bet, am I ready yet?"

The now really ancient superintendent whispered, "Have you still your autocratic mien and chronic backache; your easy willingness to inflict discomfort on all around you; your arbitrary and capricious manner and your pride in never responding the same way twice; your constant self-pitying demeanor from feigned overwork, your penchant for loud swearing at inappropriate times, and your total contempt for all opinions but your own?"
The now late middle-aged superintendent said, yes, he did.

"At last," pronounced his really ancient mentor, "you are well and truly qualified to write a book about educational leadership," and, content at last, he died "old and full of days."
And the now late middle-aged superintendent did that.

And this is it.

It's my hope that this book will be of value, in a myriad of ways,

(*1*) To principals, superintendents, and other educational practitioners, from helping them understand themselves and what they accomplish each day to providing experience-based observations on modern public educational leadership and offering a measure of practical counsel for their labors—this through perceptual analyses by someone who survived more than a quarter of a century in the superintendency trying to "get it right" and occasionally succeeding

(2) To teachers and others who may be entertaining an interest in public school leadership, as one view of what all leadership positions require with suggestions for meeting such requirements, and to make clearer to teachers the high esteem in which they are held, by experienced school superintendents and principals, for all that teachers do each day on behalf of their students

(3) To university professors and their students as an alternative to traditional texts and references in graduate preparation programs for aspiring administrators

(4) To undergraduates planning teaching careers who are also curious about school district leadership and to their professors who want to help undergraduates become better acquainted with an experienced practitioner's views of public school education and modern educational leadership

(5) To personally secure board of education members with well-insulated nerve endings who have an interest in, and can live comfortably with, the inner thoughts of at least one of those who knows them well

(6) To business leaders as a basis of comparing their approaches with those of educational leadership—In spite of uninformed thoughts to the contrary, public education is a very real part of a very real world, and ideas in the book on leadership may translate well to corporate leadership

Over the past ten years, I have taught graduate courses (including personnel administration, education law, administration and supervision, school finance, school and society, and various seminars and other subjects) and have remained dissatisfied with many of the available leadership reading and textbooks. Too many are dull, filled with viscous prose that beats the obvious about the head and shoulders, stuffed with overripe research and pseudoresearch, and far removed from the real world of principalships and superintendencies. It is my hope that this book may add a modicum of life and color to texts and references used for graduate courses in school leadership and administration—both through a breadth of practical knowledge acquired over many years of public school experience and from a highly developed sense of the absurd.

Full appreciation of the abounding humor in public education environments enabled me to survive, almost totally intact, twenty-five years as superintendent of schools in five communities; years of statewide professional activities with state superintendent organizations, including a tour as president in Connecticut; classroom teaching; a principalship; as a submarine officer afloat (and submerged); and as an instructor and division director at the U.S. Naval Submarine School.

Almost every individual piece in the book is either intended to make a serious point leavened with humor or to be humorous and make a serious point; a few may only express a point of view and dance off unsmilingly—or even stalk off angrily.

Although it's important for long-term leadership success to appreciate the abundance of humorous situations and people that infest public schools, while trying to avoid both pretentiousness and portentousness, I remain serious about school leadership and its importance to the nation's future.

Most recently, as an interim superintendent of schools after a two-year hiatus from the superintendency, I again enjoyed the late nights and the early mornings; the exposed nerve ends endemic to many personal and professional relationships; interesting board of finance meetings and budget cuts; anxious parents; angry taxpayers; a myriad of staff concerns and worries; transportation issues; leaky roofs; eight-hour budget (and attitude) adjustment sessions when nobody even leaves the table to visit a bathroom; special education hearings and compliance reviews; an entire galaxy of meetings at which there is rarely any real risk of productivity or progress; and, generally, the sweat and gristle of the superintendent's calling—it was great!

And I couldn't stop thinking of the movie *Patton* and the scene in which George C. Scott and his adjutant view the aftermath of a tank platoon's brutal, unexpected, and lengthy night encounter with German armor and infantry. After hours of savage hand-to-hand combat, the battlefield is littered with twisted and charred tanks, one still aflame in the foreground, and dozens of bodies from both armies. An American tank commander is the lone living witness to what has occurred there. After General Patton kneels and confers a warrior's salute for gallantry on the surviving American soldier, he stands back drinking in the tragedy of modern mechanized warfare. Intoxicated with his love of battle, he declares passionately, "I love it! God help me, I do love it so!"

Well, God help me as well, because I remain enamored of the "Sturm and Drang" of daily superintendent life and realize how much I've missed it all. Sure, it's easier as a short-timer for all the obvious reasons, and my attention span wouldn't last another twenty-five years this time around. But in spite of many difficult days, and even longer periods of troubles, I experienced this same pleasure from the superintendency over the twenty-five years in which I served various districts in that role—as I did during my years as principal and a classroom teacher.

Leadership has become increasingly tougher because of social changes and financial constraints and continues to become even more so as the nineties roll on and a new century approaches. All that being true, public education remains among the most important, most necessary, personally rewarding professions available. Leaders who are and who will be the most successful are, for whatever psychiatric flaw that makes it so, those who really enjoy their calling in the face of inevitable daily and perpetual issues, problems, obstacles, and frustrations.

MUCH OF THE material in "Legal Issues," Chapter 5, although reorganized and newly titled, is from my article "Keep Your School Attorney in Hand," in the May 1981 edition of *The Executive Educator* and is reprinted with permission, from *The Executive Educator* (May), copyright 1981, the National School Boards Association, all rights reserved. Essays having their genesis there are, "Faxing Policy Manuals Is Expensive," "Fred and Ginger," "It's the Kids, Stupid!" "Junkyard Dogs – I," "Junkyard Dogs – II," "Legal Pen Pals," "Legal Poultices, Potions, and Elixirs," "Lou Holtz, Esq.," "Some of My Best Friends Graduated from Law School," "Think First, Then Reach for the Telephone," and "Take Two of These and Call Me in the Morning."

After thirty-five years in public education as an elementary and secondary teacher, in a principalship, as a university graduate assistant, as a part-time professor at five colleges and universities, and twenty-five years as a superintendent of schools, there are too many good people to thank each by name for all their caring, support, and assistance – and for all they taught me through selfless, unceasing dedication to the welfare of their students.

I have been fortunate to work for and with outstanding superintendents of schools, exceptional principals, and a phenomenal group of dedicated and competent classroom teachers. Also, some of the best and most able public school friends I've known were secretaries, clerks, aides, teaching assistants, bus drivers, bus contractors, custodians, buildings and grounds directors, cafeteria workers, school volunteers, and probably some categories I've forgotten – all of these singular men and women contributed immeasurably to the lives of thousands of children and young people. Whatever successes we may have achieved together are primarily from all their personal efforts, hour by hour, day by day, week by week, month by month, year by year, and career by career.

Throughout my life, any knowledge or wisdom I've acquired has come from associations and friendships with and my love for teachers, including my wife Anne and her mother Ruth; from my own childhood and university mentors and hundreds of teachers with whom I worked; from my children and grandchildren Mary Jeanne, Suzanne, Lisa, Bill, Ben, Dan, and Lee—they know who is which; from mothers and fathers, especially my own; from my brothers and sisters Bob, Mike, Mary Ann, and Carolyn—and from their wives, husbands, and children who comprise a vast assemblage of nieces and nephews, many of whom now have families of their own; from grandparents and great-grandparents, especially mine; from uncles and great uncles, aunts and great aunts, cousins, and other relatives, all of whom have been important to me.

Professionally and personally, I've also learned much of what I know from brother and sister superintendents, principals, special education directors, and other educational colleagues of all descriptions and kinds; from public school and university classmates; from commissioners of education and their minions; from board members; from town officials, elected and appointed; from a reasonable number of good friends, including submarine and minesweeper shipmates; from two each of loving dogs and cats; and especially from innumerable students—all of whose lives have enriched and brightened mine beyond measure or description.

Many of these people who meant so much to me personally and professionally, and to so many others as well, are gone now. They leave behind unfilled spaces in the lives of those of us they touched. I'd change that if I could, but I can't.

In spite of my occasional harsh treatment of board of education members in this book, I've had the privilege of working with many of the most competent, selfless, secure, supportive, insightful board members who ever graced a superintendent's career—and only a relatively small percentage who were incompetent, selfish, insecure, destructive, and obtuse. As superintendent of schools, I would have, in a heartbeat, traded any one of the members in the latter group for "Vlad the Impaler" and an unnamed third-round draft choice.

Educational life and times really don't get any better than this—in spite of restructuring, total quality mismanagement, and all the pathetic fads and gimmicks so dear to political charlatans and educational jellyfish with sea-level thresholds of self-delusion. They, and too many from other invertebrate species, refuse to recognize the reality of societal contributions to modern educational problems and attempt to shift responsibility to educators for solutions to all social ills—educators who have been strong enough to accept more than their share of responsibility for the state of our nation and to live with their partial successes and even their failures.

My own professional band of saints and sinners struggled along together over five decades from the fifties through the early nineties, always taking two steps forward and one step back in futile pursuit of the perfectibility of American public education and of each other. We never even came close to producing a single perfect human being among those we taught and guided or among ourselves—but we contributed significantly to the lives of all those imperfect children who so closely resemble their imperfect teachers, principals, superintendents, and other humanly flawed mentors.

A poem I read many years ago described looking back into our pasts not as peering through the wrong end of telescopes, but as views over old stone walls into neighboring fields. For most of us, our past appears that close to our present.

If I had the opportunity, and the energy, I'd do it all again—and, I hope, even better the second time.

PUBLIC SCHOOL LEADERSHIP is a constant search for balances, between and among conflicting ideas and forces, to shape difficult choices. All effective and successful leadership must intuitively understand, appreciate, and apply the concept embodied within Aristotle's "Golden Mean." Aristotelian golden means are virtues found between undesirable extremes, usually nearer one extreme than the other, as courage is nearer to foolhardiness than to fear and responsiveness nearer to servitude than to contempt for others. Courage and responsiveness are two examples among golden means that characterize effective leadership.

The golden mean is not vapid compromise, but a hard search for the morally correct position, often between immoral extremes—although there are times when the Aristotelian ideal either can't be identified or acted upon, and compromise finds a place in the educational decision maker's pantheon of imperfect choices.

Leadership that place itself firmly at the right point on the continuum between extremes is not passionless or weak leadership. To the contrary, identifying a rational mean and acting upon it, while resisting pressures from both sides, requires more character and strength than surrendering to extremist views. A reasoned position between excesses can be, and should be, as impassioned, and is certainly more reasoned, than the extreme positions all too prevalent in all aspects of life today.

The search for "golden means" comprises a recurring theme throughout this book's various chapters, sections, and individual essays. In all its parts, the book dedicates itself, directly or by implication, to educational leadership's search for golden means to resolve endless issues and problems productively and effectively. The outcomes of leadership's search for reasonable and balanced choices will have major consequences for American public education, both in the remainder of this century and the next.

CHAPTER 1

Leadership

WHAT IS IT?

AS IS TRUE of many other abstractions, leadership is easier to recognize than define. We know it when we see it, but it's hard to describe precisely. "It is a riddle wrapped in a mystery inside an enigma" [1] was first used to express Winston Churchill's uncertainty about future Russian military action at the beginning of World War II, but it may be equally appropriate to explain the imprecision of many leadership definitions. The Supreme Court might have as much difficulty describing leadership as it does determining the appropriateness of books and movies.[2]

Among other attributes, effective leadership articulates commonly held values and beliefs, develops shared commitments to common goals, and inspires others to do what they ordinarily wouldn't do. Whether on athletic teams, in military life, or in public education, good leadership elevates and transforms as it creates group dedication to shared goals. As crucial as education is to the nation's future, too often there is no clearly stated, widely accepted, group commitment to school or district success. Teachers may be immersed effectively in their individual disciplines, but unified group efforts and common school or district direction may be lacking. Effective educational leadership seizes each opportunity to bind teachers, administrators, and parents together in the common cause of student educational and personal achievement.

Public leadership in the nineties, at any level, is much more difficult than it was in past decades—and it's never been easy. Together, financial constraints, single-issue constituencies, and media feeding frenzies on large and small professional and human foibles add synergistically to pressures faced by public leaders today, including superintendents of schools and other educational administrators.

[2]The only X-rated leadership analogy I'll make.

1

One of life's greatest professional satisfactions comes from being part of worthwhile and inspired group commitments to shared goals, and American public education offers the potential for these experiences in every school district, every day, of every year, of every career.

WHAT DOES IT LOOK LIKE WHEN YOU SEE IT?

Although speakers and writers tell us constantly that modern leadership styles must be very different from those of the past, they are only partially correct. Autocratic leadership is an anachronism, and decisions need to be shared more freely today—but the same personal qualities that made good leaders in the past are still necessary for the current generation of school principals and superintendents. While not all characteristics fit all leadership in all situations, there are predominant and recurring characteristics among good leaders, and they include the items listed below in this section (in addition to the usual scout descriptors of "brave, loyal, trustworthy, kind, reverent, obedient, cheerful, thrifty, clean . . .").

Personal Security and Self-Confidence

Although none of us is altogether free from anxiety or self-doubt in every situation, good leaders feel good about themselves and about their abilities—not arrogance or smugness, but a quiet confidence in their own abilities. If there's time for reflection, no matter how confident leaders are in their own judgment, important decisions should be made only after soliciting other views, examining them from a myriad of perspectives, and melding other people's ideas with the leader's own personal and professional judgment and experience.

Although leaders should base difficult decisions on their own best judgments, sometimes their judgment may be that they lack adequate knowledge to make informed decisions. In these instances, they need a strong sense of self, and the personal security growing from it that allows them to admit they don't know enough and to defer to other expertise—even in these situations, they should poke, probe, examine, weigh, and test recommendations and alternative recommendations for soundness and consistency against their own basic values and make or ratify final decisions.

There are other instances when leaders have the luxury of accepting cooperative decisions against their better instincts, because specific decision consequences may not be as significant as the group process by which they are made.

Andrew Jackson once advised a young officer, "Don't you make any orders on your men without maturing them, and then you execute them, no matter what it costs; and that is all I have to say" [2]. David "Davy" Crockett had accompanied the young officer to hear General Jackson's advice, and when asked what the general had said, his translation was "Be always sure you're right—then go ahead!" [3]. Both versions are good leadership advice.

Ability to Make Decisions and the Ability to Live Comfortably with Decisions Once Made

Tough choices are relatively easy; living with their results is often much more difficult. Implicit in effective decision making are the experience and judgment that tell leaders when decisions must be made quickly and when they can, or should, be delayed—and at times, they should be held in abeyance until more information can be gathered.

Sometimes administrators even need to practice "transcendental indifference," remembering the cardinal rule of educational medicine—"above all do the patient no harm," make no decision, and hope the district recovers. Although to be prescribed sparingly, and with great caution, benign neglect may be the best treatment for a seemingly acute school district illness. Transcendental indifference, in spite of how it sounds, is not a tenet of the Maharishi Mahesh Yogi or others in his circuit but a legitimate educational alternative in some circumstances.

Openness to Changing Previous Decisions, but with a Degree of Reluctance to Change Course

While remaining open about possible needs to modify or reverse decisions in light of additional information, leaders' initial biases should be toward choices already made—at least for a while. After decisions are made, they should be put aside in favor of other decisions waiting in an endless queue. Agonizing over the past erodes whatever leadership capacities people may have, and, if they can't live comfortably with difficult choices, they probably don't have much leadership capacity anyway. If, however, evidence is clear that a new course should be set, leaders shouldn't allow "foolish consistency" to prevent them from changing direction as necessary.

Tolerance of Ambiguity

Leadership is a real trial for compulsive personalities who need every small issue neatly resolved, wrapped, and tied with a bow. Thoroughness is to be sought and appreciated when found, but perfection in human endeavors is rare. Although major breakthroughs are better than incremental progress, they are much less likely to happen. Keeping significant improvements as their ultimate goal, good leaders know when to accept minor achievement gratefully and when to continue taking small steps forward until, eventually, major change takes place. At times, leaders need to back away from issues and allow small improvements to simmer for a time before adding ingredients and turning up the heat again. Even modest organizational gains should be treasured.

A hallmark of organizational maturity is jurisdictional ambiguity for the sake of getting the job done. Organizational flexibility is productive among central office leadership when role freedom allows staff interchanges of problems and issues without jurisdictional hassles and when administrators are comfortable outside rigid lines of authority. If a principal calls the superintendent's office with a problem that (in the boss's absence) an assistant can handle, the issue should be resolved between the assistant and principal and the superintendent told, as soon as possible, of the problem and its resolution. Existing levels of organizational sophistication and flexibility often require compromises to ideal jurisdictional flexibility. It's a leadership error to loosen or abandon lines of authority with people who can't yet handle it, but softening the rigid lines of authority on organization charts remains a worthwhile objective.

Recognition of the Essentials

Without this ability, leadership spends much too much time on relatively unimportant issues, or parts of issues, without understanding why the organization doesn't function as it should. Seeing through the irrelevant to the essence of problems is a function of intelligence, but that skill can be cultivated and improved. Administrators must keep foremost in their minds that primary leadership responsibility is identifying important aspects of important issues and resolving them before becoming concerned with peripheral matters.

Superintendents, principals, and other educational leaders often are approached by staff members with a perceived "problem," which is really the person's solution to a yet unidentified problem. For example, three teachers, unsuccessfully sharing one large teaching area, bring to their principal the question of how the district can pay for constructing walls to separate teaching areas. Sometimes principals attack financing wall construction when the yet unidentified issue is teacher inability to organize space to function properly. Spend enough time thinking about other people's so-called "problems," and you may be surprised how often, in reality, they are someone's desired solutions to yet unspecified issues.

Five to Live By

Personal security and self-confidence; the ability to make decisions and live comfortably with them once made; openness to changing previous decisions, but with a degree of reluctance to change course; tolerance of ambiguity; and recognition of the essentials are five important characteristics for good leaders to live by.

BORN OR MADE?

Searching out the origins and components of leadership may be similar to deciding whether intelligence originates in heredity or environment; either position is difficult to advocate or defend with absolute conviction. Both personal qualities and professional experience play major roles in professional leadership, and neither is totally responsible for effective leadership. Almost every person can lead in certain situations, but degrees of specific leadership ability vary greatly from person to person. Although it seems superficial to acknowledge that irrelevant characteristics contribute to successful leadership, the advantages of physical attractiveness, size, and general appearance are impossible to deny.

That isn't to say that above average physical attributes are all that good leaders need, but they help. If Cleopatra's nose had been shorter, would the world have been the same [4]?[3] If John F. Kennedy had been "vertically challenged," fat, and spectacularly ugly, would he have been

[3]The actual quote was, "Cleopatra's nose: had it been shorter, the whole aspect of the world would have been altered," from the French scientist, philosopher, and mathematical prodigy, Blaise Pascal. When he was sixteen years of age, Pascal wrote an original treatise on conic sections and later solved the problem of "general quadrature of the cycloid," which to nonmathematicians sounds more like a swelling behind the ear than something geometric.

President of the United States of America? Possibly, but the odds are against both—although, if JFK had been short, fat, and spectacularly ugly, he may have had fewer personal distractions from his presidential responsibilities.

Good leadership requires good childhood training. In a professional periodical review of one school administration textbook for graduate courses, the reviewer spoke kindly of the author's stated goals to develop personal values such as honesty, openness, and compassion in his graduate students; to help them focus on the human effects of decisions, rather than on primarily bureaucratic considerations; and to ground leadership choices in student welfare, rather than in leadership convenience—another version of avoiding expediency in favor of hard, but correct, decisions to help children.

If students don't arrive in graduate school already equipped with apropriate personal standards, it's too damn late for professors to develop them. Most parents try to inculcate in their children those traits that the professor, and his reviewer, wanted to instill in graduate students.

A *Doonesbury* series, which began shortly after "Watergate" and its attendant scandals exploded on the nation, is particularly applicable here. The initial strip pictured a rumpled, but dignified, veteran law professor leaning on the podium of a college lecture hall, as he contemplated first year students beginning their initial law course with him. The professor, clasping his hands behind his back, began by explaining the rationale for the course and quoted Ambrose Bierce's description of a lawyer as "one skilled in circumventing the law" and connected that characterization to recent national events. The professor then asserts that knowing the law isn't enough, that law schools have an obligation to ensure that graduates understand the spirit of the law, as well as the letter of the law, and concludes with "Right and Wrong 10-A is one such stab in the dark."

We all know about recalcitrant mules and the "two-by-fours" often needed to ensure a mule's attention. Figuratively applied "two-by-fours" are also useful at times for educational leaders to gain other educators' attention; sometimes only then is it possible to explore previously unexamined values with them. People not already armored with strong moral character and good instincts are difficult to transform into effective leaders; faced with obvious choices between good and bad, appropriate and inappropriate actions, these truncated personalities instinctively, without hesitation, make the wrong decisions. Examples are a superintendent's automatic disapproval of an expensive special education student placement to avoid discomfiting the board of education with an unexpected and major expenditure at an awkward time of the budget year and an administrator attempting to conceal a problem from the world because his or her personal insecurities don't allow revelations of even small cracks in an educational facade.

Problems are often complex with many shades of gray—not usually dichotomies of obviously correct and incorrect answers—if school leaders can't act easily and correctly on clear right and wrong moral issues, they won't have the inclination, the instincts, or even the time to cope successfully with the infestation of more difficult problems populating public leadership today like fleas on an old hound. Difficult issues appear before us *ad seriatim*, as waves break on the shore, without clearly marked courses of action for administrative choices and decisions.

Good leadership has always needed a consistent moral compass to point the way—it still does.

IN SEARCH OF GOLD

Aristotle believed the "mean" to be a great virtue lying between two vices, both undesirable in themselves, normally not midway between the vices, or extremes, but almost always nearer one than the other—as courage, the Aristotelian mean, is nearer to rashness than to cowardice; as liberality is the mean between prodigality and meanness, closer to prodigality; as proper pride is the mean between undue humility and empty vanity and probably closer to undue humility. "There are three kinds of disposition, then, two of them vices, involving excess and deficiency respectively, and one a virtue, viz., the mean, and all are in a sense opposed to all; for the extreme states are contrary both to the intermediate state and to each other and the intermediate to the extremes; . . . to the mean in some cases the deficiency, in some the excess is more opposed . . . one extreme is nearer and liker to the intermediate" [5].[4] Again, Aristotle believes that the proper mean, while between both lies closer to one extreme than the other—not halfway between extremes but located through a thoughtful search for the best position or course of action between them—but always nearer one than the other.

[4]Aristotle's extant works are largely a collection of edited compilations of notes for lectures delivered to his Athenian disciples. One of Plato's pupils, this son of the court physician for Amyntas III of Macedonia was also a teacher in Myteline and in Athens as head of the Lyceum.

"But as virtue receives her proper station in the mean, so all extremes decline from that mark" [6]. "Reason lies between the spur and the bridle" [7], between rushing forward and restraining. "Share your heat between earth and sky . . . safety lies midway" [8].[5] "The golden rule in life is moderation in all things" [9].

Each of these quotes speaks to avoiding extremes and of the eternal search for reasoned positions between them. Three hundred years after Aristotle's *Nichomachean Ethics,* Horace borrowed the idea and labeled it in his advice to Licinius: "Better wilt thou live, Licinius, by neither always pressing out to sea nor too closely hugging the dangerous shore in cautious fear of storms. Whoso cherishes the *golden mean* safely avoids the foulness of an ill-kept house . . ." [10].

It's important to recognize that proper leadership may be extremely arbitrary and efficient in crises and extremely humanitarian when employees suffer personal tragedy; in these two examples, the "golden mean," as conceived by Aristotle and labeled thus by Horace, can be seen and judged only in the overall context of both circumstances and of many others like them—not just in one situation alone.

Every school leader, every day, in every school, in every school district, in every state, faces endless decisions, each of which should involve a search for the golden mean between extremes:

(1) *Data and intuition:* Making decisions on one of these alone without consideration of the other can be dangerous, overly time-consuming, rigid, bureaucratic, etc. Leadership needs to find the proper point on the line between locating or developing important data and the use of intuition founded upon experience and intelligence.

(2) *Educational philosophies and personal standards:* Philosophies may be the only moving force in the lives of a few card-carrying pedagogues, but, for the rest of us, educational philosophy needs to be balanced with personal conviction.

(3) *Student needs and district finances:* As educators, our responsibility is to present and defend necessary student programs; yet even the most passionate student advocate must balance programmatic advocacy with the realities of limited funding.

---

[5]This advice from Publius Ovidius Naso, or Ovid as he's better known, came originally from Phoebus, the sun god, to his son Phaethon as he reluctantly gave his offspring, who didn't even hold a learner's license, the keys to the family chariot for a quick whirl across the sky to a celestial mall. The quote from Ovid is from his major work, a narrative poem, *Metamorphoses,* which tells of marvelous transformations from creation until J. Caesar's time.

(4) *Student, staff, parent rights and student, staff, parent responsibilities:* Everybody's got rights and everybody's got responsibilities, and knowing exactly when one must give way to the other isn't always clear, morally or legally, but these must also be maintained in balance.

(5) *Policy/regulation and common sense:* The trick here is to use policy and regulations effectively but not to the exclusion of common sense. That doesn't imply violations of policy, but it does mean their limitations should be recognized and that policies need to be changed when they don't fit particular circumstances.[6]

(6) *Public's right to know and employee confidentiality:* Although often a legal issue governed by state statutes, regulations, state "sunshine committee" decisions, and board of education policy, these conflicting rights often must be examined and appropriate points determined between them.

(7) *Board recognition of superintendent of schools as chief executive officer of the board and its legitimate need to hear other staff views and perceptions:* Although boards should recognize superintendents as their primary contacts on school district issues, they can't be totally closed off from casual communication with staff; as a good example of the Aristotelian mean, the correct balance is much closer to the superintendent as the source of primary board information.

(8) *Efficiency and effectiveness:* Efficiency saves time—effectiveness takes time; efficiency doesn't weigh human concerns heavily and is bureaucratic—effectiveness is humanitarian, reflective, and selective; efficiency is more dictatorial—effectiveness is more democratic. School leadership can't function successfully if it's always either totally efficient or totally effective. At times, efficiency and time saved through solitary, quick decisions are paramount; at other times, a search for long-range effectiveness may slow decision making through greater staff, parent, student, or board involvement.[7]

(9) *Consistency and flexibility:* Leadership consistency is important and desirable as long as it isn't foolish consistency that produces rigidity; sometimes, situations change and so must previous decisions, leaving leadership open to charges of "inconsistency"—and changing decisions is inconsistent, no matter how

[6]See also, Chapter 4, "And So Do His Sisters, His Cousins, and His Aunts," p. 172.
[7]See also, Chapter 3, "Efficient or Effective—Choose Any Two," p. 73.

minor the degree of inconsistency. This particular golden mean, although always found between two extremes, lives next door to consistency and on a different continent from inconsistency.[8]

(10) *Details and the big picture:* Possibly even more than most of the other balancing acts, this one typifies the point made about judging only in the overall context of a number of circumstances, not the basis of one incident. With some issues, the golden mean can only be seen and judged in the overall context of many circumstances—not just in one of them alone; at times, the leader must engross him- or herself in detail, while at other times back away from specifics and take a larger perspective. In balancing attention to detail with monitoring the "big picture," it's probable that the appropriate mean may only be achieved through movement toward one extreme at times and toward the opposite extreme at other times.[9]

(11) *Confronting problems directly and avoiding others:* School administrators should, more often than not, tackle problems head on and quickly, but there are too many of them for that to happen in each instance; necessary prioritizations hold some solutions in abeyance while more crucial issues are being resolved; at times, "benign neglect" is the best approach. This golden mean is another that is closer to one extreme than the other—closer to direct action than avoidance.

(12) *Making difficult decisions personally and delegating them appropriately:* Leadership should strive to make itself unimportant by developing colleagues to their fullest and, if others are to grow professionally, through delegating decisions appropriately; conversely, the person responsible must also monitor closely the effects of delegated decisions and must solve many difficult problems personally—always accepting responsibility for all decisions at all times, whether delegated or made personally and alone.

(13) *Open acceptance of other people's motives and development of a highly functional "BS detector":* This is a good example of "creative schizophrenia,"[10] which requires leaders to impute good motives to everyone until proved wrong, while at the same time developing an acute sensitivity to the "Nineteen Sneaky B's": babble, balderdash, baloney, bile, bilge, blabber, blarney, blubber,

---

[8]See also, Chapter 4, "And So Do His Sisters, His Cousins, and His Aunts," p. 172.
[9]See also, this chapter, "The Devil Is in the Details," p. 18.
[10]See also, Chapter 3, "Creative Schizophrenia," p. 66.

bluff, bluster, boastfulness, bombast, boneheadedness, bootlick-
ing, bowdlerization,[11] breast-beating, broadsides, bronchitis,[12]
bullheadedness, and BS.

(*14*) *Acquiring adequate information to make decisions and making
timely decisions:* To some degree, this is a kissing cousin of both
efficiency and effectiveness; leaders need adequate information to
make decisions, but if they wait until they know everything,
they'll never made a decision. Knowing how to balance these conflicting needs is crucial – another good example of determining
the golden mean in the overall context of all known circumstances, rather than from a single instance. Some decisions
must be made quickly at greater risk of error; others could take
almost forever with no great organizational harm; most fall
somewhere in between.

(*15*) *Seriousness of purpose with enjoyment of professional life:*
Recognition of grim reality must be balanced with optimistic
imagination, and frustration should be balanced with pleasure;
leadership balance should be maintained between seriousness of
purpose and enjoyment of life. Educational leaders need to recognize and enjoy the pomposity, banality, illusion, delusion, ambiguity, misdirection, lunacy, boredom, and just plain old "nonsense" that surround them daily – as well as appreciating the
excitement, challenge, and importance of educational leadership
and the dedication and competence that characterize most colleagues and friends.

Leadership balances, or golden means, need to be sought each day
between: data and intuition; educational philosophies and personal
standards; student needs and district finances; student, staff, parent
rights and student, staff, parent responsibilities; policy/regulation and
common sense; the public's right to know and employee confidentiality; board recognition of the superintendent of schools as chief executive officer of the board and its legitimate need to hear other staff
views and perceptions; efficiency and effectiveness; consistency and inconsistency; details and the big picture; confronting problems directly
and avoiding them; making difficult decisions personally and
delegating them appropriately; open acceptance of other people's

---

[11]The act or result of "bowdlerizing," from Thomas Bowdler, an English editor who expurgated
books through omission of words he considered vulgar – for example, "bullshit" to "BS" or even
"nonsense."

[12]Just checking to see if you're paying attention and reading the footnotes.

motives and development of a highly functional "BS detector"; acquiring adequate information to make decisions and making timely decisions; and seriousness of purpose with enjoyment of professional life.[13]

SITUATIONAL LEADERSHIP

Some people generally, and some leaders specifically, are crisis-oriented and don't function well in tranquility. Their need for issues to resolve may even lead them to create their own problems to exercise their special abilities. This reality is illustrated in an unfortunate volunteer firefighter syndrome—if there aren't enough fires, occasionally, a member of the department will set one to have something important to do.

Most teachers and administrators have worked with principals or superintendents who fit this description—leaders who, under great pressure, produce remarkable results but, in times of relative calm, lose interest, flounder, or withdraw. In positions requiring major damage control, these leaders are superb, but they probably should move on to another disorganized setting after straightening out current organizational inadequacies. Other leaders are much more comfortable in caretakers' roles in outstanding systems with few problems. These professional posts are becoming harder to find, and if you must choose one type of leadership over the other, go for the troubleshooter—odds are he or she will be kept busy today and at least won't be bored.

School systems provide various kinds of leadership in different situations: (1) Peer leadership is the natural ascension of one or more faculty members to informal leadership positions among the faculty. This can be made more formal through union/association involvement. (2) Team leaders, department chairman, and central office subject matter supervisors are staff with greater than ordinary knowledge and expertise in particular fields who can be considered district "noncoms" providing a form of "expert" leadership. (3) General leadership is analogous to military "line officers," including building administrators, central office personnel with direct line authority, and superintendents of schools. General leadership requires admixtures of personal/professional leadership qualities and is, to a great degree, also situational.

[13]See also, Chapter 3, "Creative Schizophrenia," p. 66.

People and leadership situations are so different that not every strong leader can be successful in every position. Matching leadership with positions is a complex business although, fortunately, among the very best people, a number have the ability and flexibility in their leadership style to succeed in almost any job.

SUBMERSIBLE LEADERSHIP

Forty years ago now, after completing submarine school in New London, Connecticut, as a member of its 100th Officer Class, a young naval officer reported aboard the U.S.S. BUGARA in Pearl Harbor, Territory of Hawaii—in 1955, the islands hadn't yet achieved statehood. BUGARA was a World War II submarine refitted as a "Fleet Snorkel Submarine" with a higher battery capacity, a snorkel mast to run the engines underwater, and a streamlined "guppy"[14] type superstructure.

For the four decades since then, he has kept a letter from the submarine's captain when the junior officer reported aboard—not only as memorabilia from an interesting and vividly recollected time in his life, but because it presents important leadership concepts in such straightforward, unaffected, simple, albeit sometimes lapsing into rococo, prose.

As a compulsive editor of anything that passes through his hands, there were inevitably minor changes he would have liked to make, but, all in all, in spite of an occasional phrase that might have been changed slightly, the CO's letter fared well without his editorial assistance. Sure, the editor would have preferred to lose some capital letters, but, in their military context, most are acceptable. Ellipses indicate that a few words were omitted because they were technical references or otherwise peculiar to the specific naval setting, and the editor couldn't restrain himself from cleaning up one or two typographical glitches.

Although it may not be the definitive treatise on the subject and although the once young officer confesses to being at an impressionable age at the time of this correspondence, the four-page letter remains a singular effort to help him understand important elements of leadership and also to establish the commanding officer's expectations of a line officer's leadership responsibilities—in this instance, naval leadership, but much of the advice translates well to other settings even today.

---

[14]"Guppy" stood for greater underwater propulsive power, with the "y" added for euphony.

U.S.S. BUGARA (SS 331)
Fleet Post Office
San Francisco, California

From: Commanding Officer
To: Lieutenant (jg) David L. Cattanach, USNR

Subj: Your Role Aboard the BUGARA

1. Welcome Aboard! I am pleased to have you aboard as one of my
officers, and I look forward to sharing a pleasant and enlightening cruise
with you. As your Commanding Officer, I take this opportunity to present to you my viewpoints on the subject of leadership and the star upon
your sleeve. I expect, through allowing you some insight on matters in
which I am interested, that a mutual understanding will ensue and that
you will have cause to reflect not only on your past actions as a Naval
Officer, but also on your future as a new arrival.

2. Up to this time, you have been provided with a vast amount of training activity in the form of schools, short courses, motion pictures, correspondence courses, and on-the-job training as both a Division and
Department Head. Many and various publications have been made
available to you by both the Navy and the Submarine Force to guide and
train you not only as an Administrator and a Naval Officer, but also as
a Submariner in your particular assignment to duty in the BUGARA. A
prodigious number of pamphlets and articles have been published to further aid you in the transition from surface craft to submarines, or from
civilian to commissioned Naval Officer, thence to surface vessels, and,
finally, to duty in the Submarine Force. Every conceivable requirement,
every possible hardship, every unexpected embarrassment has been anticipated by words of caution, advice, and illustrative story in all of the
officer training schools the Navy provided for you.

3. Inevitably, a proportion of this training given you will have lost some
of its force and effect after you have gained experience afloat and accli-
mated yourself to the necessities of your actual task. But remember, as
a Submarine Officer, the primary objective in your training for duty in
submarines has been to equip you with the needed initial knowledge to
perform this highly specialized duty and, secondly, to provide you with
the tools with which to broaden your knowledge of General Line subjects. . . . However, there remains one basic requirement for every
Navy Officer. . . . This requirement must be fulfilled competently
throughout your entire Naval Career if you are to hold the commission
given only by an estimate of your potential fitness and your achievement
of prescribed academic standards, and if you are to wear and retain the

coveted "Dolphins"[15] awarded to you by virtue of your having completed established minimum requirements. This requirement is your ability to uphold the character and fulfill the stature of a <u>Line Officer</u>.

4. You, as a Submarine Officer, are an Officer of the Line. You wear the five-pointed gold star upon your sleeve to denote that you are an Officer of the Line. That star has no embroidered parentheses containing symbols that specialize or limit your Line responsibility. Not only in the United States Navy, but since time immemorial in all Navies, an Officer of the Line has been the Officer charged with the <u>Exercise of Military Command</u>. He is so defined in the United States Navy Regulations. All too frequently, that definition has come to mean to many Officers merely the exercise of Military function or of Command function. The Exercise of Military Command means neither. It is not the trappings of your uniform that proclaim you as being of the Line — it is your ability to lead. . . .

5. It is of little importance that you, as a new Submarine Officer reporting aboard for the first time, comply with all the customs and usages of the Naval and Submarine Service with the accustomed ease of a salty veteran. However, it is of the greatest importance that when you first cross the Quarterdeck,[16] whether saluting it properly or improperly, that you had firmly fixed in your mind the mechanics by which you can successfully use your character, your personality, your confidence, your executive capacity, your previous military experience, to effect the transition to acceptable military leadership. Any observant new Officer, in but a few weeks of shipboard life, can become indistinguishable from officers who have spent years in the Submarine Service insofar as Submarine and Naval Customs and terminology are concerned.

6. All the training that you receive aboard the BUGARA, all the information you may receive, should be taken with only one point in view: Its contribution to your assumption of Leadership. For example, there are innumerable recommendations about uniforms . . . necessary on a cruise. The importance of the number of work shirts and trousers in your sea bag is only that you shall always present the example of a neat and military appearance. . . .

7. I place great stress on your maintaining a high order of physical fitness. The rigors of service encountered in various submarine patrol

[15]Uniform breast insignia awarded upon "Qualification in Submarines" — completion of specific requirements in each technical area of the ship and after demonstrating familiarity and expertise in all aspects of submarine operations, including diving and surfacing and maneuvering, or "landing," the ship alongside a pier or submarine tender.

[16]The area at the top of the gangway where persons coming aboard salute the flag on the stern and exchange salutes with the Officer of the Deck. On subs and small ships, the Officer of the Deck is busy elsewhere, and the Quarterdeck watch stander is a petty officer.

areas require this. Those officers who have served with me in the past are well aware of my feelings on this subject. The relationship and the importance of your physical fitness to your personal welfare is great, but it is even greater in the example which you must exhibit before your men. The physical stamina of an individual Officer is of little value if . . . it cannot be communicated as a highly desirable achievement for every man under that Officer's command.

8. I feel sure that you are familiar with the periodic Fitness Report[17] and the important part it plays on the road to promotion. The Fitness Report can have little meaning if the Officer concerned does not devote himself to the advancement of his men as well as himself. The professional knowledge derived from the specialized training with which you are equipped may see you through your contacts with more senior officers. It cannot prevent you from being an abysmal failure if you do not direct it downward, through supervision and education, to increase the proficiency of your men. I might add that your Fitness Report is a direct reflection of the efficiency of your department or division organization as to administration, operation, and material. Along the line of first impressions, it has been stated that the most important moment for the new officer reporting aboard is not, as commonly believed, his introduction to his Commanding Officer. Rather, it is his first appearance before the crew at Quarters.[18] It is there that he erects the first milestone in his submarine career. It is often there that his "fitness" is determined.

9. Those of you who are Reserve Officers may be sensitive, by civilian conditioning, to inequalities of privilege. Assignment of staterooms and bunks, locker space, leave and liberty, position and frequency on the Watch Bill, assignment of collateral duties, are all more or less zealously guarded rights which you may feel should be distributed with proper equity. Only time and . . . observation will indoctrinate you in these factors in order for you to make the necessary adjustments to submarine shipboard life. Personally, I am "sensitive" about officers aboard who abuse or treat lightly these cherished Naval and Submarine customs, traditions, and practices. All of these factors similarly apply to enlisted men, with like degree of appreciation, and it is to you that your men look for the equitable distribution and guardianship of those rights and privileges.

---

[17]A personnel evaluation system somewhat akin to a teacher evaluation checklist, but the importance of a fitness report to a naval officer's career is much more crucial than teacher evaluations are to teachers—unless an evaluation becomes the impetus for or basis of teacher termination.

[18]"Quarters" are daily musters of shipboard division personnel, in a designated area on deck, to start each work day, whether at sea or in port, and includes attendance checks, sick list reports, announcements, and reviews of daily divisional work plans and assignments and other routine shipboard, departmental, and divisional business. The observance of morning colors, the ritual raising of the flag, is an integral part of each daily quarters.

10. It is difficult to set up a pattern for good leadership by merely stating general principles. In practice, the exercise of leadership consists of doing a multitude of <u>little</u> things as part of daily routine. A very few of these are given below:

   a. Be present at Quarters. Always be there on time. Let there be no absence on your part that would not be equally valid for the crew.

   b. Irrespective of what you may have done the night before, when you stand before the crew at Morning Quarters, present yourself as a smart, interested, and alert officer.[19] Let the crew see and feel that you were well chosen.

   c. Make a daily check of educational progress for advancement in rating of those men under your command. Do not hesitate to offer your personal assistance to those in need of it.

   d. Should any man under your command be placed on the binnacle list,[20] it is your obligation to make a daily visit to him, to check his progress personally, and to talk with him.

   e. Each day make an inspection of the living spaces and those other areas for which you are responsible, not to find fault, but to indicate your interest to your Petty Officers so they can maintain the standard you desire.

   f. When the crew engages in intra- or inter-ship activities, be present at the events. Never hesitate to participate if your help is needed to win.

   g. Take a personal interest both in the Watch, Quarter, and Station Bill[21] and the Liberty Sections. Let your Petty Officers know that you are not overlooking anyone, even the newest submarine recruit.

   h. When you have something to say to your department, division, watch section, or to a separate few, have them fall out of ranks and gather around you so they can all hear and see you clearly. Be explanatory, but be concise. Use a voice that is firm and confident but not austere and unfriendly. There is no record in Naval history where profane,

---

[19]Easy for him to say. Since the submarine's executive officer neither drank nor debauched himself in any way, only a year later it fell to me as Operations Officer to accompany the Captain ashore on liberty—where we at least had one or two beers from early evening until dawn. Returning aboard in the early morning, the Captain retired to his small stateroom for a nap, while the hurting junior officer went to quarters, sometimes with a "foul weather jacket" covering a civilian blue shirt and red striped tie, hoping his eyes weren't bleeding visibly. (CO's only made rare appearances at morning quarters to make particularly important announcements. So the Captain wasn't abusing his position with his brief morning catnaps while his previous night's liberty buddy suffered well-deserved pain trying to appear alert at quarters and not cry in front of the troops because his head hurt so bad.)

[20]The "binnacle list" identifies any crew members who are too ill to perform their assigned duties.

[21]The ship's listing of personnel assignments and responsibilities in different shipboard evolutions, activities, and situations.

vulgar, or obscene language produced any better results than simple, plain words properly delivered.

i. Whenever possible, when your men are on watch or at battle stations, relieve one for a time, if the occasion warrants, for the constructive purpose of showing him, first, that you know how to do the job yourself and, second, how you expect it to be done.

11. Leadership is often divided into two qualities—those naturally possessed and those acquired. The Officer having no acquired qualities of leadership can hardly be expected to gain them in the relatively short period of training afforded him before he reports aboard BUGARA. However, every Officer reporting aboard has some acquired qualities of Leadership gained both from civilian experience and from brief military experiences, and he can easily place them in full force and effect as a military leader with remarkably little adaptation. It is here that the greatest opportunity lies for the Line Officer. If you have led before, you can lead now . . . and your task is infinitely easier because these men have the stimulus of moral obligation to duty and the assignment of heavy, individual responsibilities.

12. Leadership—that is the significance of the star upon your sleeve. Make leadership your first goal, make all else subordinate to it. Do this, and we shall see "eye to eye" during our cruise together.

E. R. Ettner

In one way or another, almost every idea in the Captain's letter, modified or eased appropriately to reflect changes of time and milieu, translates well to leadership in any public education setting and position.

THE DEVIL IS IN THE DETAILS

"The man [*sic*][22] in charge must concern himself with details. If he does not consider them important, neither will his subordinates. Yet 'the devil is in the details' [11]. It is hard and monotonous to pay attention to seemingly minor matters. . . . Most managers would rather focus on lofty policy matters. But when the details are ignored, the project fails. No infusion of policy or lofty ideals can then correct the situation" [11]. This quote, although arising from a background in the nuclear navy, applies equally well to public educational leadership.

Concern for detail is not mutually exclusive of broad, conceptual

[22]Read both genders throughout this paragraph. The quote had military origins at a time when there were even fewer military women "in charge" than there are today, when the number remains modest.

thinking or of picturing and understanding the overall organizational design and function. Instead, public school leadership's attention to detail dramatically increases chances for educational success in each school district. "Genius means transcendent capacity of taking trouble" [12].[23]

Effective leaders are driven to question colleagues regularly, intensively, thoroughly, and in detail to assure themselves that those who work for them understand completely all implications of their efforts in specific projects and to reveal shortcomings, inadequacies, errors, conceptual flaws, or any other defects that could jeopardize particular programs or educational processes. This ability and this practice do not belie appropriate and necessary trust in other administrators and teachers; instead, they help teach the importance of each component of plans, reports, analyses, evaluations, preparations, summaries, recommendations, and all other aspects of educational leadership.

Other administrators will not always enjoy these "interrogations," but there is no better way to assure quality performance and the success of the enterprise. The more effectively the leader manages these work sessions, the better prepared administrative colleagues will be when they arrive at one of them—and the more effectively district leadership will present issues to other staff, boards of education, the media, and the public.

"All animals are equal, but some animals are more equal than others" [13].[24] To some degree, skillful questioning is a function of intelligence; the unfairness of some administrative "animals" being smarter than others might imply they have an advantage in acquiring questioning skills—they do. But even the brightest people need to focus on questioning techniques and hone them even sharper—the rest of us need to work harder to develop them. But everyone can improve questioning skills and abilities when they are afforded the high priority they should receive.

Superintendents and other school district leaders should anticipate all reasonable, and many unreasonable, questions that may be asked

---

[23]Thomas Carlyle was a Scottish essayist and historian and another who earned his living at one time or another in his life as a teacher; he taught in Annan and Kirkcaldy. It took him almost fourteen years, from 1851 until 1865, to complete the history of Frederick the Great—the next year, possibly needing a rest, he became Rector of Edinburgh University. The quote cited was used in connection with "little Fritz," or Frederick the Great as a child, who understood even then that getting the job done properly required close attention to detail.

[24]Not many educators know Eric Blair, or George Orwell, was also an assistant superintendent—albeit an assistant district superintendent of the Indian Imperial Police, stationed in Burma from 1922–1927.

about recommended courses of action and should be able to answer them effectively. They need to develop an ear for discord amidst harmony. Often, the "facts" presented to them aren't "facts" at all, but estimates, conjectures, or the even more dangerous "SWAGs".[25]

When leaders hear wrong notes, they should pursue those sounds and run down the branching paths of ideas like good hounds coursing a scent. When possible, they need to take time to reflect on important decisions, come back to them more than once, and shake them the way junkyard dogs worry old bones.

When leaders don't examine proposals or solutions thoroughly, inevitably, someone else will to their embarrassment—and, often, their carelessness extracts a high price to be paid with the currency of eroded confidence in professional leadership.[26]

FOUR KINDS OF LEADERSHIP

Variously attributed to a German admiral and a German general officer, and possibly also to Robert E. Lee and Hannibal, there are four categories of military leaders. In the nautical version, they are (1) hard working and brilliant—these are qualities that make particularly good staff officers; (2) lazy but brilliant—these qualities are compatible with seagoing command of ships and submarines, where crucial intellectual assets are needed even if only for brief periods of time during combat; (3) lazy and not too bright—these qualities in officers present formidable problems for admirals, but properly pointed and frequently pushed, or even kicked, there are places in the navy for them where they can make significant contributions; (4) industrious and stupid—this combination produces men and women too dangerous for leadership positions who should be removed from the military at any cost. Their ignorance, combined with boundless energy, makes them a lethal force.

The analogies aren't all that bad for leadership positions in public education. Hardworking and brilliant administrators make good curriculum directors, assistant superintendents, etc. The brilliant, but less compulsive, workers can be wonderful principals and superintendents if an adequate supporting cast is provided for them; otherwise, the

[25]"Stupid, Wild A-- Guesses."

[26]See also, this chapter, "Ten Cardinal Principles of Leadership," p. 21; Chapter 4, "Dress Rehearsals," p. 149; and Chapter 8, "Frequently Understandable, Often Forgivable, Never Acceptable," p. 246.

comparison fails. Even downright lazy and not too bright leaders can function in some assistant principalships or lesser central office positions if their bosses are demanding enough and persistent enough to aim them each morning and propel them frequently throughout the day. And, as in the Germany navy, there is no place in public educational leadership for hardworking, but stupid, people. Their energy and misguided enthusiasm wreak havoc in the best of organizations through their energetic impersonations of the proverbial bulls in china shops.

TEN CARDINAL PRINCIPLES OF LEADERSHIP

Some years ago, at the Connecticut Governor's Conference on Excellence in Education, Yale University President, A. Bartlett Giamatti, later Commissioner of Baseball, spoke of "creative tensions"—equilibriums of contending and conflicting forces, or balances between polarities, or even more simply, differing perspectives—all of which work together, when a reasonable balance between them is maintained, to make organizations better.

In a somewhat related television editorial, Harry Reasoner of *CBS News* examined changes in national attitudes since the birth of our nation. It was his premise that early American statesmen envisioned democratic government in an environment of moderation between more radical views, with public opinion on major issues falling within a bell-shaped curve—differences to be sure are inevitable, but not almost total polarity on every important matter. Reasoner further asserted that our founders would be shocked and saddened today by the recklessness of modern American extremist views, which can only be portrayed as a bimodal distribution of the electorate. This nation, designed to be run by a moderate center between fringe groups, is now riven by a series of single-interest issues that trample the moderate minority trying to survive in the center.

The views of both men, while not lessening the importance of diverse convictions among the citizenry, also argue that moderate positions don't require characterless compromise or a lack of strong convictions. Courage isn't the midpoint between cowardliness or foolhardiness; it is, instead, a desirable position between two foolish extremes—an example of the "Aristotelian Golden Mean."[27] Americans

[27]See also, this chapter, "In Search of Gold," p. 7.

have the same right to be impassioned about reasoned, balanced beliefs as do zealots, on either end of the political spectrum, about their all or nothing opinions—but moderate voices, often perceived incorrectly as prima facie evidence of weak character, often can't be heard over the din of extremist shouts:

> *Turning and turning in the widening gyre*
> *The falcon cannot hear the falconer;*
> *Things fall apart; the centre cannot hold;*
> *Mere anarchy is loosed upon the world,*
> *The blood-dimmed tide is loosed, and everywhere*
> *The ceremony of innocence is drowned;*
> *The best lack all conviction, while the worst*
> *Are full of passionate intensity [14].* [28]

The following "Ten Cardinal Principles of Leadership" attempt to maintain creative educational balances and recognize that balances between extreme views are preferable to extreme positions on educational issues, problems, attitudes, and behaviors. Some of them are explored in greater detail in other sections of this book. [29]

First Principle

Understand current educational philosophies, but temper them with the standards your parents gave you in making educational decisions.

Educational philosophy may excite the philosophers among us, but if we look closely, we'll find a hell of a lot more philosophies than licensed philosophers. Education needs leaders who apply strong personal standards to situations and decisions; standards developed by nurturing parents and teachers; unfortunately, those standards may not be as prevalent today as they once were. Enduring virtues still lie between conflicting extremes of relativism, and they possess a dignity and strength that all the relativists in the world, on either fringe, can't erode.

---

[28]William Butler Yeats won the Nobel Prize for literature in 1903. One of his major efforts was titled *Ideas of Good and Evil* published in 1903, and "The Second Coming," from which the quote was taken [14], was also concerned with this same subject of good and evil.
[29]See also, this chapter, "In Search of Gold," p. 7.

Second Principle

Be efficient, but beware of ineffectiveness, which may grow from efficiency.

Policies, regulations, forms, and procedures for solving recurring problems are essential. Leaders don't have the time to address every issue without recourse to established procedure and precedent, but general solutions to specific problems must be applied with caution and with awareness that they are imperfect approximations of ideal solutions. Policies and regulations are always subject to change as their shortcomings are shown to exist. They are not socks with one size that fits all. Excessive leadership efficiency may result in eroded leadership effectiveness.[30]

Third Principle

Be consistent, but don't be afraid of necessary deviations from consistency.

"A foolish consistency is the hobgoblin of little minds, adored by little statesmen, philosophers, and divines" [15]. <u>Foolish</u> is one of two key words in this concept, and <u>consistency</u> should be tempered as necessary to avoid rigidity. Human considerations often require departures from past practices. Emerson also advised us, "Speak what you think now in hard words, and speak differently tomorrow if need be, for tomorrow will be a new day" [15]. When you make a bad call, admit it, cut your losses, change the decision and the course it has set. Shifting directions is painful but, in the long run, won't hurt as much as persisting in folly; just be sure you've given your decisions enough time to be evaluated thoroughly.[31]

Fourth Principle

Pay close attention to the details, not to the exclusion of larger issues, but to the extent details affect larger issues.

[30]See also, Chapter 3, "Efficient or Effective—Choose Any Two," p. 73 and Chapter 4, "And So Do His Sisters, His Cousins, and His Aunts," p. 172.
[31]See also, Chapter 4, "And So Do His Sisters, His Cousins, and His Aunts," p. 172.

Administrative genius, as other kinds of genius, "means transcendent capacity of taking trouble" [12]. The "devil is in the details,"[32] and "if we don't consider details important, neither will colleagues; if small items are ignored, our educational venture will fail, and no infusion of policy or lofty ideals will correct the situation" [11].

Fifth Principle

Work hard, but don't run at every windmill.

There is so much to do and so little time to do it; we need to focus our energies effectively and not expend them recklessly. An old bull and a young bull were strolling in a field one day when the young bull's keen eyesight identified a herd of cows in a distant meadow. Stimulated by this vista, he nudged the old gent and said, "Let's run over to that field and be friendly with a couple of those cows." The old bull counseled, "No, son, let's stroll over and be friendly with them all." (I recognize the potentially sexist characterization of this story, but think how politically incorrect it would have been if, instead, I'd said, "An old cow and a young cow were strolling in a field one day. . . .")

Sixth Principle

Don't avoid difficult professional decisions, but also trust those who work with you to make them when appropriate.

The better we do our jobs, as leaders, the less necessary we become. Maybe it's fortunate that few of us are so good we become unnecessary, and it's difficult to let go of control so others can act on their own. It's even more difficult to let them fail on their own, but we learn only through taking risks and occasional failures. It's still wise to avoid catastrophes whenever possible.[33]

Seventh Principle

Accept other people's motivations as good, but develop a highly sensitive BS detector about information others provide.

This is a difficult balancing act, and it's easy to fall off the wire. Although you should be generous about others' motives and abilities,

---

[32]See also, this chapter, "The Devil Is in the Details," p. 18.
[33]See also, Chapter 8, "It's What You Do That Gets Me in Trouble," p. 248.

you still need to question, probe, and test the soundness of ideas and information characterized for you as "facts." Anticipate all reasonable, and many unreasonable, questions that may be asked about a course of action, and be able to answer them effectively. Develop an ear for discord. When you hear a wrong note, pursue the sound. Run down branching paths of ideas like a good hound coursing scents. When possible, take the time to reflect on important decisions; come back to them more than once; worry them the way a dog worries a bone. You can be sure that when you don't examine proposals or solutions thoroughly someone else will—to your embarrassment.[34]

Eighth Principle

Balance your needs to gather information prior to decisions with the need to make timely decisions.

Learn as much about issues as time allows, but realize that if you wait until you know all there is to know you will never make a decision. None of us will ever know everything about anything anyway.[35]

Ninth Principle

Make the right decisions for the right reasons, emphasizing the principles underlying the decision.

Stress pupil safety not to avoid lawsuits, but to protect young people from injury. Making good decisions for the wrong reasons makes it more likely that wrong choices will be made eventually for the wrong reasons. Concentrate on central issues, and cast out the peripheral the way prototypical linebackers shuck blockers in single-minded searches for ball carriers.[36]

Tenth Principle

Balance grim reality with imagination and frustration with pleasure.

Maintain the balance between seriousness of purpose and enjoyment of life. Your educational world will be immeasurably better if you can identify and enjoy the pomposity, banality, illusion, delusion, ambi-

---

[34]See also, this chapter, "The Devil Is in the Details," p. 18.
[35]See also, Chapter 3, "Efficient or Effective—Choose Any Two," p. 73.
[36]See also, Chapter 3, "Puritans and Bears," p. 85 and Chapter 5, "It's the Kids, Stupid!" p. 195.

guity, misdirection, lunacy, boredom, and just plain old BS, which surround you daily—as well as appreciating the excitement, challenge, and importance of educational leadership and the commitment, competence, and caring characteristic of most of your educational colleagues.[37]

CONCLUSION

Educators are members of the only profession that expects to be perfect—and that the public expects to be perfect. Doctors can't cure all patients, but we accept medicine's limitations—albeit grudgingly. Lawyers, except for Perry Mason and he's dead, don't win every case. It is both public education's honor and its tragedy that its practitioners accept each student failure as their failure; we embrace this Quixotic notion because to act any other way would be an abandonment of responsibility. Accepting this challenge is painful, and the best way to ease that discomfort is through recognition and appreciation of education's many successes; with a sense of humor; and with a sense of personal, professional, and historical perspective.

DISCUSSION QUESTIONS

(1) What is your definition or conception of leadership? With which assertions in "What Is It?" do you agree and/or disagree?
(2) From "What Does It Look Like When You See It?" to what degree do you believe the five qualities listed are important in educational leadership positions? Why?
  • personal security and self-confidence
  • ability to make decisions and the ability to live comfortably with decisions once made
  • openness to changing previous decisions, but with a degree of reluctance to change course
  • tolerance of ambiguity
  • recognition of the essentials
(3) To what extent do you agree or disagree with assertions in "Born

[37]Maybe I "overceed" in that last sentence. See also, Chapter 3, " 'The Emperor's New Clothes,' " p. 94.

or Made?" Can anyone be taught to be an effective leader? If you think not, what are the qualities necessary for effective leadership that cannot be taught?

(4) Have you worked with educational leaders who had difficulties locating the Aristotelian mean between any of the qualities or attributes or issues described in "In Search of Gold" (data and intuition; educational philosophies and personal standards; student needs and district finances; student, staff, parent rights and student, staff, parent responsibilities; policy/regulation and common sense; the public's right to know and employee confidentiality; board recognition of the superintendent of schools as chief executive officer of the board and its legitimate need to hear other staff views and perceptions; efficiency and effectiveness; consistency and inconsistency; details and the big picture; confronting problems directly and appropriately avoiding others; making difficult decisions personally and delegating them appropriately; open acceptance of other people's motives and development of a highly functional "BS detector"; acquiring adequate information to make decisions and making timely decisions; and seriousness of purpose with enjoyment of professional life)? Have you personally been faced with finding the gold between extremes, and, if so, in what kinds of educational settings or situations?

(5) Would you be, or are you, more fulfilled through leadership crises or in a position of relative calm, which permits more time for reflection and/or a slower pace?

(6) Which parts of E. R. Ettner's advice from "Submersible Leadership" do you believe could be applicable to you in your particular educational setting?

(7) Reflecting upon points made in "The Devil Is in the Details," with which do you agree and/or disagree? Why?

(8) Match the descriptions of the four kinds of leaders from "Four Kinds of Leadership" with educational leaders with whom you have worked: hard working and brilliant, a bit lazy but brilliant, downright lazy and not too bright, and hard working and stupid. Into which category have most of the leaders for whom you've worked fallen?

(9) Identify and write your own "Ten Cardinal Principles of Leadership." How many are the same as, or similar to, those in this chapter?

CHAPTER 2

Getting Started

WHERE DO WE COME FROM?

FOR CLASSROOM TEACHERS, public education is an increasingly important, almost always interesting, and often exciting profession; principalships, superintendencies, and other leadership positions in public education offer their own special highs and lows and are highly recommended for the right people.

Good teachers remain the best group from which to find good school leaders, and easing administrative certification requirements to encourage people outside education to become principals or superintendents of schools won't change this reality. Although there is a current school of thought that believes successful business leaders would automatically be major successes as school district leaders, public education has specific organizational knowledge, its own special culture, and a special ambience that can only be learned and absorbed through years of public school experience.

CEOs of large corporations should be given the opportunity to tackle large city school districts or other kinds and sizes of school districts as superintendents of schools. Possibly, they would perform wonders heretofore unseen, and superintendents who have given their best leadership efforts for many years would suddenly find out what they should have been doing all along, but a more likely possibility is that CEOs would retreat quickly to their corporate boardrooms—having learned the hard way the differences between very real corporate power and the limited authority of the superintendency, with even that small portion impaired by board of education micromanagement, local politics, association and union relationships, and parents whose interest in and ability to shape educational direction far exceed the relatively disorganized stockholders of large corporations.[38]

[38]See also, Chapter 6, "Blah, Blah, Blah, Natasha," p. 203.

HOW LONG DOES IT TAKE?

Some educators with only minimal experience have become administrators and believed themselves to be successful in spite of experiential deficits. Possibly, those of us for whom that occurred were
precocious exceptions, or maybe we had low thresholds of self-
delusion—or maybe both. Our self-perception (or the lack of it) may
have caused us to underestimate the value of experience, and it may
still mislead us once in a while. It has taken many superintendents too
long to understand that we may be harsher critics of others than of ourselves, and, at least partially for that reason, we have underestimated
the importance of maturity and experience in effective leadership.

School districts with administrative salaries below area norms must
often, of necessity, place greater weight on a candidate's personal
potential and accept his or her relative lack of professional experience.
It's not uncommon for superintendents to be unpleasantly surprised by
significant administrative inadequacies in carrying out even routine
leadership responsibilities, from inadequate preparation and experience, among very bright but inexperienced school leaders. There
are always exceptions, and a few administrators manage well in spite of
experiential deficits.

Although we should always seek outstanding personal qualities in administrative candidates, ultimately, we learn to value the wisdom that
comes only from experience and maturity. Most analogies are imperfect, and medicine is too often dragged kicking and screaming into
educational discussions, but when people need gall bladders removed
(only one per customer), they are much better off with journeymen sur-
geons who have sliced and diced hundreds of the offending organs, instead of in the hands of brilliant recent medical school graduates who
haven't done many, if any, on their own. Good hands and practice will
outperform young intellect alone—although experience and brilliance
remain the best combination. In spite of all this, occasionally, we may
still be charmed by personal qualities into forgiving less than desirable
experience.

In preparing for administrative leadership, teachers should become
involved in as many learning opportunities outside the classroom and
assume as many additional professional tasks as reasonably possible—leadership positions outside school settings are also valuable.
Committees, activities, and memberships alone won't bedazzle inter-

viewers, but potential learning from different experiences makes each one important.

Good arguments can be made that administrative jobs require approximately similar overall experiences, but in different configurations. While desirable experiences and the quality of previous experiences vary among administrative aspirants, a rough guide to minimum experience requirements for various initial administrative positions might be:

- elementary principalships (or for the relatively rare elementary assistant principalship)—eight to fifteen years of teaching and other good background (A few people are ready sooner, but they are exceptions even more so today than twenty years ago.)
- secondary school assistant principalships—eight to fifteen years divided between classroom and department chairmanships
- high school principalships—fifteen or more years as a teacher, in departmental leadership, and probably as an assistant principal
- assistant superintendencies and other central office administrative positions—fifteen or more years total educational experience, including five to ten years of classroom teaching and successful administrative leadership, preferably including a principalship
- superintendencies—fifteen to twenty years total educational experience, including five to ten years of classroom teaching, and ten or more years of administrative leadership, including a principalship; previous central office experience is also helpful

Clearly, any standards for experience requirements must be applied with caution—from person to person and situation to situation; successful exceptions occur with regularity, and not every superintendent views experience prerequisites the same way. Employers often are moved by the force or personality of particular candidates, but most strongly prefer varied and adequate backgrounds in addition to outstanding personal qualities.

There is, however, a point of diminishing returns, beyond which extensive experience causes prospective employers to suspect seemingly late-blooming leadership aspirations.

AM I READY YET?

Just about a year following completion of his doctoral study, a beginning superintendent of schools was asked to be a speaker at a conference on graduate programs preparing educators for public school leadership. As he figuratively bit, clawed, kicked, scratched, pummeled, denigrated, and probably desecrated a sizable portion of his educational preparation at the state university, his former professors' reactions were intriguing. Those whom he respected immensely were offended, angered, or hurt by what he said; those who had offered little to their graduate students smiled and nodded agreement as if to say, "Give those incompetents hell!" They were his "Teflon®" professors to whom no criticism would ever stick. It has been almost thirty years since then, and for the past ten or so years, I've been one of those professors about whom I had such mixed feelings.

Will Rogers said that he never met a man he didn't like, and similarly, many of us never completed a graduate course from which we didn't learn something of value—much of what we took with us from courses came from outside reading, writing, and other study—and, of course, outside of class learning is what education is about. That's the good news; the bad news is that it shouldn't have been necessary to drive eighty miles round-trip for bad lectures and vapid discussions, both of which characterize many graduate courses in educational administration.

In the early sixties, professors in graduate administration programs were frequently former, or current, practitioners of administrative martial arts, and, many had not been leadership superstars. In many universities, toward the middle and late sixties, there was an influx of younger professors with some, but usually modest, administrative experience in public school leadership. They were, for the most part, more oriented toward "theoretical administration," which to many of us appears almost worthless in the hurly-burly real world of principalships and superintendencies.

As we've gained more experience, our convictions about that pseudo body of knowledge called "theoretical administration" hasn't changed; much of what we thought was useless then remains useless today. Normally bright people acquire the best of it from living a while, but they don't confuse their hard-won knowledge by immersing it in prose with an SAE index of about sixty. Not only can't relatively unimaginative people pour certain liquids out of a boot, there are leadership theories so viscous that even the most able person would find them difficult to pour out of anything. The courses and their ideas are just too thick, too slippery, and too murky, and many educational leadership textbooks fall into this category.

The problem seems to be an inferiority complex that drives people who feel inadequate without a knowledge base comparable to that of law schools or medical schools or schools of engineering to make one up—to find professional fulfillment, they need their own esoterica. Instead, they should be proud to be important parts of practical, real-world efforts to prepare school leaders.

Wherever three of more professors manage to snare common sense in a leghold trap and transmogrify their captives through fifteen theoretical lectures on school district leadership, a degree-granting institution inevitably springs up. Fortunately, many fine programs remain centered, without apology, on the complex, practical, human enterprise of public educational leadership, even if they have introduced theoretical leadership elements. Using appropriate research bases, effective graduate programs examine, analyze, and improve leadership and leadership styles while remaining focused on the centrality of public school administration—leadership.

An intrinsic problem for graduate preparation of educational administrators is unrealistic encouragement of educators who don't have the personal qualities and the presence to even consider educational leadership—but as long as the continued existence of graduate schools depends upon student financial support of programs, this inherent conflict will remain. Many responsible professors cope with this issue successfully, but others don't, and a number of graduate students learn the hard way that their career goals are unrealistic. Too many pursue inappropriate goals for too long at too great a cost to their psyches before the accumulated evidence weighs them down, and they finally give it up.

RABBIS—I

Ed McBain is a former New York City policeman who writes the

87th Precinct police novels (*enjoyable reading*). In his books, police-men and detectives often have "rabbis" — not only Jewish cops, but others as well. In police circles, as in religious institutions, *rabbi* means "teacher" or "mentor," but it also implies a well-connected departmental superior who provides guidance, advice, and necessary contacts for a policeman's professional advancement. Educational "rab-bis" are extremely important to aspiring administrators, far beyond helping them secure interviews and providing recommendations to pro-spective employers; they also serve as role models and mentors who can draw upon their experiences to teach educators how effective educational leadership should be delivered.

Affiliation with universities having graduate administration pro-grams with good reputations and well-connected professors, as well as a candidate's professional working relationships with his or her superintendent or principal, help in administrative job searches. While applicants aren't hired just because they have good "rabbis," they are in-terviewed more often — and you can't get a job if you aren't interviewed. People who aren't hired because they are interviewed might require even more than an outstanding "rabbi" can provide — maybe an estimate for a personality transplant.

Superintendents are more likely to interview applicants presenting placement papers from universities or resumes accompanied by letters from other superintendents or college professors they know profession-ally. University placement services are well respected by educational employers, and if prospective administrators don't have an active folder from a graduate school, they should start one. It makes them seem part of an academic and administrative family instead of as poor, orphan match girls. Letters of application in homemade placement folders usu-ally aren't as well received as university papers, even when they are well assembled. Although a few outstanding people may use commer-cial placement services, most superintendents are skeptical about ad-ministrative applications from those sources.

Search consultants to boards of education for superintendencies nor-mally don't serve as mentors or "rabbis," but sometimes they come close. For principals and other administrators seeking school superin-tendencies, personal contacts with search firm consultants are in-valuable; although such "headhunters" are sensitive to charges of operating "stables" of preferred candidates, and most do not, usually they are willing to speak with and advise candidates about particular positions and about career prospects generally. When consultants have had direct professional contact with strong candidates, they are much more likely to suggest boards of education interview them.

WHERE ARE WE FOUND?

Almost all school districts post openings locally and seriously consider applicants from within the system. Most districts also advertise in area, state, and sometimes in national newspapers and publications. For superintendent "wannabees," nationally *Education Week* and AASA publications (American Association of School Administrators) are prime sources of administrative vacancy information.

Many districts save money at the expense of the applicant pool by using newspaper advertisements too small to catch candidates' attention or to make the desired impression. Cost differentials for large ads compared to the smallest classified are not that great. It's a good idea for district administrators to collect different sizes of personnel advertisements from weekday and weekend papers, with notations about costs of different sizes of advertisements, for various numbers of days, and on both weekdays and weekends. For the cost differentials involved, substantial ads are more cost-effective than four-line classifieds, and they make a major difference in who applies.

Superintendents and university professors are often asked to recommend qualified people, and, in turn, they often contact eminent "rabbis" for candidate referrals.

One dilemma faced by school districts is whether or not to search afar. For superintendencies, school districts will almost always reimburse candidate transportation and other expenses, and, for those positions, it's customary to conduct national searches; for assistant principalships, on the other end of the spectrum, it's a rarity for districts to subsidize airfare and other significant applicant expenses, and the odds are so against any one person being selected, it's awkward to require candidates to underwrite travel and other expenses for as many as four interviews before the final selection is made for a position.

Most districts advertise for entry-level positions within candidates' driving distances; for example, most Connecticut school districts advertise in New England, Middle Atlantic States, and maybe as far south as Virginia and the Carolinas. Selected candidates drive to their initial interviews and take care of overnight and other incidental expenses. Depending upon the district's affluence, sometimes ultimately successful candidates, or finalists, or all candidates interviewed may be reimbursed for travel and incidental expenses—but often, it's only finalists who are reimbursed for expenses.

"SOBER, STEADFAST, AND DEMURE" [16]

In addition to placement papers, specific letters of application and other materials are also integral parts of administrative applications and affect the outcome of position searches. Letters of application are particularly important and should demonstrate both literacy and, if possible, at least a modicum of knowledge about the district. It's a good idea to have friends or associates review generic letters of application. Superintendents have received letters of application on yellow tablet paper; written in pencil; on scraps of paper; replete with major grammatical errors and misspellings; and with a's, e's, and o's filled with typewriter dirt or holes punched through those vowels—uncommon today with word processors widely available.

Materials accompanying letters of application also vary widely from slick, printed resumes with gratuitous candidate pictures to the rag-tag, toilet paper varietals. Understated quality is best, and it makes a difference how an application is perceived. Superintendents have also received letters of application such as the one in which a particular applicant challenged all other candidates to a series of public debates over who was better qualified—in that same letter, its author employed the beautiful phrase "pusillanimous poppycock" to describe most textbooks—an early educational circular torpedo run that destroys its own ship or, in this case, its own candidacy.

Candidates would do well to have their application papers reflect at least those qualities from *Il Penseroso* which are the title of this piece.

GAINING ENTRANCE TO THE PARLOR

It's not an easy task for school district personnel to wade through the many applications received and choose the best candidates for interviews. Even with good letters of application and well-organized accompanying papers, for a given candidate selection for interviews is still problematic. Because it is so difficult to assess candidate worth and potential from applications alone, it's a good practice for prospective employers to schedule personal interviews with as many candidates as possible. However, not every superintendent can, or is willing to, invest the time required to see even most of the good applicants—which increases the importance to candidates of good application papers.

To improve chances of being chosen for personal interviews, candidates should use whatever likely contacts they have—their superintendent, his or her professional colleagues and friends, past or current university professors, and anyone else who might help them receive personal interviews. Superintendents don't mind unsolicited references, as long as the caller is clear that interview consideration is all that's sought. Superintendents call other superintendents regularly on behalf of applicants in whom they have a personal or professional interest, and these calls normally help candidates' chances to be interviewed. Anything that can help a candidate be seen personally is worth thinking about.

Many school districts recently have experienced an upturn in public school enrollments, but the burgeoning school populations of the sixties won't return any time soon. School closings in the seventies and eighties, along with reductions in central office positions, have reduced the numbers of administrative positions available. Baby "boomlets" we may have, but probably no big time booms. Ironically, at the time when women finally are receiving fair consideration for leadership positions, the number of available administrative jobs for them and others is dwindling.

Although applicant pools vary from town to town and from season to season and although in the nineties fewer good teachers are prepared to leave the classroom for leadership positions, districts still receive reasonable numbers of applications for administrative openings—some from obvious losers but also many from good, competent, experienced professionals. Statistically, finding the initial position in school leadership is a steep hill to climb, even for outstanding educators, but if they persist in their search, well-prepared candidates eventually secure good administrative positions somewhere.

HOW DO I GET TO CARNEGIE HALL?

For people very familiar with daily homework, it's amazing how many educators don't do their own. Although, as preparation for job interviews, nothing is more effective than previous job interviews, thorough investigation of and preparation for each situation is warranted. In the early stages of his legal career, a young attorney took quite a few weak cases to trial—real "bowsers." Although his chances of winning ranged from nonexistent to negligible, the courtroom experience was later invaluable when he had better cases to try—owning his own ambulance helped also. Educators should consider similar rehearsals and preparation, without the ambulance, to begin their own leadership careers.

When selected for interviews, candidates should learn as much as possible about the job they seek—the school, the district, its personnel, and the community. Internal candidates obviously know quite a bit to begin with, but even they shouldn't assume they know all that's required and should speak further with other staff and community members to gain additional perspective.

If applicants are from out of town, they should inquire of anyone they know who lives and works locally; ascertain public perceptions of particular schools (or school districts if looking for central office positions), their strengths, and the characteristics people believe need improvement. When candidates detect specific dissatisfactions about schools, or previous administrators, they should expect interview questions to determine their own styles, abilities, knowledge, or propensities in those areas of concern. Additionally, candidates should read newspapers and district publications, talk to others, and sharpen possible responses to questions about those particular issues of concern in the school or district or both. Interviewers' judgments (fair or unfair, accurate or inaccurate) of incumbent superintendents, or principals, are easily discernible through interviewers' questions, which always reveal perceived deficiencies of previous administrators.

It's wise for candidates to arrange with a friend, or friends, to simulate interviews; from previous administrative interviews, from study of the particular position, or from examples of questions provided in this chapter, applicants should assemble probable interview queries. A variation on "How do I get to Carnegie Hall?" might be "How do I get to the principal's or superintendent's office?"—the answer to both questions is "Practice! Practice! Practice!"

Because many interviews are conducted by multiple interviewers, simulated group sessions around an interview table are important; even though they're not actual interviews, answering questions in group simulations will prove helpful later in the real thing. Previous experiences in similar interviews, even simulations, make the ambience of actual interviews far less threatening.

Candidates should prepare, and videotape, opening and concluding interview statements; videotape simulated interviews, both one-on-one and group interviews; critique their tapes personally; and have associates review the recordings with candidates and offer constructive criticism.

This kind of careful, thorough preparation isn't illegal, immoral, or fattening—it's just doing the homework that should be done for a possible principalship, superintendency, or for any other educational leadership position.

GRAB ON TO THE ROPE!

A radio commercial in the New York City area extols the virtues of a particular home supply store through attacks on a mythical competitor. In their hypothetical rival's vast warehouse, shoppers are forever getting lost as they wander helplessly from one department to another. The commercial features a husband and wife trudging wearily through miles of labyrinthine aisles to find the hardware department; finally, they see a sign that says, "Next rest area five miles." Then they hear the clatter of an approaching helicopter, and a stentorian voice from above directs the lost and forlorn couple to "Grab on to the rope! Grab on to the rope!"

On local, state, and national levels, school leaders should also "grab on to the rope" from their various professional organizations. If they accept those professional offers of assistance, they benefit immeasurably from membership and participation in area, state, and national administrative organizations. Major national leadership associations include:

- American Association of School Administrators (AASA)—Although all levels of school administration may belong, superintendents make up the largest single group in the membership of this organization. AASA is an active participant in legislative development activities of the U.S. Congress and with the U.S. Department of Education and also works closely with state superintendents' associations.
- National Association of Secondary School Principals (NASSP)—NASSP is the national parent body for secondary school administrators.
- National Association of Elementary School Principals (NAESP)—NAESP is the national parent body for elementary school principals; both NASSP and NAESP solicit membership from junior high or middle school principals.

- Association for Supervision and Curriculum Development (ASCD)—This is a professional organization focused on curriculum and instruction; many administrators also belong to ASCD, as well as one of the other major administrative groups for their school district leadership level. For curriculum directors and assistant superintendents for curriculum and instruction, ASCD often is the major professional association in which they are active.
- National School Boards Association (NSBA)—As the parent body for boards of education and their state board associations, NSBA programs, activities, and services are heavily attended and contributed to by school superintendents, as are the programs, activities, and services offered by state boards of education associations.

Although percentages of active administrators participating on the national level are smaller than percentages involved at state and regional levels, the numbers of participants are substantial at all three levels—national, state, and local—in all five groups identified earlier. Leadership benefits from membership and active participation include (1) additional leadership opportunities and service in different settings, from national leadership, through state leadership, and in regional leadership, among administrative peers and between administrators' particular associations and other major leadership groups; (2) professional learning activities from national conferences, from state conferences and workshops, and from area meetings of administrative groups; (3) access to professional publications and periodicals; (4) opportunities to affect public legislation and policy at both the national and state legislative and regulatory levels—particularly state commissioners of education and state education departments; (5) professional networking in professional advancement and in job searches; and (6) opportunities for professional and personal socialization and collegiality with administrative colleagues. The psychological benefits from associational activities and meetings with friends and colleagues is important throughout an administrator's entire career in public education—and for that matter, for the rest of his or her life. In few situations, especially at the superintendent's level, can his or her administrative organizations salvage a situation when relationships with boards of education have deteriorated irrevocably; however, the psychological and moral support they give, and sometimes their good legal and practical advice, are invaluable for leaders in crisis with their employers.

If there were a typical career pattern for participation in professional administrative organizations, it might be as follows: (1) Administrators become active in their regional groups and take the escalator to the top through their leadership positions, for example, serving as secretary, vice president, and president of an area superintendent's group; many have no interest in moving beyond this level of peer involvement and participation. (2) Among a number of those who may be interested, a few might move from regional participation to state superintendents' associations, by whatever name they may be known, possibly first as area representatives to the central governing bodies of state associations, and then through the chairs, to the presidency. (3) For a few hardy souls, national leadership may be sought, and even fewer are successful in their quest. To be elected to AASA's board of directors, and possibly later to a national AASA office, involves heavy-duty campaigning reminiscent of candidates seeking typical national political offices. Only the most ambitious and energetic can manage both the superintendency and national organizational responsibilities in addition—they also must be fortunate and be employed by a very understanding board of education that encourages them in their broader professional pursuits.

Even when school leaders have no burning ambitions to become associational leaders, participation on regional and state levels is very important for the reasons already cited—plus the satisfaction received from being part of an even larger group dedicated to improving American public education for its students and, ultimately, for the entire nation. The added dimension and perspective from this involvement and participation is both worthwhile and satisfying to educational leadership.

FRANK BUCK IS ALIVE AND WELL—I

Superintendent Search Firms

Consultant services are used for many, if not most, superintendent searches. There are occasional perceived problems with search consultants, and, although these problems may have appeared more frequently in the past, they occur today as well. A few consultants, especially if closely connected to particular universities, have been accused of favoring candidates from a particular "stable" of prospective superintendents; when a candidate is one of the horses in their barns, that doesn't seem so terrible. But, when applicants forage alone, then it can be difficult to be seriously considered as an entry in the race.

Almost all experienced superintendents, especially those who have had more than one superintendency, have been both beneficiaries or victims of the consultant system in superintendent searches. In balance, it is a legitimate process that adds greatly to a board's ability to locate and select the right person to lead their school system, but school boards must choose their consultants carefully and weigh their judgments and recommendations the same way.

Many school board members only experience a superintendent search once, and they have very little knowledge of the process against which to evaluate search consultants. Even those who have previously experienced a search with consultants often have little insight into the backstage machinations that sometimes accompany finding a new superintendent. It may not be appropriate to say that a superintendent search is similar to sausage making and that a person doesn't really want to know what goes into either—but it's a temptation.

Superintendent of schools searches are divided into three phases, by whatever names the three phases are called and by whomever they may be conducted whether search consultant or board of education.

PREPARATION (FOUR WEEKS)

In the "preparation phase" of a search after the search consultant is selected, all consultants, in one way or another, follow steps 1–6: (1) Organize search committee. Procedures vary from district to district, and arrangements may include the following among others: boards of education that conduct the entire search with the consultant without any other participation by citizens or staff; boards, augmented with one or more administrators, teachers, support staff, parents/citizens, elected officials, and sometimes students, that serve as the search committee and selection committee; board committees that will do the initial screening and then recommend finalists to the entire board of education for a final selection; board committees, augmented with one or more administrators, teachers, support staff, parents/citizens, elected officials, and sometimes students, who do the initial screening and then recommend finalists to the board of education for a final selec-

SEARCH FLOW CHART

Preparation—4 Weeks

1. Select consultant
2. Organize search committee
3. Approve search schedule
4. Establish salary and benefits
5. Consultant interviews with board of education, citizens, town officials, and staff
6. Consultant report on interviews
7. Consultant preparation, and board of education approval, of brochure and advertisements

Search—8 Weeks

8. Advertisements, personal contacts with prospective candidates; letters, telephone calls
9. Applications received, processed, verified complete
10. Preliminary reference checks
11. Regular progress reports to board of education search committee
12. Candidate screening; consultant recommendation of best candidates for board of education/search committee interviews
13. Board of education/search committee receives all applications and materials

Choices—4 Weeks

14. Consultant review of recommendations and preliminary reference checks with board of education/search committee
15. Candidates selected for semi-finalist interviews by board of education/search committee
16. Semi-finalists interviews (eight to twelve)
17. Selection of finalists (three or four)
18. Completion of reference checks
19. Board of education interview of finalists
20. Decisions on candidates and site visits
21. Selection/election of new superintendent of schools

tion. (2) Approve search schedule. The process usually requires twelve to sixteen weeks to prepare, search, select, and sign a contract with the selected superintendent. The number of weeks cited in this outline (four, eight, and four weeks) is of a typical search without greater than usual pressures to select a new superintendent. From the time of selection and contract signing, there may be up to ninety days until the new superintendent can free himself or herself from current contractual obligations and report to his or her new district. (3) Establish salary and benefits. (4) Consultant interviews board of education, parents and citizens, town officials, and staff. (5) Consultant reports on interviews to board of education. Although it's true that there often are strong similarities in qualities that districts seek in a new superintendent, because of the particular circumstances in each district, there are also differences that should be identified. (6) Consultant prepares, and board of education approves, brochure and advertisements.

SEARCH (EIGHT WEEKS)

Most consultants place similar advertisements in *Education Week* and the AASA newsletter and correspond with major colleges and universities, state superintendents of schools, and some with the AASA executive directors of superintendents' organizations in each of the fifty states.

A high, although unknown, percentage of the same candidates respond to vacancy advertisements regardless of who places them, and going beyond the ads with personal contacts is one major variable among search consultants. To avoid charges of having a "stable" of candidates, many firms won't initiate contacts with prospective candidates and, instead, rely entirely upon advertising. But some will recruit people they believe to be well suited for a particular position, and often an invited candidate may become a finalist—and sometimes, ultimately, even the anointed one, selected not by the consultant, but by the board of education. This more active, personalized approach often is the difference between an acceptable search and an outstanding one.

All consultants receive applications, process them, and verify completeness. All consultants claim to screen candidates, although some are reluctant to make specific recommendations and to name the best candidates as they see them—other than putting them in three files like the Sears, Roebuck categorizations of good, better, and best. Some don't do reference checks, leaving that responsibility to their client board of education, although many do; the quality of reference checks conducted is also crucial to good selection. All consultants maintain contact with boards and/or search committees, but with different degrees of openness and interest.

There are still some search firms today that don't make all candidate applications and associated paperwork available to the board or screening committee along with consultant recommendations; today, however, many searchers provide board of educations everything received from applicants.

CHOICES (FOUR WEEKS)

This phase of a search normally consists of intensive reference checks, if not already performed by search consultants, and first-round interviews of semi-finalists—candidates chosen from paper screening for personal interviews with the board or search committee; second-round, often final, interviews of three of four selected candidates from the initial round of interviews; another round of reference checks, including site visitations of the final candidate, and sometimes of all finalists, prior to selection by the board of education; occasionally, one final interview prior to appointment or election of the board's choice.

Differences among services provided by various search consultants become more apparent in this phase of the process. Some consultants are effectively finished with their work after turning over the applications—although they may provide a sample superintendent contract for use in negotiating contract terms with the selected superintendent. These firms may have done a good clerical job, but the most important work remains ahead after applications are received.

It's important for consultants to conduct complete reference checks on the best candidates, to arrange and sit in on interviews as an observer (if the board requests), and to share informed perceptions and knowledge with the search committee and the board—and with candidates.

Some consultants offer various guarantees that they will perform the search again with no further search fees if the chosen candidate vaporizes before beginning work or leaves within a specified period. That's a minor risk when the search has been done properly, but unexpected behavior and events can happen—even in the best of families.

Superintendent searches are often conducted by other than rocket scientists, but good consultants are worth the fees they charge when they have a good working knowledge of the superintendency and its demands and of the different approaches, styles, strengths, and weaknesses among its practitioners and their communities.[39]

FRANK BUCK IS ALIVE AND WELL—II

Administrative Searches

Procedures for principal and other administrative searches parallel those of search consultants for superintendencies but are normally conducted by the superintendent of schools or, in larger districts, often by an assistant superintendent of schools or the director of personnel.

A thorough search process adds greatly to identifying and employing the right leaders for a school system. The search process should be developed thoroughly and involve staff, including teachers and other administrators, parents/citizens, and often secondary school students. Superintendents, or other responsible administrators, should clarify participants' roles clearly and explain the limits of their authority and/or participation in the search.

Although a few superintendents may be prepared to abide by majority decisions of search or screening committees, most explain that the committee's responsibility is limited to sharing its perceptions with the superintendent to help him or her decide who should be chosen for the position or recommended to the board of education for further interviews and final board selection. Generally, a superintendent will not, and should not, hire or recommend someone he or she doesn't personally support for a position; nor will he or she go forward with someone receiving generally negative reviews from a committee. While reserving the right to make final choices, the messages to the search committee should be that, absent some almost nonexistent circumstance, final selection will come from a meeting of minds between the superintendent of schools and search committee members.

Administrative searches may also be divided into three phases, as for superintendent searches, with typical time requirements shown in parentheses for each phase.

---

[39]See also, the Search Flow Chart, p. 43.

PREPARATION (FOUR WEEKS)

In the "preparation phase" of a search, superintendents generally follow steps 1–5: (1) Organize search committee. Procedures vary from district to district, and arrangements can include superintendents who conduct the entire search without any other participation by staff, citizens, students, or others; superintendents, working with a search or selection committee of administrators, teachers, support staff, parents/citizens, elected officials, and sometimes students; and committees, such as described above, which conduct the initial screening and then recommend finalists to the superintendent of schools for a final selection or for a final choice of an administrator or administrative finalists to be interviewed by the board of education for interviews and a final selection. (2) Develop search schedule. The process usually requires twelve to sixteen weeks to prepare, search, and select the new administrator; the number of weeks cited in this outline (four, eight, and four weeks) is for a typical search without greater than usual time pressures to select a new administrator. From selection and contract signing, there may be up to sixty days until the newly selected administrator can free himself or herself from current contractual obligations and report aboard. As a matter of professional ethics, the superintendent in the receiving district should work out transition arrangements with the superintendent in the district where the new administrator is currently employed. (3) Review salary and benefits and, if not covered in negotiated agreement, establish them. (4) Superintendent discusses position with staff, parents, and often students. (5) Prepare the brochure, if used, and position advertisements.

SEARCH (FOUR TO SIX WEEKS)

Superintendents, or designees, place advertisements in local and area newspapers, *Education Week*, and the *AASA Newsletter* and correspond with major colleges and universities and with in-state superintendents of schools. Some superintendents actively recruit particular administrators whom they believe are well-suited for a particular position locally. As in superintendent searches, this personalized approach can be the difference between acceptable searches and outstanding ones.

Superintendents, or designated assistants, receive applications, process them, and verify completeness. The superintendent, or designee, sometimes with search committee members, screens applications and selects a number of candidates for personal interviews.

CHOICES (FOUR WEEKS)

This phase of an administrative search normally consists of intensive reference checks, which are also crucial to good selection of principals and other administrators and first-round interviews of semifinalists—candidates chosen from paper screening for personal interviews with the superintendent or designee or search committee; second-round, often final, interviews of three or four selected candidates from the initial round of interviews; another round of reference checks, including site visitations of the final candidate, and sometimes of all finalists, prior to selection by the board of education; occasionally, one final interview prior to appointment by the superintendent or board of education.

As with superintendent searches, appropriate time and care in administrative searches and involvement of teachers, other administrators, and parents/citizens/students will greatly improve chances for a district's selection of the right candidate for its position.[40]

LOVE AT FIRST SIGHT

The first few seconds of an interview are critical; some say the first thirty seconds, and the first two or three seconds are unquestionably the most important moments of the first half minute. Good carriage, the right clothing, and a smile are important in these opening moments; we're not requiring classic good looks here, but a strong presence and an ineffable, unmeasurable life force, which emanate from some people more strongly than from others, are crucial to interview success. It's rare that extremely negative initial impressions evaporate during an hour-long discussion; more often, initially favorable impressions are eroded by candidate obtuseness, insensitivity, or other personal or professional shortcomings.

Small mannerisms and personal characteristics contribute to initial interview impressions—many of these traits can be cultivated, changed, or eliminated. Although everyone knows a limp handshake is a turnoff, a few candidates who never got the word still proffer them.

[40]See also, this chapter, "How Do I Get to Carnegie Hall?" p. 37; "A Baker's Dozen of Interview Suggestions," p. 49; and "Some Have Greatness Thrust upon Them," p. 52.

If your hands sweat, before shaking hands with interviewers, dry them (your hands) on your backside when nothing better is available—especially at interviews, somebody else's backside is always a "no-no." Mastery of the surreptitious swipe is an acquired skill, and the risk of being caught at it is still better than a damp, clammy handshake. If your hands are always cold, find a lavatory and run warm, or hot, water on your hands, and dry them thoroughly just moments before the interview begins.

A BAKER'S DOZEN OF INTERVIEW SUGGESTIONS

(*1*) If you don't know the local geography well, take the time to look it over before your interview. Drive through the town noting prominent features, and locate the interview site to insure your timely arrival for the interview. When candidates are even superficially conversant with landmarks, topography, and local features, their knowledge can be used to advantage in typical interviews. Don't begin an important interview in a semi-hysterical state, having arrived two minutes late after running three traffic lights, cruising through a couple of stop signs, and barely avoiding capture by local police after a high-speed chase.

(*2*) Maintain good eye contact with interviewers without trying to outstare him, her, or them. If you manage that, you may never be forgiven. If there is an interview team, share visual attention among all its members, but avoid looking like a windup toy as you shift your eyes around the table. Don't be unnerved by frowners; often, they are only concentrating on what you're saying and aren't angry with you at all. However, when you do sense problems with particular interviewers, work with them for a bit and see if you can change their overt reactions to you. Don't, however, become fixated on lost causes; if it's not working with one interviewer, smile, cut your losses, and focus on others around the table—with a token return to the seemingly hostile folks now and again. Don't take the nodders and smilers for granted either—continue sharing your attention with them to maintain, reinforce, or solidify your perceived position.

(*3*) Watch your body language. Hands above the table are probably more appropriate than below it—interviewers may wonder if they're trembling uncontrollably when out of sight. If they are shaking noticeably, take that chance and hide them. In that situation, the reality equals an interviewer's worst speculation. Leaning forward is usually better than leaning backwards—it shows interest, rather than indifference. Varying your position occasionally is even better—occasional changes, not constant motion that conveys nervousness and distracts interviewers. Leaning back to reflect on a response and leaning forward to deliver it are usually effective.

(4) It's okay to think a moment before answering. Don't be pressured to fill every empty second with your own voice.

(5) Periodically vary the tone, pitch, amplitude, or whatever vocal qualities you can change. Exhibit enthusiasm interspersed with reflectiveness and calm. An unchanging pattern of vocal responses can be either soporific if it's too calm, or it may jangle interviewers nerves if it is too enthusiastic for too long.

(6) Don't panic if a questioner puts you under some stress. Although most interviews aren't "stress interviews" designed to test emotional stability, it's reasonable to push an applicant occasionally to see how he or she responds under modest pressures. If an interviewer asks, "Have you ever had any failures?" to disorient you momentarily, they might add, "I'm not referring to unfortunate sexual experiences." If that totally discombobulates administrative candidates, their interview experiences may turn out badly—although, today, they may have a legal case because of the question about past failures.

(7) Avoid jargon. Most people don't want to hear a constant flow of "schoolspeak" such as "gross motor problems" when you mean the kid is clumsy, or "fine motor control difficulties" to describe bad handwriting. Know the current educational buzzwords, but avoid using them to excess. Be alert to verbal patterns or traps to which candidates occasionally fall prey—for example, using a favorite word over and over. If you say *rubric* once, you'll probably survive the interview, but after you've said it two or three times, people are counting the occurrences and ignoring what you're saying. I've had it happen (fortunately not with "rubric), and it was as if every time I needed a good nickel word, the same fifty-center popped out before I could wrestle it down. Each time it happened, I bit my tongue, but the word kept jumping unbidden out of my mouth.

(8) Use humor if it's natural and unforced. No jokes please—we're

talking humor and wit. Don't try to become someone you aren't; it doesn't work anyway. If you're a straight arrow without a highly developed sense of the absurd, go with your strengths; there's plenty of room in administration for all personal styles, and if yours doesn't suit one interviewer, probably it will be perfect for another.

(9) Feel good about yourself, the foundation of successful leadership, and let others know that you do—not insufferable conceit, but solid self-assurance. Don't be afraid to let people know that, after listening to other views, when you still feel your own is right for the situation, that's the one you will follow. It's not arrogance to value your own judgment over others as long as colleagues know your judgment will be to rely on somebody else's judgment when you don't know enough—and when you know you don't know enough. We like people who appreciate sound opinions—their own as well as those of others.

In a particular administrative interview, interviewers were really impressed by one candidate who, at the end of his interview time, was asked if there was anything he'd like to add in clarification or support of his candidacy. After a few seconds of reflection, he said he believed he had presented himself as well as he could have and that, whatever the final outcome, he was at peace with himself and with his presentation of himself. His manner was easy, not at all smug, reflecting honest feelings about a job well-done. It was very well received, and he got the job—although he wasn't selected only because of that one statement, it really helped him.

(10) Keep your responses briefer than you think you should. When you have answered a question succinctly and well, ask if the questioner wants more information—"Have I answered that to the extent I should have, or would you like me to amplify my statement?" That's preferable to talking until somebody shoots you to put a stop to your pain—and to theirs as well. If there is a single, common candidate failing over all others at interviews, going on much too long in response to each question would be high on the list.

(11) Develop strong opening and concluding statements. You will usually have an opportunity to use them, and they contribute strongly to interviewers' final interview impressions.

(*12*) Expect some nervousness and make it work for you. No matter how well you prepare, a degree of heightened consciousness and increased adrenalin flow are to be expected and are positive side effects of interviews. It's not desirable to begin an interview appearing either too relaxed, often seen as patronizing or indifferent, or overly tense, obviously rampant insecurities, and candidates should strive for the Aristotelian Golden Mean of demeanor somewhere between panic and complacency.

(*13*) Above all else, make the interviewers like you as a person! If you can manage the first twelve interview suggestions, the commandment that completes the "baker's dozen" is, "Make the interviewers like you!" An ingratiating manner won't work and likely will have the opposite effect; showing you know all the latest educational theories and buzzwords won't put you over the top either; demonstrations of professional knowledge and skills, while critical in helping you achieve the final round of interviews, won't by themselves make the interviewer or interviewers choose you from among other good finalists; to make it past initial interviews and to and through the final round into the winner's circle, candidates must make the interviewers like them as people.

There is no easy formula to achieve this goal, although careful attention to the twelve earlier suggestions will help, but as a candidate you must keep this need to "make them like me" fresh in your thoughts. While being honest and open about yourself, also convey to those around the interview table that you like them, too. If you can manage this, while at the same time showing you can do the desired job, your chances of being selected for the position you are seeking become immeasurably better. Of course, candidates who suffer from OPD, or obnoxious personality disorder (the newest psychiatric darling of the EEOC), have a rough road to travel to arrive at an administrative position; however, once chosen, the most mellow among us will be seen as often afflicted with OPD even on our best days.[41]

"SOME HAVE GREATNESS THRUST UPON THEM" [17]

A secret that many educators know, but which few admit openly, is

[41]See also, Chapter 7, "Grabbing the Brass Ring," p. 233 and Chapter 8, "Divergence and Convergence," p. 244.

that final choices are based primarily on visceral human reactions, instead of on candidate responses—almost always, however, they are made within acceptable ranges of professional competence among well-qualified finalists.

Candidates should be informed, articulate, and confident, but among the best who demonstrate most, or all, of the qualities sought for particular positions, final determinants are more often individual personal reactions to particular people. Interviewers often justify choices on candidates' answers—sometimes even answers to irrelevant questions because they can't acknowledge that their human reactions to candidates have been more important than professional credentials or interview responses. We all can react favorably to dozens of people we would never think of employing, and decisions made from human chemistry should only be among relatively equal and professionally competent finalists.

Somehow, though, you've got to make them like you, or you won't get the position no matter how well-qualified you may be.

"THE PHONE STILL AIN'T RINGING, SO I GUESS IT STILL AIN'T YOU" [18]

This title from a country western song[42] captures many administrative aspirants' feelings well. Most experienced administrators have applied unsuccessfully for administrative positions more often than successfully; occasionally, they never even heard from districts after they applied; sometimes they received letters of rejection without being interviewed; often, they were interviewed; and the best of them were frequently finalists for positions. They've had interviews that convinced them they had the jobs in their back pockets, but didn't; interviews that they thought went only modestly well but from which they received enthusiastic job offers. Most veteran candidates normally have at least an approximate sense of how well they did at interviews—but not always. Administrative candidates who are chosen for one in four positions are excellent hitters in the job search game—a batting average close to an infielder's batting average years ago; today, infielders don't usually hit that well, even earning two or three million dollars a season.

Some of us may have been misled because we received the first prin-

---

[42]This country western singer was describing a different kind of telephone call in his metaphysical song title, but the parallels are strong between his situation and those of equally anxious administrative candidates waiting to find out how they fared in an interview.

cipalship and/or superintendency for which we applied, and early successes can make subsequent near misses all the more incomprehensible. There are times applicants don't feel bad about missing out on particular positions because they have such great respect for the person eventually chosen. Sometimes, you won't understand how districts chose the people they hired while passing you up; but they did; they do; and they might again even when you believe that a movie made about a particular competitor or a board of education should be classified PG—not "parental guidance," but "perverts and goofballs."

Unsuccessful candidates for administrative positions usually fit one of three categories: those who apply and are never or rarely interviewed; those who apply, are interviewed frequently, but rarely get past initial interviews; and those who apply, are interviewed more than once, and often finish as finalists.

Category 1

If you find yourself in the first category, rarely if ever receiving interviews, examine your paperwork, review references, and try to improve what prospective employers are seeing on paper. Also, consider whether resumes reveal too little experience. In that case, you may have to be patient until you can add legitimate heft to your professional accomplishments. Touch base with your "rabbi" and see what advice he or she might have about improving your chances for interviews.

Although it might offend some prospective employers (but what the hell, nobody is seeing you anyway), call a few days after your papers should have been received; ask to speak with the superintendent of schools; if successful, express sincere interest in the position and ask if you might visit the school or district. Depending upon the prevailing tone of the conversation, you might also venture a hope that you receive an interview because you are so interested in the particular school or district. Any or all of these extra efforts may help you get an interview.

Category 2

If you fall into the second category, interviewed often but rarely twice, the problem obviously isn't the paperwork or the resume, but in how you conduct yourself at interviews—or "The fault, dear Brutus, lies not in our resumes but in ourselves." In these instances, recall the suggestions for simulated interviews and ask professional colleagues to help you do a better job with interviews. Some commercially advertised public speaking and personality overhaul courses are excellent and might help. If, after trying hard to improve interview skills, unsuccessful interviews continue, you may need to consider changing professional goals.

Category 3

If you're good enough, and sometimes lucky enough, to find yourself in the third category, often a bridesmaid but not yet a bride, you're in good shape if you stay with it. Even when outstanding teachers and administrators are often close without achieving final success, it's normal for them to feel discouraged and believe there must be something wrong with them, or they would have been offered a position already. Among good finalists, different interviewers choose different people, and factors influencing choices of one good person over others are almost as numerous as grains of beach sand.

There are always areas in which you can improve, but if you continually clear your first hurdles, chances are you're doing a good job. At that point, it's just a matter of finding the right match between you and other people's expectations and perceptions—it will happen.

PSYCHIC[43] BENEFITS OF ADMINISTRATIVE LEADERSHIP

Each man or woman who enters school administration today has a special opportunity to be part of inspired team efforts and group commitments to achieve worthwhile goals. If you are, or have ever been, fortunate enough to be a vital part of a team striving collectively to reach worthwhile goals, you already know the powerful feelings such commitments can generate—and the satisfaction that comes from even partial accomplishment of difficult tasks. If you have never felt that excitement, you should before you retire. Today, public school leadership offers such opportunities even more than ever before—not guaranteed successes, but abundant opportunities for worthwhile service.[44]

---

[43] I once allowed a note to the faculty to get by me with "psychic" spelled as "physic"—a mistake, which I asserted, in a make-up memo, "measured the distance between soul and large intestine." I'd never been so humiliated in all my life.

[44] See also, Chapter 11, "Educational Colleagues and Friends," p. 366.

GOLDEN SHOVELS

"The Golden Shovel Award" is presented to selected Connecticut superintendents for special efforts to combat destructive elements within or without public education and for appropriate resistance against school district villains. The award evokes the mental picture of a dedicated superintendent shoveling a noxious substance against an endless tide of odiferous material. On one special occasion, the award was presented to all superintendents in the state, and the presentation text follows:

> Ernest Hemingway defined courage as "grace under pressure." The "Golden Shovel Award" recognizes the courage shown by each year's award recipient for his or her strength in defense and support of public education and in opposition to individuals, groups, or ideas who or which would do harm to children or youth, to a school district, to public education generally, or to the superintendency itself.

> Although this year's award winner hasn't slain dragons in full view of admiring crowds, or performed dramatic acts resulting in widespread public recognition, each day has required ample measures of courage, or grace under pressure; pressure from unrealistic board of education expectations; from angry, confused, or frightened parents; from increasing constraints imposed by federal and state governments and bureaucracies; from boards of finance; from employee unions and associations; from national, state, and local economic and budgetary crises; from insufficient time; from imperfect health and personal frailties; and from a host of other pressures which surround superintendents each day as air surrounds our bodies. Although others in education feel pressures, superintendents are at the forefront of any important issues, rallying support for students and good education from among those who would give it, with professional reputation and position vulnerable and at great risk of loss.

> This year's Golden Shovel recipient worked each day with quiet courage, understanding that the best of efforts would be met with nonexistent to modest recognition or appreciation. The day to day honest striving to provide the best possible education for kids; the sharing of credit for successes and the personal assumption of responsibility for failures; the belief in a job well done, because all jobs should be done well whether noted by anyone else or not; all of these are unheralded daily examples of the integrity and commitment which mark the careers and professional behaviors of this year's honorees.

> For your courage, your grace under pressure, your style, we present an

equal share of the Golden Shovel Award to each of the state's Superintendents of Schools.

Every American superintendent of schools should receive this award annually—even if he or she must present it to him- or herself. It's well deserved.[45]

DISCUSSION QUESTIONS AND ACTIVITIES

(1) Compare your views to those expressed in "Where Do We Come From?" on whether business and corporate leaders could move easily into educational leadership.

(2) Prepare your own preferred experiential guidelines/requirements for candidates for school district leadership:
- elementary principalships
- secondary school assistant principalships
- high school principalships
- assistant superintendencies and other central office administrative positions
- superintendencies

(3) Review existing or past letters of application for administrative positions and edit them as necessary to make them potentially more effective; if you haven't written one, do that as a basis for such letters in the future; assemble a set of placement papers, including letter of application, resume, four letters of reference, and college and university transcripts.

(4) With associates, simulate an employment interview with you as the candidate for the administrative position of your choice. Practice the ideas from "A Baker's Dozen of Interview Suggestions"; videotape the interview, and critique it with your interviewers.

(5) Have you had experiences with superintendents or other search consultants? What are your views on this phenomenon?

---

[45]See also, Chapter 6, "Taming the 450-Pound Media Gorilla—A One-Act Morality Play," p. 212 and Chapter 11, "Lanterns in the Window," p. 348; "May I Have the Envelope Please," p. 349; and "Educational Colleagues and Friends," p. 366.

CHAPTER 3

Attitudes, Behaviors, Practices, Skills

ANKLE BONE CONNECTED TO THE FOOT BONE . . .

EFFECTIVE SCHOOL LEADERS need to be sensitive to undercurrents, ripples, and eddies in, between, and among different groups that comprise educational communities—within groups of teachers, principals, other administrators, boards of education, parents, and students and between and among all of them. As Earth's tides are attuned to its moon, superintendents, principals, and other administrators must ascertain the pull from gravitational fields emanating from constituent groups and understand the synergistic effects of one body on the other, to such a degree that they: (1) remain suspicious, if not totally disbelieving, of seeming coincidences between similar or related events—especially when they have significant problem potential; (2) recognize and understand existing connections between and among seemingly disconnected events, including, but not limited to, individual and group behaviors, actions, attitudes, questions, and correspondence; news articles; and recommendations and propositions that possibly they should refuse; (3) connect the dots and visualize overall patterns emerging from apparently independent events; (4) use connections and identified patterns to investigate and analyze similar or even tangential past events to determine existing relationships between or among them; (5) develop connections and patterns from relationships among present conditions, including emerging issues and current problems identified; and (6) take effective steps to correct existing problems before they worsen and to prevent new problems from spinning off the old ones.

The two different scenarios that follow illustrate how well all of these important and necessary recognitions, connections, analyses, corrective actions, and preventative steps might occur in one situation with one superintendent and not at all in another situation with another superintendent.

59

The Case of the Comatose Careerist

In its most recent negotiations with teachers' bargaining representatives, which concluded in the fall of last year, a school district added contract articles, effective in the current school year, providing teacher aides to cover lunchroom and playground duties "to the extent practicable"—and, correspondingly, the new provisions also increased the number of teachers' instructional preparation periods each week.

At the close of the last school year, three district teacher aides retired, and, during the summer, unexpected budget problems persuaded board members that the superintendent shouldn't fill those three positions until further notice from them. At that point, the superintendent should have reminded the board of its collective bargaining obligation to ensure the school district had sufficient teacher aides to comply with the added and the revised contract provisions. If he can't comply, he must report that to the board and review anticipated staffing problems with union leadership. He did neither of these things.

In early September of the current school year, the superintendent walked into a teachers' room to say hello to the staff having lunch there, and, as he entered, he heard a teacher express indignation about perceived inequities in lunch and recess duty assignments. The teacher didn't see the superintendent come into the room and didn't complain for his ears. The context of the criticism was unclear to the superintendent, and all he knows at this point is that the teacher has an unspecified complaint about duty assignments.

Although the principal is just down the hall, the single teacher comment doesn't seem to be anything more than occasional grumbling, which happens in the best of families; the superintendent ignores it. At this juncture, all the preceding events involving contract changes, aide resignations, and his meetings with board and union leadership—if he had been astute enough to have held them—should flood back into the superintendent's mind, and he should initiate a second conversation with the union president to review the situation again—and further, notify the board of an incipient grievance.

A few days later, the superintendent received a late afternoon visit from the union president, who asked the superintendent for his interpretation of the new contract article on teacher aides. The superintendent reviewed its intent with the union president. If the superintendent hadn't figured it out before, this should have caused the light to dawn, and he should take the steps, indicated in the previous analysis, that he should have taken initially—not to mention asking a number of pointed questions to ascertain union intentions.

At the next administrative council meeting, a principal reported that she has received comments from teachers about lunch and playground duties, but she believes it's just routine complaining. Another principal mentioned that teachers in his building met with the union's building representative after school on some unspecified topic. If, following this administrative meeting, the superintendent hasn't made connections between and among these events and doesn't take the kind of actions suggested earlier, he is undoubtedly comatose and totally flatlining his brain wave monitor.

Three days later, a principal called the superintendent to report a grievance has been filed on teacher lunch and recess assignments; the superintendent was stunned by this unexpected turn of events. By this time, there's ample evidence that the superintendent is oblivious to the world around him and possibly too stupid to be a superintendent any-place, anytime. These issues and events are simple ones, and, if he can't even recognize them as potential problems, he's guaranteed to miss subtleties by an even wider margin.

The Case of the Able Administrator

Early in the fall, a suburban superintendent of schools attended a Saturday night football game. Although the crowd was well behaved, a number of elementary school age children were playing pickup football games or just running around aimlessly in a poorly lighted area behind the bleachers; they were unsupervised as older brothers or sisters or parents watched the varsity football game from the stands. The super-intendent had observed a bit of this previously, but the numbers of kids involved and the aimlessness of their activities seem to have increased.

On the following Monday morning, the superintendent spoke with the high school principal, and they agreed, while there aren't serious crowd problems at home games, that minor rowdiness has increased among younger kids not really interested in watching high school foot-ball. Three steps were decided upon: (1) The principal will send home a letter that, though uncritical and easy in tone, addresses the issues identified with younger students at football games and asks for parental cooperation to improve the situation. (2) At the next administrative council meeting, the superintendent plans a discussion with all princi-pals (elementary, middle school, and high school) about younger children's behavior at games to enlist their assistance with the kids. (3) For all remaining night games on the home field, the high school principal will add a second, off-duty, uniformed policeman with a special responsibility to monitor peripheral behavior of young people. These were the superintendent's first three smart decisions—even though the only related events at this time were loose supervision of younger children and increased numbers of unsupervised children at football games.

In a conversation that afternoon with the board chairman, the superintendent reviewed her concerns, and the steps she and the principal had taken, stressing that, although there aren't major problems presently, she's trying to prevent any. The chairman was relaxed about what he heard and thanked her for the call. This type of casual, informational conversation is always the right thing to do with a board of education chairman.

The following Monday morning, the high school principal called to report a near fight between a black male student from the neighboring city school district, who was a guest at a local school dance, and a local white male student; teacher chaperones separated the two before an exchange of nonracial insults, along with serious pushing and shoving, could escalate into a full-blown fight. There were no further issues at the dance.

The local high school has a fifteen percent black minority enrollment, and, to this time, race relations have been smooth—at least on the surface. The principal and superintendent both obviously hope this was an isolated incident and not racially motivated; however, the superintendent has heard, from other area superintendents, of increased racial tensions in neighboring schools. She scheduled a meeting with her assistant superintendent and the high school faculty to discuss any existing and/or potential black/white student issues. This was the third correct move and the fifth good decision that the superintendent made. The dance incident and the neighboring reports may be unrelated, but they may also be connected. Whether they are isolated events or not, she doesn't assume coincidence and takes appropriate steps to learn more about student relationships in the local high school.

The meeting with the high school faculty took place on Thursday afternoon, but the staff reported nothing significant. As a follow-up, the superintendent asked the principal to arrange a session, as soon as possible, with both black and white student leadership to solicit thoughts and feelings on student racial issues at the high school and any suggestions they may have to ease existing or potential tensions. After the nonproductive high school faculty meeting, the student meeting was the next correct step taken by the superintendent.

The next Tuesday, over her morning coffee and the morning newspaper, the superintendent read about an altercation at a fast-food restaurant in the neighboring city (where the black youth involved in the high school dance scuffle attends high school) between four of her suburban white high school students and an undetermined number of black city youths. City police are investigating the incident.

As she read about the restaurant fight, the superintendent saw the possible connection between it and the dance incident, realizing even if there isn't a direct link (and there is a good likelihood the two events are connected), the emerging pattern should be immediately addressed by high school staff, students, and parents. School district leadership should make this connection in this instance.

When she arrived in her office that morning, the superintendent scheduled an early afternoon appointment with the high school principal to review the probable connection between the dance problem and the civil disturbance — another appropriate action because of the likely relationship that exists between the two events. She also scheduled a brief meeting that morning with the local chief of police at his office to discuss the incident at the dance, the fight in the fast-food restaurant, and her new concerns about security at the annual football game between the city high school and the suburban high school — a night game under lights at the home field in less than two weeks.

At the meeting with the police chief, the superintendent asked him to touch base with his counterpart in the adjacent city about the restaurant brawl; the superintendent and the chief also agreed on a follow-up meeting date with school principals to review recent events. She did the right thing in meeting with the police chief to inform him of her concerns and to ask for his assistance; it was also astute to ask him to check with neighboring police and to bring the local chief of police into the meeting with principals and other administrators. As far as the superintendent knew, the student meeting she requested at the high school had not yet taken place. She also called the city superintendent of schools and reviewed recent issues with him.

When the superintendent returned from the police station, she received a telephone call from a parent she knows well and whose judgment she respects, reporting allegations of unnamed local white adolescents carrying baseball bats in their cars for use in fights with students from other school districts. She called the police chief to tell him of this story; in return, he told her he has learned the restaurant fight had definite racial origins, and further that threats of follow-up "rumbles" were made by both city black students and their white suburban counterparts. Another good move; the chief needed to hear about the baseball bat business, and the superintendent needed to know about the racial basis of the city fight and about the threats—both of which she found out because of her initiatives with the police chief.

When the superintendent and the principal met later in the day, the superintendent told the high school principal about her meeting with the chief of police, the baseball bat rumor, the information about the racial origins of the restaurant hassle, the subsequent threats, and about the upcoming administrative council meeting with the police chief (good moves to keep him informed); the principal in return told her he just learned from a black female student that a white female classmate directed a racial slur at her as she left the dance where the near-fight occurred a little over a week ago. This piece of news intensifies the superintendent's concerns and supports the wisdom of her recent actions.

Now, the superintendent directs the principal to: (1) meet with the neighboring city high school principal to enlist his help and that of his students, to plan discussions, meetings, or other steps to cool down what could otherwise become a meltdown of serious racial incidents; (2) discuss with him the possibility of changing the time of the upcoming football game between the two schools from Saturday night to Saturday afternoon; (3) inform the principal's contact at the local police department of the change in game time and request another pair of off-duty policemen to attend the game in addition to the one previously added—a total of four policemen for the game; (4) expedite scheduling the student meeting at the high school, now to review additional information that has become known, as well as for its original exploratory purposes; (5) schedule a high school faculty meeting to inform teachers about all recent events; (6) at both the student and faculty meetings, explore a weekend retreat or series of meetings of black and white student and faculty leadership to be led by a qualified outside facilitator; and (7) call a meeting of his high school parent council to bring them up to date on recent happenings and request their assistance with the steps under discussion. The superintendent also prepared a summary of her actions, which she faxed to the neighboring city superintendent including an invitation for him to call her after reading the fax.

The city principal and his superintendent were involved appropriately at this point; serious consideration of moving the football game from darkness to daylight makes sense, since even played in the daylight, additional game security is wise—also, the superintendent considered the general helter-skelter behavior of younger kids at football games and wants to ensure this doesn't add any additional problems at night games to the racial issues the district may face; the second faculty meeting is appropriate, as is the possibility of a student/faculty retreat or series of meetings; and informing parents is a good move, even though inevitably there will be exaggerations emerging from the session—but the odds are good that rumors already abound, and it's better to provide accurate and factual information and deal with its fallout openly and honestly, rather than try to keep important information hidden.

Following her meeting with the principal, the superintendent prepared a lengthy memorandum to board members in which she included all pertinent information about events to this point, including planned corrective and preventative steps in both districts, all to be reviewed further at the next meeting of the board of education. She also promised to keep them informed of any relevant devlopments.

Conclusion

The differences are phenomenal between the first superintendent's mishandling of a relatively simple situation as he remained totally unconscious of relationships between and among related events and the clearly emerging pattern that required his intervention, and the second superintendent's immediate perception of potentially connected events and their unfolding pattern and her decisive actions to deal with what had already happened and to prevent what could happen in the future from happening—all the while keeping the necessary parties appropriately informed of what she had done and planned to do.

"CLOSERS"

Walker Percy's novel *The Last Gentlemen* [19] contains a vignette from an automobile dealership where "dozens of salesmen in Rebcolonel hats and red walking canes threaded their way between handsome Biscaynes and sport Corvettes." The manager of the dealership engages in the following instructional conversation with a salesman: "Do you see those fellows out there?. . . I'll tell you a funny damn thing. . . . They know everything in the book about selling. But there is one thing they can't do. They can't close. . . . Now you know it's a funny thing but that is something you can't teach a fellow. . . ."

School leadership must hope the sales manager is wrong and that "closing" can be taught—or at least learned through experience. Educational leaders sell ideas and recommendations instead of Chevrolets, but when they're not born with native ability to close sales easily and intuitively, they need to acquire and cultivate important "closing out" skills in their sales of educational concepts to staff, boards of education, and communities.

Administrators occasionally continue talking until they lose what they've previously gained. We need to develop abilities to read our audiences and recognize when signs, omens, and portents point toward consensus and success; at that point, above all else, we must resist the temptation to continue talking to exhibit our vast storehouse of knowledge and expertise. At that point, above all else, we need to shut up, sit down, and thereby "close out" sales on the recommendations we have made, remembering always the wisdom from the Old Testament: "Have windy words no limit? Or what provokes you that you keep on talking?" [20].

CREATIVE SCHIZOPHRENIA

As unlikely and contradictory as it might seem without further explanation, school superintendents, principals, and other educational leaders must become creatively schizophrenic if they are to retain their sanity and remain as productive as they might be. Although educational leaders can consider regular schizophrenia as just another OSHA workplace hazard, it may be seen as a typical administrative characteristic by our detractors; the creative version, however, is much less common and harder to come by.

Creative schizophrenia requires that school leaders live comfortably with divergent views—except, in this instance, the divergent thoughts are found within themselves. A primary example is recognizing and accepting both of the following perspectives as true: (1) people are clearly no damn good, and if there's a reasonable way for them to screw up a situation and other lives, they will, and (2) the world is filled with wonderful souls who will do anything within their power to bring joy to other human beings.

On a given day, based on undeniable, empirical evidence of recent personnel performance and/or behavior, you would have every justification to believe, with all your heart and soul and mind, that people are no damn good. The next day, from the same undeniable, empirical evidence of recent personnel performance and/or behavior of the very same staff, it would be easy to believe, with equal fervor, that people are truly wonderful. Both times, you would be partially correct and partially incorrect.

A small minority of people in the world are clearly no damn good, and if there's a reasonable way for them to screw up situations and other lives, including those of school administrators, they will.[46] Although this group practices such behavior almost full-time, fortunately, few of them inhabit public schools. Many people are basically full-time wonderful souls who will do anything they can to help others — including school district administrators.[47] Unfortunately, although there are a number of these folks in school systems, you can never have enough of them.

Most people practice some of both behaviors that characterize the extremes. Public education is loaded with human beings in this category; the great majority of them are generally decent, well-intentioned teachers, principals, superintendents of schools, and other who also come equipped with human frailties that occasionally nudge them toward imperfect behaviors and actions in response to situations and other people.

Other examples of leaders holding contradictory, or at least contrary, thoughts comfortably in their heads might include (1) acknowledging student academic growth and achievement in the district while recognizing how much remains to be done to help them achieve even more; (2) believing the district has a fine staff, but at the same time, recognizing real staff deficits; (3) appreciating all the district still must accomplish but understanding that the world's best school districts will never accomplish all that they aspire to achieve; (4) knowing district parents care deeply for their children and recognizing many obvious exceptions to that thought; (5) espousing a new curricular approach, although recognizing it also has some negative side effects compared to existing curriculum; and (6) supporting extracurricular athletics for the benefits they confer on young people while understanding that they are overemphasized.

The "creativeness" in the schizophrenia comes from how leadership works to make an organization even better than it is, while comfortably balancing polar viewpoints in leadership minds: (1) holding divergent thoughts and believing both, while always striving toward achieving the

[46]See also, Chapter 11, "Some Days You Might Think Tom Hobbes Had It Right," p. 355.
[47]See also, Chapter 6, "Why Sometimes I've Believed as Many as Six Impossible Things before Breakfast," p. 218.

better of the differing realities; (2) recognizing staff strengths and ac-knowledging them to the staff, while simultaneously identifying exist-ing school district problems clearly and accepting how much further the district must travel to achieve true excellence; (3) intellectual and emotional acceptance of both difficult and supportive staff behaviors arriving in alternative waves and cycles—with some of each behavior occurring simultaneously, and in ever-changing configurations of pro-fessional "heroes and villains"—tolerance of frequent staff mood swings, and staff behavior changes from troublesome to helpful, with-out letting them make you really crazy; and (4) a constant conviction, regardless of recent empirical evidence to the contrary, that colleagues are individually and collectively basically good, competent profession-als who almost always intend to do the right thing.

Leaders need to trust other administrators and teachers while, through regular, intensive questioning and holding them to the highest standards of performance, pushing them constantly to excel. Tough "in-terrogations" aren't necessarily distrustful of the staff's ability; they are teaching situations and learning opportunities for both leaders and their colleagues. Leadership insistence on high standards in personnel per-formance isn't because leaders believe that most people don't set their own high standards; it comes from a recognition that, generally, even though people do set high standards for themselves, they still benefit from being pushed beyond them.[48]

If leaders aren't comfortable holding divergent points of view simul-taneously in their thoughts and appreciating the value of each, they won't be successful leaders.[49]

DANCE WITH THE ONE WHO "BRUNG" YOU

For many years, Darryl Royal coached the Texas University football Longhorns and now serves as the university's athletic director. As coach, often before an important "bowl game," he was asked if major changes should be expected to his usual emphasis on running the foot-ball almost exclusively and more forward passing added to the "game plan." Replying to this question, typically, he'd say, "You've got to dance with the one who brung you"—meaning if Texas University had gotten

---

[48]See also, Chapter 8, "Frequently Understandable, Often Forgivable, Never Acceptable," p. 246.
[49]See also, Chapter 6, "Taming the 450-Pound Media Gorilla—A One-Act Morality Play," p. 212 and Chapter 11, "Some Days You Might Think Tom Hobbes Had It Right," p. 355.

to the big game primarily through running the football, its quarterback wasn't likely to throw thirty-five passes in the upcoming bowl game.

School leaders also should cling to strengths that have made them successful to the point in their careers at which they find themselves. They were chosen to be superintendents or principals or special education directors because of those particular attributes, but people with whom they work will often work hard to change them—leadership strengths are often barriers to someone else's professional or personal interests. Relationships where one party chooses another because of particular personal strengths and then perversely becomes intent on stamping out those same characteristics are usually called marriages—these human behaviors also characterize school leadership relationships and lives.

Although holding firmly to core values, personal beliefs, and professional attributes, leaders should take every opportunity to evaluate their own specific administrative attitudes, styles, and behaviors. When their instincts and convictions tell them changes are required (often in reaction to other views, suggestions, or recommendations), they should be personally secure enough to make them when they are convinced such changes are either necessary or the right thing to do—and are not being considered solely to please either supporters or critics. When they weigh other advice carefully and disagree with it, they should thank the person for the advice and continue on the same course—always remaining open to reevaluation of an identical or related suggestion at a later time as new information or circumstances warrant.

Teaching and administrative constituencies, as well as the board of education members who chose the superintendent, were instrumental in bringing school leaders to particular districts and in the successes they may enjoy there. If superintendents aren't fiercely loyal to these groups, they are not remembering the people who "brung" them. This doesn't imply blind loyalty to the degree that it hurts the staff, because a superintendent won't push them to become even better than they already are or that the superintendent won't rid the district of incompetents—loyalty to staff must be tempered with other interests, and those interests must take precedence if the staff member or staff members can't or won't change and grow.

Openness to changing administrative behaviors, use of fortuitous opportunities for change such as a new position, and constant self-assessment—all three of these are important to school leadership. Leaders should avail themselves of these opportunities for personal and professional growth and change while holding firmly to the best basic elements in their psychic centers, which have defined them as individual human beings and as leaders, throughout their lives from childhood until the present.[50]

DISCLAIMERS MAKE THE WORLD GO 'ROUND

As frustrating as it may be for oratorical and compositional purists, leadership survival requires disclaimers, often to accompany the simplest assertions, which evidence awareness of every other possible human thought remotely relevant to the original point being made, along with barely relevant and many irrelevant notions.

For example, if a superintendent told board members that some of them were less than brilliant, we know it would start World War III. Why? The truth is probably that more than half aren't brilliant, and the other half may be *non compos mentis*. Regardless, if superintendents want to acquaint board members with harsh realities, while still hanging on to their administrative careers, they must always follow up original statements by pouring linguistic oil on troubled waters: (1) but of course, some board members are extremely brilliant—geniuses even; (2) and, of course, not every superintendent is brilliant either (including particularly the superintendent who began this discussion): self-deprecating disclaimers count double; (3) in fact, some superintendents are really stupid![51] (4) and, of course, even those board members and superintendents who aren't brilliant have a great deal to offer, and their children probably think they're wonderful; (5) and, of course, etc.

Granted, the above example isn't the most tactful to be found, but there are many routine statements that, today, for tactical reasons, must be softened with disclaimers. A more realistic example might be a perfectly reasonable observation about a group of high school students who recently scored poorly on a statewide achievement test. If superintendents want to make a serious point about members of this group who lack motivation, they also should understand the need for disclaimers—if for no other reason than to avoid having the same ideas directed back to the superintendent as proof that he or she hasn't thought deeply enough about this issue.

In a perfect world, statements in the examples below would stand alone without disclaimers, but, in the only world we have, without ap-

---

[50]See also, this chapter, "Who Is This Person?—I," p. 103.
[51]Especially the superintendent who started this particular discussion.

propriate disclaimers, they can cause a superintendent world-class difficulties.

- **Superintendent:** "A good number of our less able students lack strong motivation to learn." Possible superintendent disclaimers to preempt board members' or citizens' natural inclinations to lay objections on the superintendent, as if he or she wasn't already aware of them, might include: (1) "Of course, the great majority of our students have a real desire to learn." (2) "And even some of our most able kids aren't as motivated as we'd prefer them to be either." (3) "And, of course, many of our students with modest abilities are as highly motivated as our most able students." (4) "Many of our unmotivated students have problems outside of their control, which interfere with their education—and we are working to help with those problems."
- **Superintendent:** "Higher educational expenditures don't guarantee higher standardized test scores." Reasonable superintendent disclaimers to forestall the otherwise inevitable questions, or dumb comments, such as "Well, why should we support increases in spending then?" or "Spending more seems stupid if we're not going to get our money's worth!" include: (1) "But, of course, spending more improves our chances of raising scores." (2) "Spending less would definitely hurt student test scores to some unknown degree." (3) "And we still need to maintain present expenditure levels to at least guarantee reasonable opportunities for kids."

Again, purists understandably may complain about the need for disclaimers to soften the effects of simple statements that logically shouldn't require cautionary, or explanatory, or clarifying comment—but without an intuitive knowledge of how and when disclaimers are appropriate, school leadership frequently will be frustrated, and sometimes embarrassed, by people who just don't seem able to grasp the beauty of simple declarative prose unadorned with written or spoken baubles, bangles, and disclaimers.

Although they are only tools, disclaimers are important tools, but like "the law," disclaimers are good servants and bad masters.[52] Sometimes it's also enjoyable to let chaos ensue and defend a defensible

---

[52]See also, this chapter, "Fireside and Other Chats and Communications—I–V," pp. 75, 78, 79, 80, 81.

statement aggressively and competently just to gain people's attention. Everyone's not going to love you anyway.

DREAMING DREAMS

Many veteran educators came to adulthood in the days of "Joe Cool," when understatement was the preferred style and hyperbole was anathema—motivational and visionary speeches or writings would have curdled our psyches. As a result, there were tons of assumptions made by educational leaders that everyone on the team shared their vision and motivation—wrong.

None of us is ever likely to speak or write words as moving as those of Dr. King in his famous Washington speech. But as clumsy as our efforts may be compared to his eloquence, it's incumbent upon all leadership to accept responsibility for articulating a clear vision of each leader's hopes for, and expectations of, district colleagues, the school, or the particular department within the school system—and to continue, at each reasonable opportunity, writing and speaking thoughts to remind listeners or readers of the leader's vision for education and what he or she is committed to accomplish on behalf of young people entrusted to the local public schools. School leaders also need to share their educational dreams with students, parents, other citizens, town officials, boards of education, and with each other.

Recurring occasions offering opportunities to share leadership goals include welcome back letters to staff following the summer vacation; welcoming letters to new staff members; new teacher welcomes and orientations; opening day staff meetings; national, state, and local "teacher appreciation" months, weeks, or days; weeks immediately preceding vacations; end of school year correspondence; board of education meetings; parent/teacher organization meetings; budget hearings; graduation exercises; honor society inductions; sports banquets; school "open houses"; and any two or more people pausing on the street in front of your office.

Although each opportunity listed, along with many others not listed, requires significant variations in presentation length and style, they all should be used appropriately to convey and reinforce a leadership vision for the district's schools and especially its students.[53]

---

[53]See also, this chapter, "Fireside and Other Chats and Communications—I–V," pp. 75, 78, 79, 80, 81 and " 'Strutting and Fretting Your Hours upon the Stage,' " p. 90.

EFFICIENT OR EFFECTIVE—CHOOSE ANY TWO

"Reason lies between the spur and the bridle" [7] or, for school leadership, between the proper balance of efficiency and effectiveness. In most professions, each day is filled with choices between efficiency and effectiveness, and leadership requires balancing these two qualities.

If a leader's focus is to be sure "the railroad runs on time," he or she doesn't need to be concerned with the long-range effectiveness of whichever dictatorial approach is most efficient for achieving this limited goal. If, conversely, leadership is more concerned with helping the train's crew satisfy its passengers through exemplary service, leaders may need to be satisfied with slower progress toward meeting arbitrary timetables.

Decisions made most efficiently are made in isolation by one person; dictatorships personify efficient government. Effective decisions are made, often inefficiently, by many people, but they are more meaningful than those made by fiat[54]—and they survive the inevitable stresses and strains from living with the results of decisions. Democracies may exemplify effective government, which, though effective, is often painfully inefficient.

Endorsing the concept of the golden mean between extremes, which is almost always found closer to one than the other, leadership has no satisfactory alternatives except taking the long view, involving other people appropriately in major district educational decisions, and accepting resulting inefficiency on behalf of long-range educational effectiveness—as long as vital educational services function at acceptable levels.

However, the further away from basic educational concepts particular decisions may be and the closer they are to daily operational decisions, the more justified greater focus on efficiency might become. For example, in building cleanliness and maintenance, with transportation schedules (for buses not railroads), or with district purchasing practices, efficiency may be a primary consideration—after student safety, of course.

People outside of education often confuse management aspects of school operation in which they should expect high standards of efficiency with those in which the human aspects must receive greater attention. Students, staff, administrators, board members, and citizens

---

[54]No, not the Italian automaker!

together have great potential to become effective—but, collectively, have an almost insurmountable threshold of efficiency.

As is so often true in leadership, the ever-changing golden mean between efficiency and effectiveness must be sought and applied, situation by situation, hour by hour, day by day, week by week, month by month, year by year. . . .[55]

FINISHING THE RUN

John Madden, now the Fox color commentator for NFL football, praises good running backs by saying, "He finishes the run." Madden means by this that the ball carrier continues struggling forward until pinned to the ground by ten members of the other team, while the eleventh drives a wooden stake through his heart—even then, Madden expects the ball carrier to crawl a few more inches to ensure the first down.

An even broader implication for this football phrase is that every single leadership or instructional task, regardless of magnitude or visibility, should be focused upon, worked at, and completed as if it were the most important responsibility of a person's professional career.[56] In a novel about aircraft engineers and technicians, the protagonist founded a near religious movement around this concept. As impossible as it may be for all educators to achieve completely, the closer each professional comes to attaining it, the better our American system of public education becomes.

Thinking about each day's work within the context of giving each task before us our best leadership efforts, and, while holding the same thought paramount, focusing on each assignment as it's begun, as it's in progress, and as it's completed, will go a long way to help leaders achieve this supremely worthwhile goal. Though daunted, we press on one task at a time, one day at a time, until we can someday say we have finished the race and have run our educational race to the very best of our ability.

Along about the final week in April, superintendents and principals should concentrate on completing the school year as productively as it usually begins and on maintaining forward educational momentum until the year ends; it's further incumbent on school district leadership to

---

[55]See also, Chapter 1, "In Search of Gold," p. 7 and "Ten Cardinal Principles of Leadership," p. 21.
[56]See also, Chapter 1, "The Devil Is in the Details," p. 18.

work with teachers to ensure they also finish each year's educational run.

FIRESIDE AND OTHER CHATS AND COMMUNICATIONS—I: GENERAL

Although not all school leaders can write masterfully, if willing to work at it, we can all correspond clearly, plainly, and unaffectedly with staff, students, parents, board members, town officials, and others. For administrative reports, correspondence, and presentations to be effective, they must be given a high priority by superintendents, principals, and other school administrators. Presentations should be considered important elements of writing, because in many, if not most, cases they are written and rewritten many times prior to delivery.[57]

Although superintendents' direct personal contacts with other administrators, teachers, students, board members, and many parents are most important in shaping perceptions of him or her, correspondence and presentations add or detract significantly to judgments of professional competence and personal characteristics. To a surprisingly large number of parents and other citizens of the community, the written word is almost all they know about their superintendent.

Many older administrators have gone through stages in professional correspondence toward their eventual evolution to word processors, which today all school leaders should have available and use competently in all forms of professional writing as well as for other effective personal computer functions.

For many school administrators, yellow lined tablets were their first "Fred Flintstone Model" word processors, and initial drafts were handed to secretaries for typing. The number of follow-up drafts, before settling on a final version, depended upon the particular writer's degree of perfectionism, the amount of time available, and the importance of the correspondence or the presentation. For important speeches, some of us required as many as fifteen to twenty editings before we were satisfied, and we continued editing them until we stood up to deliver them.

For many of us, the next step in our evolutionary ascent was direct dictation to clerks or secretaries who wrote their versions of our oral administrative pearls onto steno pads, using whatever variety of short-

---

[57]See also, this chapter, " 'Strutting and Fretting Your Hours upon the Stage,' " p. 90.

hand or notehand they possessed; then, on their trusty Underwoods or Smith/Coronas, and later IBM Selectrics, they typed a draft for author review. Again, the number of rewrites varied according to the care taken by the author, time available, and the importance of the document. This is a particularly inefficient method of writing because it requires two people to be involved the entire time. Although it was easier for the writer than using yellow pads, it was also even less efficient.

The Dictaphone, handheld or otherwise, represented the penultimate level in our crawl out of the prehistoric slime toward word processing and more complex forms of communications. Dictaphones were great improvements over steno pads, because the author worked at his or her own pace, as did the transcriber of the dictation. Interestingly, during this stage of many careers, students were just beginning to use personal computers for their compositions, and some initial administrative reactions, which in more perceptive administrators soon disappeared, were that word processing was somehow un-American, and that kids should learn to write with pencil and paper the way we did, conveniently forgetting that our "writing" now consisted of talking and editing. We hadn't actually "written" anything for years. Within the past decade, many administrators ended careers without ever having fired a shot in anger with a word processor.

Unfortunately, there may be leadership dinosaurs even today, whose compositional DNA is frozen in amber at one of the three major evolutionary stages previously described and whose professional writing would benefit immeasurably from the use of word processors—the lives of their secretarial and clerical assistants would also be transformed. Probably many of these pre-Gutenberg fossils weren't lucky enough, or smart enough, to have ever learned to type, and this is a real impediment to personal use of word processors—a problem, however, which also can be solved if administrative motivation is strong enough. Retirement is another solution.

Administrators who have mastered word processing and use computers effectively wouldn't consider returning to the primitive procedures of yesteryear—unless power fails and they have no emergency backup power sources for their electronic marvels.

Regardless of an administrator's initial method of composition, frequent editing remains a necessary chore to be performed with monotonous regularity and an important skill to be acquired and practiced diligently. Word processors are almost infallible in detecting combinations such as "vp,[iyrt" (or "computer" typed with all fingers one key off to the right), but, even spell-checks permit typos to slip through undetected when they form real, though incorrect, words for particular contexts.

Administrators shouldn't feel guilty about recycling good material and should save personal copies of all important correspondence and presentations, especially those that may be useful again someday after adaptation to new situations. Of course, they can't give the identical opening day speech or tell the same joke about "Old Nell and the Three Wishes" four years in a row (at least a few people would notice), but themes may be modified as necessary and brought back five years later, or even next year in a new position—unless that particular speech was the impetus for your move to the new job, in which case you might reconsider using it again at all. Significant letters to staff, properly tailored, often are also worthwhile for parents—or the other way around, and some board correspondence may also be appropriate, if modified slightly, for parents or staff or both, etc.

Basic compositional artifacts necessary for dedicated professional writers, in addition to a computer and a good word processing program, include: (1) a desk dictionary such as the latest version of *Webster's New Collegiate Dictionary,* or any one of many other good ones available; (2) a large, library dictionary on its own stand, either freestanding or a smaller swivel stand on a flat surface at a functional height; (3) Strunk and White's *The Elements of Style* or other such outstanding guides to clean prose; (4) a good thesaurus (many software programs include them, but a hardcopy version is still useful); (5) a set of encyclopedias with which the administrator is comfortable—it's amazing how literate a person can appear through the use of *Brittanica* or even *World Book;* (6) other reference manuals on composition, and for publication guides in editing, typesetting, and proofreading, *The Chicago Manual of Style* (14th Edition, University of Chicago Press); and (7) an English teacher who writes well, shackled to a corner of your desk—if this arrangement proves impractical, for whatever unlikely reasons, don't be too proud to develop working relationships with skilled teachers in the high school, or in any school, who are willing to review especially important administrative writings with an eye to suggestions for improvement of such composition and correspondence.

Within school districts, primary written communications recipients, in order of probable correspondence volume, not necessarily in the order of each group's importance to superintendents, are boards of education, administrators, teachers, other staff, parents, town officials, and students.

For principals, the list includes (in the order of probable communications volume) teachers and other staff, the superintendent, parents, students, and occasionally board members and town officials. Much of principal/superintendent communications takes place on the telephone and in person.

At any given time, any of the named groups may become uppermost on a superintendent's communications priority list, but boards and staff remain high priorities always. Similarly, at any given time, any of the groups named for principals may be uppermost on a principal's communications priority list, but staff and parents remain high on their lists at all times.[58]

Appendix B includes samples of many of these kinds of administrative correspondence—not as perfect examples, which they aren't, but illustrative of various kinds of staff communications.

FIRESIDE AND OTHER CHATS AND COMMUNICATIONS—II: STAFF

As often as superintendents see staff personally, and even as often as principals interact directly with staff, correspondence remains important to school leaders for staff communications. The larger the school district, the more important written correspondence becomes. (Again, since many presentations are not impromptu and were originally written, they are also considered a form of written administrative communications.)

In both oral and written communications, frequently, the genesis of educational inertia is from directions to, or through, the wrong human channels. Often, when it would be more effective to speak directly with principals, superintendents may rely too heavily on administrative assistants or secretaries or assistant superintendents and communicate with building personnel through them. Avoiding direct contact with the right people, for whatever reason, lessens the chances of educational change occurring as expected.

Also, as initiatives for change, which begin with initially strong administrative enthusiasm, support, and encouragement, move further away from their origins and are translated through additional personnel, they grow weaker—the educational results of indirect instructions

---

[58]The titles of these pieces on communications came from FDR's "fireside chats" and also from a newspaper photo I once saw, which pictured a superintendent at his desk speaking to PTA representatives. The superintendent had had a working, gas-fired fireplace installed in the office for his conversations with parents and others. The man had a sense of history.

reflect this inevitable attenuation of the directive's or request's original purpose.

It's also, unfortunately, not uncommon for the flow of anger, frustration, or hurt feelings to be transmitted from group to group within the educational enterprise; it's crucial to at least change the tone of an angry directive recently received as we enlist help from other administrators to carry it out. Otherwise, it is often transmitted the same way to classroom teachers with an eventual loss of student learning.[59]

The facility of word processing makes it more possible today than even ten years ago for administrators to initiate frequent written communication with staff members collectively, by school, and individually—as well as with parents and students. Regular and recurring opportunities for superintendents to communicate with administrators and teachers include welcome back letters to staff following the summer vacation; letters to new staff members; new teacher welcomes and orientations; opening day staff meetings, breakfasts, and luncheons; national, state, and local "teacher appreciation" months, weeks, or days; significant staff achievements or district milestones; weeks immediately preceding vacations; letters to mark the end of the school year; information from board of education meetings; results of budget hearings; and before or following school "open houses."

The origins of all administrative communications to staff should be easily identified visually as superintendent or principal correspondence through consistent and easily recognizable formats—including mastheads or logos, shapes, colors, styles, and paper qualities, as well as from their contents and signatures.

FIRESIDE AND OTHER CHATS AND COMMUNICATIONS—III: PARENTS

Superintendents regularly see relatively few parents in person, and principals, though having more opportunities than superintendents for frequent, direct contacts with parents, also have relatively limited parental contacts—correspondence, supplemented with presentation opportunities, remains a primary method of administrative communications with parents.

Word processing facilitates frequent and recurring written communications with parents, individually and collectively, as well as with staff

[59]See also, Chapter 8, "Consensus versus the Right to Differ and to Be Different," p. 243; "Divergence and Convergence," p. 244; and "The Captain Made Me Do It,", p. 263.

and students. Regular and recurring opportunities for school district administrators to communicate with parents include regular school, departmental (special education, for example), or school district newsletters; special school, departmental, or school district newsletters; welcomes to new school years; letters to new families; letters to district parents of newborn children; national, state, and local "teacher appreciation" months, weeks, or days; significant student achievements or district milestones; preceding vacations; letters marking the close of school years; communicating important information from board of education meetings; budget hearing and budget vote results; news from PTOs or PTAs or parent liaison councils; and before or following school "open houses."

The origins of all administrative communications to parents should be easily identified visually as superintendent or principal correspondence through consistent and easily recognizable formats, including mastheads or logos, shapes, colors, styles, and paper qualities, as well as from their contents and signatures.

FIRESIDE AND OTHER CHATS AND COMMUNICATIONS—IV: BOARDS OF EDUCATION

Superintendents work directly with entire boards of education once, twice, or, God help them, sometimes more often each month. If they are unlucky, they also regularly attend meetings of one or more board committees if their boards are enamored of committees and have both standing and ad hoc varietals. Regardless of these constant personal interactions, superintendents' written communications with their boards of education are almost continual. Regular and recurring written superintendent communications with boards of education include

(1) Memoranda or letters to inform members of significant district events and activities prior to opportunities to discuss them at board meetings: Examples are important staff resignations, major property damage to school buildings, pending educational legislation, serious injuries to students, or almost anything that may be reported by the newspapers. Each superintendent must come to an understanding with his or her board about how much, and what kind of, information the board wishes to receive. In spite of a superintendent's best efforts to reach that understanding with a

board, satisfying individual board member's special preferences on amounts and kinds of information is always difficult, if not impossible. For superintendents, the optimum frequency, kind, and amount of information to be provided for boards of education is always a moving target.[60]

(2) *Board meeting agenda notes in which the superintendent provides explanations and supportive information about agenda items*

(3) *General notes to accompany board agendas covering items not on the agenda but important enough for board members to know something about:* Often, these general notes can replace informational items on agendas—reserving more meeting time for important action items.

(4) *Special administrative reports to the board:* Although there are times when superintendents prefer to present important information to everyone simultaneously at meetings,[61] generally, board members receive information, including reports, prior to meetings. Often, a superintendent's contribution to particular reports will be in the form of cover letters or memos reviewing the report's history and adding some personal comments—usually including specific superintendent's recommendations when a report precedes a board of education decision.

The origins of all superintendent communications to board members should be easily identified visually as superintendent correspondence through consistent and easily recognizable formats, including mastheads or logos, shapes, colors, styles, and paper qualities, as well as from contents and signatures.

Superintendents' written communications with their boards of education are keys to their success in the district and merit constant and intensive administrative nurturing.

FIRESIDE AND OTHER CHATS AND COMMUNICATIONS—V: STUDENTS

Although some superintendents see students regularly, and most prin-

---

[60]See also, Chapter 4, "How Much Information Is Enough?" p. 123.
[61]See also, Chapter 4, "Let's Be Sure We're All on the Same Page Here," p. 151.

cipals interact directly with students each day, much of the discussion of superintendent/student correspondence that follows is also appropriate for school principals; for superintendents, student correspondence is important; the larger the school district, the more important written correspondence becomes with students, as well as with staff, because of the relatively few regular, direct contacts large district superintendents have with students. Because many presentations to students are usually written before delivery, they are also considered administrative communications.

Word processors make it more possible today than ever before for administrators to expand written communications with students, individually and collectively, as well as with parents and staff. Regular and recurring opportunities for superintendents to communicate with students include welcome back letters to students following summer vacations; letters to students moving from elementary to middle school, from middle schools to high schools, and to graduating seniors; letters to local high school graduates for significant achievement in college and/or in the field of work; letters to new students or to students for significant academic, athletic, or other personal achievements; and letters to students making the honor roll—or students who disappear from honor rolls; and end of school year letters.

The origins of all superintendent communications to students should be easily identified visually as superintendent correspondence through consistent and easily recognizable formats, including mastheads or logos, shapes, colors, styles, and paper qualities, as well as from contents and signatures.

I ALWAYS KNEW THIS WOULD HAPPEN SOMEDAY, AND IT FINALLY DID

"I always knew this would happen someday, and it finally did" is the epitaph on a Connecticut pessimist's tombstone, and it should also be tattooed on the biceps of particular educators and board members as the antithesis of one of the most vital qualities of leadership—the ability to inspire a sense of optimism in those around us.

Many teachers have survived new superintendents who regularly moan to teachers and administrators about the many difficulties and obstacles of leadership duties and responsibilities. First of all, the staff has its own troubles, which are even more significant than the superintendent's, but more importantly, they just don't want leaders who are either overwhelmed with their professional responsibilities or don't have enough common sense not to show it—or both. If administrators feel they can't do their jobs, they should change jobs.

Whenever colleagues sense leadership despair, their commitment to achieve shrivels up inside them, and their enthusiasm wanes; educators don't want leaders who feel their jobs are too hard for them. Conversely, although entertaining private professional doubts and even anguish, when leaders communicate positive enthusiasm for ongoing, or proposed, educational programs and activities and appear confident and relaxed about meeting leadership responsibilities, the staff is much more likely to respond in kind with the necessary energy and drive to accomplish what needs to be done.

The superintendent's or principal's optimism or pessimism is communicated through other than verbal messages. Facial expressions, the way he or she walks down the halls, and his or her body language all tell careful readers of administrative psyches how their leaders feel about district education.

Superintendents and principals need to emulate the hardiness and the dogged persistence of aluminum siding salesmen; these folks are rejected hundreds of times for each success, yet they keep on calling, and knocking, and smiling, and selling, and driving homeowners nuts—but they make a living, and, when struck by hailstones, tens of thousands of houses today "clank"[62] instead of "clack" as God originally intended them to do.[63]

"IF YOU CAN KEEP YOUR HEAD WHEN ALL ABOUT YOU . . ." [21]

Rudyard Kipling often receives a bum rap from self-anointed intelligentsia, but the opening line of his verse "If" contains a powerful message for leaders: "If you can keep your head when all about you are losing theirs and blaming it on you. . . ." To the degree educational leaders handle stressful situations with the calm, self-possession encouraged by Kipling's poem, their leadership will be strengthened.

Leadership behaviors are highly infectious, and when superintendents, principals, or other school district leaders don't manage crises well, neither will colleagues. If, conversely, leaders exhibit a sense of

[62]A particularly inept New York Mets outfielder was called "Clank" for the sound the ball made as it hit his glove.
[63]See also, this chapter, "If You Can Keep Your Head When All About You . . . ," p. 83.

ease and an ability to cope with any problem that may arise, that also is communicated to the staff.

Some of the worst manifestations of leaders losing control of themselves, and their reactions, under external pressures include (1) attempts to shift responsibility to others when they should be focused on resolving problems, instead of trying to transfer blame to other people; (2) denying there are problems when everyone knows there are problems. Leadership should provide confident reassurance to colleagues that any and all issues can and will be handled calmly and effectively— instead of a blind refusal to acknowledge real problems that need to be addressed and resolved even if they are difficult ones; (3) shouting, yelling, screaming, or sputtering, instead of speaking in even, normal tones of voice, or through written forms of yelling, screaming, or sputtering, instead of communicating with even, normal tones in memoranda or letters; (4) body language in difficult public situations, for example, at board meetings or public hearings. Putting your head on the desk, especially if accompanied by audible moans, makes it too easy for people to realize that you're distraught and not in charge of the situation; (5) running, instead of walking purposefully but calmly. During fire drills, principals normally should have teachers and/or students report to them at a predesignated place outside the building, instead of dashing madly themselves from group to group to ensure everyone is out of the building and accounted for. There may be times when sprinting is essential, but they are rare; administrative high gear should be reserved for those special circumstances;[64] (6) loss of composure, although controlled anger may be effective in certain situations.[64] Sensing significant opposition among a superintendents' group, an effective state commissioner of education would frequently single out one unfortunate superintendent and react angrily and forcefully to his or her remarks or questions. It's difficult to recommend this technique, but it usually quells any incipient rebellion. This approach is, however, much different from the kind of temper tantrum more appropriate for two year olds.

Following a major school district problem, an administrative assistant asked, with apparent bewilderment, how the superintendent managed to remain calm throughout a recent major crisis, yet daily when she couldn't find a letter he wanted within thirty seconds she had to scrape him off the ceiling.

His response was that, in true crises, he didn't have the luxury to be

---

[64]And, of course, you should never run with scissors.

a horse's behind even among his closest coworkers, but, unfortunately for those who worked closest to him, in minor matters he could indulge himself a little. Clearly, it's better to maintain an even disposition most of the time, and it's always better to avoid becoming excited and obnoxious, but, if it must happen, be sure it happens when it doesn't matter as much. If it occurs in the middle of major problems, it can have almost catastrophic results to the educational enterprise.

Effective leaders (whether men or women, sons or daughters) manage to "keep their heads when all about them are losing theirs and blaming it on them" [21]. Are they effective leaders because they can remain calm, or can they remain calm because they are effective leaders? And does the answer to that question really matter as long as leaders can and do remain calm under pressure?

PURITANS AND BEARS

"The Puritans hated bearbaiting not because it gave pain to the bear, but because it gave pleasure to the spectators" [22][65] — a classic case of the right decision for the wrong reason. Leadership life in public education today, as well as Puritan life in seventeenth century England, provides ample opportunities for each of the following: (1) incorrect decisions for the wrong reasons — leaders who do this are easily recognized as unsuitable for leadership, or for much else for that matter; (2) incorrect decisions for the right reasons — an example of well-intentioned, but inept, leadership; (3) correct decisions for the wrong reasons — residual leadership Puritans and others who confuse the essence of issues with attendant periphery; and (4) correct decisions for the right reasons — the right kind of public school leadership and, fortunately, the most prevalent varietal of public school leadership.

The first three options are obviously dangerous to administrative health. School district leadership shouldn't be protective of children

[65]Macaulay was a middle nineteenth century English statesman, poet, historian, and essayist, and his *History of England* (in four volumes) is considered to be his best work. Thackery said of Macaulay that he read twenty books to write a single sentence — a dramatic contrast with many authors today, who write twenty books without reading a single sentence. Macaulay also was described as vivid and colorful but sometimes inaccurate, which is seen by some as three good leadership qualities. His analysis of why the Puritans opposed bearbaiting was in the context of the seventeenth century reformation of the Anglican Church and its aftermath. After the Puritans had worked their will on the church, they also attempted to control the daily lives of the people and, to save souls, to ensure that nobody ever enjoyed anything or took pleasure from anything. (The same function today is carried out by proponents of "political correctness" and sometimes by overly earnest superintendents of schools.)

because litigation might ensue if a child is injured. Teachers, principals, and superintendents should be passionate about school safety because children will be hurt when they aren't. Although choices sometimes must be made that require weighing and considering factors peripheral to an issue's moral center, school districts profit when their leader's instincts recognize the essence of educational decisions, instead of confusing them with extrinsic legal, political, or other considerations. Focusing on legal, political, or other ramifications to the exclusion of moral or human factors leads to pernicious personal attitudes and negative organizational effects.[66]

When leaders develop patterns that allow them to make even correct decisions for the wrong reasons, it becomes easier for them to make wrong decisions for the wrong reasons. Regressions from right decisions for the right reasons to wrong decisions for the wrong reasons are gradual and subtle, but they are real and ever-present leadership pitfalls to be avoided.

Don't act like a Puritan and, above all, don't dress like one; it's damned uncomfortable and focuses a great deal of unwanted attention on you at budget hearings.

SAY HELLO TO PEOPLE AT LEAST

Maybe all experienced educators have heard horror stories, and seen examples, of superintendents who keep visitors waiting while they complete routine paperwork. A superintendent's or a principal's time is valuable, and people should make appointments when they need a significant block of administrative attention—and it's good to do so if they only need five minutes. However, on the other side of that equation, it's rare that an administrator can't break from whatever he or she is doing and at least walk out, say hello, and ask if an unscheduled visitor would like to set a later time for a longer meeting. Similarly, it's good public relations to take most telephone calls, even if only to tell callers you need to return their calls at a later time.

Sometimes, attending even momentarily to visitors isn't reasonable, and superintendents can't always be available to drop-in visitors or for telephone calls, but the public will accept these mild rebuffs much

---

[66]See also, Chapter 1, "Ten Cardinal Principles of Leadership," p. 21 and Chapter 5, "It's the Kids, Stupid!" p. 195.

more readily when there has been, and continues to be, an obvious climate of openness and receptivity to personal visits and telephone calls.

Leadership decisions to interrupt routine activities in favor of courtesy with visitors or telephone callers are based on sound professional administrative priorities; one of the highest leadership goals should be to establish an open, receptive environment for staff, parent, and student constituents alike.

Some superintendents possibly overdose on this advice, often breaking from informal meetings with principals or teachers to turn away personally a teacher applicant because there are no staff vacancies or to direct a floor wax salesperson to the right employee in the organization. It is a rare occasion when these superintendents and principals don't at least say hello to a visitor—even in instances where it is necessary to reschedule the visit.

But in balance, hyperaccessibility is better because it improves everyone's perception of school leaders—and also because it's the right way to treat people.

SIT DOWN TURKEY!—OR A ROSE BY ANOTHER NAME DOESN'T SMELL AS GOOD

A superintendent of schools in a Connecticut regional district once persuaded the board of education to bring a new high school principal on board a year ahead of the incumbent principal's announced retirement to ensure a smooth administrative transition—also, on the premise that "authority forgets a dying king" [23],[67] to provide adequate leadership in the incumbent principal's final year. Although the majority of the board agreed with the superintendent's proposal, this decision required two administrative salaries for a year. It was also the superintendent's not too brilliant suggestion to call the then unnamed person to be appointed a "principal designee." As the story unfolded, naming the position proved less and less wise—and this occurred in the late seventies, a relatively peaceful time financially, and long before the national economy went to hell in a handbasket.

Initial board approval of the "principal designee" generated a bit more than the usual newspaper coverage, and board members began

[67]Alfred Lord Tennyson, or Baron Tennyson of Freshwater and Aldworth as he was later known, wrote "Morte de Arthur" in 1842. His son Hallam was Governor General of the Commonwealth of Australia from 1902–1904, which all prospective administrators must know and understand.

receiving telephone calls from citizens asking questions and registering opinions such as: "What the hell is a 'principal designer'?" "Why do we need one of those 'principal deaconates'?" "We've never had a 'principal whatsitsname' before and everything seemed OK!" "That new 'principal whatever it is' sounds like a dumb idea to me!" "Whose stupid idea was this 'principal potentate person' anyway?" "Who the 'bleep' is supposed to pay for this 'personal designate' thing?" "We never had one of them 'principal decedents' when I was in school, and look at me!"

Understandably, these calls made board members nervous, and, at their next meeting, they revisited their earlier "principal designee" decision, and this time authorized it for only half a year, instead of for an entire year. This partial retreat was also duly noted by press representatives, but, by this time, just prior to the annual budget meeting, the "principal designee," or whatever translation each person had rendered of it, had become a "cause celebre," and critical telephone calls continued unabated until the annual regional district budget session.

The budget meeting was held in the high school auditorium and attracted three or four times its usual number of voters. The board members and superintendents all recognized the extra-large attendance and figured, correctly enough, that many citizens were present because of the "principal designee" hassle—everyone worried a bit about that. Also easily noticeable was a sizable contingent of men who arrived together, similarly garbed in volunteer firemen's jackets, but the superintendent didn't think too much about that phenomenon—as it turned out, he should have been concerned.

Early in the meeting, the audience, as had been feared might happen, focused on the cost and questioned the wisdom of this newfangled "principal designee" person. Early on, the indications of a major problem were confirmed when the region's largest landowner, an elderly gentleman who had himself served on the original regional board, but hadn't been back to a budget meeting since those antediluvian days, stood up and, passionately and at length, blasted the new administrative position to smithereens—or thereabouts. The board chairwoman looked over at the superintendent, smiled, and said, "OK, this was your idea, you handle it."

No problem! The superintendent proceeded confidently to the podium and began a lucid, articulate defense of his idea. About five minutes into his self-perceived silver-tongued presentation, he innocently believed he had the audience in the proverbial palm of his hand, with the possible exception of the district's largest landowner—until the men in fire department jackets began booing, waving their arms and their hands, not to mention individual fingers, and shouting, "Sit down turkey!" and making even more dramatic suggestions about what he should do to and with himself.

At that point, he realized he'd overestimated his charm and forensic skills, lamely concluded his remarks, and, daunted, retired from the field and sulked for the remainder of the evening.

At the conclusion of the district meeting, because the budget was rejected, the board met to review citizen comment, gently characterized, and then cut the budget—this time providing a "principal designee" for only a quarter of the school year, instead of the most recent half-year decision after the original full-year decision—and by then, the superintendent of schools was happy to get the ten weeks. By the second budget meeting, the citizenry was sated with the superintendent's blood, the crowd dwindled to pre-"principal designee" levels, and the budget was approved routinely.

One lesson, among others, that I[68] learned from this entire experience is the stupidity of giving a new idea, or concept, a new name as well—regardless of how people do, or don't, garble it, it becomes the lightning rod for taxpayer resistance and anger. In the incident previously recounted, had we simply budgeted funds for principal overlap, without calling the new person a "principal designee," the budget may well have been approved initially without public furor. At worst, there would have been some, but not nearly as much, opposition to the idea as we created from the title "principal designee." Another thing I learned was not to take my wife to budget meetings. This one was her first and last—even though she admitted she was also shouting, "Sit down turkey," she claims it was more protective than hostile.

School districts will be more successful referring to new curriculum as "The New Curriculum," rather than "Income-Based Education" (or "Outcome-Based Education" for that matter). Initials such as IBE or OBE aren't too swift either, and neither are semi-clever acronyms.

It's much more difficult for dissidents to rally against a "revised curriculum" than it is to raise an army to march against "The New Renaissance Curriculum." People butchered the term *principal designee* and its relatively simple concept; imagine the demons that would be loosed from the name "New Renaissance Curriculum"—no matter what its true intent, many people would be convinced that it's a curriculum built around Genoan, Florentine, and Roman cultures and that only Italian will be spoken in the schools. Against such widespread public misun-

[68]Yes, I was the dummy who dreamed up the title "principal designee." I considered trying to pass it off as some other superintendent's mistake, but lost that argument with myself.

derstanding, "the very gods themselves contend in vain" [24],[69] and superintendents are really in over their heads.

Lose the fancy names for simple notions, and administrative lives will be simpler and more productive.

"STRUTTING AND FRETTING YOUR HOURS UPON THE STAGE" [25]

Motivational and visionary speeches or writings would have curdled the psyches of many now-experienced educators when they began their careers in school leadership, because they incorrectly believed that everyone on the team shared their vision and motivation—many of us came relatively late to the importance of such communications.[70]

Board of education meetings offer regular administrative opportunities for public administrative presentations, at which time superintendents particularly, and other administrators to a lesser but still significant degree, can develop recurring themes on professional and personal leadership aspirations for local public education. In every response to questions from board members or staff, students, or citizens among the audience, educational leadership is given opportunities ranging from chances to sell dreams on the high end of the scale to, at the lower end, simply display administrative competence—which in itself builds public support for the school system as a stalagmite grows drop by drop, day by day, week by week. . . .

As with all forms of administrative communications, school leaders should maintain a basic inventory of compositional aides, including a computer and a word processing program; a good desk dictionary; a large, library dictionary on its own stand; Strunk and White's *The Elements of Style* and/or other such guides to clean, unaffected prose; a thesaurus; a set of encyclopedias; and other reference manuals.

For important presentations, administrators should write what they plan to say and practice it often enough, with the written words before them, so they don't appear to be reading it even when they are for practical purposes. A podium or speaker's stand on which to place notes

[69]Although well-known for both his lyric poems and ballads, Schiller also wrote historical dramas such as *The Maid of Orleans* about the life of Joan of Arc. Schiller was a surgeon in a Wurttemberg regiment and went AWOL in 1781 to see the initial performance of a play he had written. He was arrested by the Duke of Wurttemberg and, for going AWOL, was sentenced to write nothing but medical treatises as his punishment.

[70]See also, this chapter, "Dreaming Dreams," p. 72.

should be prearranged whenever possible—it's a presenter's minor security blanket.

Extemporaneous speaking is a major part of leadership life, and experience makes us better at it; also, if leaders make carefully crafted, rehearsed statements appear to be off the cuff, good for them. The way to do that is with practice, practice, practice. Taping presentations for self-analysis is very effective in improving them—audiotape helps, but videotaping is a quantum leap forward and should be used whenever possible. In reviewing tapes, watch particularly for

- facial expressions: "Open faces," where the eyes are opened wide, eyebrows are elevated, and the mouth is smiling, are much better received than "closed faces," with eyes "squinched" closed, eyebrows at half mast, and an unsmiling mouth. Check both kinds of expressions in the mirror, and you'll see the advantage of "open" versus "closed"—but, in efforts to present an open face, beware of a "frozen" one, with the open expression fixed so firmly the entire countenance appears ready to fragment at any second. This can make you look more like Alfred E. Newman of *Mad Magazine* than an educational leader with a pleasant disposition.
- body language and gestures: Use occasional strong gestures, varied slightly, as opposed to metronome-like chopping motions, which become almost hypnotic; it's also effective to change positions, periodically moving out from behind the podium or leaning forward over it. Speakers should be careful to avoid such perpetual motion that audiences become fascinated by the presenter's constant leapings and boundings from position to position and lose track altogether of the message.
- voice tone and amplitude: Variations are most effective—sometimes quiet and reflective (if the microphone works well enough for that) and other times firm and louder—and occasionally even passionate about ideas being expressed.
- humor: Humor is effective if speakers are comfortable with it and if it is easy and unforced; otherwise, it's better to be your regular, stolid, dull self—people will forgive you that if you are sincere and otherwise likable.
- audience awareness: Presenters should monitor their audiences carefully, making good eye contact with various segments of the room—but at irregular intervals to avoid appearing to be a wind-up speaker running on coil springs. Be pre-

pared to adjust remarks as necessary, having already marked sections to be omitted if the audience's attention span is being exceeded; sometimes when a presentation is going particularly well, a few paragraphs that have been held in reserve for this possibility can be included with good effect.

- brevity: Generally, speakers should be briefer than they think they should; people will love you for that, even when they'd like to hear more; it's gratifying to sit down under those conditions—and much better than remaining standing and talking while sensing the audience hates both you and what you're saying to them.
- sincerity: Speakers, while avoiding appearing overly earnest, should concentrate on projecting sincerity; if you can make the audience like you personally, they will also like your message to them.

Only cynics see leadership as "a walking shadow, a poor player that struts and frets his hour upon the stage, and then is heard no more." [25] Administrative lives are much more significant than that, and they require many hours in the glare of the footlights, instead of just one, before a variety of audiences. These hours on stage are important moments in important professional lives.[71]

TELEPHONE—I: IT'S NOT ALRIGHT UNLESS YOU HEAR FROM ME

Yes, this is a rhetorical question, but how many times on the telephone has someone said to you, or have you said to someone else, or have you overheard someone on the phone say something similar to: (1) "That new sex education material you bought seemed to cause a furor with kindergarten parents in the district next door, so before you distribute it to the kindergartners send a packet to the principal's office this morning for me to look over, but unless I get back to you before they leave for the day it's alright to pass it out as the kids get on the buses." (2) "This morning's newspaper said state police identified Charlie Smith as the person who did it. So if you don't hear from me by this afternoon, you'll have to put Uncle Charlie, your much beloved custodian, on administrative leave." (3) "I'll review the budget accounts, but unless I call you back before 10:30, fax the purchase order for the

---

[71]See also, this chapter, "Dreaming Dreams," p. 72.

dozen new buses to the manufacturer." (4) "We'll both review our copies of the annual report, and if I don't call you back before the end of the day, go ahead and mail it to the Commissioner."

Obvious problems from this practice can and sometimes do arise. What do you suppose happens when someone tells you, or you tell someone else, or someone passes along to another person, one of the open-ended, no closure, semi-slovenly messages above, and (1) one or the other telephones stops working, (2) whoever was supposed to call back to confirm the original directions gets tied up with something else and overlooks the return call, (3) one or another secretaries forgets to pass along a message, or (4) other unforeseen circumstances occur?

This haphazard approach to positive communications, although a relatively minor leadership failing, can result in bad things happening to otherwise good people. Because, through careless communications, a directive to "scrub the mission" isn't received, incorrect assumptions often are made that "all systems are go," the launch proceeds, and the rocket leaves the pad. In the initial hypothetical situations earlier, here are some of the bad things that could happen because of incomplete communications: (1) Kindergartners take home condoms in their sex education packets, and the superintendent probably needs to look for a new principal—and maybe for a new job for him- or herself. (2) Good old Uncle Charlie is suspended, and already you had discovered that a different Charles Smith was the alleged "perp." Yes, you can bring Uncle Charlie back from leave, but he'll still be understandably disgruntled about his suspension. (3) Three months later, you are surprised by the arrival of twelve shiny, new, fully equipped GMC buses at the bus garage—and you can't pay for them; OK, maybe you can send the buses back, but General Motors hates that when it happens. (4) A fouled up report is mailed to the Commissioner. This one's relatively easy—just call the Commissioner's secretary and explain that you screwed up again.

To prevent these and similar misunderstandings and the unfortunate consequences of incomplete communications, administrators should always call back and complete transactions definitively by reaffirming earlier directives as given, modifying them, or canceling them.

In every instance, confirming, follow-up telephone calls are easy and are the correct habit for superintendents to develop in themselves and among administrative colleagues. Confirming, modifying, or canceling calls prevent serious staff embarrassment—and sometimes much more than that.

"THE EMPEROR'S NEW CLOTHES" [26]

Leaders need to maintain appropriate balance between seriousness of purpose and enjoyment of life.[72] Their educational worlds will be immeasurably better if they can recognize and enjoy the pomposity, banality, illusion, delusion, ambiguity, misdirection, lunacy, boredom, and just plain old BS that surround them each day. A highly developed sense of the absurd, which makes potentially humorous situations stand out as if they were covered with dayglow, neon orange paint, should be considered a strong leadership attribute.

The bad news is that some educators and educational leaders somehow feel that enjoyment of, and seeing the humor in, professional life is either forbidden or in some other unspecified way undignified. Humor frightens them. Educators who believe humor is prohibited, unseemly, or threatening are the unfortunates who see the emperor's nonexistent new suit of clothes clearly—instead of appreciating the humor in a naked superintendent being told how well he or she is dressed.

The good news is that one of public education's greatest assets is its ability to accommodate a wide range of colorful personalities, strengths, and weaknesses. Compared to the cautious, muted behaviors which characterize many corporate bureaucracies, teachers and administrators have the freedom, and usually the desire, to be themselves—blemishes and all. The abundance of colorful personalities, the undisguised human idiosyncrasies and foibles, the opportunities to work each day with large numbers of children or young people—all of these, taken separately and collectively, provide each educational leader a lifetime of rich personal interactions rarely duplicated in other professions.[73]

Some people have the misfortune to spend thirty or forty years in a corporate position, and if asked to name the most unforgettable character with whom they worked might say, "I forget," or "There weren't any." Of course, if they had known their business acquaintances outside of work, responses would be different, but the rigidity of corporate life often hides the real people inside opaque office demeanors. In public education, the problem is choosing from among dozens of unforgettable, very transparent, colleagues—not finding just one.

Although it may be impossible to develop an easy, natural recognition of potential humor much beyond the level each person is given at birth, most people, if they can relax and focus on each day's possibilities one at a time, might be surprised to discover how much otherwise

[72]See also, Chapter 1, "Ten Cardinal Principles of Leadership," p. 21.
[73]See also, Chapter 11, "Educational Colleagues and Friends," p. 366.

hidden humor is readily available—not in deep shaft mines, but just lying all around them like uncollected seashells on the beach to be gathered easily and treasured.[74]

THE LADY OR THE TIGER?

Attempts to fit complex professional personalities into one of two, or even one of a few, discrete categories are difficult even for compulsive classifiers. However, many superintendents either act, think, and focus more on the board of education or more on district staff; the two categories don't form a pure dichotomy, but portray two kinds of superintendents who, in each case, exhibit tendencies more toward one categorization than the other.

The golden mean may be found much closer to one tendency than its opposite behavior, or it may be just nudging over an invisible line equidistant between the two—but administrative preferences usually are found closer to one than the other—and the choice so made can be between the lady or the tiger.[75]

Category 1: Superintendents Whose Primary Focus Is on the Board of Education

While not necessarily indifferent to, or disinterested in, the welfare of teachers and other administrators, superintendents focus on board members individually or collectively more closely than staff; they spend more time preparing for, and cleaning up after, board meetings than they do on staff interactions.

If there are difficult decisions between pleasing either the board or the staff and disappointing the other, the board is appeased and the staff disappointed—if someone must be unhappy with the superintendent, it will likely be the staff.

Some of these superintendents and principals may also be very effective in staff relationships, but their engines may idle with these while "revving" high in board relationships. It's not that they don't care about

---

[74]See also, Chapter 11, "A Vast Armada of Small Boats," p. 360; "Lanterns in the Window," p. 348; and "May I Have the Envelope Please?" p. 349.
[75]Throughout "The Lady or the Tiger," principals' relationships with building staff and the superintendent of schools, or a special education director's relationship with staff and the superintendent of schools, may be substituted for relationships among superintendents, boards, and districtwide staff.

and respect other administrators, teachers, and support staff, but that their primary concentration is toward satisfying their board of education; they expend more physical and emotional energy on that task than on helping staff members with their work.

Category 2: Superintendents or Principals Whose Primary Focus Is on the Staff

While not indifferent to board of education members, and recognizing the obvious need to work effectively with them, these leaders focus on staff concerns, individually and collectively, more intently even than they do on board members—particularly matters of interest only to individual board members' concerns. These leaders spend more time preparing for, and cleaning up after, staff meetings and sessions than they do on interactions with individual board members between board of education meetings.

If there are difficult choices between pleasing board members or the staff and disappointing the other group, the staff receives the edge in the superintendent's mind. If someone must be unhappy with the superintendent, it probably will be a few board members. Most of these superintendents and principals also are very effective in board relationships, but they concentrate more on helping the staff do their jobs better and expend more physical and emotional energy on that task.

Superintendents and principals sometimes rationalize certain behaviors to please their boards, even at significant cost to faculty relationships, arguing with themselves that they must survive in their positions to make worthwhile educational changes—there's something to that point of view.

However, unless the staff supports its leadership, a superintendent's almost total focus on boards of education cannot accomplish anything educationally significant. Similarly, when principals, or other district leaders, are excessively preoccupied with pleasing their superintendent, to the detriment of their daily staff responsibilities and interactions, they can't be good leaders either. Whether superintendent, principal, or other administrator, this kind of upward focus may assure administrative survival, but survival is all that it is—it's certainly not leadership, and it's rarely productive of anything educationally worthwhile.

Strong arguments exist for giving staff the higher priority if superintendents expect to do more than hang around—even if it's hanging around with annual pay raises and new three-year contracts. Teachers, followed closely in importance by building principals, do almost everything for which school districts exist—teaching and guiding children and youth.[76]

Conclusion

Obviously either of these two divergent emphases, carried to extremes, is untenable. Superintendents must always try to please both these constituencies—and the general public, local governmental leaders, the state department of education, the media, other groups, and their spouses and children.

One important caveat: No matter how much leadership is enamored of its staff and the staff reciprocates that affection, if he or she encounters big-time trouble with a board of education (or a principal with the superintendent), teachers and/or other administrators can't and won't save him or her. Many colleagues may wish they could, and leaders also might wish they could, but, in extremis, leaders are always on their own. This shouldn't be disillusioning; realistic limitations of the best, most loyal, staff need to be understood and accepted as a leadership fact of life.

The best superintendents and principals, those who manage to satisfy both their important constituencies, usually locate the golden mean somewhat closer to daily staff leadership—albeit not so much closer they can't also work well with boards of education or with superintendents. The most appropriate attitude for a superintendent toward his board (or a principal toward his/her superintendent) may well be a paraphrase of a seventeenth century English poet[77]: "I could not love thee dear board so much, loved I not teachers more" [27].

THORNS IN ADMINISTRATIVE FLESH

In his second letter to the Corinthians, Paul described "a thorn in the flesh"[78] [28], which caused him constant discomfort and which also

[76]See also, Chapter 8, "A Chest Full of Ribbons," p. 239.
[77]Richard Lovelace was the prototypical soldier and cavalier in his lyrical poetry and military career, except that he kept getting jailed for one thing or another—once in the Gatehouse at Westminster for presenting a Kentish petition at the wrong time to the wrong person and once when he returned from fighting with the French forces against the Spanish at Dunkerque.
[78]"Therefore, to keep me from being too elated, a thorn was given me in the flesh, a messenger of Satan to torment me, to keep me from being too elated." Administrators often see the origins of the Biblical thorn and administrative paperwork as from the same demon.

kept him humble and therefore better able to serve the Lord. Superintendents, principals, and other administrators will also experience a certain amount of perpetual pain from important and required paperwork with its attendant deadlines—although there's no evidence that paperwork "thorns in the flesh" make anyone better able to serve the Lord or their school districts. Effective administrators give paper shuffling a low priority, particularly during the school day. When paperwork must be done, most of it should be taken care of after school hours—not during school hours when it keeps school district leaders from more important student and staff interactions.

In addition to required reports and reading, each day's mail brings pounds of useless material, which secretaries or administrative assistants should handle effectively. A secreatary or assistant should discriminate among incoming pieces of correspondence and determine (1) which of it the boss must see that same day; (2) which of it he or she must review but that can also wait until the weekly paperwork orgy; (3) which the secretary or other central office personnel can and should handle; and (4) which is junk mail and should be junked.

Administrators should establish clear, fail-safe procedures, so if there's reasonable doubt into which of the four categories a particular piece of mail belongs it will automatically be placed in at least the next higher category for administrative attention. Administrators should train office assistants to force them, at gunpoint if necessary, to read anything each day that appears really important—and if in doubt, it should be considered important. The rest of the mail that isn't recycled, and that is clearly less important, should be held until Friday, at which time administrators should bring a large wastebasket alongside their desks and throw most of the mail away after a quick glance at it. If everything ends up in the "must see today" pile, get a new secretary or assistant.

Another approach might be to throw most daily mail unread into the recycling basket. Of course, there is important stuff that must be faced, but a great deal of correspondence anguished over by administrators with misplaced priorities could be junked, and nobody would ever know. The sun would still rise on schedule each morning, the birds would still sing. . . .

In "how to" manuals, a number of modestly competent efficiency experts share good office organizational advice with administrators, including such appropriate suggestions as handling documents only once instead of placing them in an original pile and reading them two, three, or four times after moving them periodically from one pile of paper to another—a number of these office manuals are worth the administrative time required to read them.

If mail is routed to other staff for their action, administrators should have clearly understood follow-up procedures that secretaries or administrative assistants monitor to ensure appropriate and timely response and action.

Superintendents sometimes find it difficult to allow principals and other administrators the same flexibility and freedom in prioritizing communications from their offices that superintendents have with their outside correspondence. Naturally, superintendents believe everything they send to other administrators is crucial, but, to those other administrators, daily rounds with students and teachers often supersede "administrivial" priorities. Superintendents should respect administrative dedication to more important responsibilities—as long as principals and others manage to slip acceptable responses onto the superintendent's desk within his or her timelines, which should be as generous as reasonably possible.

Administrative paperwork is important, but not a process to be worshiped, and it shouldn't get in the way of more important work day activities and responsibilities.

THERE AREN'T ANY CRACKS IN MY FACADE

Another in the endless list of human and professional imperfections that spring full-grown from dragon's teeth [29] of personal insecurities is administrative inability to acknowledge organizational problems and then work to eliminate them. Principals, superintendents, and other school leaders often invest more time and energy in papering over obvious school, district, or departmental faults than they would fixing them—and correcting public education's educational deficiencies is obviously better than denying their existence.

It's not easy to acknowledge legitimate educational problems, and some people will use administrative openness and honesty against those school leaders who do. Sometimes, a school district's teachers and/or administrators are uncomfortable with open communications and public discussions of imperfections; often, board of education members are similarly inclined against acknowledging problems openly; parents may not like it either.

There is a major difference, however, between responding honestly to board members who ask if there was a food fight at the high school today and going door to door in the community forcing this news on people who previously had zero concern about the high school's "Olympic Mashed Potato, Squash, and English Pea Hurling Triathalon." Choosing one of these two options will characterize leadership as either (1) open, secure, and honest or (2) gratuitously stupid.

While nobody actually does go house to house blabbing a school district's mortal sins, some people expect superintendents and principals to tell everything to everybody no matter how unintelligent that may be—but working too hard to tell everyone everything and to convince them that district education is crumbling unchecked around you are even more counterproductive than refusing to admit there are any cracks at all in your professional facade.

Many educators have worked with superintendents with the unfortunate habit of beginning each board of education meeting by saying, "You know, I did the dumbest thing this morning. . ." or "My mind must be going, because on three separate occasions last week I forgot to . . ." or "You wouldn't believe I submitted the annual report to the state without including . . ." or "You know, I can't remember any more to zip my fly when I leave the house in the morning. . . ."

This kind of superintendent may be volunteering his failings to convince board members he's a really regular guy or in order to be better accepted by the board members or to break the opening ice at meetings or for some other unknown reason—but by the twenty-fifth unsolicited confession of personal ignorance, malfeasance in office, and unzipped clothing, he will have thoroughly convinced board members that he is indeed as incompetent as his "mea culpas" say he is.

Although we all occasionally may forget important obligations, or in some other way err, we shouldn't feel compelled to blat them gratuitously in each pair of ears we meet, and it's a good thing we don't, or people would begin to believe we also are as incompetent as our unceasing confessions of professional frailty imply.

THIS ISN'T THE FIRST TIME IT'S HAPPENED TO ME EITHER!

A principal's lawyer friend worked for the eternally bankrupt Hartford, New Haven Railroad as a company attorney; his special task was dealing with disgruntled or irate passengers, most of whom commuted each day to work from Connecticut towns and villages to New York City. He shared one particularly fascinating letter from a commuter flecked (the letter, not the commuter) with what he later hoped was saliva, considering the story that follows, from the commuter's angry sputtering as he typed his letter.

The unfortunate traveler recounted having left the train in Greenwich, or Darien, or Westport and walking under a small railroad bridge and the train, on his way to the station, his wife, and his car, for the ride home to whichever suburb in which he lived. As he walked under the bridge, some idiot on the train dumped the contents of a lavatory holding tank on him and his $300 Brooks Brothers blue suit—in those days $300 was an immense sum—ruining it along with the passenger's disposition for two or three months. Naturally, he sought replacement of his suit and recompense for his pain, suffering, and emotional distress—not to mention loss of harmonious conjugal relations for a period of time.

After railing against the stupidity of the railroad, its management, its trains, its employees, and their ancestors and progeny, the totally distraught "dumpee" ended his diatribe with this fascinating conclusion: "And this isn't the first time it's happened to me either!"

Some people don't learn from mistakes nearly as quickly as we'd like them to, but school leadership should and must. If we've figuratively, or literally, had the contents of an educational sanitary tank emptied on us, even in less expensive clothing, we should avoid walking under the same trestle a second time while the train chuffs over our head.

"VOX POPULI, VOX DEI"—I [30]

An insightful cartoon pictures a king and a companion looking down from the parapet of the royal castle. Shoes, rocks, and other missiles fly around them as, below, an angry mob screams and glares up at the king and his attendant. The courtier speaks to his displeased boss, "You're right sire, they certainly are, but when ten thousand assholes speak with one voice, even a king must pay heed!"

This sentiment flies in the face of the advice to Charlemagne by Alcuin of York [30] who said his king shouldn't pay serious attention to the notion that "the voice of the people is the voice of God" because "the seething of the crowd is always near to madness. . . ."[79] But, un-

---

[79]Alcuin got his start as a British cleric but abandoned his English environment to establish a school for Charlemagne. His bias was closer to Machiavelli than it was to participatory management. He may have been an early Hobbesian, as indicated in his views of the people—or today's electorate.

fortunately for school leaders, often the cartoon is correct, and we must heed the angry voices we hear—although it's also often true that Alcuin comes very close to the mark with his views on the general public and its behaviors.

This divergence of thought highlights yet another in the endless list of school leadership balancing acts in its search for the golden mean[80]—in this instance, between being responsive to the will of the people and acting on personal principle contrary to strong public opinion—the subject of John Kennedy's *Profiles in Courage* as he chronicled historical figures who, as a matter of personal principle, couldn't follow the conventional wisdom of the day expressed through the clear will of their constituents; they took the road "less traveled by, and that has made all the difference" [31].

There may be many occasions in superintendents' or principals' professional lives when, after careful consideration and study of an issue, they also should stand on personal or professional principles even in the face of strong public opposition. But it's important for leaders to understand that, when they take these stands, they also signal plainly they are willing to give up their current positions and start over somewhere else—with all the attendant personal and professional discomforts from surrendering a cherished job because they can't surrender their convictions.

At other times, even educational leadership must take heed when many fewer than ten thousand parents and other citizens speak with one voice, as long as taking heed isn't illegal, immoral, or fattening, and most of these parents and citizens probably shouldn't be described as the cartoon king described them. And when even one voice whispers its point of view, and that soft voice appears correct, superintendents should hear that small sound amidst other distracting noises in their educational forests.

Deciding in a particular instance whether 'tis nobler to be principled, or a far better thing to be responsive to the will of the people, or both, are among the dilemmas that make educational leadership exciting, fascinating, and often very risky.

WE NEVER DID IT THAT WAY IN MY OLD DISTRICT

When newly appointed superintendents or principals begin tenures

---

[80]See also, Chapter 1, "In Search of Gold," p. 7.

in new districts or schools, they should swear blood oaths never to say anything such as, "Well, in my old district, or school, we always . . ."—not to administrators, not to teachers, not to board members, not to parents, not to town officials, not to students, or not even to people visiting your office because it's warm inside and cold outside. Nobody gives a damn about how it was done where you were before, and, after about the third such reference, they become increasingly hostile and don't want to hear another word about

- the ample supplies, equipment, and other educational resources available there
- the hordes of students who went to the very best colleges from there
- how wonderfully supportive the parents were there
- the competence of the board of education there
- how well schools were maintained there
- the oustanding administrators there
- the dedicated teachers there
- the community there
- the weather there
- anything there
- there

Your new colleagues will hate it when you do that, and they will dislike you personally as well. References to your old district have the same effects as fingernails scraping blackboards—both set people's teeth on edge. Eventually, your staff will begin to snicker, roll their eyes, and tune out, and, especially if such nostalgia continues unabated, may also throw erasers, chalk, and large items of schoolhouse furniture.

Try not to even think about the old days; if and when such thoughts crawl uninvited into your head, don't dare even smile in a way that might suggest to those in the room what you're thinking about, and when you can't stop remembering and smiling like Mona Lisa, don't! don't! don't! ever say out loud what you're thinking and smiling enigmatically about!

The world will be a better place for your restraint.

WHO IS THIS PERSON?—I

At special times throughout their years in educational leadership, administrative job changes present windows of opportunity for self-assessment of leadership strengths and shortcomings and for modification of professional and personal attitudes and behaviors that could benefit from changes. These behavior modifications can be made almost totally without self-consciousness and with complete assurance that they will be noticed, instead of being masked by long-standing staff perceptions of the superintendent or principal—views that are often fully justified and accurate.

It's possible, even without converting to Zen Buddhism, for leaders to monitor, evaluate, and contemplate their professional and personal leadership navels without changing jobs—such practices come highly recommended. However, as administrators begin new positions, boards, administrators, teachers, and other staff are relatively unfamiliar with past behaviors, attitudes, and leadership styles—except through references, which, at best, are superficial compared to reservoirs of unrevealed professional and personal characteristics undisclosed by even the best background investigations. The new staff's views of its new leader are fresh canvases upon which leadership is free to paint its new self-portrait.

New positions bring a freedom to completely overhaul leadership behaviors without wondering whether colleagues are asking each other, "Who is this person?—this stranger I thought we knew?" Behaviors also can be changed without wondering whether or not colleagues can set aside long-held judgments and recognize the changes you have worked so hard to bring about. Often, they cannot, and their earlier perceptions remain cast in the stones of their previous experiences with you.

For example, many principals and superintendents have been hesitant to articulate serious sentiments to staff about the importance of public education and its practitioners because many of us incorrectly believed such discussions were unnecessary.[81] Although I had previously assumed those concepts were shared fully by staff and that emotions, sentiments, and vision never needed to be discussed, by the time I'd spent a decade in the superintendency, I knew better—but I was self-conscious about altering long-standing behavior patterns. Changing positions frees us from our self-imposed shackles and also allows us to change professionally and personally without the burden of other people's rigid perceptions formed out of earlier experiences with us.

Possibly, it's as true for new administrative posts as it's purported to be in the old song: "Love is sweeter the second time around."[82]

---

[81]See also, this chapter, "Fireside and Other Chats and Communications—I: General," p. 75.
[82]See also, this chapter, "Dance with the One Who 'Brung' You," p. 68.

WHOM DID YOU SAY IS CALLING?

Whether serving as school superintendents or principals, district administrators occasionally receive unsigned letters and anonymous telephone calls. These communications generally fit one of three categories: (1) calls or letters telling you what a rotten person you are, or how stupid you are for doing or having done something, or for daring to think about doing something with which your correspondent or caller disagrees; (2) communications alleging improper behavior or actions by staff members; and (3) communications alleging something unpleasant about a school district family—either about one or more parents, or about a family relative, or about a child or children in the family.

The first category is the easiest with which to deal because, even though it provides unpleasant administrative moments, you can hang up as soon as you warn callers that you won't continue the conversation unless they give their names—or tear up letters as soon as you realize they are unsigned. Unfortunately, even when you recognize written correspondence is from an anonymous source, it's almost impossible to discard letters without reading them—which may imply that people with no backbone should write letters instead of calling on the phone.

Except in rare circumstances, the second and third varietals of anonymous communications should be treated much as you would the first. If someone calls to let you know that your high school biology teacher, Dr. Crabby Appleton, is personally rotten to the core or a no good son of a whatever, you can hang up or quit reading unless they identify themselves. You could do the same if you're told old Crabby has been seen frequenting a heterosexual bar—or any other kind of bar for that matter.

If however, an unsigned letter accuses a staff member of seriously inappropriate behavior, for example, with a student, you can't ignore it. Most administrators instinctively detest anonymous calls or unsigned correspondence—a commendable instinct—but allegations of child molestation or abuse require administrative attention, regardless of their sources. If district administrators other than the superintendent receive such calls or letters, they should inform the superintendent immediately. The superintendent will contact school counsel to inform him or her of the accusations and to discuss appropriate district actions.

If the accused is a staff member, and the administrator is given the name of the alleged victim, he or she (or someone close to the young person) needs to speak with the child without revealing more than necessary, to ascertain if the young person is prepared to confirm allegations and/or to share anything else with school personnel.

Most of us wouldn't want to call parents without supporting information, but this must be decided within particular circumstances; in some states, when superintendents receive reports from faculty members accusing other faculty members of student abuse, parents must be called [32]. When school administrators don't know the supposed victim's name, as a matter of fairness to the accused, they should inform him or her of the call and see what he or she has to say. A staff member's unsolicited confession helps at this point.

Absent corroborating evidence from the child, when his or her name is known, or an admission of guilt by the staff member, superintendents should speak with district counsel, file the call or letter away in memory, but take no other action. If, however, there is corroborating evidence, as repulsive as reacting to an anonymous call may be, leadership has no other reasonable choice except involvement of appropriate law enforcement officials. If there is evidence, or even reasonable suspicion, of child abuse, many states require a "psychologist, school teacher, school principal, school guidance counselor, school paraprofessional, or social worker to report any such concerns to the state commissioner of children and family services" [32].

Whenever possible, it's gratifying to ignore anonymous communications, but there are times when administrators don't have that luxury.

PRACTICE MAKES PERFECT/DISCUSSION QUESTIONS

(1) At faculty meetings, board of education meetings, or committee meetings, note occasions that a speaker, by talking well beyond the time his or her point has been made, demonstrates a need to read the paragraph about " 'Closers.' "

(2) Reflecting on "Disclaimers Make the World Go 'Round," over the course of the next few weeks, note the disclaimers used in informal professional conversations—and in more formal settings. Collecting ten or more makes you eligible for free admission to a white belt exhibition of "Samurai disclaiming"; in that time period, personal use of ten or more professional disclaimers qualifies you for a brown belt in that same esoteric martial art form.

(3) "Fireside and Other Chats and Communications—II–V" each speak of administrative correspondence to staff, parents, boards, and students; if you are not now an administrator, write a letter on a subject of your choosing to each of an educational leader's four constituencies; if you are a school administrator, review examples of your latest correspondence to any of these groups and attempt to identify ways to improve these letters or memoranda. Compare your efforts to those in Appendix B on a similar subject—yours will probably be better.

(4) Try to recall from your recent past examples of people either making the right decisions for the wrong reasons or other aspects of the slovenly leadership behavior described in "Puritans and Bears." What issues were involved in your real-life situations?

(5) As discussed in "Sit Down Turkey!—Or a Rose by Another Name Doesn't Smell as Good," have you experienced or observed educational issues that are worsened because of the name chosen for a program or educational activity? How were the problems manifested?

(6) Do you agree with the thesis in "Telephone—I: It's Not Alright Unless You Hear from Me"? Why or why not?

(7) Have you observed superintendent or principal behaviors as described in "The Lady or the Tiger?" Into which category do administrators with whom you have worked belong?

(8) As discussed in "We Never Did It That Way in My Old District," are you fully aware of the fate that awaits you for talking incessantly about what life was like where you worked previously? Have you known people who did this? Will they, or you, burn in hell for that or not?

PRACTICE MAKES PERFECT—MATCHING THEMES/MAIN IDEAS

Place the number of the theme/main idea of the topics following the titles, in the blank to the right of the correct titles. Answers are provided in Appendix C, p. 463.

Ankle Bone Connected to the Foot Bone . . .   _____
"Closers"   _____
Creative Schizophrenia   _____

Dance with the One Who "Brung" You   ____
Disclaimers Make the World Go 'Round   ____
Dreaming Dreams   ____
Efficient or Effective—Choose Any Two   ____
Finishing the Run   ____
I Always Knew This Would Happen Someday, and It Finally
   Did   ____
"If You Can Keep Your Head When All About You . . ."   ____
Puritans and Bears   ____
Say Hello to People at Least   ____
Sit Down Turkey!—or a Rose by Another Name Doesn't
   Smell as Good   ____
"Strutting and Fretting Your Hours upon the Stage"   ____
Telephone—I: It's Not Alright Unless You Hear from Me   ____
"The Emperor's New Clothes"   ____
The Lady or the Tiger?   ____
Thorns in Administrative Flesh   ____
There Aren't Any Cracks in My Facade   ____
This Isn't the First Time It's Happened to Me Either!   ____
"*Vox Populi, Vox Dei*"—I   ____
We Never Did It That Way in My Old District   ____
Who Is This Person?—I   ____
Whom Did You Say Is Calling?   ____

Themes/Main Ideas

(*1*) Leadership survival sometimes requires explanations of our simplest assertions. Although they are only tools, such explanations are important tools.

(*2*) If leaders aren't comfortable holding divergent points of view simultaneously in their thoughts and appreciating the value of each, they probably won't be successful leaders.

(*3*) Leaders should avail themselves of opportunities for personal and professional growth and change while retaining the best basic personal elements that have defined them as individual human beings and as leaders throughout their lives.

(*4*) Educational leaders must be suspicious of coincidences between similar or related events and should recognize and understand existing connections between and among seemingly disconnected events, visualize overall patterns from apparently independent events, use connections and identified patterns to investigate existing relationships between or among them, develop connections and patterns from relationships, correct existing problems before they worsen, and prevent new problems from spinning off old ones.

(5) Leadership should articulate a clear vision of each leader's hopes for and expectations of district colleagues, the school, or department—and regularly remind listeners or readers of the leader's vision for education and what he or she is committed to accomplish on behalf of young people entrusted to the local public schools.

(6) Every single leadership or instructional task should be focused upon, worked at, and completed as if it were the most important responsibility of a person's professional career. Educational leaders should concentrate on completing the school year as productively as it usually begins, on maintaining forward educational momentum, and on working with teachers to ensure they also finish each year's educational run well.

(7) Although choices sometimes must be made weighing factors peripheral to an issue's moral center, leadership instincts should recognize the essence of educational decisions instead of focusing on extrinsic legal, political, or other considerations that lead to pernicious personal attitudes and negative organizational effects. When leaders develop patterns that allow them to make even correct decisions for the wrong reasons, it becomes easier for them to make wrong decisions for the wrong reasons.

(8) Leadership behaviors are infectious, and when superintendents, principals, or other school district leaders don't manage crises well, neither will colleagues. If, conversely, leaders exhibit a sense of ease and an ability to cope with any problem that may arise, that also is communicated to the staff. Effective leaders manage to "keep their heads when all about them are losing theirs and blaming it on them."

(9) In most professions, each day is filled with choices between efficiency and effectiveness, and leadership requires balancing these two qualities. Endorsing the concept of the golden mean between extremes, leadership should take the long view, involve other people appropriately in major district educational decisions, and accept some inefficiency on behalf of long-range educational ef-

fectiveness—as long as vital educational services function acceptably.

(*10*) School districts should lose the fancy names for simple notions, and administrative lives will be simpler and more productive.

(*11*) Whenever colleagues sense leadership despair, enthusiasm wanes; educators don't want leaders who feel their jobs are too hard for them. When leaders communicate enthusiasm for educational programs and activities and are confident about meeting leadership responsibilities, staff is much more likely to respond in kind. School leaders need to emulate the hardiness and the dogged persistence of aluminum siding salesmen.

(*12*) To prevent misunderstandings and their consequences, administrators should always call back and complete transactions definitively, by reaffirming earlier directives as given, modifying them as needed, or canceling them. Confirming, follow-up telephone calls are easy, are a correct habit, and prevent serious staff embarrassment—and sometimes much more than that.

(*13*) School leaders should establish an obvious climate of openness and receptivity to personel visits and telephone calls and an open, receptive environment for staff, parent, and student constituents alike. Accessibility improves perceptions of school leaders, and it's a better way to treat people.

(*14*) The best superintendents usually recognize daily staff leadership as their primary task—albeit followed closely by the need to work well with their boards of education.

(*15*) Leadership job changes present windows of opportunity for self-assessment of personal and professional strengths and shortcomings and for modification of attitudes and behaviors. In new positions, behavior modifications can be made without self-consciousness and with assurance they will be noticed instead of masked by long-standing perceptions of you.

(*16*) Educational leaders need to cultivate important "closing out" skills in their sales of educational concepts to staff, boards of education, and communities and not continue talking until they lose what they've gained. We need to read our audiences and recognize signs, omens, and portents that point toward success; shut up; sit down; and "close out" the sale.

(*17*) Board of education meetings offer regular administrative opportunities for public administrative presentations for leadership to develop recurring themes in leadership aspirations for local education. For important presentations, administrators should write what they plan to say and practice it so they won't appear to be reading it, even when they are. Extemporaneous speaking is also a major part of leadership life and requires practice, practice, practice. Our hours "on stage" are important moments in important professional lives.

(*18*) As new superintendents or principals begin in new districts, they should never say, "Well, in my old district, we always. . . ." Nobody gives a damn about how it was done where you were before, and after about the third reference, listeners become increasingly hostile and don't want to hear another word about it. Your new colleagues will hate it when you do that and will dislike you personally as well.

(*19*) Leaders need to maintain an appropriate balance between seriousness and enjoyment of life. A highly developed sense of the absurd should be considered a strong leadership attribute. Humorous situations are lying all around us like uncollected seashells to be gathered and treasured.

(*20*) Administrators should give paper shuffling a low priority, particularly during the school day so it won't keep leaders from more important student and staff interactions; should establish clear, fail-safe procedures to read anything that appears really important; should have clearly understood follow-up procedures to ensure appropriate and timely response and action; and follow such common advice from office manuals as "handle documents only once."

(*21*) District administrators occasionally receive unsigned letters and anonymous telephone calls. Whenever possible, anonymous communications should be ignored and callers told that's what will happen, but if a call involves possible injury to children, administrators don't have that luxury.

(*22*) Educational leaders need to find the golden mean between covering up real problems and gratuitous revelations of minor issues to everyone who will listen. The golden mean is responsible acknowledgement of major issues and is somewhat closer to gratuitous revelations than to covering up.

(23) Leaders must learn from mistakes.

(24) Educators need to strike a responsive balance between responsiveness to the will of the people and acting on personal principle contrary to strong public opinion. Deciding when to do what makes school leadership exciting, fascinating, and risky.

CHAPTER 4

Boards of Education

RECURRING BOARD PHENOMENA

Better Odds Are All You Can Expect—In Poker or Leadership Life in General

IN FIVE CARD draw, a player's odds are better drawing one card for a flush than holding three queens and drawing two cards to fill a full house, but, in any given hand, good poker players know that they might be dealt the full house against much longer odds and not fill the flush with better odds—they know, and base decisions on, percentages and don't expect guarantees of winning because of better odds.

Boards of education and parents don't much care about better odds for success; they prefer or demand guarantees. When parents discuss transportation arrangements or bus routes at board of education meetings, they say, "There is no way you can put a price on a child's life!"—which, translated, means that whatever the parents think is appropriate, school districts should provide. In their opinion, to do otherwise is valuing money over human life. Their statements are sincere and honest, springing as they do from feelings and emotions, rather than from logic and reality.

As cold and unfeeling as it might sound at first blush, although superintendents and board members share parental interests in student safety, there are practical funding limits on ensuring children's well-being, which are relevant to parents as well as to school districts. Administrators and boards do what they reasonably can in arranging bus stops, establishing required walking distances, and reducing hazards children face walking to bus stops or to school and while passengers on buses.

However, there are always more precautions that could be taken if there weren't cost and other practical constraints. If school districts could afford a quantum leap in transportation safety, each child would be outfitted in football equipment, complete with helmet and pads, picked up in his or her own driveway, transported to school in a Sherman tank (or the current model thereof), driven by a medical doctor with a registered nurse in attendance, and provided a motorcycle escort of state troopers. Even this wouldn't guarantee children arriving safely at school, although it would dramatically increase the odds of that happening.

No matter what school districts do to improve student safety, risks can't be totally eliminated—the risks aren't as great when good decisions have been made, but some danger always remains because of practical limitations on choices and alternatives. Obviously, this concept can't be presented coldly and unfeelingly, but it must be faced honestly—even though any factual discussion of it results in school leadership being labeled cold and unfeeling by those who won't, or can't, face reality. If parents don't force the issue, don't force it upon them—you can't win.

Buses already are much safer than automobiles, from Mercedes and Volvos to Volkswagens and Suzukis, in which parents transport children on family outings and on business. Although parents can't guarantee children's safety in personal transportation, any more than schools can with bus transportation, driving larger cars clearly increases child safety—but not all parents drive full-sized cars, some because of their cost and some from simple automotive preferences; those who drive smaller cars because larger cars are too expensive aren't accused of placing a price on their children's safety.

For superintendents and boards of education, transportation safety is only a microcosm of educational life and life generally, and the best decisions only improve the odds that what the board wants to happen will happen and what they don't want to happen won't happen. Examples include improving class sizes, which doesn't assure greater student learning but improves opportunities for it; purchasing computers and training teachers in their use, which doesn't guarantee computer literacy, but which can't happen without these actions; providing better educational facilities, which doesn't ensure student learning either, but better facilities make learning more likely. These examples say almost all that can be said about educational improvement or change.

These points seem so obvious, yet boards, taxpayers, and staff want, and often demand, quantified assurances that, in return for their support of particular recommendations, decisions, new programs, or procedures, what they expect to happen will happen. Public school leadership must be honest with boards of education and their constituencies and promise them only greater chances for success—not offering unfounded guarantees of it.

Better odds are all the board of education or anyone should expect—either in poker or leadership life generally—and even when correct decisions are made, better odds for success are all you get.

But Sir, I'm Only a Poor Little Match Girl

Throughout the careers of experienced educators, until the late eighties anyway, boards of education were trusted representatives of the general public, with primary responsibilities as educational advocates for children and, secondarily, as elected buffers between communities and school leadership—absorbing many of the blows directed at superintendents and principals and providing support for school district leaders when unfairly attacked.

Although some boards of education still competently perform the original roles that God intended them to play in America's educational drama, many seem to have forgotten their lines and have even abandoned their responsibilities as child advocates and supporters and defenders of district leadership and staff.

Because of increasingly difficult financial times, boards too often abdicate their responsibilities as community advocates for adequate educational programming and function as apprentice boards of finance or town councils or other fiscal authorities. From their cries of poverty, an onlooker might believe everyone in the school district sells penny boxes of matches in Victorian England—or has joined a cloistered order and surrendered all worldly goods and comforts.

Too many boards of education today practice niggardliness without portfolio and enthusiastically play newly chosen roles as defenders of the fiscal faith while ignoring their irreplaceable responsibilities as advocates for children and for budgets adequate for their educational support. In their strident cries for zero budget increases, they are often as shrill as members of the least rational taxpayers groups, and, in their futile efforts to please budget slashers, they may be no more sensible or realistic or caring than chainsaw-wielding expenditure cutters.[83]

Too many boards of education are no longer effective in fulfilling their other original assignment that they once performed so well—representing community interests to public school leadership and supporting school leaders among community constituents. Because these

---

[83]I'll have a brief lie down now until the fever cools.

boards have lost the trust of the citizenry (not necessarily all their fault) and in spite of their attempts to curry favor with taxpayers at the expense of sound education, they no longer possess sufficient clout to be effective intermediaries between citizens and school district leadership.[84]

So is continued existence justified for those boards that have turned away from advocacy for good education and that are no more trusted by the public than their administrative Prussian mercenaries? For many of them, all that's left are nights of often useless committee activities, which only weaken a superintendent's leadership through the excessive time requirements of unproductive, or even counterproductive, committee busywork.[85] These activities also foster staff cynicism because of frequent shifts in board direction as its members react to changes in the prevailing political winds.

Once the citizenry and staff recognize board committees as decision makers, no matter how poorly based in knowledge they may be, the superintendent becomes an errand person for boards, circumvented by parents and staff who want to go where decisions are really made. In these instances, since boards of education cannot provide needed everyday district direction and since they have rendered the superintendent powerless to do so, the district experiences educational anarchy.

The best boards of the nineties continue to be as effective as the best boards ever were, and many outstanding board members still fight the good fight on behalf of kids in their districts. The trend is, however, in the wrong direction, and, today, many elected boards are the vermiform appendixes of public education.[86]

Regardless of this disclaimer, it's easy to empathize with a superintendent's despairing cry to his or her board of education members: "Miserable comforters are ye all!" [33].

Dear God, He Chewed Off the Wrong Foot!

To free themselves from leg-hold traps, wolves, foxes, coyotes, and other pelt animals in extremis have resorted to chewing off one of their

---

[84]People don't much trust any elected, or appointed, officials anymore, and, unfortunately, that distrust too often is based on painful experience.

[85]See also, this chapter, "Chinese Water Tortures," p. 147.

[86]One necessary disclaimer—I don't dislike all board members; a daughter served on a board of education in two tours of duty under very difficult circumstances; some of my best friends remain board members; and, for almost three decades, I had the good fortune to work with primarily competent, dedicated, and strong boards of education supportive of public education and performing their intermediary roles between the community and its educators effectively and with distinction.

own feet. The fundamental test of intelligence for these spartan creatures, which most animals pass handily, is choosing the correct foot. That's more than can be said at times for board members whose preoccupation appears to be chewing off their own feet to discredit school leadership through the artful practice of one or more of the following games:

- "Gotcha": Rules require board members to confront superintendents or other school administrators at public meetings with questions, charges, allegations, innuendoes, rumors, or alleged problems that school leadership has no reasonable way to anticipate—in accordance with the highly stylized rules of "Gotcha," all questions, charges, allegations, innuendoes, rumors, or alleged problems must then be allowed to fester until the next meeting, at which time, the "gotchas" will be revealed as bogus, but by then nobody cares.

  The more esoteric or the more ephemeral or the more imprecise or the more unfounded, and the greater the degree of anonymity of questions, charges, allegations, implications, and innuendoes, the higher the point total board members receive.[87]

- "Did You Hear . . . ?": A special character assassination divertissement, which takes place in the community—often, superintendents are targeted, but quite often, building principals or special education directors are beneficiaries of these creative rumors also.

  Board members move their chosen game pieces in the forms of lances, daggers, poison pills, smoking guns, or a bust of "Vlad the Impaler" around the "Rumor Board" from "Heartbreak Hill" to "Sleazy Street." The number of spaces pieces are moved each turn comes from a table of preset values awarding varying numbers of moves in various categories of unfounded rumors. Examples are: alleged affairs with a married administrator—eight spaces; suspected dalliances with unmarried teachers—four spaces; seen in an expensive restaurant with secretary—three spaces; reported alone in a grubby bar—five spaces; found asleep on the bar—eighteen spaces; driving an expensive foreign car—eleven spaces; mishandling taxpayer funds—eleven

[87]See also, this chapter, "I Found These at the Dump," p. 125, for additional information and data on this phenomenon.

spaces; a closet supporter of "Outcome-Based Education"—fifteen spaces; acknowledging to friends that the superintendent was named state educator of the year—go back twenty-five spaces and lose two turns; asserting that the superintendent's not a bad person when you get to know her (or him)—go directly to jail, do not pass go, a thousand dollar fine.

- "Body Language": Another board meeting game with points awarded for the number of times board members turn away from administrative speakers in feigned disgust, shake their heads slowly in horrified disbelief, fold their arms angrily across their chest, cover their faces with their hands as administrative recommendations are made, point a finger down their throats, snicker silently, or sneer knowingly.[88]
- "Nasty Laughs and Other Disparaging Vocalizations": The first board member to accumulate ten of the following at each board meeting wins the game: evil chuckles, audible snickers and sneers, moans, groans, snores, disbelieving gasps, uncontrolled fits of coughing, gagging and choking sounds, or other distracting noises as ruled upon by a majority of the players.[89]

Unfortunately, participants in these board variants of "Dungeons and Administrators" can't comprehend the damage to local education, in terms of lessenend public support for budgets and thereby student programs, from their misguided efforts to discredit district leadership or staff members. Although superintendents, other administrators, and staff usually survive their worst shots, public support inevitably is eroded, often at significant educational costs, in school systems that these board members were elected to support and advance.

Compared to these various board versions of administrative immolation, there are better ways to disagree with and even kinder ways to remove educational leadership from office, available at comparatively little public relations cost to local school districts. Board members who play "Gotcha," or "Did You Hear . . . ?" or "Body Language," or "Nasty Laughs and Other Disparaging Vocalizations," are "chewing off the wrong foot" in futile attempts to free themselves from governance traps that they themselves have built.

---

[88]Only examples of possible "body language" and not an exhaustive listing of such behaviors.
[89]Only examples of "nasty laughs and other disparaging vocalizations" and not an exhaustive listing of such behaviors.

Don't You Pick on My Little Brother (or Sister)

When dissident members of boards of education publicly undercut majority board positions, most board members act as if the naysayers were naughty children and chide them for their disloyalty to the board instead of beheading them as they may well deserve.

The phenomenon isn't scientifically explainable, but one conjecture is that, through their tolerance of aberrant behaviors, board members accumulate credits in some celestial board member bank on which they may draw when they themselves inevitably run off the rails—sort of like the way squirrels store nuts for the winter. Although this speculation appears eminently logical and possible, the mystery of why board bodies tolerate, with such equanimity, the virulent organisms with which they are self-infected still remains unsolved.

Even if a majority of board members sharply disapproves of board minority behaviors, when a superintendent attacks board dissidents for their destructive actions other board members instinctively become protective like families defending each other against outside threats— and the way older brothers protect younger brothers and older sisters take care of younger sisters. As much as siblings may fight among themselves, or in this case majority board members disagree with minority board members, they reflexively defend each other when attacked. Board members usually are much more uncomfortable inflicting discomfort on each other, even when they dislike each other intensely, than they are going after staff with whom they disagree—even when they may like staff members personally.

The importance of this phenomenon to superintendents is clear. Although at times required to differ strongly with board members, a superintendent's disagreement should be temperate to avoid triggering the big brother/big sister defensive reflex of the rest of the board and having them savage the superintendent for criticizing one of their own—forgetting entirely the original offense by the board member who may have done irrevocable harm to important board positions or decisions.

Lost in Space, a children's television program from the sixties recounted the adventures of the "Space Family" Robinson as it rocketed throughout the solar system along with Dr. Smith who had somehow hooked up with the Robinson clan for the journey. Smith was a truly unpleasant man, given to feeding, or trying to feed, a Robinson child to ambulatory, man-eating, broccoli plants or dropping the son or daughter into bottomless pits of molten lava or leaving them stranded on new and strange planets in the company of various hostile and badly intentioned alien creatures.

The Robinsons, on the other hand, were undoubtedly the galaxy's most forgiving matched quartet of humanoids. Each time Smith unsuccessfully tried to do in one of the kids, the family's most severe retaliation for his homicidal efforts was exiling him from the dinner table and forcing him to dine alone in his space cabin. Even small children who watched the series recognized that Smith's punishments didn't fit his crimes.

The space family remained accepting and long-suffering until the series had run its course in the afternoons, lingered for a time in late-night reruns, and finally, the cans of videotape were launched into space and seen no more on earth.

When dissident members of boards of education undercut majority board positions publicly, for example, by speaking against the budget at the school district meeting called to approve it, most board members act like the Robinson family and chide the bad guys for their disloyalty, instead of beheading them—the latter would be much easier to understand and fully justified. In this instance, the entire board of education has labored over the budget for months, and the dissidents may or may not have taken opposing positions previous to, or at the time of, board budget approval; then at the hearing with the district's fiscal authority, the contrary minority torpedoes their budget Lusitanias without any warnings before the fatal torpedoes are launched.

Normally, board of education majorities don't have any legally effective ways of disciplining their "rogue elephants"—statutory recall provisions for board members are rare to nonexistent in the fifty states. Among themselves, no matter how serious a fellow board member's crime or crimes, other board members are like the Robinson family with Dr. Smith. Such accepting and forgiving behaviors might be seen as "turning the other cheek," or saintly reactions to the devil's minions, but they also aid, abet, and encourage more such behavior.

An individual board member's free speech rights can't be taken away. The surliest of board reactions against a member's disloyalty, including board censure and strong admonition, may not prevent recurrences of unacceptable behavior, but the gentle finger shaking and "tsk tsking," often the board majority's only visible reactions to being stabbed in the back repeatedly by their own Brutuses, certainly do nothing to discourage repetitions of disloyal acts.

Some of these dissident behaviors, which undercut board majorities, are serious enough for boards to, at a minimum, make it clear, as individual board of education members and corporately as boards, that, while possibly still liking and respecting the disloyal members as people, they disapprove vigorously of their board of education disloyalty.

Educational Maritime Law

In adjudicating ship collision cases under English law, admiralty courts determine negligence proportional to each ship's faults as they contributed to the collision. As an example, consider a hypothetical collision between an aviation gasoline tanker and an ammunition ship[90] when the tanker had an inoperable stern light, but did nothing else in violation of "the rules of the road" or international maritime laws; the ammunition ship showed no running lights, changed course four times without signaling just prior to the collision, was operating at high speed in a fog, and both the captain and helmsman were drunk and had been for two weeks.

Under English admiralty law, the ammunition ship probably would be held ninety-nine percent responsible for the collision and pay ninety-nine percent of attendant damages—maybe, in this case, even a hundred percent, with the court totally forgiving the tanker's minor flaw, which contributed nothing to the two-ship collision.

In the identical situation, American maritime law would proclaim "equal responsibility for unequal fault" and would apportion negligence and damages equally between the tanker and the ammunition ship. Avoiding an equal share of responsibility for a collision requires total freedom from the most minor faults or flaws of either commission or omission, or a high seas version of Caesar's wife.

Boards of education adjudicating staff dismissals and other issues characterized by exposed nerve endings usually employ their own version of American maritime law, instead of the more sensible English approach. Superintendents and principals, working with attorneys, often lay before the board well-documented cases of staff incompetence, insubordination, or general unsuitability, only to have board members focus on a single, minor, irrelevant, procedural flaw in the administrative presentation.

Most fired staff members are decent enough human beings who, un-

---

[90]Could be a hell of a bang.

fortunately, aren't able to perform their jobs satisfactorily, but board members hate the guilt feelings that accompany terminations. There's nothing wrong with that so far; so do superintendents and principals — but it's a dirty job, and someone has to do it.

Usually, though not always, when the administrative case is strong, employees are dismissed. Often, though not always, board member guilt from their unpleasant task causes them to turn on the reluctant prosecutors and focus on tiny imperfections in strong, well-documented, ninety-nine percent perfect, administrative cases.

Boards practicing this variation of American maritime law aren't restricted to personnel issues only. Often, they respond similarly to administrative recommendations requiring difficult board decisions. Issues of this nature might include (1) parental challenges of curriculum suitability for their children — sex education was once the most likely, but today OBE may have replaced it as the controversy du jour; (2) school closings or redistricting; (3) student grouping practices; (4) grievance hearings; (5) award of transportation contracts, especially if it changes a long relationship with a local contractor; and (6) facilities projects, either new construction or major additions and/or renovations.

In these often controversial and generally difficult situations, many board of education members focus on perceived minor flaws in leadership proposals and ignore the preponderance of solid support from superintendent and staff. There's no immunity against this unfortunate practice; leaders can only prepare as nearly perfect a case in support of recommendations as possible, and, when board members are distracted by a perceived administrative defect, attempt to refocus them on a proposal's strengths compared to the minute problems that have been unearthed — or imagined.

How Much Is Board Harmony Worth?

All experienced "board watchers" are familiar with the strong tendency among board of education members to compromise on important issues in forlorn attempts to ensure every board member leaves each issue satisfied. This isn't the same phenomenon as the positive "win/win" approach to find alternative answers to questions or alternative solutions to problems that the entire group can endorse. It's after "win/win" has been explored to the best of board leadership's ability, and differences among members still remain, that these sometimes unfortunate compromises occur.

For example, a board has been wrestling with instructions to negotiators for next year's teacher salary increase. Eight of nine board members are prepared to instruct the negotiating team to go as high as a five percent salary increase. In spite of the overwhelming board position, prevailing state and area settlements, and recent arbitration awards, one member still holds out for no increase at all. Against logic, and in futile efforts to make all members happy, boards have an abysmal tendency to compromise in this situation and agree on a two and a half percent limit for their negotiators.

Instead, they should explain clearly why the majority feels as it does, give the lone ranger a final chance to elucidate his or her position, pass a motion by a vote of eight to one to carry out the majority will, and go on to the next piece of business before them.

On a more personal level, this identical kind of salary compromise often affects superintendents personally—when eight members are willing to award an x percent salary increase to the superintendent and the one member holds out for y, boards often split the difference between x and y instead of outvoting the y advocate and moving on to other issues.

Variations of these inappropriate compromises take place in other than financial areas. If one board member doesn't like the "whole-language" curriculum proposal in the elementary schools, boards may defer approval of the curriculum to appease their compatriot or table action on the curriculum indefinitely.

At times, a five to four board vote on an important issue can be a Pyrrhic victory for the majority, and, possibly in these circumstances, modifications should be made in proposals for the sake of meaningful board of education relationships; but catering constantly to one or two recalcitrant board members is counterproductive.

Superintendents need to work closely with board chairpersons to change this kind of ineffective board behavior.

How Much Information Is Enough?

For superintendents of schools, providing adequate information to boards is a moving target at which they often aim futilely. Various reasons at various times move the bull's-eye right or left, forward or backward, up or down—but the damned thing never remains stationary. A number of variables affect the degree to which the information target moves, and a half dozen of the most common include:

(1) *Board member experience:* Usually, the more experienced the board members are, the more realistic they also are in their expectations of superintendent information to help them make decisions; until they've been around for a while, they may expect far too much data, which they vainly hope will transform tough decisions into easy ones.

(2) *Board knowledge:* This is almost the same as board member experience, but, unfortunately, board members' experience doesn't guarantee knowledge of board responsibilities. In that context, their experience is worthless. The more knowledgeable the board, normally the easier the superintendent's job is.

(3) *Overall superintendent relationships with board:* If working relationships have already gone south, boards won't be satisfied with either the quantity or quality of information provided by superintendents of schools; conversely, when boards and superintendents work well together, board expectations are much more reasonable on amounts and kinds of information required.

(4) *Political climate:* If the board is a partisan political board, or strongly divided along personal or other lines, one or more of the two major parties, or one of the major board of education factions, will probably continually ask for additional information—often, to stall decisions until requesters can assess more effectively the political import of particular decisions to be made, or sometimes just to frustrate a board majority ready to move on to other issues.

(5) *Issue volatility:* The more controversial the issue before a board of education, the more the board tends to drag out necessary decisions, and the more information it demands from the superintendent. Again, the board is hoping against hope that somehow a smoking gun will be found to make one of the likely alternatives guilty and the other innocent—or one available option clearly correct with no potential negative side effects for anyone and all other alternatives obviously wrong for everyone; of course, this never happens in real-life issues before deliberative bodies.

(6) *Board of education's work ethic:* Although this cuts both ways at different times, the lazier the board, the more it usually expects to

be done for it by someone else; this means more information from the superintendent. Sometimes, however, lazy board members are much too lazy to read materials provided anyway and therefore don't want much written information; these members complain about the volume of written material they are expected to review before board meetings. However, they may also ask for more oral presentations at the meeting and less in writing before the meeting. In balance, the less industrious the board, the more information it usually expects from the superintendent of schools and staff.

All six board variables may affect, in various ways, the amount of information boards require from superintendents—some logical, some not. In determining the quantity of information necessary, a few variables, or even one of them, may dominate all others, and the superintendent never knows which one will control the others in a given circumstance.

So the answer to the question, "How Much Information Is Enough?" is that nobody knows until after the plump person performs. Experience, combined with careful reading and weighing of the identified variables plus others peculiar to particular boards of education, help superintendents come closer to the optimum information flow a board desires, but even this doesn't guarantee ultimate administrative success in reading board tea leaves.

I Found These at the Dump

The bane of a superintendent's existence is skillful "I gotcha"–playing board members whose lives are made whole only when they can spring an unholy surprise on the superintendent at board of education meetings. A board member once brought a paper bag to a meeting. When the meeting was called to order he stood up, smiled evilly, dumped the bag onto the board table, and asked for an explanation of this waste of taxpayer money. The bag contained textbooks that he found at the town dump. Although the assistant superintendent was pleased to remind the board pack rat that dump picking was illegal, neither he nor the superintendent knew, at that very public moment, how the books had arrived at the dump to be found by the board's self-appointed "chief cook and dump scavenger."

The next day, an investigation determined the textbooks were issued to a high school student who had dropped out of school only a few days before the board meeting without notifying anyone and had tossed his books into the family garbage can. This information couldn't be given publicly for three weeks, and, in the meantime, the dump picker enjoyed having discomfited school leadership.

Had the board member advised the superintendent in advance of the meeting about his contraband dump treasure, the superintendent could have answered his question outside of the board meeting, or, if there weren't satisfactory answers available to him, the board member could have asked the chairman or superintendent to include "textbook care and inventory procedures" on the next meeting agenda for full board and administrative discussion. Unfortunately, his agenda wasn't to make a possibly bad situation better; it was to embarrass school district leadership.

Although sometimes easier said than done, superintendents need board policy that clearly spells out requirements for board members to place items for discussion on agendas before meetings, and the chairperson must enforce these requirements by discouraging unscheduled items being placed on the table at meetings. No matter how well-informed school leaders may be, occasionally, they need advance notice to research an issue before answering questions about it.

Board of education members who behave as the dump picker did are a perverse board species whose only enjoyment in life appears to come from their attempts to prove that their district is seriously flawed; they revel in these efforts and use whatever false charges or data their tiny minds can create. Individual members of this carnivorous group may have served ten or more years on the board of education, yet still feel no personal responsibility for alleged school district defects. If the superintendent of schools could prove beyond a reasonable doubt that the particular school system was, without question, the best district in the entire world and completely without educational flaw, these negative board members would no longer have reasons to remain on the board—and possibly not even any reasons to live.

Superintendents should devote a reasonable amount of time and effort to these board members, seeking their support for cooperative board/staff efforts to improve local public education. If there aren't any noticeable results from this attention, superintendents should cut their losses and work around these human obstacles to progress—while treating them civilly in private and in public.

I've Had Many, Many Calls about That

Sympathetic ears are one thing, but indiscriminate empathy is something else again.

- quiz question #1: Is any school administrator confused about why some board members receive all complaining calls and others rarely, if ever, receive any?
- quiz question #2: Does anybody believe that it's coincidental that some board members get many, many telephone calls and others none or almost none?
- quiz question #3: Is it possible that the following descriptors identify and characterize those members who receive almost all the parental and citizen complaints? (1) board members who want to believe the worst about their own school system; (2) board members who undiscerningly accept at face value any and all critical comments from callers or visitors about staff members; (3) board members who won't suspend judgment on staff members until after hearing their perceptions of situations; (4) board members who never suggest to upset parents that they should speak directly to the teachers or administrators accused by a child of unfair or inappropriate actions; (5) board members who don't give the superintendent a heads-up call to alert him or her about problems or alleged problems, even after having referred callers back to the proper staff member; or (6) board members who never consider any other techniques or approach but public board meeting "gotchas" to bring issues to the superintendent's attention, but who always privately inform other board members with similar proclivities of critical calls received.
- quiz question #4: Could it be possible that there are cause and effect relationships between board of education members who behave as described and receive all, or almost all, critical and/or complaining telephone calls instead of the board members who exhibit none of those behaviors?

Answers to the four quiz questions are

- answer #1: No! We are not confused about why some board members receive all complaining calls and others rarely, if ever, receive any.
- answer #2: No! It is not coincidental that some board

members get many, many telephone calls and others none or almost none.

- answer #3: Yes! It is possible that the descriptors identify and characterize those members who receive almost all the parental and citizen complaints.
- answer #4: Yes! It is possible that there are cause and effect relationships between board of education members who behave as described and receive all, or almost all, critical and/or complaining telephone calls instead of the board members who exhibit none of those behaviors.

Quiz scoring is as follows:

- four correct—acceptable
- three correct—below average
- two correct—abysmal
- one correct—pathetic
- zero correct—brain-dead

Henry M. Robert versus Common Sense

All boards of education in America operate in accordance with *Robert's Rules of Order*—or so they claim. Except for Mr. Robert himself (and he died a long time ago, probably from frustration from attending board of education meetings), several U.S. Congressmen, and a few lost souls who should get themselves an actual life, nobody really understands the intricacies of parliamentary procedures, but, in spite of this reality, all boards seriously believe they operate in strict accordance with *Robert's Rules of Order*. In hundreds of board meetings each month, the American public watches Mr. Robert's rules generate more confusion than clarity and more heat than light—although once in a while, accidentally or otherwise, they work OK.

Parliamentary procedure, like other law, is a good servant but a poor master. Superintendents and board members are well advised to understand basic parliamentary procedures and to use them as the foundation of board meetings. A major caveat is that procedures shouldn't override common sense. All experienced board watchers have witnessed motions that everyone originally understood tortured to death by sadistic parliamentarians through unnecessary amendments, amendments on amendments, seconds, withdrawals of seconds, withdrawals of original motions, amendments of seconds, moving the questions, debates on the propriety of moving the question, arguments about the propriety of debating the propriety of moving the question, etc.

And if the board watchers are lucky, in the midst of this total parliamentary confusion, the effective board of education chairman, often strongly encouraged by the superintendent, declares it all non-sense, starts over, and saves three quarters of an hour and badly frayed tempers.

Few occurrences make boards of education look sillier in public than a thirty- or forty-minute hassle on *Robert's Rules of Order,* which often results in votes that half the board members don't understand anyway, and they say so out loud. These long minutes of empty talk evoke superintendents' versions of hell, languishing forever "unrespited, un-pitied, and unreprieved" [34],[91] trapped in the midst of endless par-liamentary debate as board members "cavil on the ninth part of a hair" [35].

Inherent dangers from a slavish adherence to parliamentary rules and procedures are clearly revealed when, lizardlike, they crawl out from under the rock where they've been hiding, and board members give them more care and attention than they do the issues themselves.

Pearls before Swine—Or Where Does It Say Precisely What I Said?

Board of education minutes should reflect primarily what boards do, not what they say. However, board members often expect that every remark they make, brief or interminable, relevant or irrelevant, will be recorded in meeting minutes. Then, in the twenty-second century A.D., their great-grandchildren's great-grandchildren can read about their distinguished ancestor who served on the local board of education before the turn of the century.

A reasonable golden mean between verbatim transcripts and only recording motions might include introductory paragraphs such as: "Following the business manager's explanation of its provisions, the

[91]John Milton led an interesting life. In 1642 he married Mary Powell, a seventeen year old, who went back home to Daddy within a month of their marriage—but they reconciled three years later. Whether or not it was inspired by his personal experience, Milton also wrote lesser known pam-phlets about divorce, including "The Doctrine and Discipline of Divorce" in 1643. These writings so offended the Presbyterians of his time that there was a threat of prosecution by a parliamentary committee—probably chaired by a right-wing Presbyterian of that era or the south of England's Sir Newt of Gingrich or his parliamentary compatriot Sir Alfonse of D'Amato.

superintendent recommended board approval of a new five-year transportation contract with Toonerville Trolley and Bus Company, Inc. Discussion followed, including various questions on contract provisions, particularly the concern of some members about its duration. Some board members thought three years was preferable. The superintendent provided further information about the lengths of typical contracts and responded to comments and questions from members of the public."

The official record of the action taken by the board, including the person who makes the motion, its seconder, and a record of votes, including abstentions, if any, may appear as: Motion #3. That the board of education approve the five-year transportation contract with Toonerville Trolley and Bus Company, Inc., effective September 1, 1995, and that the superintendent be authorized to sign the contract for the board of education. Goodrich, Johnson. (Passed 7-1-1) In favor—Goodrich, Johnson, Blackstone, Sekoll, Porteus, Smith, White; Opposed—Chapman; Abstained—McFarland.

When only one or two board members comment or ask questions, minutes often reflect a synopsis of what each said, attributed to them by name: "Peter B. Chapman strongly opposed any transportation contract for more than three years." If it goes much beyond that, similar comments are often combined into one and summarized, for example, "Some board members expressed concern about the duration of the proposed contract."

A recurring "board minutes" phenomenon is for a board member to pronounce pontifically something akin to, "I'm strongly against either staff or students drinking hard liquor in the schools during the school day, and I want that reflected in the minutes!" No matter how self-serving some of these statements may be, concessions are usually made for the sake of the board member's ego and his or her political future, and the remarks, abbreviated as necessary, are included in minutes—unless the current discussion is about the transportation contract, and a remark about alcohol consumption in schools comes totally out of right field. Possibly, in that instance, there's sufficient reason for the minutes to ignore the request, regardless of the individual board member's demand that his comments be included. The board chairman should make that ruling.

Board chairmen and secretaries are key superintendent allies with board members who expect every remark to be recorded for posterity in official board minutes and attributed to them by name. Together, the superintendent, board chairman, and seccretary should wean these members away from such unrealistic expectations. Complying with them takes far too much staff time preparing minutes, as well as board of education time at subsequent meetings arguing over who said what and revising quotes as a result.

Board of education policy should state clearly that minutes are expected to be records of board of education actions – not of its conversations and discussions, especially the musings and ramblings and speculations and vacillations and whimsy and vile and contumely and preferences and philosophies of each individual board member.

Peter Pan Is Alive and Well on Your Board of Education

Lost innocence is inevitable if you choose to grow up, and for every positive change, in education as well as life, there probably is a cost to be paid for the gain to be made. Yet some board members become adults without learning this obvious lesson: regardless of all the positive outcomes that major change may bring, there is almost always a price to be paid for it.

Effective board members, as do effective leaders, understand this reality and, in considering changes, assess foreseeable negative effects, weigh them against anticipated positive outcomes, and when positives are significantly more important than negatives, proceed. Ineffective board members and ineffective leaders aren't prepared to pay any price and can't move forward with change regardless of its benefits – and almost always there is a price that must be paid for worthwhile improvements and changes in district practices.

Ineffective board members and administrative leaders don't even seem to understand that changes have negative side effects; they often become bewildered, and then horrified, when particular drawbacks from altering past educational practices are pointed out, or God forbid, if they realize this on their own; when it finally dawns on them, however that occurs, that somebody or something will be less well off than before, they are astounded and often righteously indignant. Because of a few negative side effects, these lost souls often believe the superintendent is a "commie pinko fink"[92] for proposing change even when the overall effects of change are overwhelmingly positive with great benefits to the educational program in the school district.

[92]For younger readers, this term was commonly used during the "Cold War" to describe your political enemies.

Any curriculum departures, any changes in personnel evaluation procedures, any added safety measures for school playgrounds, any bus stop changes, any schedule changes, any school organizational changes—all have downsides that leadership must be able to demonstrate are more than balanced by the positives from such changes.[93]

Curriculum specialists and textbook writers often tout new curricula as the salvation of particular subjects, for example, changing from a science curriculum teaching all aspects of elementary school science each year to one providing more intensive coverage of fewer topics each year. A major disadvantage of this change is that some issues are covered only in early childhood when subjects must be taught relatively superficially. Changing from fewer topics each year to a spiral curriculum, wherein each topic is studied at each grade level in ever-increasing depth, is repetitive and often kids resent the repetition. This isn't to argue for either curriculum over the other but, instead, to point out that there are always pluses and minuses in every new or different approach.[94] When a district strengthens administrative evaluation or initiates it, outcomes normally justify inevitable initial, and often continuing, tensions in working relationships between supervisor and supervised. Depending upon how well it's handled by both parties, anxieties may be minor, but they will increase no matter how effectively this change is implemented.

Changing bus stops may benefit many more students than previous arrangements, but some children will lose from the change. Should changes ever be made in bus stops even though they have disadvantages? The answer is probably yes unless traffic hazards for the few increase more significantly than traffic dangers are reduced for the majority, in which case the answer probably becomes no.

Making children as safe as possible seems like a "no brainer," but that's not always so. Maximum playground security against "stranger danger" for children would mean that students never go outside—not allowing them on the playground at all obviously offers the greatest protection possible against various outdoor dangers. Most educators would agree that the added safety from such a change doesn't justify its cost.

[93]See also, this chapter, "Better Odds Are All You Can Expect—In Poker or Leadership Life in General," p. 113.

[94]Interestingly, most elementary science curricula use the upward spiral, whereas social studies curricula usually study the family in grade one, the community in grade two, the state in grade three, the nation in grade four, the world in grade five, and back to ancient history in grade six —all the while often subdividing each year's major subject into history, geography, and sometimes a primitive version of sociology.

Even safety changes upon which almost all of us would agree come with price tags attached. Removal of certain playground climbing apparatus often avoids major childhood injuries; but that removal also eliminates or reduces challenges for children to grow and to practice effective safety behaviors while benefiting from the physical and emotionl growth potential such equipment offers.

Effective leadership recognizes the need to preempt board members' tendencies to discover triumphantly (with glad cries of "Aha! I gotcha this time!") the obvious drawbacks from recommended changes of whatever nature. Superintendents and principals should lay out disadvantages completely and clearly along with administrative recommendations — and provide a complete list of advantages and reasons why the positive list outweighs the negative list.[95]

Fear of acknowledging drawbacks or not recognizing they exist in even the best proposed changes reflect poor thinking. Careless thought processes make it more likely that dumb recommendations will also be made because leaders can't accept the slippery downslope always lurking on the other side of positive recommendations — and sometimes it's true that potential dangers are greater than potential gains from change.[96]

Questions That Don't Want Answers

When superintendents are lucky, board of education members ask questions to receive information, for additional data, and to hear the superintendent's ideas and opinions — in other words to learn something that may help them make better decisions.

When superintendents aren't as fortunate, board members ask questions with one or more of the following motivations and/or expectations: (1) when they think they already know the answer, hoping for an opportunity to challenge, with self-proclaimed knowledge, the administrative response — sometimes obvious efforts to entrap the administrative object of their interrogation and nonaffection; (2) if, regardless of the administrative response, they plan to roll their eyes, shake their heads, snicker, sneer, and, in other ways attempt to discredit the answer to erode perceptions of the superintendent's integrity — of course, without actually disputing any specifics in administrative answers because board members have no information with

[95]See also, Chapter 3, "Disclaimers Make the World Go 'Round," p. 70.
[96]Nobody should ever tell you that leadership is easy. However, making decisions is easy; it's living with their consequences that makes leadership a challenge.

which to refute them;[97] (3) through asking a two-page, five-minute question, to prove they know all there is to know about the subject under discussion; (4) through asking a two-page, five-minute question to publish for posterity their particular philosophical points of view on issues of the moment—but with no real interest in an administrative response; (5) from the complexity of the issue and their questions, to embarrass school leadership or school staff because they know immediate responses aren't available—and of course, the superintendent's lack of specific response promptly is labeled administrative evasiveness; (6) to elicit the only possible answer to their question—one they know will play badly in both Peoria and in their own particular school district; (7) when they could care less about an administrative response, except insofar that it may reveal district shortcomings or flaws; or (8) for reasons nobody comes close to understanding.

The good news is that the number of board members asking questions for the wrong reasons is much smaller than those honestly seeking information; the bad news is that many boards have one or more of these unfortunate specimens apparently serving lifetime sentences.

To cope with badly intentioned interrogators, administrators should treat them exactly as they would those who ask questions to learn—but always recognizing, and never losing sight of, what is really happening and why it is happening. Also, as in answering questions from people whose motives are pure, school leadership should readily admit not having answers when good answers aren't readily available, and leaders should be more than usually alert to potential problems from careless or casual off-the-cuff responses with these people.

"Safe No's"

Dissident board of education members have perfected a perverse practice that can be described as voting the "safe no." Although on occasion, it can be a "safe yes," given the negative nature of these nattering nabobs,[98] "safe no's" are much more commonplace than "safe yeses."

To clarify the term, "safe no's" are negative votes for the record to please a dissident's like-minded constituency, but they are cast only when the "no" vote obviously won't affect the outcome. For example, when a negotiated contract is before the board of education for approval, and the tenor of a long discussion indicates to the dissident or

---

[97]See also, this chapter, "Dear God, He Chewed Off the Wrong Foot!" p. 116.
[98]I'm going to need another short lie down until my alliterative fever cools.

dissidents that approval is assured, he/she/or they can vote "no" without fear of consequences. After the contract is approved as expected by eight to one, or seven to two, teachers and other supporters of the measure, including other board members, will grumble and mumble momentarily, but because the contract was approved easily enough, they usually relax and forgive the naysayers. However, RANK[99] taxpayers will always remember their heroes or heroines who voted against spending more taxpayer money.

The way this works is that, when the chairman says, "All those in favor say aye," RANK board members hold back until other board members respond and they can quickly tally the "yeses." If it's safe, they vote "nay."

If, on the other hand, their "no" vote, or votes, would derail the negotiated agreement, thereby making them lightning rods for staff anger and the focus of intense board disapproval, even the approbation of their RANK peers won't embolden them to take the inevitable heat from upsetting the contract applecart. In the hushed room, with everyone awaiting their decision, a prolonged and obviously intense struggle with their consciences takes place, and they grudgingly vote "yes," hoping their anguished soul-searching is appreciated by RANK onlookers.

In order to create circumstances in which "safe yeses" can be cast, it's necessary to introduce motions obviously not passable but emotionally gratifying to RANK supporters. For example, just after school district counsel has explained relevant state statutes on the issue, a RANK board member introduces a motion to require morning prayer in classrooms. The newly converted "yeasayers" recognize (1) that their motion and "yes" votes are as safe as their usual "no's" because the motion can't possibly pass, and there will be no consequences from their actions; (2) that their efforts will be treasured by RANK; and (3) that they won't be sued by their political opponents, the local chapter of SLOP,[100] because nothing really happened.

Following the school prayer issue, let's stay with the First Amendment's Establishment Clause and, for discussion purposes, examine a complex, follow-up motion that an avowed RANK member on our prototypical board might introduce for "safe yeses": "I move that henceforth the superintendent shall be addressed as 'His Eminence' or 'Her Grace'; all instruction shall be in Latin; lunch shall be called 'communion'; pupil expulsion will be known as 'excommunication'; sixth grade recognition ceremonies shall be identified as 'confirmation'; physical

[99]"Retired Anxious Neanderthal Klub."
[100]Surly Liberals on Patrol.

education shall be referred to as 'mortification of the flesh'; and signs on principals' offices shall say 'Confessional.' And, in spite of warnings against my motion by 'Her Grace' that this additional provision in my motion will make the staff more than usually surly, I further move that we introduce a requirement for teacher celibacy into their next negotiated contract."

The other RANK member of this unfortunate board will routinely second this proposal (known as the "safe second"), fully aware that, even on this benighted board of education, the motion has an extremely slim chance of passage, and therefore it won't kick SLOP's beehive.

Smoking Guns—Or How Much Proof Do You Need Anyway?

Everybody knows the old "smoking gun" expectation of prosecutors who aren't happy with evidence in a murder case unless detectives can testify they found the accused holding a "smoking gun" and standing over a recently dead body. Then the decision to press charges becomes one even the least competent prosecutors can make.

Boards often resemble prosecutors in their demands on superintendents for data or information to make their decisions easy. In real life, golden means must always be sought between (1) intuitive decisions with no data upon which to base them and (2) decisions that are made only when they won't cause decision makers the slightest discomfort— in other words, decisions that most reasonably enlightened primates could make before breakfast.

Sometimes, boards and, occasionally, superintendents cling to forlorn hopes that sufficient data or information will allow intellect and judgment to become optional accessories inside their hats.[101] The best superintendents help boards learn to distinguish between essential and superfluous information and lead them to timely decisions on important issues. The worst boards make this impossible.

Together, superintendents and board chairmen need to help boards arrive at reasonable positions between (1) "seat of the pants" decisions and (2) a thirst for data, which makes your favorite celebrity boozer of choice appear to be a social drinker. Clearly, boards need databases for important judgments, but generating an endless flow of information, in

---

[101]There really may be a special place in hell for leadership unable to make difficult choices among conflicting alternatives.

futile attempts to make each decision easy, overloads decision-making circuitry and fuses the entire school district into the educational equivalent of an inert, charred lump.[102]

The Old Rubber Stamp Gambit

Among frustrations experienced by effective superintendents of schools is board members becoming sensitized to, and defensive about, public charges that they are "rubber stamps" for the superintendent or that they are the superintendent's "puppets" or "marionettes." This only happens when boards and superintendents share common educational goals for district schools and when, because of those common understandings, boards generally are supportive of and act favorably on leadership recommendations.

Most of these accusations of rubber stamping boards of education or of superintendents as puppeteers manipulating their board member puppets arise from public misunderstandings of a board's role as policymakers and from the public's miscasting board members into daily educational managers. Some of it also stems from good working relationships between boards and superintendents. And these usually absurd charges may even be true in rare school districts where boards may be subservient to superintendents and follow their recommendations blindly.[103]

No matter how false the rubber stamp accusation may be, even strong board members are uncomfortable being perceived as dancing with superintendents who lead. The result is that often they feel obliged to prove their independence. They may even act contrary to their natural inclinations to distance themselves from kindly old Superintendent Gepetto, the master marionette maker and manipulator. The stronger the terminology used in the insult to the board member, the stronger is the board member's natural desire to separate himself from the superintendent.[104]

It's good strategy for superintendents to confront potential charges of administrative puppeteering or rubber stamping openly and directly

[102]See also, this chapter, "Educational Maritime Law," p. 121; "How Much Information Is Enough?" p. 123; and "Peter Pan Is Alive and Well on Your Board of Education," p. 131.

[103]In twenty-five years of the superintendency, whenever the board/superintendent relationship was what it should have been, I expected this song to be sung—and I was never disappointed.

[104]It disconcerts most board members to be called any of the many names used frequently by the "I Man" on "Imus in the Morning," as he comments on people he doesn't like at any given moment: weasel, lying worm, pantload, empty suit, scum, girly man, etc.

with boards at annual superintendent performance reviews and/or board of education self-evaluation sessions, even before such charges are made. Without appearing obsessed by the issue, the concept of an effective board and an effective superintendent working well together should be explored as often and in as many ways as possible.

When politicians, citizens, or board members themselves assert that, because a board generally follows administrative recommendations, there is too much administrative control of district education, it might help if the superintendent asks them to choose from among the following options for board/superintendent relationships in the school district: (1) an extremely competent board of education that rejects ill-advised recommendations from an incompetent superintendent of schools; no rubber stamps here, but who needs it? (2) an incompetent board of education that constantly rejects informed recommendations from an extremely competent superintendent of schools; no rubber stamps here either, but again, who needs it? (3) a well-informed, competent board of education that generally agrees with well-researched recommendations from a competent superintendent of schools; no rubber stamps here either, but things are working the way God intended them to.

Fortunately, most people prefer the third option among the three presented. Of course, superintendents should be prepared for particularly insightful and obnoxious dissidents who agree that, among the three choices presented to them, the third is obviously preferred, but who also maintain that what really exists in your school district is an incompetent board rubber stamping a dumb superintendent's recommendations. You may just have to write these folks off as casualty losses on your Form 1040.

"Vox Populi, Vox Dei"—II

It's frustrating for educational leaders to craft a presentation carefully and present it articulately, only to find the board still timorous or undecided about an offer administrators thought they couldn't refuse. Then a parent, or a custodian, speaks in support of the superintendent's position, using a rationale that had been advanced clearly in the earlier administrative presentation. Board members sit up, look interested, pay attention, ask questions, take notes, laud the speaker for his or her brilliance and insight, and approve the recommendation as if they can't understand why the superintendent didn't explain it that way in the first place—even when he or she obviously did.

There is something sufficiently different about new voices in front of boards of education that makes them more persuasive than the voices they hear often—even when a board and its superintendent work well together.

In the order of their effectiveness with boards, the strongest and most effective voices are often primary age children, adolescents, town officials, custodians, parents, paraprofessionals, secretaries, teachers, assistant principals, principals, central office administrators, talking mules, superintendents of schools.[105]

The order of acceptance occasionally can be altered by especially strong personal qualities of particular speakers; for example, a vivacious, attractive, well-spoken adolescent may do better than a surly kindergartner who picks his nose. At times, even a sober superintendent, if he or she is one of the very best, might be slightly more effective than an inebriated custodian—but you shouldn't count on it working that way, and the above order of effectiveness usually runs true to form.

Understanding this phenomenon, a Machiavellian school leader may sometimes enlist the assistance of new voices to accomplish a particular goal. Although that approach is only one arrow in a full quiver, it shouldn't go unrecognized or unused.

SUPERINTENDENT / BOARD RELATIONSHIPS

"And the Greatest of These Is . . ."—I

Meanwhile, these three qualities remain: personal security, objectivity, and positive enthusiasm; of these three, the last shall be first, and the greatest of these is positive enthusiasm.

Personally secure and objective board of education members can be self-confident and even objective, in a calculated way, and also can be negative, destructive board members—the kind too numerous in prototypical southern politics, without vision or goals except political survival; the kind of politician who when faced with difficult and substantive issues offers fear of minorities as a substitute for leadership.

It is all too easy today for negative politicians and negative board members to maintain themselves in office by focusing dissatisfaction on various nonethnic minorities: (1) the superintendent of schools or other

---

[105]Some people see no distinction between the last two in this hierarchy.

school leaders, (2) the perceived shortcomings of state and national governments, (3) student behavior and achievement levels caused by factors not of the school district's making, (4) other board of education members with whom they disagree, (5) and the beat goes on. . . .

Demagoguery and manipulation of public opinion might, at times, enhance a board member's reelection chances, but these acts seriously harm public education in districts where they flourish. Almost the only bad board of education members are those whose satisfaction comes from tearing down, those who need power to bolster fragile egos, and those who crave authority for what it does for them—not for any constructive good they might accomplish through it.

Again, these three qualities of good board of education members remain: personal security, objectivity, and positive enthusiasm, and the greatest of these is that positive attitude toward public education generally; toward the school district's administrative leadership; toward teachers and other staff members; toward students and parents; toward the town and its leadership; toward being effective, constructive board members; and, of course, the one that gives rise to all the others—toward life and the living of it.

Brave, Loyal, Trustworthy . . .

School districts are so different from each other that universal truths for boards of education and their chairpersons[106] are difficult to come by. Chairmen of 200-pupil elementary districts have dramatically different problems and responsibilities from those in large city school districts. Both may have major issues before them, but they usually face vastly different kinds of problems, both in numbers and intensity.

If superintendents, board of education members, and others were asked to describe the perfect board chairman, responses from all might include special interpretations of the usual descriptors for scouts—brave, loyal, trustworthy, etc. However, the following are the real interpretations of those desired traits, synthesized from collective responses of superintendents and other citizens nationwide who were asked to

---

[106]As a concession to modern practice, I have used this word once; henceforth, however, "chairman," "chairmen," "chairmanship" and "chairmanships" are used for both men or women instead of "chairperson," "chairpersons," "chairpersonship," "chairpersonships," "chairwoman," "chairwomen," "chairwomanship," "chairwomanships," "chair," "chairs," "chairship," or "chairships." These attempts at gender neutrality look and sound absurd to me. My choice is in no way intended to be disrespectful of the clearly equal ability of women in board of education "chairmanships," but, instead, to avoid what to my ear are awkward constructions—such as "woperson" instead of "woman."

amplify the scout descriptors for an ideal board chairman. When the pronouns "I," "my," or "mine," are used, it is as if a single individual is responding as spokesperson for all other respondents.

(1) Trustworthy—always to me
(2) Loyal—to whatever particular interest I find important at any given moment
(3) Helpful—especially to friends of mine
(4) Friendly—to everyone, but especially to me
(5) Courteous—to my friends, but not my political enemies
(6) Kind—but not to people who don't want what I want
(7) Cheerful—no matter how much the public insults or criticizes him or her
(8) Brave—in defending all sides of each controversial issue and resisting the wills of all special interest groups except mine
(9) Clean—at least for those who must sit close at meetings
(10) Reverent—in the same church that I attend, but not at board of education meetings
(11) Obedient—to my educational and political wishes and preferences
(12) Thrifty—to me and to all taxpayers whose homes have been recently revaluated, the highest virtue to be sought in this position

Except for the special twist in each of the twelve descriptors, these expectations aren't tailored for board of education chairmen and could also fit teachers, bankers, school administrators, plumbers, engineers, or truck drivers—as well as scouts or board chairmen. Practitioners of these other professions might be excused for lacking one or two of the twelve desired traits, but all would be superb at what they do for a living if they had all twelve.

Moving deeper into the attempt to clone the perfect chairman, from long experience, five qualities seem most important, in addition to the scout descriptors. The final three qualities are the same as for board members generally; the first two are also important for all board members but are especially so for board chairmen: (1) knowledge—of appropriate board of education procedures and of major issues faced by his or her school district; (2) demonstrated personal leadership—previously as a member of the board of education on tough or controversial issues; (3) personal security to deal successfully with the many pressures around board issues and board of education decisions on these issues—the bedrock on which other positive personal attributes are based. Chairmen will be ineffective if their egos are so fragile they need constant bolstering and support and if they seek the position for what it can do for inadequate psyches instead of what their positional authority allows them to do for others; (4) objectivity—which allows them to change personal beliefs when given appropriate information, data, or reasons to change;[107] (5) constructive enthusiasm—crucial because, unfortunately, people can be self-confident, knowledgeable, efficient leaders, and even objective—and also negative, destructive, board members if they are not also constructively enthusiastic.

As in other public leadership positions, chairmen should guide other board members in searching for "golden means" to make tensions creative instead of destructive. Six common creative tensions that need constant attention for board success include the following.

EFFICIENCY AND EFFECTIVENESS[108]

Although most people want both, these concepts often oppose each other. On assembly lines, efficient is generally also effective, but, in democratic government, this isn't always so. Efficiency, although faster and simpler, often produces short-term benefits at the expense of the group process and relationships—which probably means long-term ineffectiveness. Effectiveness, although slower and more complicated, produces lasting benefits and strengthens the group process and relationships.

A major part of the board chairman's art is in recognizing when efficiency and effectiveness can coexist peacefully and when those two ideas are incompatible. When they are compatible, they should work in tandem, but when they can't, proper balances should be sought between them.

DATA AND INTUITION

As bases for decision making, these two can be polar opposites: both

[107]See also, Chapter 1, "Ten Cardinal Principles of Leadership," p. 21 and this chapter, "And So Do His Sisters, His Cousins, and His Aunts," p. 172.
[108]See also, Chapter 3, "Efficient or Effective—Choose Any Two," p. 73.

extreme, and both bad. The board needs guidance in its search for a reasonable position between "seat of the pants" decision making and a craving for data to make the toughest decision somehow simple and easy. Clearly, boards need adequate information for their judgments, but too much data clogs decision makers' arteries. Effective board chairmen help their fellow board members to distinguish between essential and superfluous information and to make timely decisions on important issues.[109]

OBJECTIVITY AND LEADERSHIP RESPONSIBILITY

It's important for board chairmen to address board issues objectively and fairly and to avoid permanent personal alignments with factions on the board. Balanced against this desirable objectivity and impartiality is a moral responsibility to take and express leadership positions on major issues and to make her or his views public.

STUDENT NEEDS AND DISTRICT ABILITY TO PAY FOR THEM

Although at one time theorists may have argued that only student needs should preoccupy boards because other bodies were responsible for finances, the reverse may be the issue today. Too often, in recent years, boards have abandoned their traditional role as student advocates to become fiscal body homunculi who demonstrate more concern about tax rates than student education.[110]

PUBLIC MEETINGS AND MEETINGS HELD IN PUBLIC

Public meetings are meetings for the primary, if not exclusive, purpose of hearing from the public; board meetings are meetings held in public for the board of education to conduct board of education business. Although, in this instance, the appropriate point between these two positions is closer to the latter, it would be unrealistic for a board to exclude the public from speaking at meetings. The chairman must strike a moving balance between encouraging public expressions of opinion and public interference with the board's ability to conduct necessary district business.

---

[109]See also, this chapter, "How Much Information Is Enough?" p. 123.
[110]See also, this chapter, "But Sir, I'm Only a Poor Little Match Girl," p. 115.

PARLIAMENTARY PROCEDURE AND COMMON SENSE[111]

Parliamentary procedure, like the law, is a good servant but a bad master. Chairmen should know basic parliamentary procedures and use them in board deliberations but should not let them get in the way of common sense. Nothing makes a board look more ineffective than a prolonged hassle on unnecessary amendments, amendments on amendments, seconds, withdrawals of seconds, withdrawals of original motions, amendments of seconds, moving the question, debates on moving the question, arguments about the debatability of moving the question, etc. In the midst of this kind of flailing about, good chairmen declare it all nonsense, start over, and save time and frayed tempers—not to mention making the board look both more effective and less bureaucratic.

Effective board of education chairmen, as is true of effective board of education members, resist inappropriate outside pressures; analyze issues thoroughly and request assistance and advice from the superintendent of schools and other staff as necessary; really listen to and understand other views; guide the board to make timely decisions on difficult issues with reasonable amounts of information and data; and relax about decisions once they are made, but remain open to changing positions in light of additional information that might later become available.

Additionally, effective board chairmen deal fairly with all members and factions on the board; act independently of partisan political interests; keep board meetings on track, discussions on topic, and minimize later additions to board meeting agendas—especially those proposed at board meetings; establish and maintain a tone of courtesy and respect at meetings; understand parliamentary procedures and when they should be eased for the sake of board effectiveness; take the lead in public presentations of budgets and similarly important board issues before other town bodies and agencies; are instrumental in development, revision, and use of board of education policies; keep up with statewide educational issues and legislation; and inform the superintendent of subterranean community and board of education currents and issues. In return, the superintendent owes the board chairman similar timely information on significant school district problems and controversies before they become public; must publicly support the dis-

---

[111]See also, this chapter, "Henry M. Robert versus Common Sense," p. 128.

trict's administrative, teaching, and other staff; and should work effectively with reporters and representatives of other media.

To superintendents of schools, board chairmen are sometimes right and left arms, life buoys and flotation devices, and often even good friends.

Care and Feeding of Board Members—I

As a school principal in a small Connecticut K–8 district, I attended board meetings with the superintendent and worked closely with board committees. For twenty-five years following that initial administrative position, I served as superintendent of schools in three jobs in two states. Two of the positions, my first in New York state and my final superintendency in Connecticut, were typical, single board of education, one school district organizations. The middle position involved eleven years with three separate elementary school district boards of education in three Connecticut towns; a separate secondary school board with a junior and senior high school serving the three elementary communities; and a fifth board, composed of representatives from the other four—a total of thirty-three board of education members in four separate district jurisdictions. The fifth board was responsible for central office staff and functions and its requisite budget.

With a significant number of the total from eleven years in the four-district regional organization, I worked directly with at least 200 board members over my administrative career. In addition, through state organizations, I shared time with many more. Among those I knew well were homemakers; attorneys; a variety of corporate middle managers; engineers; college and university professors; public school teachers, administrators, and paraprofessionals who worked in other school districts; salespersons; secretaries, receptionists, and other clerical personnel; business owners; ministers; insurance executives; doctors and nurses; computer specialists; artisans and craftsmen; inventors; telephone company linemen and technicians; retirees from many fields and professions, including retired superintendents, principals, and teachers; nuclear power plant employees; contractors and builders; assembly line and other blue collar workers; and others I can no longer identify by profession or trade.

Even the interesting experience of serving with approximately 200 board of education members didn't come close to teaching me all there is to learn about the species, but working with that number for close to thirty years taught me plenty—some of which I'd like to forget. Although extremely fortunate to have worked with predominantly good to outstanding board members, the complete spectrum ranged from malevolently incompetent to dedicatedly brilliant; again, the vast majority fell into the upper end of the board member–shaped curve.

Effective "boardsmanship" doesn't appear to correlate highly with any particular occupation or educational stratum, but more with personal qualities that board members bring with them to their avocation. The single characteristic that appears solidly predictive of productive board members is a strong sense of personal security that enables them to resist outside pressures, think issues through and accept needed assistance and advice from the superintendent of schools and other staff, really hear and understand other views, make timely decisions on tough issues with reasonable amounts of information and data, and relax about decisions once made but remain open to changing previous positions in light of additional information that might later become available.

I've worked with board members who almost made sense when they spoke at board of education meetings, but didn't quite; it sometimes seemed to me that if they could have been tuned even slightly everything they said would suddenly have been miraculously clear instead of incomprehensible. Unfortunately, that never happened.

A few of the worst were harpooned and lampooned in various places in this book,[112] and it gave me great pleasure to do this on their behalf—but the vast majority of the 200 with whom I worked directly were dedicated, able, caring men and women.

Care and Feeding of Board Members—II[113]

Throughout twenty-five years in the superintendency, in addition to working with approximately 200 board members, many of them in eleven years with a five-board regional superintendency, I've probably also served with thirty-five to forty different board of education

---

[112]See also, this chapter, "Recurring Board Phenomena," p. 113 and "Superintendent/Board Relationships," p. 139.

[113]Repeating much of an earlier footnote, "chairman," "chairmen," "chairmanship" and "chairmanships" are used for both men or women instead of "chairperson," "chairpersons," "chairpersonship," "chairpersonships," "chairwoman," "chairwomen," "chairwomanship," "chairwomanships," "chair," "chairs," "chairship," or "chairships." These attempts at gender neutrality look and sound absurd to me. My choice is in no way intended to be disrespectful of the clearly equal ability of women in board of education "chairmanships," but, instead, to avoid what to my ear are awkward constructions—such as "woperson" instead of "woman."

chairmen. In some situations, chairmen held their posts for only one year, and, at the other extreme, one woman was chairman over my entire eleven-year experience with her board—and long before and after my time there.

The longest tenure as board chairman, of which I'm aware, dates back to the middle sixties in upstate New York. A small rural district to the north had a chairman, at that time, probably in his mid-eighties, who often was spotted dozing through county and regional school board meetings. Nobody criticized him for his frequent naps, and they shouldn't have. At that time, he had been chairman of his board for well over fifty years, and the odds were good he had already heard everything being said many times before. I've lost track of him, and, although the odds don't favor it, he may still be chairman, working on his eighty-fifth year of continual service. Sleeping through local and area board meetings may be the best way for anyone to survive fifty plus years on a board of education—especially as chairman.

As was true for board members generally, good board leadership didn't seem to correlate highly with any particular occupation or educational stratum, but more with personal qualities that chairmen brought with them to their leadership of a board. And as with board members generally, chairmen came from many different vocations and professions, including homemakers, attorneys, a variety of corporate middle managers, engineers, college and university professors, salespersons, business owners, ministers, insurance executives, doctors and nurses, artisans and craftsmen, inventors, telephone company linemen, retirees, nuclear power plant employees, contractors and builders, and probably others I can no longer identify by profession or trade.

Almost all of the dozens of chairmen with whom I worked were competent in their board leadership roles and very supportive of school leadership, as well as of the entire school district, its programs, and its staff. Although that should be a given for board of education chairmen, every district isn't that fortunate, and for superintendents without such strong working relationships based on mutual trust and respect with their chairmen, professional life resembles a Hindu *fakir's* wedding night on his proverbial bed of nails—and district education suffers commensurate difficulties and pains.

Chinese Water Tortures

Board committees are the devil's own invention, and the steady drip, drip, drip on administrative heads of eternally slow minutes endured in board committee meetings is the closest thing to the old Oriental water torture that modern education can inflict upon chief school officers. Superintendents and boards of education should review board committee structures, both the number of standing and ad hoc committees and their responsibilities and operations. Board committees, compared to their productivity, require significant amounts of the superintendent's time preparing for, attending, and following up committee meetings — not to mention blotting his or her forehead.

Decisions made and actions taken by board committees, and by assignments or directives from such committees to the superintendent of schools, are passed along to other central office staff, building administrators, and teachers. Many experienced superintendents strongly believe that the only standing board of education committee should be the policy committee; all others should be for specific purposes with specific tasks and specific time schedules — and the fewer in number the better.

Advantages to elimination or reduction in the number of board committees include (1) boards of education can ease their own workloads and those of superintendents and administrative staff in preparation for and follow-up of board committee meetings; (2) superintendents can devote more direct administrative attention to educational and staff issues, because time required of them to prepare for and follow up on board committee meetings is reduced; (3) discussion at board meetings becomes more meaningful, and boards will not be as quick to follow unquestioningly, through automatic or routine approval of committee recommendations, the supposed expertise of board committees that have spent more time studying issues than the rest of the board membership; (4) board decisions will be made only after public discussion and debate, rather than as a result of decisions made at committee meetings — boards too often tend to accept committee recommendations without adequate scrutiny; although committee meetings are often open sessions, the public doesn't usually attend these meetings, and neither do media representatives; and (5) superintendents will be seen as district leaders, rather than primarily as errand persons for board committees — district governance is thereby strengthened.

When the amount of service and assistance required from superintendents to multiple board committees becomes so great that their professional time is primarily used for tasks centering around committees, the district has no true leadership. Staff quickly recognizes that important decisions are made by board committees and that the superintendent is a "gofer"[114] for board subgroups instead of the professional, educational decision maker that he or she should be.

Once this understanding dawns on a staff, teachers and administrators begin to work around superintendents to reach and influence a district's real power structures—board of education committees. When that occurs, school systems slide into anarchy; neither boards of education nor their committees can really manage school districts on a day by day basis—no matter how many committees are created—and the superintendent is recognized as without significant authority, ergo, nobody is really in charge, and local education suffers.[115]

"Dammit, I Can So Accept Criticism!"

At a board of education evaluation session of the superintendent of schools some years ago, a particularly effective and perceptive board of education chairman gently informed the superintendent that he had at least minor difficulties in accepting criticism—to which the superintendent's angry, unperceptive, and totally self-incriminating response was, "Dammit, I can so accept criticism!"

Although most of us run a few quarts low on self-knowledge, it's easy to acknowledge the general premise that we are imperfect human beings and even imperfect educational leaders, but mention a specific imperfection and we'll deny it exists until hell freezes over. "Sure I have faults, but not that one; no, not that one either; no, certainly not that one; nor that one; nor. . . ."

There is no easy cure for this human defect, nor is there any certain immunity from its debilitating effects. Maybe the best we can do to build up a psychic resistance to this disease is accept its epidemic nature and be alert to its symptoms, both incipient and full-blown. And we should recall the satirical message of a well-known Scot who wrote, "Oh wad some Power the giftie gie us to see oursels as ithers see us!" [36].

Dress Rehearsals

A major part of superintendents' reputations are made or destroyed at board of education meetings. It is logical then that they prepare them-

---

[114]Go for pencils, go for paper, go for reports, go for information, etc.
[115]See also, Chapter 3, "The Lady or the Tiger?" p. 95.

selves, their administrative staffs, board of education members, and the public carefully and thoroughly in advance of board meetings.

Specific actions superintendents should take to prepare and inspire all the players for board meetings include (1) reviews with administrative staff of potential meeting agenda topics; (2) discussions with board chairmen about possible agenda items; (3) preparation of tentative agendas and associated explanatory support materials, including informational "general notes" to the board – the board should understand from past practice that these items are informational and that if board members want to discuss them (although it shouldn't happen all the time) they will be part of future meeting agendas; (4) dress rehearsals for board meetings with administrators and teachers who share responsibility for meeting presentations, specifically to: practice actual presentations and recommendations as they will be given or made at meetings; identify all reasonable and many unreasonable questions that might be asked following presentations and recommendations, including likely alternatives to recommendations – and also to be prepared to deal with unacceptable alternatives; develop answers for anticipated questions and positions on alternatives to recommendations that are to be made; detect discord amidst presentation elements and in suggested responses to anticipated questions – when wrong notes are heard, those sounds should be pursued, and at least short walks taken down all visible paths branching off the main ideas; probe, test, and examine "facts" in presentations, recommendations, planned responses to anticipated questions, and in the explanatory or supportive material to be included in board members' meeting "packets" – ensure that "facts" really are facts, instead of estimates, conjectures, groundless estimates, unfounded opinions, or "SWAGs".[116] (5) When possible, take the time to reflect on important recommendations; come back to them more than once; worry them the way dogs worry bones; prepare final agendas with presentations, recommendations, and associated backup or explanatory material revised as necessary; review the final agenda with the board chairman; and distribute board meeting packets to board members, the press, staff, town officials, and the general public in accordance with accepted district practice.

The day of the meeting, briefer versions of earlier dress rehearsals are also good to review outcomes from more extensive earlier sessions, along with highlights of presentations and recommendations to be made at that evening's board of education meeting. When leaders don't

---

[116]"Stupid, Wild A-- Guesses."

examine proposals or solutions thoroughly in these meeting rehearsal sessions, someone else will to their embarrassment—and at the expense of confidence in the district's staff and in its professional leadership.

So if someone asks you how to get to Carnegie Hall, tell them, "Practice, practice, practice."

Let's Be Sure We're All on the Same Page Here

Prior to board meetings, superintendents almost always provide board of education members adequate information on issues to be decided at the meeting.[117] If board members are expected to approve a new program at next Tuesday's meeting, they should receive information on the program well ahead of next Tuesday.

There are, however, times when superintendents may prefer, because of the complexity, volatility, or history of the issue to be acted upon or because of all of those factors combined, to present specific information to all board members together at a meeting, then distribute supportive information, and defer action until the subsequent meeting.

Not expecting decisions until later board meetings, superintendents give board members even more time for study and reflection, as well as additional information on which to base decisions. Even more importantly, through presentations to all board members simultaneously, superintendents keep them together on the same page—at least partially avoiding dramatically different interpretations of material distributed before meetings and forestalling members locking themselves into intractable positions before fully understanding the issues involved.

Written material is always subject to varying readings and degrees of understanding, from zero, through partial, to complete; some board members arrive at meetings well-prepared, others not having glanced at the data painstakingly assembled by staff, and some having done just that. They looked at the pages of material, shook their heads, and replaced everything in the large manila envelope—possibly never remembering their good intentions to go back to it and read it thoroughly.

Giving everyone the information simultaneously and then providing a period for study and reflection helps assure a common understanding of issues, rather than expecting each member to manage on his or her own. It also helps prevent one board member from confusing or persuading another over the telephone before everyone has the opportunity

---

[117]See examples of Agenda Notes in Appendix B.

to begin from the same point—especially those members who haven't had the time or the inclination to read the supportive data and, because of that, are relatively easy to sway.

Distributing handouts only after presentations are completed helps presenters achieve relatively undivided board member attention, because they can't lose themselves in the written material just distributed. It's distracting to pass out information just before or, even worse, during a presentation; if board members need to see particular data during the presentation, overhead projectors help everyone focus together on desired data.

A few board members resent either receiving information at the meeting instead of before the meeting—even when superintendents ask that no action be taken until the following meeting; this attitude appears to stem from some form of perverse reasoning understood only by them—or receiving written material at a meeting after a presentation is made instead of before the presentation.

Because some people are more visual than aural, preferring the security of the written word in front of them, superintendents often honor their learning styles and preferences; sometimes, they must do so whether they like it or not. Again, overheads may also help visual learners, and, if presentations are short and simple enough, superintendents occasionally ask boards to indulge them to avoid distractions during presentations.

Board members' preferences for receiving explanatory material prior to meetings are recognized by administrators, and superintendents generally provide information in advance when meeting decisions are expected. When superintendents are prepared to defer board decisions until later meetings, meeting presentations, with material and data following immediately, should be acceptable to reasonable people. But then not every board member is a reasonable person.

Board chairmen are key allies to superintendents generally, and, in dealing with these issues, it's crucial for superintendents to persuade board chairmen to remain on the same page with them and to understand superintendents' reasons for occasionally presenting information to everyone simultaneously or for withholding handouts until presentations are completed.

Oh Yeah!—And You're Another!

Question: Why should boards of education evaluate their own performance?

Answer: For the same reasons any performance self-evaluation takes place: to establish standards of performance for the board as a whole and for its individual members—when boards agree on comprehensive evaluation rating scales or checklists, the individual items, traits, skills, performances, or whatever collectively become board of education job descriptions. These job descriptions are crucial in guiding board of education behaviors and also to boards' abilities to evaluate superintendents of schools—until evaluators know their own responsibilities, how can they properly evaluate anyone else? For example, before a board of education judges a superintendent's performance in meeting board of education expectations, the board should take a close look at how clearly it has set forth its expectations of the superintendent.

As a help for individual board of education members to become more effective in their jobs (although boards of education in action are greater than the sum of their individual parts) individual performance growth is necessary for overall board improvement. Experienced board watchers have seen the effects, both positive and negative, of a one-member change on the board of education; if a new member can change the board as dramatically as they often do, the same kind of change, but always in the proper direction, can take place from improving individual board member job performance.

Evaluation is also to increase board of education effectiveness. It's important for boards to examine their operation and effectiveness if they are to improve them. Board self-evaluation is essential to improving both its operation and its effectiveness.

Question: What should be evaluated?

Answer: (1) Performances, traits, characteristics, processes, responsibilities, behaviors, etc., upon which the board agrees and which define its appropriate functions; (2) achievement of yearly board goals; (3) actual conduct of board of education meetings; (4) individual board member performance, although not necessarily by name, through individual member self-evaluation.

Most often, in those rare instances in which boards examine their own operations, the first of the four areas usually becomes the focus of board evaluation through rating scales or checklists; if two of the three areas are scrutinized, board goals are the most likely second item to be added; the conduct of the meetings themselves would be the third area to be judged; individual performance, even through self-evaluation, is rarely included in a self-evaluation process. However, complete board of education evaluations must examine individual contributions and impediments to both board effectiveness and to board efficiency.

Performances, traits, characteristics, processes, responsibilities, and behaviors to be evaluated might include

(1) Meeting procedures and conduct with written guidelines for conduct of board meetings, including agendas – length, organization, quality; members' preparation for meeting; meeting length – appropriateness of; allocation of time to issues – major issues allocated greater board time and attention; participation by board members and willingness to take positions and express opinions; atmosphere and tone of meetings; focus on issues and avoidance of personality differences; attention to speakers – public, board, staff; and executive sessions – proper use and procedures

(2) Relationships with superintendent of schools, including differentiation between policy role of board and administrative responsibilities of the superintendent of schools; adherence to defined channels of authority and responsibility; appropriate use of board committees; referral of concerns, complaints, and criticisms to appropriate school staff with information to superintendent of their action; mutual respect and trust between board and superintendent with commendation where earned and constructive criticism as needed; consideration of superintendent recommendations prior to making decisions; use of superintendent as primary source of information to board; public support of superintendent, especially in pressure situations; and handling of differences between board and superintendent

(3) Problem solving and decision making, including definition of task at hand or problem to be solved; objective examination of alternatives with consideration of advantages and disadvantages of each; identification of blockages to desired change and strategies to remove them; consideration of group goals, as well as personal points of view; ability to reach closure and decide; minority board member support of majority decisions; and determination of specific evaluation procedures for outcomes of, or programs resulting from, major decisions

(4) Delegation of tasks to superintendent, including clear definition of tasks to be accomplished; development and use of criteria to measure superintendent's success or failure in carrying out delegated assignments; provision of adequate resources to superintendent for accomplishing tasks assigned; and establishment of necessary checkpoints to evaluate superintendent progress with delegated tasks

(5) Board chairman: use of appropriate parliamentary procedures, keeping discussions on topic, and conflict resolution techniques and results

(6) Instructional program: board actions consistent with district educational philosophy and goals, differentiation of curriculum and program responsibilities between board and staff, and program decisions based on student welfare

(7) Financial management: decisions made with appropriate regard for fiscal responsibility and financial priorities established for decision making

(8) Community relationships: knowledge and understanding of community attitudes and special interests; appropriate balance between public opinion and board judgment; ability to work with, and resist if necessary, special interest groups; ability to adopt and maintain board positions under public pressure; relationships with news media; and citizen attendance and participation at board meetings

The next two evaluation criteria are administrative responsibilities but tied so directly to board of education meetings that they may be evaluated as integral parts of a board evaluation: (1) presentations of superintendent or other staff: adequacy of information, organization, clarity, specific recommendations from superintendent of schools — alternative courses of action given as appropriate; and (2) superintendent information to board: quality and amount.

Without consideration of individual member performance, it wouldn't be clear whether particular ratings, for example, average marks on "board members' preparation for meetings," indicate that all board members do an average job preparing or that half are outstandingly well prepared and half are totally unprepared, or that a third are outstanding, a third average, and a third poorly prepared. Each situation described produces an average mark — but pictures very different boards of education. Without ratings, even anonymous ratings, of individuals, the essence of board performance in this area is never clear, and chairmen don't have the necessary tools to effect board change.

Question: Who should evaluate the board of education?

Answer: In a real clockwork universe, the general public would be the logical evaluators of the board that it elects. Unfortunately, although the ballot box remains one means of board evaluation, there are usually too few citizens with the necessary knowledge of board operations to evaluate the board. The usual available options are outside consultants, board members themselves, and district leadership—usually the superintendent of schools and possibly assistant superintendents who regularly attend meetings.

Of these three, boards normally will find board of education self-evaluation most productive, but it should be coupled with evaluations by superintendents and other administrators who have adequate experience and knowledge of the board. With especially dysfunctional boards, or for specific board meeting processes and other relatively narrow issues, outside experts (such as the director or other staff from the state board of education association) can be of great assistance, particularly to assess a single meeting operation. Also, outside consultants may guide boards through development of effective processes for board self-evaluation.

Many district boards of education are composed of a majority of members with fewer than four years of experience and many who are in their first or second years on the board; most superintendents have worked with many more boards of education than their members have with different superintendents. Because of the relative experience of boards and superintendents, it's wise for boards to add a dash of administrative experience to their evaluation stew. Superintendents and other administrators provide objective and experienced views of boards, and in spite of attendant hazards from superintendents evaluating their collective bosses, their evaluations should not be merged with others but should stand apart as his or her evaluation of the board.[118]

Question: What are major differences between a superintendent evaluating a board and a board of education evaluating a suprintendent?

Answer: An evaluation of a superintendent is composed of many people's judgments focused on one person (convergent), and a board of education's evaluation by a superintendent is one person's assessment of a group and its group process (divergent). A superintendent evaluation, good or bad, accurate or inaccurate, describes him or her on the job and nobody else. Board evaluation describes only one machine, but one that has many moving parts, any one of which, if defective, can stop the machine or at least cause it to run poorly.[119]

Question: If boards of education and superintendents both had

---

[118]Possibly, the board could place a big gold star, or leftover Thanksgiving turkey stamp, on the form to be used by the superintendent but tell him or her not to sign the form—sort of a rudimentary I.Q. test for the superintendent.

[119]Yes, I know most superintendents also have moving parts, in spite of contrary arguments by malcontents—but not in this sense.

tenure, which or whom would be easier to fire on the basis of incompetent performance?

Answer: Under these hypothetical circumstances, it would be much easier to fire an incompetent board. Boards are easier to catch in the act of being themselves and doing what they do than it is for them to observe superintendents performing the variety of tasks for which they are responsible. Except for executive sessions or illicit board activity, boards function in public at prescribed times and places, and their decisions and actions are visible and clear to evaluators.

Question: How would you contrast the nature of a board evaluating a superintendent compared to a superintendent evaluating a board?

Answer: A board evaluating a superintendent is the natural order of things—the way God intended it to be; a superintendent evaluating a board is an unnatural act—something akin to donning a chicken suit and visiting one of Colonel Sanders' restaurants at dinner time. Although personal security is a prerequisite for successful superintendents, unmitigated foolhardiness is not. To receive candor from superintendents in board evaluations requires boards to convince the superintendent of their collective security and openness to administrative criticism and suggestions. On the other side of that, even holding all the high cards in the board/superintendent game, few board members are prepared to have their personal evaluations of the superintendent attributed to them by name.

Further, a superintendent's evaluation of a board is like a flashlight that may provide illumination but no heat; a board evaluation of the superintendent is like the sun's rays through a magnifying glass, which produces both bright light and white heat on the focus of its scrutiny.

Evaluations of superintendents affect their salaries and job security, and, although administrative motivation to change in response to evaluation may not always be pure, it's strong—superintendents care deeply about board judgments of them. Board members have no extrinsic motivations to improve, except possibly their desire for reelection. The reality understood by most board members, however, is that individual board member performance is rarely observed by significant numbers of voters.

Question: Is board evaluation for everyone?

Answer: No! Although most boards would be healthier if they took the medicine, there may be contraindications to it: (1) When board members are already working effectively together and with the superintendent, when public relations between the board and staff and the board and the community are good, and when students are achieving well, it may be better not to swallow any new compounds. Nature's balance can be a delicate one, and when things are going well, don't change the prescription; unfortunately, there are only a few districts where everything works this well. (2) When members are resistant to board evaluation, it will likely do no good and can exacerbate board and board/superintendent relationships. (3) If the board won't commit itself to serious efforts to use results for individual and board growth, it's a waste of time. (4) If political, or other external pressures, are primary driving forces on the board, superintendents should relax and try to enjoy the ride—evaluation won't help.

Any board considering board of education evaluation should discuss its own circumstances thoroughly, along with its readiness for the journey. If, after careful consideration, there seems to be consensus supportive of the process, it should begin. Although the results might be painful, board of education evaluation can also provide real benefits for district education and its students.

One Last Great Act of Defiance

A cartoon of unknown provenance pictures an enormous eagle filling most of the page with its outstretched wings, enormous cruel eyes, vicious beak, and talons spread to strike as it swoops down on its imminent prey. At the very bottom of the picture, you see the back view of a lonely little mouse. This isn't your basic macho, NFL linebacker type mouse; this one is a skinny, vulnerable, frail little creature standing as straight up on his hind legs as he can, long hairless tail curling out behind him, courageously holding his right arm (or foreleg) straight up in the air, with the extended middle digit of his right hand (forepaw) thrust into the face of the predatory eagle. The picture is captioned, "One Last Great Act of Defiance."

Sometimes, when board of education members have histories of unfounded and unfair public attacks on individual staff members, or the entire staff as a group, superintendents may at times feel obliged to emulate the mouse, figuratively speaking except in very unusual circumstances, and take on publicly a few of the people who control their professional destinies. Sometimes, the results approximate a moment in time after the eagle/mouse confrontation described, and the superintendent may fare no better than did the mouse.[120]

---

[120]But it can still be fun.

Often, fair-minded board members or superintendents believe it's better for other board members and the superintendent simply to ignore snide remarks or facial expressions derogatory to staff or unfounded criticism of them; at times, that makes sense, because it's tough to "refute a sneer" [37]. At other times, it may not, and if negative board members continue with outrageous public accusations and criticisms without refutation from people who know better and who have the information to provide the rebuttal, there's a stronger argument that these already "ripe" misstatements, if left to ripen further, will be accepted as true by many who hear them.

On occasion, educational leadership has an obligation to tackle these folks frontally, firmly, and unapologetically but with as much gentility and civilized behavior as they can muster. It's as true for superintendents and principals as it is for other leaders that "he makes no friend who never made a foe" [38], and for school district leaders to avoid this unpleasant task is an abdication of professional responsibility to the very people who do the important work of education.

The Parable of the Superintendent and the Duck

One February, a Connecticut superintendent's spouse was away on a cruise with her mother, and the superintendent decided to visit his old friend Charlie who lived out in West Texas in a small town called Ozona. When Charlie picked the superintendent up at the Ozona Airport late in the evening, he said he had to go in to work the next morning, but he would be back by early afternoon. In the meantime, the superintendent was encouraged to make himself at home.

Charlie said, "There'll be coffee; you can watch television; and I know you like bird hunting. This is duck hunting heaven, and although what we call Texas Desert Ducks may be a little different from what you're used to, they're a real challenge because of their evasive flight patterns. If you'd like, you can just sit out in the backyard and fire away—even though there are houses nearby. You can see one neighbor's house over the fence to the north—it's the one with the ladder leaning up against the side. Don't worry though, people around here are used to gunfire, so feel free."

The next morning, the superintendent rose early, had some coffee, and watched a little Oprah on TV. Becoming restless, he strolled out back, and sure enough, game birds flew over regularly in amazing displays of aerial acrobatics characteristic of "Texas Desert Ducks." The superintendent went back inside, picked out a Purdy "over and under" from the shotgun rack, loaded it, put a couple of extra shells in his jacket pocket, walked outside, and sat down on the stoop. Within a few seconds, a duck zigzagged overhead, and when the superintendent snapped off a quick shot, the duck fell dead on the flat roof of the neighbor's house with the ladder alongside.

Pleased by his marksmanship, the superintendent scrambled over the fence, climbed the ladder, and collected the bird from the roof of the house. After backing carefully down the ladder, he turned and found himself face to face with a large, angry Texan: "What the hell you doing up on my roof, son?"

"I was only retrieving my dead duck. I'm staying with Charlie, and I shot the duck, and my duck fell on your roof."

"Ain't your duck. It's my duck. Out here, it's not who shoots the bird, but where it lands says who owns it."

"I don't agree with that concept, but how can we settle this?"

The Texan reflected for a moment, and said slowly: "Well, the way we resolve all kinds of troubles out in West Texas is stand face to face and kick each other until one of us can't kick any more. The one standing is the winner, but I doubt Yankees are tough enough for that."

The superintendent thought to himself, "Holy crushed egos, Batman. I don't like this a bit, but I can't back down from this Neanderthal. It would embarrass my old friend Charlie," and so he said, "OK, I agree."

"Me first!" said the Texan. And he lifted the superintendent off the ground with a vicious, well-placed kick. The superintendent sprawled in the dust, moaning and writhing, and carrying on something fierce. He was down, completely incapacitated, for almost a half hour while the Texan grinned and watched him.

Finally, he struggled to his feet, and feeling some strength returning, gasped, "Now it's my turn."

To which the Texan replied, "Oh hell, what's a neighbor for anyway? You keep the duck."

The meaning of this story is obvious. Not every dead duck is worth the pain—your pain, and/or, if you're good at what you do, the pain you inflict on others. Superintendents don't need to run at every windmill or fight with boards of education over each dead duck; sometimes, it's smart to be a good neighbor and let them keep the duck. Unfortunately, occasions do arise when leaders must be prepared to stand up for issues, even at some risk to themselves and their professional careers, and to some painful kicks.

Superintendents have sometimes heard, from one of their colleagues, assertions such as, "I'm not planning to die on that hill," an expression meaning someone isn't willing to charge up an educational hill in the face of heavy board of education, staff, or public firepower. There are times when this practical attitude makes great sense, but, when the expression is overused, people begin to wonder if there are principles for which the superintendent will place his or her professional life on the line—and sometimes their speculation is well founded. There may be no issues over which that particular superintendent will risk losing a position through taking a stand or running up a dangerous issue—in which case he or she should be in some other line of work.

The trick is to recognize when the fight is worth the potential prize. It's got to be more important than a dead duck, but deciding how much more important requires a combination of character, experience, and judgment.

Ray Bolger and Other Straw Persons

Ray Bolger, as the semi-lovable Straw Man in *The Wizard of Oz* was, for many of us, our first experience with a straw man, but, in modern political circles and in other public positions, a phenomenon referred to as the "straw man approach" flourishes. For the innocent or uninitiated, the "straw man technique" offers up a sacrificial, weak argument contrary to a chosen position and then easily demolishes it; once people discredit their sacrificial straw man rationale, they then indicate, in both words and manner, that all other positions different from theirs are naturally of the same pathetic quality, soundness, and durability.

Adolescents often employ variations of this maneuver on parents—anticipating the weakest parental defense against a desired course of action, offering it up, dealing with it easily and often even contemptuously, and expecting immediate and total parental surrender of all other arguments against allowing their progeny to be out carousing until four in the morning.

National leaders and local politicians, including board of education members, have developed, refined, and transformed the straw man into someone closer to Arnold Schwarzenegger than the character played so "heartlessly" by Ray Bolger in *The Wizard of Oz*—although there are similarities between the rubber-legged underpinnings of the inhabitant of Oz and those on which "straw men" arguments move about in educational circles.[121]

---

[121]Mixing metaphors can sometimes be humorous, but OK then, "straw-legged" instead of "rubber-legged."

Superintendents of schools should resist temptations to enlist "straw persons" in their own professional administrative armies but, more importantly, should avoid placing themselves into vulnerable positions that are easily assaulted by straw men. As is true with offspring, whenever too many reasons are given in support of positions, board members, staff, parents, and children will go for the least defensible rationale and destroy it through opportunistic variations of the "straw man technique"—in those instances, you've given your opposition their straw man free of charge, and they didn't need to build their own.

School leaders should remain with their strongest positions and not offer weaker ones as easy targets. When they don't have sufficiently strong positions, they are better off waiting until they do.

Rotate the Dancers a Quarter Turn to the Left

Among Jack Paar's regular guests in the sixties were Genevieve, Guido Panzini the fictitious Italian golf pro, and artist and raconteur Alexander King. King had one of those large, droopy, walrus mustaches and, as was typical of the times, smoked incessantly. One reason some people watched the show when he was scheduled was to see if he would finally ignite his upper lip. He was an amusing conversationalist with a good sense of the absurd.

One of his stories concerned a painting commissioned by a major cruise line, in which he was to show couples dancing on deck under the stars—clearly to help sell the idea of a romantic ocean cruise to potential customers. King explained that, when he turned in his painting, company executives placed it on an easel in a large office, studied it intently for some time, and, in all seriousness, the vice president in charge of "dancing paintings" turned to King and said, "Alex, I think you should rotate the dancers a quarter turn to the left."

After the artist was retrieved from the overhead, he explained the inefficacy of revising his painting as requested. The vice president still insisted he "rotate the dancers," so King did the work over again. In recounting the story, he said to Jack Paar that, from that time on, he always included some easily detected and easily corrected defect in each commercial painting. For example, in a dance scene similar to the one already discussed, he'd place a man's hand too low on his partner's back. Very low on his partner's back. Actually, his hand was just south of his partner's back and not really on her back at all. King's intention was to ensure he would only be asked to make obvious and easy corrections.

Similar practices are often followed by deviously successful superintendents of schools in dealing with boards of education. They may also be practiced in modified form by principals or other administrators working with the superintendent.

If superintendents have a series of recommendations to present to the board, they may insert an obvious "clunker" among the others. Their hope, often realized, is that boards will reject the obvious losers, and then, having satisfied themselves that they are indeed in charge and make no mistake about that, they will approve pro forma the other recommendations—and everyone lives happily ever after. This is particularly effective shortly after boards have become sensitive to charges of "rubber stampism."[122]

A couple of caveats are presented here for Machiavellian administrative manipulators: (1) The obvious "loser" recommendations must be for goods or services school districts really could use—in case something unusual happens and boards decide to spring for them. Typically, they're desirable purchases or contracts that superintendents don't believe boards will support financially. Recommending the purchase of 150 new Macintosh computers for your elementary schools is an outstanding example superintendents can use again and again; nobody on the board will say anything bad about efforts to improve technological education in the district, but a hundred fifty thousand dollars. . . . (2) Really stupid, sacrificial agenda items, although providing even greater distractions for board members than the more logical but still obvious losers, tend to stick in board members' individual and collective memories. Later, over coffee or other beverages, they will be exhumed and dissected—accompanied by fits of giggling about how "the old boy" or "the old girl" really is losing it lately. (3) Overuse of this approach, even with computer purchases, will often cause the same board reaction as even infrequent use of really dumb board distracters. (4) When superintendents load up administrative sleds, they should place key fish in just the right agenda location so board members will be distracted by them while allowing their sleds through with the other fish intact— often, a good spot is just before the most important item superintendents want boards to approve. If the "giveaway" is placed too far from key issues, boards may reject that recommendation as expected, pass a few others routinely, and then unexpectedly put on their game faces and jump back into their rejection mode to kill the superintendent's most cherished recommendation—often, for no better reason than they haven't done anything that much fun in the last half hour or so.

A collection of obvious losers, fish off the sled, a superintendent's fine hand placed too low on the board of education's backside, or giving the board an easy kill by whatever name it's known, should all be assembled and stored away where they can be brought out at very special occasions and thrown on the table as distracters.

BOARD POLICIES

"Accidents Will Occur in the Best-Regulated Families" [39]

Board of education policies play a role similar to that played by women in the home as described by Charles Dickens[123]: ". . . Accidents will occur in the best-regulated families; and in families not regulated by that pervading influence which sanctifies while it enhances. . . . In the lofty character of Wife, they may be expected with confidence, and must be borne with philosophy" [39]. With policies, problems in solving problems will occur frequently enough; without them, as without the influence of woman as wife, problems in solving recurring problems will be major problems for school leaders.

Intellectual understanding and specific knowledge of board policies and administrative regulations are both vital, but they are of little value without deep visceral commitment to their development, revision, and daily use. In their importance to board members and school administrators, the golden mean of policy importance should fall somewhere between food and sex—maybe a bit closer to food.

Board of education policies translate beliefs and desires of elected officials into action through superintendents of schools. Except for specific meeting decisions, policies are a board's only appropriate means of shaping district education—board members delude themselves in believing they can manage local education effectively through decisions made at board meetings. In any given school year, meeting time is re-

---

[123]Charles J. H. Dickens knew from experience about troubled family life. As a child, he worked as a "drudge" in a blacking factory, and in 1824 his father was jailed for debt. American compulsion to create euphemisms for words such as *drudge* probably would have resulted in Dickens being called a blacking factory junior technician. But count on the English to call a "drudge" a "drudge."

stricted, and the number of significant decisions emerging from board of education meetings is relatively small. Cynical superintendents of schools might argue that unlimited board meeting time wouldn't change the number of significant decisions made at board meetings anyway.

Boards of education amplify values and aspirations most legitimately through written board of education policies – and through insisting that written policies be followed by superintendents of schools and all staff members. Thoughts in the previous sentence are paralleled in superintendents' administrative regulations, which provide an administrative "how it will be done" to accompany board of education policies that establish more generally "what is to be done."

Although a few central office dinosaurs may believe policy vacuums permit, or even encourage, untrammeled administrative discretion, that's wrong; if we believe that, the real vacuum is between our ears. It's difficult enough, even for outstanding superintendents, always to meet expectations of boards of education, and it's impossible for even the best unless school district direction has been agreed upon in board of education policy and clearly understood by all involved. Policies set forth written board of education expectations to superintendents of schools and make it clear, at least by implication, that superintendents are not expected to act according to each individual board member's every whimsical, or even sincere, wish.

An "Army of Unalterable Law" [40]—Not!

If you asked average citizens of a given school district, "For whom are board of education policies written?" their responses probably would be, "For the board, of course!" Seems logical, but dead wrong. Board policies, except for bylaws, guide superintendents of schools and their administrative staffs in day-to-day school district leadership choices. It is, however, the board's responsibility to ensure superintendents use policies in making decisions; it is, similarly, the superintendent's responsibility to insist that both policies and their amplifying administrative regulations are followed by everyone else in the school system.

It should be a cardinal sin, in the eyes of school superintendents, for other administrators to say, "Oh, we've never paid any attention to that policy (or regulation); it's not practical, and it doesn't work." They may well be correct, but then the policy or regulation should have been changed long ago. The unforgivable transgression is in not calling policy and regulatory problems, real or imagined, to the attention of the right people for necessary corrections. When particular policies and regulations are flawed or unworkable, the staff has an obligation to share its perceptions with the superintendent, and the superintendent has a parallel responsibility to refer inadequate policies to the board of education, along with suggestions for correcting or improving offending policies or regulations and reports of necessary administrative violations of current policies or regulations—or superintendent justifications for acting outside of or contrary to existing policies and regulations.

In the best of circles, even those with outstanding policies and policy practices, problems requiring policy modifications will occur periodically, and policies shouldn't be viewed as divine law—or as characterized by the fallen archangel Lucifer, "the army of unalterable law" [40].

"As He Brews, So Shall He Drink" [41]

Although significant school district differences in policy and regulation development exist, there are even greater commonalities among the characteristics, procedures, and philosophies of organizations having effective policies and administrative regulations. In such school systems, the following conditions are present: (1) Policies and regulations have been assigned high priorities by boards and superintendents of schools; (2) many people at different levels participate in development and review of policies and regulations; (3) procedures for development and revision of policies and regulations are clear and well understood; (4) participants know their roles and authority; (5) board of education, administrative, and staff lines of communication are observed; (6) use of policies and regulations as guides to action is stressed at all organizational levels, and policy or regulatory violations by school district personnel are not overlooked or condoned; (7) policy and regulatory effectiveness are monitored regularly by boards of education, superintendents of schools, and other staff; and (8) board members and administrators are aware of and guard against intrinsic problems of policies and regulations.[124]

In Ben Jonson's[125] dramatic comedy, George Downright uses a version of the biblical admonition, "As Ye Sow, So Shall Ye Reap" when

[124]See also, this chapter, "And So Do His Sisters, His Cousins, and His Aunts," p. 172.
[125]Ben Jonson is a good quote on board policy because he was apprenticed as a bricklayer to his father. Developing policies is like that, with one policy layer at a time instead of a layer of brick at a time.

he says, "As He Brews, So Shall He Drink" [41] characterizing the behavior, and its implied consequences, of his half-brother Wellbred. Adequate time and effort expended in developing and maintaining effective board of education policies and attendant administrative regulations produces a better brew for leadership consumption.

The Lost Commandments Found

According to tradition based on divine law, policy manuals contain three basic types of entries—board of education policies, superintendent of schools regulations, and board of education bylaws. Some policy "wonks" don't see enough differences between bylaws and policies to justify considering them in entirely separate categories; instead, they consider bylaws a particular species of policy found in a particular policy section. Either view makes its own kind of sense. (1) Policies are guides for discretionary action by superintendents of schools and their staffs; not all policies require administrative regulations. (2) Regulations are superintendents' amplifications of board policies into specific staff actions; not all administrative regulations require policies. (3) Bylaws are rules governing board of education internal operations.

According to the aforementioned divine law, policy manuals include policies on blue paper (or blue stone tablets) and regulations on yellow paper (or yellow legal tablets.)

Two common codification systems for policy manuals are used. One uses a four-letter[126] alphabetical organization of individual policies, which drives some people nuts: "AAAA, BBBB, CCCC . . ." for major policy sections; the other, somewhat more popular arrangement uses four digits, plus decimal subdivisions as necessary—the ten major series numbers are 0000 through 9000 containing Board Goals and Objectives (0000); Community/Public Relations (1000); Administration (2000); Business (3000); Personnel (4000); Students (5000); Instruction (6000); Buildings (7000)—rarely used; Special Board Operations (8000)—almost never used; and Bylaws of the Board (9000).

Series 8000 is the vermiform appendix of policy manuals and the only person who used it died many years ago.[127]

---

[126]It's not what you may be thinking.

[127]Recently discovered in a recent archeological dig in Egypt was an early Pharaoh's policy and regulations manual on blue and yellow papyrus with an 8000 Series used for "Internal Board Operations."

"And the Greatest of These Is . . ."—II

The relationship between negotiated employee contracts and board of education policies is very clear—contracts supersede or take precedence over board of education policies in all cases of conflicts between the two. Policy sections on personnel, which before collective bargaining spelled out salaries, benefits, sick days, leaves, etc., are now, for the most part, simply cross-references from old policy titles to articles in negotiated agreements with employee bargaining groups.

Board policy manuals often retain personnel sections, partially from habit and partially because they still contain guidance for the superintendent of schools on some aspects of personnel management that are not specifically spelled out in negotiated agreements. For example, a board policy article may not prescribe three personal days annually per teacher if the teacher contract calls for five—that's a conflict with the contract and therefore impermissible. On the other end of the seesaw, when contracts are silent on the issue, board policies or administrative regulations may prescribe forms for administrative implementation of personal leave articles. Generally, boards or superintendents have some leeway in administering negotiated contracts as long as their policies or regulations are not inconsistent with the intent of negotiated agreements.

When the contract doesn't speak to the issue, a policy or regulation also authorizing superintendents to require written statements from teachers justifying personal day requests, as an added accompaniment to leave forms, falls somewhere between the two extremes—but probably much closer to impermissible than permissible. Somewhere between the two extremes (but probably closer to permissible than impermissible) might be policies or regulations requiring teachers to complete personal day requests within three work days after emergency use of personal leave if it wasn't reasonable for teachers to have obtained prior permission from administrative supervisors.

In gray areas of authority between policy and contract, the grievance procedure is available to both parties to clarify issues when informal discussion cannot—although it's almost unheard of for a board to file a grievance, it's possible within some grievance procedures.

"An Abundance of Counselors" [42]

The more people who are involved in policy and regulation development and the greater their involvement, the more acceptance and effect policies and regulations have. As with other human endeavors, the problem is finding the Aristotelian mean between efficiency and effectiveness.[128]

The most efficient, and the least effective, way to develop board policies and administrative regulations is to have one person do it alone; the least efficient, and most effective, way is involving everyone in the district. Neither of these two opposites is appropriate or even possible; board of education and administrative wisdom lies in knowing where to act between these polar opposites.

Policies and regulations on district business practices may be developed, both efficiently and effectively, by the board of education, the superintendent, and the business staff; on or near the other end of the spectrum, meaningful and effective drug education policies require widespread participation of board members, administrators, and other staff, students, parents, and various community groups, including local law enforcement authorities.

Superintendents of schools are responsible to boards for carrying out policy, and they should be heavily involved in policy review and development. In turn, superintendents should consult frequently with other administrators and staff, and a superintendent's policy advice to boards should be given only after careful consideration of other staff views — and it should identify any major staff differences about particular recommendations and reasons for those differences. Similarly, in preparing administrative regulations, superintendents should involve staff, students, the general citizenry, and community groups as appropriate.

Frequently, legal advice or other expert assistance should be sought in drafting new policies or regulations and/or in reviewing existing policies and regulations, particularly those involving student suspension/expulsion, teacher reduction in force, etc. The intent of these recommended reviews by school attorneys is not to have legal holy water sprinkled on policies and regulations by jurisprudential potentates, but for analysis of and recommendations on those with the greatest potential for legal fallout.[129]

---

[128]See also, Chapter 1, "In Search of Gold," p. 7 and "Ten Cardinal Principles of Leadership," p. 21 and Chapter 3, "Efficient or Effective—Choose Any Two," p. 73.

[129]I can't say the word *fallout* where I live because we have three nuclear plants in the town—our euphemism for *fallout* is *plume exposure path*, which somehow doesn't seem as ominous.

"Fearfully and Wonderfully Made"[130]

McSorley's Wonderful Saloon, a book about a real bar in New York City and the interesting people who frequented it, contains an account of a possibly brilliant, certainly mad, and generally fascinating indigent professor who always carried with him the manuscript for his book, which he had titled *The Unfinished History of the World.* He died somewhere in the city's subway labyrinth or in one of its parks or in a flophouse, and his "unfinished history" was lost forever to the world [44]—unless Mel Brooks found it and used it as the plot for his movie with a similar plot.

Too many board members and superintendents in the fifty states carry around tattered and unfinished policy manuals, conceptually at least, resembling the professor's manuscript. If they are waiting to adopt policies, or to approve regulations, until each policy and regulation is perfect or as described by the unknown psalmist, ". . . fearfully and wonderfully made" [43], they will never have workable sets of policies and regulations.

Perfect policy manuals do not exist, and school boards need to place policies into the hands of school superintendents—even when they may be incomplete or imperfect. Then the district begins its unending process of refinement and improvement, which, in contrast, makes Sisyphus[131] seem underemployed.[132]

Where Do You Put the Point on the Line?

Boards of education and superintendents of schools are always striving together (and often fighting with each other) to find the golden mean between policies so general they are useless and policies so specific they are bureaucratic nightmares that unnecessarily constrain superintendents' freedom to make appropriate decisions. Board of education policies should tell superintendents "what" should be done, but shouldn't tell them "how" to do what the board wants done. Among the most complex tasks for boards of education and superintendents in

[130]"For it was you who formed my inward parts; you knit me together. . . . I praise you, for I am fearfully and wonderfully made. Wonderful are your works that I know very well." Possibly, this is a bit overblown as a policy manual description, but it's very nearly correct.

[131]You remember the legendary CEO of Corinth condemned to roll a heavy rock up a hill in Hades where it always rolled back down when he finally reached the top. Board policy manuals are like that rock and superintendents and board members like Sisyphus.

[132]If you can't do better, have the board of education approve the *Board of Education Unipolicy Manual* found later in this chapter.

developing new policies or revising old ones is achieving an appropriate balance between the need to allow superintendents of schools ample discretion to do "what" boards want done and board members' compulsions to specify exactly "how" things should be done, as well as "what" should be done.

Six generalized variables in policy-writing equations that help determine where boards are likely to place their discretionary points on the continuum between generality and specificity are (1) statutes and governmental regulations, which often require or suggest very specific policies allowing little, if any, administrative discretion; (2) board members' understandings of their roles as policymakers—usually, the clearer the board's understanding of their policy roles, the more administrative freedom is allowed in board policies; (3) superintendents' understandings of their administrative role—if superintendents attempt to overcontrol policy issues, they may be successful for a while; however, after a time, boards of education may, in retaliation for administrative power grabs, approve policies even more restrictive than they would have otherwise been; (4) competence and leadership of school superintendents where the more competent they are, the more administrative freedom usually is allowed; part of a superintendent's competence and leadership is manifested in his or her willingness and ability to defend appropriate freedom and administrative discretion needed to carry out board policies effectively; (5) unanimity of board thought— the greater this unity, the more policy specificity is likely; specific policies are less probable amidst major diversity of board member opinions; agreement is difficult enough, even on very general wording, among board members who think alike; and (6) who drafts policies— this variable cuts both ways. Frequently, when superintendents of schools prepare policy drafts, proposed policies allow greater administrative latitude because superintendents congenitally prefer freedom from excesssive policy restrictions. On the other hand, the greater superintendents' participation, the less threatened they may be by relatively specific policies—if I write it, how can it threaten me?

Although the words *variables* and *equation* are used in this section, there is little that is consistent or scientific in either policy equations or their variables. All six factors play various parts in policy development and policy revision, along with others not identified, some logical, some not. In shaping the specificity of board of education policies, a few of the variables, or even one variable, may dominate all the other "equation variables"—and you never know which one is controlling all the others.

Boards of education should hold policy balance firmly in mind, always conscious of the degree of discretion superintendents are allowed in board policies. If such discretion is too limited or nonexistent, they need either to change policies or be able to explain, rationally and honestly, to the superintendent why the board prefers the policies as controlling as they are. Similarly, superintendents of schools should maintain an administrative regulatory balance in the degree of leadership discretion that principals and other administrators are permitted by administrative regulations. If administrative discretion is too limited or nonexistent, superintendents also need either to loosen regulations or be able to explain, rationally and honestly, to other school district administrators why the boss prefers regulations as specific as they are.

Absolute standards or guidelines for policy development are difficult to find; however, there is a well known, though informal, educational policy assessment standard often called the "Baby Bear Test of Board Policies." In this test, policies are compared against strict test norms to insure they are neither too hot nor too cold, too hard nor too soft, too general nor too specific, but just right.

"And So Do His Sisters, His Cousins, and His Aunts" [45]

In public education, as elsewhere, good things are often illegal, immoral, or fattening, but board of education policies and administrative regulations are rarely immoral and never fattening—although they be illegal. Good policies, used well, translate a community's educational aspirations for its children and youth into school district achievements and help solve recurring problems effectively with great economy of board and staff time and effort. Although superintendents and other administrators don't have the luxury of addressing each issue anew, without regard to past procedures and written precedents, school districts are always confronted with two perpetual policy and regulatory problems: the time it takes to develop and update them and the difficulty of developing administrative and staff commitment to their importance and to their regular use as problem solvers.

These problems, as significant as they are, are small potatoes compared with administrative insensitivity, its concomitant mindless adherence to rules, and a slavish following of authority reminiscent of Sir Joseph Porter's adoring female relatives on "H.M.S. Pinafore";[133]

---

[133]"H.M.S. Pinafore" was Gilbert's third libretto to Sullivan's music.

it's always dumb to try and stuff ten-pound problems (or ten pounds of small potatoes) into five-pound policy or regulation bags—unlike socks, "one size policies" don't always fit each situation or every pair of feet.[134]

To guard against policy and regulatory misuses and abuses, administrators should understand intellectually and feel viscerally that general answers to specific questions must be applied with caution; that policies and regulations are often imperfect approximations of ideal solutions; that, if the world were a perfect place and administrative time were unlimited, each issue could be approached afresh without any restrictions from preconceived solutions set forth in policies or regulations; that policies shouldn't be viewed as divine law—or as characterized by the fallen archangel Lucifer "the army of unalterable law" [40]; and that policies and regulations must always be subject to changes and improvements as specific circumstances reveal their shortcomings.

Foolish consistency may be the "hobgoblin of little minds, adored by little statesmen and philosophers and divines" [15]. Often, superintendents are required to "speak what we think now in hard words and speak differently tomorrow if need be, for tomorrow will be a new day" [15].[135] These ideas neither contradict nor lessen the value of policies and regulations but, instead, highlight an ever-present potential for bureaucratic misuse of guidelines. Superintendents must be willing to recommend policy changes and to make regulatory modifications accommodating individual needs and human considerations more important than "foolish consistency"—and, when necessary, to act outside of or even contrary to policy and report policy or regulatory violations to boards of education at the first available opportunity, including suggestions for policy changes or reports of regulatory changes and justifications for actions outside of or contrary to existing policies and regulations.

Board of Education Unipolicy Manual

The superintendent of schools shall cause, through his/her leadership, example, and the writing of appropriate administrative regulations, the effective and efficient operation of all aspects of the district's educational and other programs to develop each student beyond his/her maximum potential. In doing so, the superintendent shall abide by all

---

[134]In naval parlance, a "swivet" is ten pounds of something other than potatoes stuffed into a five-pound bag.
[135]See also, Chapter 1, "Ten Cardinal Principles of Leadership," p. 21.

federal, state, and local statutes, ordinances, and regulations, as well as applying and causing to be applied by each employee and student in the district, to every area of school life and operation, the accumulated wit, wisdom, and culture of all world civilizations, both major and minor, both past and present.

The superintendent shall report regularly to the board of education providing complete, specific, and objective data on school district progress toward achievement of this policy's goals and shall render such reports in a manner that guarantees the contentment and happiness of each board of education member and the entire community.

The superintendent of schools shall comply with all aspects of this policy by next Thursday.

PRACTICE MAKES PERFECT—SUMMARIZING THEMES/MAIN IDEAS

Summarize in three or four sentences the themes/main ideas of each of the following recurring board phenomena and essays under superintendent/board relationships. Summary examples are provided in Appendix C, pp. 467–474.

(*1*) Recurring Board Phenomena
- Better Odds Are All You Can Expect—In Poker or Leadership Life in General
- But Sir, I'm Only a Poor Little Match Girl
- Dear God, He Chewed Off the Wrong Foot!
- Don't You Pick on My Little Brother (or Sister)
- Educational Maritime Law
- How Much Is Board Harmony Worth?
- How Much Information Is Enough?
- I Found These at the Dump
- I've Had Many, Many Calls about That
- Henry M. Robert versus Common Sense
- Pearls before Swine—Or Where Does It Say Precisely What I Said?
- Peter Pan Is Alive and Well on Your Board of Education
- Questions That Don't Want Answers
- "Safe No's"
- Smoking Guns—Or How Much Proof Do You Need Anyway?

- The Old Rubber Stamp Gambit
- *"Vox Populi, Vox Dei"*—II

(2) Superintendent/Board Relationships
  - "And the Greatest of These Is . . ."—I
  - Brave, Loyal, Trustworthy . . .
  - Chinese Water Tortures
  - "Dammit, I Can So Accept Criticism!"
  - Dress Rehearsals
  - Let's Be Sure We're All on the Same Page Here
  - Oh Yeah—And You're Another!
  - One Last Great Act of Defiance
  - The Parable of the Superintendent and the Duck
  - Ray Bolger and Other Straw Persons
  - Rotate the Dancers a Quarter Turn to the Left

PRACTICE MAKES PERFECT—BOARD OF EDUCATION EVALUATION

Attend one or more board of education meetings and evaluate the board of education in the areas given in the list below. Rate each applicable item for the board of education as a body using the following indicators: (+) for (choose one) outstanding, superior, strong, above average, excellent; (0) for meets standards, average, adequate, satisfactory; (−) for needs improvement, below average, poor, unsatisfactory; or (NO) for not observed.

Also rate each applicable item as it applies to the board as a collection of individuals or to the collection of administrative individuals in attendance (double asterisks indicate characteristics which cannot be so rated): (1) for relatively uniform knowledge, attitudes, or performance among board members or administrators; (2) for significant variance in knowledge, attitudes, or performance among board members; (3) for major variance in knowledge, attitudes, or performance among board members; or (NO) for not observed.

(1) Meeting procedures and conduct: written procedures for conduct of board meetings**; agendas—length, organization, quality**; members' preparation for meeting; meeting length—appropriateness of**; allocation of time to issues—major issues allocated greater board time and attention; participation by board members and willingness to take positions and express opinions;

atmosphere and tone of meetings; focus on issues and avoidance of personality differences; attention to speakers—public, board, staff; executive sessions—proper use and procedures**

Observations: _____

_____

_____

(2) Relationships with superintendent of schools: differentiation between policy role of board and administrative responsibilities of the superintendent of schools; adherence to defined channels of authority and responsibility; appropriate use of board committees**; referral of concerns, complaints, and criticisms to appropriate school staff with information to superintendent of their action; mutual respect and trust between board and superintendent, with commendation where earned and constructive criticism as needed; consideration of superintendent recommendations prior to making decisions; use of superintendent as primary source of information to board; public support of superintendent, especially in pressure situations; handling of differences between board and superintendent

Observations: _____

_____

_____

(3) Board problem solving and decision making: definition of task at hand or problem to be solved; objective examination of alternatives with consideration of advantages and disadvantages of each; identification of blockages to desired change and strategies to remove them; consideration of group goals, as well as personal points of view; ability to reach closure and decide; board members in the minority on supporting majority decisions; determination of specific evaluation procedures for outcomes of or programs resulting from major decisions

Observations: _____

(4) Delegation of tasks to superintendent; clear definition of tasks to be accomplished**; development and use of criteria to measure superintendent's success or failure in carrying out delegated assignments**; provision of adequate resources to superintendent for accomplishing tasks assigned**; establishment of necessary checkpoints to evaluate superintendent progress with delegated tasks**

Observations: _____

_____

(5) Board chairman: use of appropriate parliamentary procedures**; keeps discussions on topic**; conflict resolution techniques and results**

(6) Board relationships with instructional program: board actions consistent with district educational philosophy and goals; differentiation of curriculum and program responsibilities between board and staff; program decisions based on student welfare

Observations: _____

_____

(7) Financial management: decisions made with appropriate regard for fiscal responsibility; financial priorities established for decision making

Observations: _____

_____

(8) Community relationships: knowledge and understanding of community attitudes and special interests; appropriate balance between public opinion and board judgment; ability to work with, and resist if necessary, special interest groups; ability to adopt and maintain board positions under public pressure; relationships with news media**; citizen attendance and participation at board meetings**

Observations: _____

_____

_____

The next two sections are administrative responsibilities but tied so directly to board of education meetings that they may be evaluated as integral parts of a board evaluation:

(9) Presentations—superintendent or other staff presentations: adequacy of information; organization; clarity; specific recommendations from superintendent of schools—alternative courses of action given as appropriate

Observations: _____

_____

_____

(10) Superintendent information to board: quality**; amount**

Observations: _____

_____

_____

PRACTICE MAKES PERFECT—BOARD OF EDUCATION POLICY EXERCISE

Review your district's, or any district's, board of education policy and regulations manual against the following criteria:

(*1*) Policy's age and currency, including (a) date of most recent major policy revision and (b) frequency of policy changes or the number of years in which one or more policies have been revised. (This criteria indicates the presence or absence of an active board of education policy committee, as well as superintendent interest in use of board policy as a guide in decision making.)

(*2*) In your judgment, have policies and regulations been assigned high priorities by boards and superintendents of schools? What evidence do you have for that point of view?

(*3*) Do administrators, teachers, parents, and sometimes students participate in development, review, and revision of policies and regulations?

(*4*) Are procedures for development and revision of policies and regulations clear and well understood?

(*5*) Do participants in policy development, review, and revision understand their roles and authority?

(*6*) Are board of education, administrative, and staff lines of communication observed?

(*7*) Is the use of policies and regulations as guides to action stressed at all organizational levels?

(*8*) Are policy or regulatory violations by school district personnel overlooked and/or accepted?

(*9*) Is policy and regulatory effectiveness monitored regularly by boards of education, superintendents of schools, and other staff?

(*10*) Are administrators and board members aware of, and do they guard against, intrinsic problems of policies and regulations?

CHAPTER 5

Legal Issues

HOW DID WE GET HERE FROM WHERE?

EARLY AMERICAN LAWS were rooted in English codification of cultural practices into the "common law" adopted by English courts as guides to judicial decisions. Common law still forms the basis for much of modern American jurisprudence.

At federal, state, and local levels, the various elected and appointed legislative, regulatory, and governmental officials, documents, and judicial systems sharing legal control of American public education are divided among federal, state, and local governmental bodies; federal and state courts; and the U.S. Constitution, state constitutions, and local charters and ordinances. The organization of these entities includes (1) constitutions, federal and state, and local charters and ordinances; (2) federal and state judicial systems; (3) legislation, federal and state, and board policies; (4) federal and state agencies and regulations; and (5) local governmental bodies and elected and appointed officials:

- federal: United States Constitution; federal courts including the United States Supreme Court, Circuit Courts of Appeal, and federal district courts; congressional legislation; federal regulatory departments
- state: state constitutions; state judicial systems; state legislatures and state statutes; state agencies created by legislatures, including state departments of education and agency regulations
- local: town, county, and other consolidated legislative and regulatory bodies and fiscal authorities; local ordinances, charters, and regulations; boards of education; board of education policies; superintendents of schools; superintendents' administrative regulations

In combination and separately, each of these fourteen entities and their part in shaping American education are discussed briefly in this section.

Federal—United States Constitution

The U.S. Constitution establishes the framework within which Congressional acts, state constitutions, state legislation, local government ordinances and rules, and board of education policies must fall. Although the Constitution is important to public education, it doesn't refer specifically to education; however, the contracts clause of the Constitution and its first, fourth, fifth, tenth, and fourteenth amendments have been and continue to be important to American education.

ARTICLE I, SECTION 10

"No State shall enter into any Treaty, Alliance, or Confederation; grant Letters of Marque and Reprisal; coin Money; emit Bills of Credit; make any Thing but gold and silver Coin a Tender in Payment of Debts; pass any Bill of Attainder, ex post facto Law, or Law <u>impairing the Obligation of Contracts</u>, or grant any Title of Nobility."

This article of the Constitution is often referred to as the *contracts clause,* and the underlined portion of this constitutional provision has been cited relative to state legislative enactments changing state retirement statutes, teacher tenure, etc. Those opposed to such changes cite Article I, Section 10, along with assertions that the particular statutory relationship is contractual between the state and its employees. If courts agree and view existing statutory retirement or tenure provisions to be contractual, legislative acts "impairing the obligation of contracts" would be rendered unconstitutional by the contracts clause.

FIRST AMENDMENT

"Congress shall make no law respecting an (1) <u>establishment of religion</u>, or (2) <u>prohibiting the free exercise thereof</u>, or (3) <u>abridging the freedom of speech, or of the press; or the right of the people peaceably to assemble, and</u> (4) <u>to petition the Government for a redress of grievances</u>."

Prohibitions in the first amendment apply only to the U.S. Congress, but Supreme Court interpretations of a fourteenth amendment provision (prohibiting a state's denial "to any person within its jurisdiction the equal protection of the laws") make first amendment provisions applicable to states, as well as the federal government. The first amendment contains four concepts, which historically have been and which continue to be, major influences in shaping American public education. Key words of each concept in the text of the first amendment printed above are underlined and identified with numbers from (1) through (4).

(*1*) The prohibition against "an establishment of religion" by Congress is the establishment clause of the U.S. Constitution and figures prominently in arguments by those opposed to federal funds being used in private schools with religious affiliations; Supreme Court decisions have allowed state and federal expenditures for specific services in private schools under its "child benefit theory," first enunciated in a Louisiana decision on state funding for private school textbooks, and disallowed others that, on the surface, seem very similar to those approved. Although patterns are sometimes discernible in the high court's decisions, it has also rendered seemingly contradictory pronouncements, with labyrinthine reasoning to explain why certain practices are or aren't constitutional, and there are even greater variations among decisions from the fifty different state court systems. Fortunately, individual school district actions involving the "establishment clause" are clearly prescribed in or proscribed by state statutes, and school superintendents, in this area of school law at least, administer a system "designed by geniuses to be executed by idiots"—sometimes this can be comforting as well as infuriating.

(*2*) The Constitutional bar against Congressional prohibition of the free exercise (of religion) thereof, although important historically and currently in assuring religious freedom, doesn't figure prominently in daily educational life; however, it may be invoked against employers who act against persons because of some religious affiliation not considered appropriate by employers—as would the fourteenth amendment's prohibitions against abridging the privileges or immunities of citizens and against denying "to any person within its jurisdiction the equal protection of the laws."

(*3*) Its "freedom of speech" section is invoked to uphold rights of educational employees and students to express views contrary to management positions; free speech includes symbolic expression, as well as verbal expression, either written or oral.

(*4*) The right of the people peaceably to assemble and to petition the government for a redress of grievances section of the first amendment is invoked in defense of employees' rights to picket schools during strikes or in other group actions to affect educational policy or decision making.

FOURTH AMENDMENT

"The right of people to be secure in their persons, houses, papers, and effects, against unreasonable searches and seizures, shall not be violated, and no warrants shall issue, but upon probable cause, supported by oath or affirmation, and particularly describing the place to be searched, and the persons or things to be seized."

The fourth amendment bears on administrative actions, and the results thereof, in student personal searches, in property searches within school buildings or on school grounds, and on administrative involvement with law enforcement officials' investigations, on school property, of alleged crimes. Court decisions allow school personnel greater latitude in searches of students and school property; "reasonable" instead of "probable" cause is the usual standard to be met, and the difference is substantive, usually obviating the necessity of warrants prior to searches. Regardless, there are sensitive issues in personal searches, and even in property searches, which indicate the need for administrative caution in these areas—although often it's "commonsensical" to carry out searches.

FIFTH AMENDMENT

"No person shall be held to answer for a capital, or otherwise infamous crime, unless on a presentment or indictment of a Grand Jury, except in cases arising in the land or naval forces or in the Militia, when in actual service in time of War or public danger; nor shall be compelled in any criminal case to be a witness against himself, nor be deprived of life, liberty, or property, without due process of law, nor shall private property be taken for public use, without just compensation."

The fifth amendment prohibition against being "a witness against himself" hasn't been held to apply in typical student disciplinary cases—unless law enforcement officials are investigating a crime with which the student will be charged. However, the section about taking private property for public use is involved in "eminent domain" issues, where a school district wants a particular piece of private property for educational purposes.

TENTH AMENDMENT

"The powers not delegated to the United States by the Constitution, nor prohibited by it to the States, are reserved to the States respectively, or to the people." It is from this "express powers" clause that states derive their control of public education. Education is therefore a state function, and states have the authority over local public education. Boards of education are subservient to state control, and board members are agents of the state.

FOURTEENTH AMENDMENT, SECTION 1

"All persons born or naturalized in the United States, and subject to the jurisdiction thereof, are citizens of the United States and of the State wherein they reside. No State shall make or enforce any law which shall abridge the privileges or immunities of citizens of the United States; nor shall any State deprive any person of life, liberty or property, without due process of law; nor deny to any person within its jurisdiction the equal protection of the laws."

As stated earlier in comments on the relationship between the fourteenth and the first amendments, Supreme Court interpretations of the first section of the fourteenth amendment make first amendment provisions applicable to states, as well as to the federal government. Of the five sections in the fourteenth amendment, the first applies significantly to public education, and the two important parts of Section 1 are underlined. "Due process" applies to (1) legislative acts (substantive due process) to ensure they are within the legitimate authority of the legislative body and also to (2) ensure that due process, or all legally required actions, have been taken in administrative attempts to follow or enforce legitimate statutory intent (procedural due process.)

Supreme Court decisions on procedural due process in student discipline require simply that students be told what they are accused of having done wrong and given the chance to explain their version of issues to school authorities who will listen to their explanations with open minds; when those procedural requirements have been met, due process has been afforded to students.

The "equal protection clause" of the fourteenth amendment and individual state constitutional provisions have been widely used either together or separately in cases involving state educational expenditure formulas for financial support of local school districts. As a variation of that, the fourteenth amendment equal protection clause has also been invoked in cases of alleged de facto segregation, especially involving minority student concentrations in cities and larger school districts.

Federal Judiciary

UNITED STATES SUPREME COURT

This nine-member federal court is established by the U.S. Constitution and is superior to all other courts on federal issues—Constitutional or legislative. The Supreme Court can hear appeals from the Federal Circuit Courts of Appeal or from decisions of the highest state courts when federal Constitutional issues or federal statutes are involved.

FEDERAL CIRCUIT COURTS OF APPEAL

There are twelve circuit courts nationally, which hear appeals from rulings of the United States District Courts of the federal judicial system. Appeals from the twelve circuit courts' decisions are heard by the Supreme Court.

UNITED STATES DISTRICT COURTS

District courts, throughout the nation and its commonwealths, territories, and the District of Columbia, decide legal issues arising from federal jurisdiction over Constitutional or federal legislative issues. Appeals from district courts are heard by the appropriate Circuit Court of Appeal.

CONGRESSIONAL LEGISLATION AND FEDERAL DEPARTMENT REGULATIONS

Federal legislation stems from enactments of the U.S. Congress and its regulatory agencies created by congressional action.

State

STATE CONSTITUTIONS

Paralleling the function of the U.S. Constitution, the fifty state constitutions provide frameworks for state legislation and have authority over it. State constitutions are interpreted by state judiciary systems and they fall within the authority of the U.S. Constitution.

STATE JUDICIARY SYSTEMS

State court organizations vary among the fifty separate state jurisdictions; however, they all provide lower trial courts and usually two appellate court stages, for example, superior courts, a state court of appeals, and a state supreme court. State courts are judicial equals of federal courts, except for the U.S. Supreme Court in interpreting the U.S. Constitution and the meaning of federal legislation; their pronouncements on federal issues are reviewable by the U.S. Supreme Court. Legal controversies end in the highest state court unless they have Constitutional or federal legislative implications, in which case they may be heard by the Supreme Court of the United States.

STATE LEGISLATURES AND STATE STATUTES

Through their legislative enactments, state legislatures have primary control of public education in the respective fifty states, subject only to judicial review of actions to ensure consistency with their state constitutions and other state legislation and U.S. Supreme Court review of the legal compatibility of state legislative enactments with the national Constitution and/or federal legislation.

STATE AGENCIES, STATE DEPARTMENTS OF EDUCATION, AND AGENCY REGULATIONS

As creatures of their respective state legislatures, state education departments by any name promulgate regulations that control public school operation. Although state departments of education have direct responsibility to legislatures for administering state public education, other state agencies also issue regulations affecting public school districts and their students—state health departments, child protection agencies, state labor departments, etc. State departments may be overseen by state boards of education, or similar bodies (often appointed by state governors), and their commissioners of education (sometimes with other titles) who administer the state education department; relationships of commissioners and their boards are analogous to those of local boards of education and superintendents of schools.

State boards of education and commissioners of education need to maintain good working relationships with state governors and legislatures to advance the cause of public education in the states. Commissioners of education have a national organization, a council of chief states officers, who meet at intervals to review educational issues of common interest and probably to exchange war stories about politicized state boards of education, inept legislators, and unruly governors.

Local

TOWN, COUNTY, AND OTHER LEGISLATIVE AND REGULATORY BODIES AND FISCAL AUTHORITIES

Although public education is a state responsibility, its complexity suggests the need for state legislatures to share some aspects of its governance. Therefore, state legislation delegates responsibilities to various local governmental units. Most often, for example, control of educational expenditures lies within the jurisdiction of towns or counties or parishes. On the national level, New England states' public school districts are coterminous with town or city boundaries (sometimes in regional groupings of towns), but in many southern states and the west, county school districts (or variations thereof) are the norm.

Fiscal control of education at the local level varies widely among various state jurisdictions; among specific bodies having fiscal control of local educational programs can be found boards of education that are "fiscally independent," town or city councils, boards of finance (in New England states), and others. In some instances, the same groups serve as fiscal authorities and as the legislative authority over boards of education that are not fiscally independent, and, at other times, the electorate carries out this function in referenda or school district meetings such as town meetings or regional school district meetings.

LOCAL ORDINANCES, CHARTERS, REGULATIONS, COMPACTS

In local governmental jurisdictions, these documents parallel state and federal constitutions in providing frameworks within which town, county, and other legislative and regulatory bodies and fiscal authorities function in their exercise of control over local public education.

BOARDS OF EDUCATION

Local boards of education are delegated, through state legislation and regulation, significant control over local public education, its personnel, and its students. Each state's laws will differ in details; as one example of major educational statutes, among a myriad of other related statutes, delegating authority and providing direction to boards of education, Connecticut general statutes provide

(*1*) *Duties of boards of education [46]:* Each local or regional board of education shall maintain good public elementary and secondary schools, implement the educational interests of the state as defined in Section 10-4a, and provide such other educational activities as in its judgment will best serve the interests of the school district in accordance with provisions of the general statutes and shall give all the children of the school district as nearly equal advantages as may be practicable; shall have charge of the schools of its respective school district; shall make a continuing study of the need for school facilities and of a long-term school building program and from time to time make recommendations based on such study to the town; shall have the care, maintenance, and operation of buildings, lands, apparatus, and other property used for school purposes and at all times shall insure all such buildings and all capital equipment contained therein against loss in an amount not less than eighty percent of replacement cost; shall determine the number age and qualifications of the pupils to be admitted into each school; shall employ and dismiss the teachers of the schools of such district subject to the provisions of Sections 10-151 and 10-158a; shall designate the schools that shall be attended by the various children within the school district; shall make such provisions as will enable each child of school age residing in the district to attend some public day school for the period required by law and provide for the transportation of children wherever transportation is reasonable and desirable and, for such purpose, may make contracts covering periods of not more than five years or may arrange with the board of education of an adjacent town for the instruction therein of such children as can attend school in such adjacent town more conveniently; shall cause each child seven years of age and over and under sixteen living in the school district to attend school in accordance with the provisions of Section 10-184; and shall perform all acts required of it by the town or necessary to carry into effect the powers and duties imposed by law.

(2) *Boards of education to prescribe rules, policies, and procedures [47]:* Boards of education shall prescribe rules for the management, studies, classification, and discipline of the public schools and, subject to the control of the state board of education, the textbooks to be used; shall make rules for the control, within their respective jurisdictions, of school library media centers and approve the selection of books and other educational media therefor; and shall approve plans for public school buildings and superintend any high or graded school in the manner specified in this title.

From the breadth of delegated authority in Connecticut statutes, it would appear that boards of education exercise primary governance and operation of American public education.

BOARD OF EDUCATION POLICIES

Board of education policy translates beliefs and desires of elected officials into action through the superintendent of schools, and, except for specific board meeting decisions, policy development is a board's best way to provide school district direction. Policy manuals contain three basic types of entries: board of education policies (guides for discretionary action by superintendents of schools), superintendent of schools regulations (amplifications of board policies into specific actions), and board of education bylaws (rules governing boards of education internal operations).

Typical policy manuals contain major sections on board goals and objectives, public relations, administration, business, personnel, students, instruction, buildings, and bylaws of the board.

SUPERINTENDENTS OF SCHOOLS

In selecting superintendents of schools, boards of education may seek the advice and counsel of interested individuals or an advisory committee, and it may hire consultants to assist. Superintendents must be properly certified by the state; however, boards may require qualifications in addition to those prescribed by state boards of education. A typical board policy outlining duties and responsibilities of superintendents of schools might include the following.

Introduction

The superintendent of schools shall be the chief executive officer of the board of education and shall be responsible for the management of the public schools in the district within federal and state laws and regulations and board of education policies. He/she shall be responsible to the board as a body and not to individuals on the board and shall be responsible for the execution of all decisions and the administration of board policies and directions concerning school system operations. The superintendent shall have the power to act in matters not covered by board policy, subject to such actions being reviewed by the board at a regular meeting.

Board Relationships and Responsibilities of the Superintendent of Schools

(*1*) Serve as ex-officio member of all board committees, except those dealing with the personal status of the superintendent.

(*2*) Act as professional advisor and executive agent of the board.

(*3*) Attend board meetings with the right to speak on all issues before the board.

(*4*) Participate in local, state, and national professional organizations.

(*5*) Develop and direct an active and effective program of community relations.

(*6*) Maintain a cooperative working relationship with the community and its agencies.

Personnel Responsibilities of the Superintendent of Schools

(*1*) Develop effective professional relationships with and among administrators, teachers, and other staff.

(*2*) Organize, arrange, and direct the administration and the staff.

(*3*) Develop and operate a system of staff evaluation of each employee of the board.

(*4*) Develop and operate staff in-service programs and activities.

(*5*) Recommend to the board new positions or reductions of positions.

(*6*) Assign, transfer, and classify employees for salary purposes.

(*7*) Employ staff as authorized by the board of education and report such actions to the board (or recommend employment of personnel to the board for its approval). Suspend, terminate, accept resignations, approve leaves for support staff; recommend terminations, suspensions, and leaves of absence for certified personnel (in accordance with current agreements – individual or collective).

Educational Program Responsibilities of the Superintendent of Schools

(*1*) Direct and manage the instructional program of the school system.
(*2*) Develop and maintain curricula for all subjects and programs and recommend curriculum changes for board of education review and action.
(*3*) Recommend to the board basal textbook adoptions.
(*4*) Recommend to the board changes in district educational goals and/or objectives.
(*5*) Develop and operate a program of standardized testing and reporting.
(*6*) Develop and manage the system of reporting to parents on student progress and achievement.
(*7*) Develop standards of student achievement and for student promotion and placement.
(*8*) Organize and operate appropriate programs of special education and related services.

Business and Fiscal Operation Responsibilities of the Superintendent of Schools

(*1*) Prepare an annual school budget for review and action by the board of education.
(*2*) Implement and manage the school system budget within appropriated funds.
(*3*) Develop and direct a system for requisitioning, purchasing, contracting, and bidding district goods and/or services within budget limits.
(*4*) Develop and supervise a system for payrolls, payment of bills, and financial record keeping.
(*5*) Operate the schools efficiently with careful use of public funds.
(*6*) Direct and supervise the district's food service program.

Facilities Responsibilities of the Superintendent of Schools

(*1*) Develop procedures for and direct school building operation, cleanliness, and maintenance.

(*2*) Identify building needs and recommend corrective or other measures to the board of education.

(*3*) Prepare educational specifications for new schools or additions.

Pupil Transportation Responsibilities of the Superintendent of Schools

(*1*) Develop and manage the pupil transportation system, including bus schedules and routes.

(*2*) Develop bus safety and emergency procedures and direct a program to ensure staff and student understanding of such procedures.

Records and Reporting Responsibilities of the Superintendent of Schools

(*1*) Develop and maintain necessary and required records for students and personnel and for the operation of the school system, including financial records.

(*2*) Prepare and submit to the board of education regular status reports on the budget.

(*3*) Prepare and submit to the board of education reports on educational programs, activities, and school system operations as requested by the board and as he/she deems necessary.

(*4*) Prepare and submit all required state, federal, and local reports.

(*5*) Prepare and submit an annual report to the board on the condition of local education with recommendations for changes as appropriate.

General Duties and Responsibilities of the Superintendent of Schools

(*1*) Execute decisions of the board of education requiring staff action.

(*2*) Prepare the agenda for meetings of the board and deliver the agenda and associated materials in advance of the meeting.

(*3*) Recommend policy change to the board of education and maintain official policy manuals.

(4) Develop and approve administrative regulations.

(5) Develop and recommend school attendance areas.

FAXING POLICY MANUALS IS EXPENSIVE

School attorneys should be provided copies of important school district information to help them help school districts in critical legal circumstances. Among district materials that attorneys should be provided, before specific legal problems arise, are board policies, administrative regulations, negotiated employee agreements, board meeting minutes, school and parent handbooks, correspondence on issues that may have potential for litigation, town charters and ordinances, and other mutually agreed on information.

Having complete sets of district publications and other background material already at the attorney's office saves both significant administrative and legal time and money wasted in repeated transmission of documents that already should have been in counsel's files.

FRED AND GINGER

If all school district administrators are free to communicate directly with school attorneys, without clearances from superintendents of schools, the usual results are confusion, unnecessary problems, and very large legal bills.

Relationships built from frequent interactions and communications are almost always more efficient and more effective than those between people who rarely deal with each other. One person, normally the superintendent, working closely with an attorney bypasses the need for gratuitous professional and personal familiarization and the ritual dances that frequently take place in business contacts between people who don't know each other well—if dancing there must be, the partners should know each other's moves as well as Fred Astaire and Ginger Rogers who danced in all those old movies together. Two people who have worked together effectively on many other occasions can get down to business quickly and conduct it efficiently without wasted motion or time.

Often, superintendents can answer other administrators' legal questions easily, and they should be the first persons asked by other administrators. They work cheaper than lawyers; in fact, their advice is free because they are being paid already—and their semi-judicial pronouncements often taste almost as good as the high-priced legal spread.

IT'S THE KIDS, STUPID!

During a recent presidential campaign, one of the candidates was constantly reminded by his advisors, "It's the economy, stupid!" to keep him concentrated on the primary issue of the '92 election. As necessary, school leaders should be reminded, whether by themselves or others if necessary, to focus on kids instead of on arcane legal considerations.

Principals shouldn't be protective of children because litigation might ensue if a child is injured; they should be passionate about school safety because children can be hurt if they aren't. Although choices sometimes must be made that require weighing factors peripheral to the issue's moral center, school districts profit when leadership instincts address the real essence of decisions instead of extrinsic legal considerations. Focusing on legal ramifications to the exclusion of human factors leads to pernicious personal attitudes and negative organizational effects.

When leaders develop patterns of making correct decisions for the wrong reasons, it becomes easier for them to make wrong decisions for the wrong reasons. Regressions from right decisions for the right reasons to wrong decisions for the wrong reasons may be gradual and subtle, but they are real and ever-present leadership pitfalls to be avoided.

Focusing on important issues to the exclusion of less important problems also should apply to life in general—not just to legal issues and attorneys.[136]

JUNKYARD DOGS—I

If a school district ever finds itself saddled with an attorney who habitually prescribes inaction unless he or she can find specific statutory/regulatory authority or specific case law to support what appear to be reasonable actions, those lawyers should be placed in cardboard boxes and abandoned on some other school district's doorstep. An

---

[136]See also, Chapter 1, "Ten Cardinal Principles of Leadership," p. 21.

attorney's lack of confidence may avoid litigation, but it can also immobilize a school district.

School districts should choose legal representatives who are confident enough to give the go-ahead when proposed actions are well considered, rational, and without clear legal precedent against them and who, if problems arise, can provide competent courtroom or other defenses for those actions.

Avoid nervous attorneys who sidle up to the law, watching it constantly out of the corners of their eyes; instead, seek educational counsel who will grab issues firmly the way junkyard dogs latch onto intruders' ankles.

JUNKYARD DOGS—II

No matter how sharp superintendents are about education law, there are particular educational issues that, because they can be as mean as junkyard dogs, require, or at least strongly suggest, legal review and advice: (1) professional staff contract nonrenewals, terminations, and other significant personnel matters; (2) aspects of professional or noninstructional collective bargaining, especially those involving unit certifications, bargaining representative elections, etc.; (3) staff disputes or controversies likely to end up in grievance arbitrations, at state labor relations boards, or at similar administrative proceedings; (4) major differences with parents on children's special education placements and related problems; and (5) board of education policies or administrative regulations with greater than usual potential for legal problems: pupil records, student safety, transportation, student disciplinary procedures, special education, controversial curriculum materials or textbooks, censorship, and church/school issues, etc.

The first line of a middle-aged song goes, "Have you ever been mellow . . . ?" and ends with, "Have you ever let someone else be strong?" That's also good legal advice—even when provided in a musically Socratic style. When superintendents encounter one or more of these legal issues, they should communicate expeditiously with their attorneys and bring them up to date on what has already happened and/or what's about to happen.

LEGAL PEN PALS

Although telephone conversations often are useful to obtain clarifications, follow-up information, or answers to particularly easy questions, written requests for legal recommendations help focus administrative thinking and help attorneys shape their responses. If your lawyers are (as you would hope they would be) professionally successful and, therefore, busy and overworked, written queries also help them keep track of your issues and their suggestions to you.

Also, written questions to attorneys usually generate written answers, which are very helpful when translating attorneys' opinions to boards of education or other third parties. If legal pronouncements must be received over the telephone, administrators should prepare dated summaries of conversations—they may come in handy at some future date.

LEGAL POULTICES, POTIONS, AND ELIXIRS

Lawyers, even very good ones, can't guarantee administrators immunity from the consequences of their leadership decisions or actions. If school leaders are faced with difficult problems and ask their attorneys, "Can we be sued for that?" the answer inevitably is, "Of course, you can, dummy." School districts can be sued no matter what they do—or even if they do nothing at all.

In a Herman Wouk novel, an old doctor was queried about a patient's medical outlook: "Are there any serious risks in his condition? Anything that can go suddenly wrong?" Dr. Eversill replied ". . . As I often tell people, it's a damn risky thing to be born, and the prognosis is a hundred percent bad" [48]. The doctor was correct. Risks make the rounds with superintendents and board members as they exercise their special educational responsibilities as well as in their personal lives. When decisions and actions are logical, right for students and staff, and educationally sound, school leaders must accept a degree of legal uncertainty and do what they believe is right.[137] Fortunately, unlike the ultimate medical prognosis about human life, the legal prognosis isn't always bad for educational decision makers.

The cost of futile attempts to totally immunize yourself from legal risks is just too high for a school system dedicated to getting its job done effectively and expeditiously—and it's impossible anyway.

LOU HOLTZ, ESQ.

Once while visiting a legal relative who allegedly keeps an am-

---

[137]See also, Chapter 4, "Better Odds Are All You Can Expect—In Poker or Leadership Life in General," p. 113.

bulance in his office, I fell into conversation with Geoff, a member of the law firm, who had just returned from court where he watched the group's flamboyant, string tie with big hat, criminal counsel successfully defend a client charged with driving under the influence. Geoff was bubbling over with enthusiasm about the legal skills of the firm's criminal attorney, so I asked him to tell me about the case. He replied, "Well our client was observed, by two policemen in a squad car, driving very slowly and carefully down Navigation Boulevard. He came to a complete stop at each of three red lights, gave a proper right-hand turn signal, and turned right onto a side street. Proceeding up the side street, he also made three complete stops at three stop signs and slowed through two caution lights. Just past the second blinking yellow signal, although he hadn't committed a single traffic offense, the Houston police were suspicious, turned on their red flashers, and pulled him over. When our client got out of his car, he stumbled and fell back against the left front fender, and, when questioned by the cops, he had difficulty communicating clearly and making himself understood to them. At this point, they arrested our man on a DUI charge."

I said I thought the prosecution had what seemed to be a good case, but my lawyer friend said it wasn't nearly good enough. When I asked how the firm's attorney had managed to gain his client's acquittal against such strong evidence, Geoff continued, "OK, here's how he did it. He intentionally brought his client into court a little late for the trial and had him walk from the rear of the courtroom all the way up to the witness stand. As he sort of lurched up the aisle, it was clear to everybody there that our client's right leg was six inches shorter than his left leg, and walking was very awkward and difficult for him. When he got up to the witness chair, he sort of fell back into it helplessly. This made the prosecutor's statements about him stumbling as he got out of his car inconclusive. Then, through ingenious questions requiring answers with particular vowel/consonant combinations as he denied all charges against him, he highlighted our client's serious speech impediment—this wiped out the prosecutor's evidence on the driver's unintelligible speech. As soon as this happened, the judge dismissed the case. Our guy was magnificent."

My response was, "Hell, I could have won that case!" My cavalier dismissal of such legal brilliance definitely hurt Geoff's feelings.

As superintendents work with their school attorneys, they will encounter this strange legal phenomenon regularly. Their lawyers will never be satisfied with administrative documentation and support of the case at hand; they will moan endlessly and loudly about how difficult the district's case will be for them—in the same manner Lou Holtz cries to sportswriters about his next Notre Dame football game against The Little Sisters of the Poor or some other team he expects to beat seventy-three to zip. But, as soon as our attorney appears before the board or the judge or the jury, that same counsel will pronounce, with total conviction, that this is one of the most righteous cases, that the district's legal position in this matter is unshakeable, and that his case is supported by the most damning evidence ever presented before a tribunal—and if you've done a good job assembling the necessary documentation, he's correct.

Nobody wants anybody to think his or her job is simple or easy—but when Lucy Brown, Esq., wins her case, she'll expect you to notice her naturally curly hair; Charlie Brown, Esq., will expect you to overlook his total absence of hair.

SOME OF MY BEST FRIENDS GRADUATED FROM LAW SCHOOL

Correspondence, telephone calls, or visits from solicitors threatening legal action should be referred immediately to your own counsel. Resist temptations to deal personally with opposition lawyers. Referring them to your attorney not only soothes your stomach and calms your disposition, it also lets the lawyers wearing the black hats know you're not someone who recently rode into town on a wagonload of wood. More importantly, it involves your attorneys in the white hats early enough to deflect potential lawsuits or to prepare effectively for trials or hearings if legal escalation of disputes can't be prevented.

THINK FIRST, THEN REACH FOR THE TELEPHONE

An attorney's knowledge of case law is of great value when issues have relevant precedents. The trick is understanding when legal interpretations, or previous judicial decisions, should preempt use of common sense to resolve an issue.

Superintendents should arrange for school attorneys to meet with boards of education and explain their legal limitations—what they can and can't do for school districts. Bad ones, especially real bad ones, might peddle the notion to boards that their legal dispensations, blessings, and wisdom are required for almost any decisions made in school districts. This is one of the primary reasons for school districts to choose their legal counsel so carefully.

Although it is important to know what we don't know, it's also important to know what other people don't know any better than we don't know it.

TAKE TWO OF THESE AND CALL ME IN THE MORNING

Like the multicolored pills that ease emotional stress, attorneys on retainers can be dangerous and habit forming, and a possible side effect is overdependence. Often, legal advisors are asked to do more than they are able to do and to solve problems they shouldn't be asked to solve. Attorneys, even really good ones, can't see into the future—or predict with infallibility judges' decisions or juries' reactions. Judicial outcomes may be ordained by the personalities of plaintiffs, defendants, or opposing counsel; by the temperature in the courtroom; by the judge's sex life,[138] or by any number of other factors that nudge people in one direction or another.

The most serious side effect of having attorneys on call is administrative over-reliance on them to resolve problems that could, and should, be managed with board policy, administrative regulations, references to past practice, an administrators' own professional knowledge, and common sense. Overdependence on outside legal authority produces morally sluggish school leaders and petrified school boards—a poor crop anytime.

PRACTICE MAKES PERFECT—SUMMARIZING THEMES/MAIN IDEAS

Summarize in three or four sentences the themes of each of the following from Chapter 5. Summary examples are given in Appendix C, pp. 474–476.

- How Did We Get Here from Where?
- Faxing Policy Manuals Is Expensive
- Fred and Ginger
- It's the Kids, Stupid!

[138]Or lack thereof.

- Junkyard Dogs—I
- Junkyard Dogs—II
- Legal Pen Pals
- Legal Poultices, Potions, and Elixirs
- Lou Holtz, Esq.
- Some of My Best Friends Graduated from Law School
- Think First, Then Reach for the Telephone
- Take Two of These and Call Me in the Morning

DISCUSSION QUESTIONS

Suggested answers/responses are provided in Appendix C, pp. 476–478.

(1) Distinguish common law from constitutional and statutory law.

(2) Summarize (key words as highlights are sufficient) major educational implications of (a) Article 1, Section 10 of the U.S. Constitution; (b) first amendment; (c) fourth amendment; (d) fifth amendment; (e) tenth amendment and (f) fourteenth amendment.

(3) Identify the two categories of school cases governed by the first amendment on religious freedoms.

(4) Distinguish between substantive and procedural due process.

(5) Identify types of education cases under the fourteenth amendment.

(6) Explain briefly the relationship between the federal constitution and state constitutions.

(7) What is the primary source of statutes affecting public schools?

(8) How do Constitutional limitations affect board of education policies, administrative regulations, and individual teacher regulations?

(9) Identify the three levels of federal courts.

(10) Discuss briefly precedential effect of higher court provisions on lower courts.

CHAPTER 6

The Media

BLAH, BLAH, BLAH, NATASHA

IN ONE OF Gary Larson's *Far Side* cartoons, a dog we'll call Natasha was on the receiving end of a lengthy corrective lecture from the man of her house, in which he was saying something similar to: "Be a good dog, Natasha! Stay at home, Natasha! Keep out of the flower beds, Natasha! Leave the garbage cans alone, Natasha!" etc. The cartoon also showed what the puppy was actually hearing, which was, "Blah, blah, Natasha! Blah, blah, blah, Natasha! Blah, blah, blah, blah, Natasha!"

Because of the media's incessant admonishments of public education and public educators, as they read newspapers or news weeklies, watch and listen to television, and listen to radio, teachers' and administrators' minds actually may be registering, "Blah, blah, blah, *public education;* blah, blah, blah, blah, blah, *principals,* blah, blah, blah, blah, *teachers;* blah, blah, blah, blah, blah, *teachers' salaries;* blah, blah, blah, blah, blah, *SAT scores;* blah, blah, blah, *rising expenditures;* blah, blah, blah, blah, blah, blah, blah, blah.

This may be the communication media's version of the boy who cried wolf—at least as far as educators are concerned. Even many parents are tired of hearing it. The news is often bad, and if there were some realistic balancing of responsibility for it, instead of all the blame landing on schools' doorsteps, and if it were more selective instead of incessant, it might be attended more carefully by all.

According to the media, members of the business community, and many among the general public, public schools should be run like businesses: "If you ran your schools the way I run my business . . ." (insert here the most wonderful thing you could imagine to happen).

As examples of business ethics and acumen, consider the savings and loan scandals of the eighties, the failed banks, stock market rapaciousness and illegalities, the steel industry's (and a number of others) inability to survive foreign competition, the lack of customer attention at

203

many department stores, the quality of automobile repairs, and consumers' inability to speak directly to real people in the age of telephone mailboxes and touchtone telephone conversations with recorded voices. "Hell is a highly organized, computerized, dignified, and virile place with almost but not quite perfect management" [49] – employees in businesses, industries, and corporations, and those who deal with them, can attest to the accuracy of that description in their work lives.

The late eighties and the nineties have seen the "downsizing" of one large corporation after another in the name of competitiveness and survival, and some of it undoubtedly may have been justifiable. Cynics and others may believe it was tied to stock prices and the effect of those on CEO salaries, bonuses, and benefits; they may be at least partially correct.

As the inertia of forward momentum fades under the accumulated weight of fifty- and sixty-hour work weeks and as corporations find it increasingly more difficult to respond to customers and clients, these mammoth personnel reductions will need to be reversed for businesses to function properly. But, after collecting their swollen paychecks, bonuses, stock options, bigger and better club memberships, other perquisites, and their lucrative golden handshakes, those same corporation presidents, who today tell school districts they should run their schools the way the CEOs run their businesses, will retire, leaving behind corporations that are, functionally, only shells of their former selves, or they will move on to plunder other companies or to accept positions on laissez-faire corporate boards where they preside benignly over more of the same short-sighted decisions made by their new little CEO buddies. "Today the villain most in need of curbing is the respectable, exemplary, trusted personage who, strategically placed at the focus of a spider web of fiduciary relations, is able, from his office chair to pick a thousand pockets, poison a thousand minds, or imperil a thousand lives. It is the great scale, high-voltage sinner that needs the shackle" [50]. This quote is from 1907, and its author would seize-up completely if he were a witness to modern business practices.

The press and the American public should examine these realities more carefully, and think twice about telling school superintendents they should run their districts the way American businesses are run. In addition to examples of corporate imperfection[139] cited in this section, each American could recite his or her own litany of personal frustrations and disappointments with defective products; indifferent or un-

---

[139]Actually, much closer to infamy than imperfection.

friendly service; insensitive, indifferent, and unconscionable treatment of employees; and a host of other complaints.

Privatization of American public education is no answer to our abundance of social ills; imperfection is at least as common in corporate enterprise as it is in public education. Fortunately, America also enjoys many outstanding, well-operated privately owned corporations and businesses of all sizes in a variety of endeavors.

The nation also benefits immeasurably from its many outstanding, well-run, public school districts of varying sizes; neither private enterprise nor public education has a monopoly on either efficiency or effectiveness nor on inefficiency or ineffectiveness, and each can learn from the other—but it's dead wrong to propagate the enduring, but totally false, mythology that school people don't understand good business procedures or that businesses, corporations, and industries present perfect models for American public education to emulate.

DEATH UNDER TRACTOR CANCELS
RETIREMENT PLANS OF MAN, 64

This headline appeared in a 1968 edition of an upstate New York newspaper [51], and its accompanying story began: "A 64-year old Connecticut man due to retire to a home he has been planning . . . near here was killed yesterday when the wheel of a farm tractor he had been riding passed over his body." The news story could have as easily been titled "Death under Tractor Ruins Weekend of Man, 64." Sometimes, newspapers and other media "just don't get it."

In 1983, the media gave widespread publicity to particular sections of the *Report of the National Commission on Excellence in Education* [52], *A Nation at Risk,* and the quote that people usually remember from that document, repeated again and again in print, on television, and on the radio, is "If an unfriendly foreign power had attempted to impose on America the mediocre educational performance that exists today, we might well have viewed it as an act of war" [52].

The media also acquainted the general public with the report's recommendations to strengthen high school graduation requirements; to focus secondary school curriculum on English, mathematics, science, social studies, computer science, and foreign languages; for more rigorous and measurable standards; for higher expectations of academic performance and student conduct; for increased admissions requirements to colleges and universities; for an end to grade inflation and social promotion; for more effective use of standardized tests; for improvements in textbooks and other teaching materials; for more student homework; for more effective use of school time and for fewer extraneous demands on instructional time; for longer school days and/or longer school years; for better discipline; for strict attendance policies; for intensive teacher evaluation, merit pay, eleven-month teaching contracts, and career ladders for teachers; for master teacher involvement in teacher preparation programs and new teacher supervision; for administrative professional development in leadership; and for increased leadership roles for superintendents of schools and principals [52].

It was these recommendations, with which most educators would agree strongly, that the media emphasized, along with the inflammatory "unfriendly foreign power" quote. However, the commission report also spoke to parents, students, citizens, the general public, and state and local officials—unfortunately, the media didn't communicate these thoughts from the report clearly, if at all, to the public.

Speaking to parents, the commission charged them with strengthening the character of their children; inculcating a "deep respect for intelligence, achievement, and learning"; setting goals; instilling an "intolerance for the shoddy and second rate"; being adult examples of what children should honor and emulate; encouraging diligent study and discouraging mediocrity; monitoring children's study; nurturing children's curiosity, creativity, and confidence"; being an "active participant in the work of the schools"; exhibiting a "commitment to continued learning" in their own lives; and teaching children that "excellence in education cannot be achieved without intellectual and moral integrity coupled with hard work and commitment" [52].

Students were told they forfeit their chances for a full life when their best educational efforts are withheld; that to give a minimum effort to learning assures a minimum return on that effort; that in the end, it is their work, "that determines how much and how well" they learn; and that they must take hold of their lives, apply their natural gifts and talents, work with dedication and self-discipline, have high self-expectations, and convert every challenge into an opportunity [52].

Citizens and the general public were told there is an urgent need for greater moral and financial support of public schools and for increased public involvement in education; that teachers' salaries are inadequate and must be increased dramatically; "that schools are routinely called on to provide solutions to personal, social, and political problems that the home or other institutions will not or cannot solve;" and that there is a "shoddiness in many walks of American life" and "that this shoddiness is too often reflected in our schools and colleges" [52].

State and local officials were charged with implementing commission reforms and recommendations. The federal government was called on to identify the national interest in education and to provide funds to support those interests; to meet the needs of key groups of students such as the gifted, the handicapped, the disadvantaged, and language minorities; to protect student civil rights; to collect data and research; to underwrite teacher training in areas of shortage; and to provide student financial assistance in research and graduate education [52].

The real meaning of the commission report, when read in its entirety and without preconceptions, is that public education is a national interest, that there is challenge enough for all, and that schools can't solve educational and societal problems alone. The report is an imperative for educational reform and for major societal reform, for higher educational standards and expectations and for higher parental standards and expectations, for stronger administrative leadership and greater support for professional development opportunities, for more rigorous curriculum and for increased student effort and commitment, and for better prepared teachers and higher teachers' salaries. For each of the commission's charges to educators, there were counterbalancing requirements for other elements in American society.[140]

The overall conclusions in the commission report were that strong and effective public schools are crucial to America's future; that students, parents, teachers, principals, superintendents, boards of education, legislators, publishers, the business community, and all citizens must recognize their mutual interdependence; and that, recognizing their common need to place public education at the top of our national priorities, appropriate national resources must be devoted to the task at hand.

For whatever reasons, the national media didn't confront the difficult recommendations to parents and students or recognize the significance of the commission's charges to these key educational constituent groups. They "just didn't get it" then, and they still "just don't get it" today.

---

[140]A number of the more manageable recommendations have been achieved in the twelve years or so since the report made headlines, including significant increases in professional salaries, but charges to parents and students have not been successfully confronted.

DON'T ARGUE WITH PEOPLE WHO
BUY INK BY THE BARREL

Mark Twain is alleged to have cautioned against arguing with those who buy ink by the barrel; that's good advice about the futility of battling the press. No school administrator enjoys reading critical news coverage of his or her educational activities or indictments of the school district or even stories that, although correct, report undesirable happenings within the school system; sometimes letters to the editor rebutting articles or editorials that school leadership believes are unfair may lower their blood pressures, even if the undesirable coverage can't totally be undone.

No one should argue that negative news stories are as welcome to school district leadership as positive ones, but school administration should take some comfort from the following real-world realities: (1) Only a fraction of the school district's parents have time to read the newspaper with all the other responsibilities they have and the multiple obligations they must meet; (2) only a fraction of the fraction of the school district's parents and other citizens who have time to skim the newspaper at all will even notice the article causing you such pain— unless it's on the newspaper's front page with a large damning headline, such as "Death under Conference Table Cancels Retirement Plans of Superintendent, 64"; (3) only a fraction of the fraction who even notice the article at all, of the fraction who have time even to skim the newspaper will read it completely; (4) only a fraction of the fraction who read it completely, of the fraction who noticed it at all, of the fraction who have time even to skim the newspaper will read it correctly; (5) only a fraction of the fraction of those who read it correctly, of the fraction who read it completely, of the fraction who noticed it at all, of the fraction of those with time enough even to skim the newspaper will understand its import; and (6) only a fraction of the fraction of those who understand its import, of the fraction who read the article correctly, of the fraction who read it completely, of the fraction who noticed it at all will give a damn anyway.[141]

Even if bad press isn't as awful as you might think, superintendents and other school administrators should observe a few commonsense rules of dealing with reporters and other media representatives: (1) Recognize that, regardless of what nice people they may be, their responsibilities are very different from yours, and they represent interests

---

[141]So maybe three people in town are unhappy—you can live with that.

that depart from yours. (2) Be receptive to calls and inquiries from the media; return calls promptly if you weren't available when they originally called. (3) Be honest, but put the best light you can on the issues, while at the same time being open about district problems under discussion and what you are doing to resolve them. (4) Provide them, unasked, board meeting agendas and as much backup material as reasonably possible. (5) Speak with reporters immediately after meetings if it can be arranged with an offer to amplify or clarify anything that might be helpful. (6) Offer to call their office with late-breaking meeting information or decisions that take place later in the meeting after newspaper deadlines had required them to leave the meeting. (7) Don't expect them not to print any part of what you tell them unless they volunteer to you that they won't, and be careful even then. It's also better not to initiate conversations prefaced by statements, or even requests, that what you are about to say should be off the record. Once you've opened a topic that way, even if they agree to keep administrative comments out of the paper, you can be sure they'll be intrigued by your concern about publicity and poke around trying to discover what's happening. (8) Avoid the phrase "no comment" because it's so reminiscent of statements from convicted felons fleeing courtrooms with coats over their faces. Instead, say something closer to, "Keith, you know legal constraints and the feelings of those involved don't permit me to talk about that with you." If Keith then quotes you as saying, "No comment," explain to him, the next time you're together, that wasn't what you said and that you'd appreciate accurate quotes instead of "canned" phrases. (9) Don't react angrily or inappropriately to provocative or naive questions. Once when some knuckleheaded kid had exploded a homemade pipe bomb in the corridor during classes, we were deluged with newspaper reporters and TV talking heads with microphones. The state police public relations officer who was at the scene along with his troopers suggested I have a press conference with the mob on the school's front steps. When I watched the evening news, the first shot was of the superintendent of schools laughing, apparently about the bomb, but really because the first question I was asked by a television reporter was, "When you left home this morning, did you expect this was going to happen?" After I stopped laughing, I explained that no, I was surprised by the event, which had never occurred before in that district or any other with which I'd been connected over a moderately lengthy educational career. (10) Understand a reporter's limitations. The odds are high that persons covering school news will be young men or women in their first reportorial positions, who are just beginning to learn their craft. They probably possess boundless energy, for a time at least an idealistic view of the world, and a desire to do the best possible job. Support them with your patience and understanding, and when their stories are confused, review them gently with the reporter, thoroughly explaining errors, ambiguities, or misunderstandings. All administrators should be teachers anyway, and, without being obvious or patronizing, help these young men and women better understand the educational issues they cover. When school leadership follows these and similar guidelines, the press may still hand them their heads, but the odds grow less that this will happen, and they're the right things to do anyway, regardless of whether or not it improves your media coverage. Chances are, however, it will.[142]

PRELUDE TO A VAST ARMADA OF SMALL BOATS

The primary meaning of Chapter 11's "A Vast Armada of Small Boats" is obviously that superintendents should retire when they finally hear voices. But an important secondary theme is that too many elected and self-anointed officials, dignitaries, and sometimes even superintendents speak with little understanding about perceived educational problems and offer such peripheral solutions as school choice, privatization, or restructuring—examples of more recent, generally specious, notions among an endless series of fads, gimmicks, and cheap answers to complex problems that threaten to swamp American public education.

That said, many new ideas, theories, and concepts should be explored realistically and thoroughly. Often, educational problems stem not from new programs or educational approaches, even when they're no more effective than the ones that they replace, but more often grow out of inflated expectations from mindless attempts to impose universal solutions onto the complicated business of teaching and learning and from the aggressive, commercial marketing of every professorial or corporate belch, or other eructation, as the salvation of the public schools.

If only school districts would do this new thing they are being told to do, instead of what experience tells them is right, all public education's problems would go away. Yeah, sure! The "corporate/legislative/university/state education department/media complex" is just as dangerous

[142]See also, Chapter 4, "Better Odds Are All You Can Expect—In Poker or Leadership Life in General," p. 113.

to public education as the "military/industrial complex's" danger to the nation as characterized by a retiring president.[143]

Throughout their careers, many superintendents have resisted those who promote each new educational toy as if it assures a public school millennium. Anyone in a position of educational leadership has made mistakes and embraced ethereal new programs that never seem to work out as promised—or may have grossly oversold legitimate innovations. That's not surprising because education must develop different approaches if it wants to improve, and educators must recognize salutary educational and public relations benefits from telling constituents about worthwhile new educational ideas and activities.

But it's crucial for superintendents, principals, and board of education members to hold foremost in their thoughts that the simple, but enormously complex, day-to-day interactions between teacher and pupil are, always have been, and always will be the essence of the educational enterprise. There are no organizational shortcuts to good education. Teachers achieve success with students "the old fashioned way—they earn it." They earn it with dedication, hard work, and daily attention to important details.

The nation should wish, for all its school districts, educational leadership that is simultaneously progressive and cautiously conservative; leadership that is open to careful examination and trial of new approaches and ideas, but that holds firmly to what is most important in education—classroom teachers' daily efforts with kids, one at a time, in small groups, class by class, day by day, year by year; leadership that has a highly developed version of what Ernest Hemingway called his built-in B.S. detector; and finally, leadership that, while acknowledging public education's imperfections, defends teachers and principals against misplaced attacks on them, instead of on the real cause of public education's perceived defects. A brief quote from a newspaper column at least skirts the edges of the last point:

> Americans once expected parents to raise their children in accordance with the dominant cultural message. Today, they are expected to raise their children in opposition . . . [to that message].

> Once the chorus of cultural values was full of ministers, teachers, neighbors, leaders. . . . Now the messengers are Ninja Turtles, Madonna, rap groups, and celebrities pushing sneakers. It isn't that parents can't say no. It's that there's so much more to say no to. That's what makes child raising harder. [53]

[143]For our difficult fight against the "corporate/legislative/university/state education department/ media complex," educators would be pleased to enlist Dwight Eisenhower in our army.

Good for Ms. Goodman. Her message is true enough as far as it goes, but today's schools are expected to educate kids, also in opposition to the dominant cultural message and its messengers, and successfully teach students, many of whose parents haven't been able to say no to them as often as they should have—and some may never have said it. All of this makes education incredibly more difficult than it once was, but the public wouldn't understand that from reading their newspapers and national weeklies, listening to their radios, or watching their televisions.[144]

"ROUND UP THE USUAL SUSPECT . . ."

Claude Rains had an often quoted line from "Casablanca." As a world-weary inspector of the Casablanca gendarmerie, he cynically directs his subordinate (who has just reported the murder of a German general) to "round up the usual suspects"—all the while knowing Humphrey Bogart is the guilty party but wishing to protect him. It's here that Rick, or Humphrey, says, "This is the beginning of a beautiful friendship."

When unpleasant events or actions take place in a school district, the board of education, media, parents, and sometimes even staff, are always prepared to round up their usual suspect—the superintendent of schools. If school leaders aren't willing to serve as the singular "usual suspect" for whatever educational ills befall a school district, they're in the wrong job because they will be rounded up and held responsible for every aberrant act of any district student or employee. Of course, it's not fair, and life often isn't, but somebody must be responsible no matter how unpleasant that is for the person responsible—and that person is inevitably the educator at the top of the local pyramid.

Now matter how much authority is delegated, responsibility can't be delegated along with it—regardless of a district's commitment to site-based management and decentralized decision making.

TAMING THE 450-POUND MEDIA GORILLA— A ONE-ACT MORALITY PLAY

A midwestern superintendent received a call at his office one morning from his distraught wife.

[144]See also, this chapter, "Taming the 450-Pound Media Gorilla—A One-Act Morality Play," p. 212 and "Why Sometimes I've Believed as Many as Six Impossible Things before Breakfast," p. 218.

"Honey, you've got to come home right away. There's a gorilla in the garden!"

"A what? Where?"

A gorilla! In the garden!"

"Stay calm, and stay in the kitchen. I'll be right home."

The superintendent arrived from the office in record time. Cautiously peering around the edge of the house into the garden, he couldn't see any gorilla. Emboldened, he walked a bit further and realized the gorilla had climbed a large oak tree just outside the garden area—the beast seemed at least momentarily content drowsing amid the branches.

The superintendent went back into the house and into the kitchen where his anxious wife awaited him. "Well?" she asked.

"It's a gorilla alright. A big one, too."

"What are you going to do?"

"I'm not sure. Hand me the yellow pages."

Sure enough, under "Gorilla," there were quite a few entries in the yellow pages, including "Used Gorillas Bought and Sold," "Gorilla Mimes," "Gorilla Rentals and Leasing," a "Gorillaphobes Support Group," "Gorilla Tuxedos and Other Formal Attire," "The Gorilla School of Dance—Tap, Jazz, Acrobatic, Ballroom, and Ballet," and many others in a half dozen pages of "Gorilla" entries; finally, he spotted what he was looking for—"Smith and Robinson, Gorilla Catchers." Excitedly, he dialed the gorilla catcher's number, and a man's voice answered: "Smith and Robinson, Gorilla Catchers, Smith speaking, can I help you?"

"Oh, God, yes, this is Bill Brent, and there's a gorilla in a tree at my house."

"Relax, what's your address?"

"It's 110 Lakewood Road."

"I know the area. I can be there in ten minutes. But my partner Robinson is on vacation, so I may need a little help from you."

"I don't know. . . ."

"Look it's not dangerous at all, and I'll explain when I get there, but in the meantime I need to know whether the gorilla is male or female."

"I'm not really sure. I was so excited when I saw it. Does it really matter?"

"Trust me. This is my business. I really need to know. But look, I'll come prepared for either. When I get there, it will help though if you can tell me whether it's a male or female."

"OK, I'll try."

"Good. Meet me at the curb at the front of your house in ten minutes."

"I will, and hurry!"

Hanging up the telephone, the superintendent told his wife to stay right there in the kitchen, and he tiptoed cautiously through the garden to find the gorilla still resting in the oak tree. As the superintendent crept closer, he was able to identify the animal's gender—a male alright. He ran to the front of his house to wait for Smith.

A couple of minutes earlier than promised, a dilapidated old pickup truck rattled up to the superintendent's house. A handpainted sign on the door of the truck reassured the superintendent this was indeed the truck from "Smith and Robinson—Gorilla Catchers." The cargo area in the rear confirmed his diagnosis, filled as it was with traps, lines, shackles, pulleys, and assorted other gorilla catching hardware, and, on the front seat alongside the driver, there were also a stepstool, net, cage of white mice, shotgun, pair of handcuffs, and a gigantic near-sighted English bulldog with an obviously nasty disposition and the largest teeth you've ever seen.[145]

Jumping quickly out of his dilapidated pickup truck and hurriedly donning his special purchase, hand-sewn, Banana Republic gorilla catcher's jacket, Smith demanded: "Well, what's the story? Are we looking at a male or female here?"

"I'm sure it's a male," answered the superintendent, "but what's the difference?"

"Big difference! If it were a female, I'd need the stepstool, the net, and the cage of white mice. But since it's a male, we'll take the shotgun, the pair of handcuffs, and my friend the gigantic nearsighted English bulldog with the nasty disposition and the largest teeth you've probably ever seen. And since it's a male, I'm definitely going to need your help. I'll explain when we get around back."

"Oh man, I'm not so sure I want to get close to that thing."

"Don't worry about it; I've done this for years. Just come on with me."

At that, Smith strode confidently around to the back of the house carrying the handcuffs in the special purchase, hand-sewn, Banana Republic gorilla catcher's special handcuff pocket of his special purchase, hand-sewn, Banana Republic gorilla catcher's jacket, the shotgun

---

[145]See also, Chapter 8, "The Strange Case of the Gigantic, Nearsighted, English Bulldog," p. 264. I'm not sure Smith's bulldog was from the same lineage as the one I knew in Houston, but it's quite possible. They certainly looked like brothers.

tucked under his left arm, and dragging his friend the reluctant, gigantic, nearsighted, English bulldog with the nasty disposition and the largest teeth you've ever seen.

As they approached the large oak, the bulldog could smell the gorilla, and he became so excited he had to be restrained. Smith stopped, leaned the shotgun against the tree, looked up, located the gorilla, and said quietly, "So here's what we'll do. You take these handcuffs. I'll walk over to the tree and turn loose the gigantic nearsighted English bulldog with the nasty disposition and the largest teeth you've ever seen. Then I'll climb the tree and shake the branches the gorilla is sleeping on. I'll shake them so hard the gorilla will fall right out of the tree. As soon as he hits the ground, that bulldog grabs him with those large teeth in a way I'd rather not describe. The gorilla's eyes will roll back in his head. He'll be completely docile at that point. You can easily slip the cuffs on him. Just lead him to the truck. He'll climb in and behave himself until we get back to the zoo."

"If you're sure it's safe. . . ."

"No problem! When that bulldog grabs him where he grabs him, it's all over."

"Well, I guess I can do that."

"Sure you can," and with that Robinson swung himself into the lowest branch of the oak.

"Wait a minute," said the superintendent, "you didn't tell me what I was supposed to do with the shotgun."

Smith immediately scrambled down from the tree, grabbed the shotgun from where it was leaning against the trunk, ran back with it to the superintendent, and thrust the weapon into the superintendent's hands. Smith looked pale, and he had begun to perspire. "Oh man, I've never forgotten that before. Even the thought of not explaining about the shotgun makes my blood run cold. That shotgun . . . Omigod, that shotgun . . . Now, that shotgun is in case I fall out of the tree instead of the gorilla. If that happens, you aim that shotgun carefully—and kill that goddamn bulldog!"

If you believe the media bulldog, education "is not what it used to be," and in this instance, the media is absolutely correct. It's only been since the middle sixties, in the last thirty years of America's approximately 350-year educational history, that public education has begun seriously addressing student differences and exceptionalities with compensatory, remedial, and special education programs and services. It was also in this most recent period, this thin slice of our nation's educational life, that meaningful school desegregation began throughout the nation—and major problems with integration and heavy concentrations of minorities in cities and city schools still remain unsolved.

However, beginning in the seventies and becoming significantly even better toward the end of the decade, both the numbers and professional quality of prospective teachers have soared dramatically. In those fifteen to twenty years, teachers good enough to be chosen from among hundreds of available candidates for almost any given vacancy have been superb, and they are much more able than many of those who preceded them.

Today's media and national, state, and local political and business leaders can't, or won't, acknowledge the real causes of educational mediocrity, which, unfortunately, characterize many American school districts and their student educational outcomes. It's much simpler for the press and public figures to suggest school leadership should solve societal problems through "educational restructuring" or with "total quality management" or with whatever new and ethereal notion has momentarily captured the national media's fancy than it is to confront the real causes of inner city and rural poverty, suburban rootlessness, or a very real "national malaise"—the bare mention of which got Jimmy Carter run out of Washington a number of years ago; although a fact even then, national social problems weren't even a patch on the social problems prevalent today.

Republican presidents, many senators and congressional representatives of any persuasion, governors, state legislators, local politicians, big business, television, newspaper reporters, and syndicated columnists with a plethora of quote boys at their beck and call are all eager to dump national problems on educational doorsteps, instead of honestly and openly acknowledging the increasing disintegration of American families; problems of drug and alcohol use and abuse; the intellectually numbing effects on children of thousands of hours spent in mindless, semi-comatose, television viewing; the glorification of false public idols, not even mentioning Beavis, Butthead, and Bart Simpson— every classroom teacher's worst nightmare; racism; grinding urban and rural poverty and homelessness and its obverse—suburban affluence and excess; the decline of traditional values such as honesty, respect for others, a work ethic willing to defer immediate gratification for the sake of a larger future reward; the erosion of respect for any kind of authority other than our own; environmental pollution and toxic wastes; increasing crime, including child abuse and neglect; and a myriad of other social ills that the nation has not been willing, or probably able, to correct. Public schools have been assigned responsibility for remedying all of these problems.

Today's national preoccupation is with preventing tax increases or with cutting taxes and to hell with human services, including public education, which the media keeps repeating isn't working anyway in spite of continual increases in educational expenditures; this as our city school districts are facing, and some are experiencing, almost total disarray; even good suburban schools are feeling tremendous pressures to make changes that somehow, miraculously, will ameliorate or banish, to "never-never land," major societal problems currently labeled school deficiencies.

Often, educators are their own worst enemies; we've tinkered with peripheral changes for decades while most teachers, thank God for major blessings, went about their daily business of educating children as superintendents and principals touted their latest educational fads. Even more substantively, our collective willingness to assume problems not of our making, and we make enough of our own, has allowed educators to be victimized by first rate political "scapegoating."

Combine all the foregoing with the seemingly contradictory reality that education, except at the highest professional levels, produces thousands of university graduates each year who scramble to find jobs that will provide them anything close to the standard of living their parents could manage twenty-five years ago after graduating from high school. Great numbers of American secondary school students have internalized this "deserts in the middle of oases" transmogrification of earlier national economic trends and have decided that the odds of education paying off for them aren't what they were—further dulling their desire to work hard, lessening their willingness to defer gratification for the sake of greater future rewards, which now appear problematic anyway, and reducing their commitment to educational excellence.

Education, as other major human enterprises, too often exhibits the twin physiological defects of softheadedness and shortsightedness; we are sometimes victims of our own inertia, defensiveness, selfishness, jurisdictional pettiness, and masochistic compulsion to leap onto every bandwagon with a single bound. Critics of public education have identified a number of real educational deficits for which we bear responsibility. And if they are ever to be solved, we must continue to address problems not of our making, as well as those that we did create.

Although teachers can't save the world alone, major world, national, and state issues can't be resolved without effective public schools. In the particular media and morality play as it speaks to public education, it's not always clear whether the media's role is played by the gorilla or by the bulldog, but considering the damage either protagonist in this one-act play can do and the havoc they both can wreak on public education, does it really matter? Probably not, but if you want to be absolutely safe, get your own gigantic, nearsighted, English bulldog with a nasty disposition and the largest teeth you've ever seen, and don't leave home without him.

"WHY SOMETIMES I'VE BELIEVED AS MANY AS SIX IMPOSSIBLE THINGS BEFORE BREAKFAST" [54]

Throughout their careers, many superintendents and principals have resisted jumping on each new educational bandwagon guaranteed to bring about the public school millennium. Others have overenthusiastically tried all of them without discrimination. All educational leaders have erred, at least once, through embracing slick new programs that didn't work out as promised—and some continue to be guilty of practicing hyperbole without a license as they grossly oversell even legitimate innovations.

In today's rapidly changing social environment, education must develop and use new approaches if it is to improve or even hold its own, and educators badly need to take maximum advantage of potential public relations benefits from trying new ideas and telling their constituents about them. The American public wants to feel better about its schools, and if new organizations or instructional techniques might help, they should be tried—as long as they aren't oversold with hype and hyperbole.[146]

The drumbeat of media criticism, beginning with Sputnik in the late fifties through the *Nation at Risk* report of the National Commission until today, has focused public attention on the alleged and the real shortcomings of American public education. State commissioners of education, superintendents, principals, teachers, and boards of education are desperate for quick fixes to make educational problems go away so that newspapers, television, news weeklies, politicians, and others will let them breathe freely for a while. In this nineties climate, with motives as mixed as their products, educational snake oil salesmen abound, along with genuine educational reformers: (1) many innovators sincerely believe in their ideas, and their sin is overselling

[146]See also, this chapter, "Prelude to a Vast Aramada of Small Boats," p. 210.

new programs and promising much more than the best of them can deliver; (2) others see their new notions as stairways to educational stardom and to public recognition and acclaim; and (3) some attempt to impose their external educational solutions onto complex organizational and societal problems because of the money they can make doing it.

To avoid the failures and their attendant disappointments from romancing one or more of these new approaches, school leaders must remain or become simultaneously progressive and cautiously conservative; open to careful examination and trial of new ideas while holding firmly to the primacy of classroom teachers' daily efforts with kids, one at a time, in small groups, class by class, day by day, year by year; and be equipped with a personal and professional, well-tuned, built-in B.S. detector, which helps them separate effluent from pure spring water.

Teachers have become cynical about frequent shifts in educational directions, approaches, ideas, concepts, techniques, and programs.[147] If teachers are to buy into legitimate change, educational leadership needs to be up front and open with them about its own blends of enthusiasm and skepticism, idealism and practicality, trust and suspicion — and above all, must avoid the overstatements and inflated expectations exemplifying that "Alice in Wonderland" strain of administrative satyriasis, which compels school leaders to love six new and impossible educational theories or organizations or instructional innovations each morning, even before they eat their Wheaties®.

PRACTICE MAKES PERFECT/DISCUSSION QUESTIONS

(1) In a given period of at least one month, clip or copy stories of more than passing comments in newspaper articles, columns, letters to the editor, and editorials; similar kinds of writing in news weeklies; or statements and analyses from television editorials, news, or other programs relating to school events, activities, or happenings at local, state, and national levels. Summarize these news stories in a sentence or two and list your summaries in two columns: those supportive of one or more aspects of public education and those critical of one or more aspects of public education. Guess beforehand which column will be lengthier.

(2) According to the media, members of the business community, and

---

[147]See also, this chapter, "Prelude to a Vast Armada of Small Boats," p. 210.

many among the general public, public schools should be run like businesses; the comment, "If you ran your schools the way I run my business . . ." is often heard. What's your view on that suggestion? In which respects do you agree with or differ with the author's point of view as expressed in "Blah, Blah, Blah, Natasha."

(3) In "Don't Argue with People Who Buy Ink by the Barrel," the author provides ten suggestions for dealing with media representatives. Develop your own list of ten (or more or fewer) suggestions for such interactions and compare them with those in the article.

(4) In "Taming the 450-Pound Media Gorilla—A One-Act Morality Play," identify ideas with which you agree and those with which you do not agree. Give your reasons for either agreeing or disagreeing.

(5) How many instances of business or corporate error can you recall within the recent past? How many instances of perceived inappropriate treatment of customers or clients? What were these circumstances, and what would the public reaction have been had similar behaviors been evidenced by school personnel?

(6) What have been the greatest changes in public education since you were a student? Explain why you believe they have been either positive or negative for public education. Which currently discussed reforms, restructurings, or changes in American public education hold the greatest promise for significant change? Do you believe public education has declined or improved? Support your point of view.

(7) Read, or reread, *A Nation at Risk*. What do you believe it accomplished, or what changed because it was written and publicized?

(8) To what do you attribute the prevailing newspaper attitude toward reporting school and school district news? Can this be changed in many or most instances, and, if so, how?

(9) How do you see the differences and similarities among the following groups on educational innovation and change?
- parents and other community members
- teachers
- principals
- superintendents of schools
- boards of education

- business and industry
- the media
- state education agencies
- the U.S. Congress, state legislatures, and other political leadership

CHAPTER 7

Recruiting, Interviewing, Selecting

RECRUITING

It Hasn't Always Been This Way

IN THE FIFTIES and sixties, superintendents of schools often made recruiting trips to colleges and universities—a quaint practice that has all but disappeared because of the buyer's market enjoyed by school districts in the seventies, eighties, and continuing in the nineties.[148] In spite of this trend, special area shortages remain in some parts of the country, for example, in speech teachers/clinicians/pathologists. But except in isolated parts of the country, and in some large cities, teachers have come to the prophets instead of the prophet being required to travel to the universities.

However, even with such an abundance of good candidates, it's still important for school leadership to seek out the best possible prospective teachers for a district's specific personnel needs. Also, when the supply of experienced teachers and the backlog of relatively new graduates have found positions through retirement of existing staff, the flow of teachers in the college and university pipelines again may be inadequate for district needs, and the ancient art of recruiting will rise again.

Although teacher versatility is important today because of frequent reassignments caused by staff reductions, it's still better to choose the best available talent for the specific position you are filling.[149]

Educational Piracy

Because personnel directors or superintendents seek the best available teachers, it's tempting to follow the private sector's practice of

---

[148]See also, this chapter, "The Second Great Flood," p. 229
[149]See also, this chapter, "Choose the Best Available Athlete," p. 232.

223

overtly recruiting individuals—in this case, pirating them from other school districts. The American Association of School Administrators' code of ethics, endorsed by state superintendents' organizations, requires honoring teacher and administrator employment contracts. Even when candidates apply unsolicited, prior to employing selected teachers, superintendents are expected to discuss their contract status with current employers and to work out appropriate release conditions for them.

In addition to leadership responsibilities in their own school systems, administrators have a larger responsibility to the educational profession. Stealing teachers from another district isn't helping students overall; it's benefiting children in recruiting districts at the expense of other districts. Sometimes we teach children more by example, even though our actions are not always easy for students to observe, than by what we say.

Preparing the Schematic

Effective personnel recruitment and selection procedures to determine who rides on the ark include position analyses, preparation of vacancy announcements, advertising the position, receiving applications, selecting candidates for interviews, candidate interviews, checking candidates' references and credentials, selection, appointment of selected candidate, and notification of unsuccessful candidates.

Job analyses should be completed before writing job descriptions, and the resulting job descriptions should determine selection criteria for screening, interviewing, and selection.

Vacancy announcements should be based on job descriptions. The superintendent, or someone designated by the superintendent, prepares advertisements for vacancies and publishes them, allowing adequate time to receive applications—typically, three or four weeks for teaching positions and usually four to six weeks for administrative and executive positions.

For administrative openings, there are two schools of thought on listing salary to be offered. It might be appropriate to use the words "salary consistent with experience and qualifications," when districts really are prepared to pay the successful applicant, without local restrictions, based upon his or her experience and qualifications. But if the district's salary range is established, and/or there is a maximum salary that is available, that should be stated. Otherwise, you waste people's time, including your own, interviewing candidates who are overqualified for your position, or, if a district has a high salary potential and doesn't make that clear, outstanding but expensive candidates may not apply.

Most boards and superintendents believe it's more effective to fight the battle up front, determine the amount to be paid (or a range at least), and advertise the position with specific salaries or within salary ranges. Salaries for principalships and other middle management positions often are determined by negotiated agreements or contracts, and districts should be forthright about that; if there is no salary flexibility, there shouldn't be implications to the contrary or omissions in advertisements or brochures that might mislead applicants. Avoiding specific salary information in advertisements wastes personnel time and creates bad feelings about a district's hiring practices, which eventually hurts its recruiting.

Looking for Mr. or Ms. Right—I

Existing staff is a primary source of candidates for open positions, particularly administrative positions. This doesn't imply that inside candidates always will be employed, but only that district personnel are often given an opportunity to apply for openings and strong consideration for them. However, some negotiated agreements place great weight on the selection of insiders for open administrative positions and sometimes make it difficult to look outside the system. Because of the greater potential pool of possible internal applicants, larger systems are even more likely to recruit from within.

Major arguments for internal promotions include (1) better employee moral because of internal opportunities in the system; (2) knowledge of the existing system, which internal candidates bring to their new position; and (3) cost savings from not having to advertise and recruit outside the district. The strongest argument against districts promoting its leadership from within is that eventually it may produce staffs as inbred, and possibly as unproductive, as European royal families.

Positions may be filled by people referred by other employees, and, similarly, superintendents share among themselves the names of outstanding teaching or administrative applicants for whom they have no openings. Often, these are teachers who have been "riffed," or laid off, from the referring superintendent's district. Also, graduate school professors often suggest excellent students from their classes for open administrative positions.

Over the past few decades, few school districts have benefited significantly from employment agencies, and most superintendents are wary of agency candidates. This bias against professional or paid referrals usually doesn't apply to consultants who help choose top executives for a system.[150]

College and university placement services are respected by superintendents and other staff with personnel responsibilities; prospective administrators who don't have active placement folders should consider assembling one if their graduate colleges or universities offer the service.

Although hardly a highly sophisticated recruitment technique to be taught to aspiring superintendents, uninvited walk-in applicants have been, for the past decade, a very productive source from which districts have filled open positions.

In seeking an administrative position, the odds against any individual are always great at the outset, but someone always gets the job. Many districts are somewhat reluctant to advertise nationally for positions, other than superintendencies, unless boards of education are willing, and able, to pay candidate's travel expenses. It's difficult for districts to require candidates to pay travel expenses from the West Coast to the East Coast as one of fifteen or twenty people to be interviewed, when their chances, in the early stages at least, are statistically so small.

But, again, someone is always chosen, and it could be you or me—well, you anyway.

Looking for Mr. or Ms. Right—II

Ample time should be allowed for advertising and the receipt of applications. Instead of using the word deadline, some districts use more flexible wording such as "please submit applications or letters of interest by "date." It can be overly rigid to exclude outstanding candidates from further consideration because of a late reference; the major loser in such cases can be a school district. Sometimes, however, applications or associated materials are received so late that there are no appropriate alternatives to rejecting the application because of untimeliness.

Many districts save money at the expense of candidate quality through the use of advertisements too small to catch the attention of candidates or to make the kind of impression desired. Cost differences to run a two by three inch boxed advertisement compared to smaller inconspicuous classified ads are not that great.

---

[150]See also, Chapter 2, "Frank Buck Is Alive and Well—I and II," p. 41 and p. 46.

For comparison purposes, someone in the central office should collect a variety of personnel advertisements from the newspapers and price these advertisements of differing sizes and styles for running them various numbers of times, including price differentials between weekday ads and weekend ads. Depending upon the jobs to be filled, districts can then select from among advertisement possibilities with full knowledge of how much each will cost. An advertisement sample booklet frequently will be helpful each year.

If the search is local, the superintendent should know which newspapers are best for advertising, both price and circulation, and if the search is to be a national one identify professional journals, magazines, or newspapers that are most productive considering their advertising costs.

A Veritable Garden of Eden

Brochures on superintendencies, central office positions, principalships, and, occasionally, department chairmanships and other administrative positions are appropriate. During the fifties and sixties, when recruiting was an art practiced by almost all superintendents, brochures were used to describe a school district to prospective teachers, and a few districts may still use such brochures to good effect.

These local publications typically include glowing statements about the innumerable joys of living in the district and immediate area, including all the cultural, educational, and recreational benefits available to prospective staff members and their families; information on the town or towns comprising the district; data on the number and sizes of district schools and student achievement (if it's noteworthy); certification requirements and state education department telephone numbers and addresses to help prospective applicants check certification requirements; possibly a map of the area of the state in which the district is located; and other information to encourage applications.

For superintendencies, principalships, and other administrative positions, it's also a good idea to maintain a listing of colleges and universities to which notices of open administrative positions and brochures will be mailed.

Do You Play the Piano?

Although most applications do some of both, each district should determine whether its application form will focus on factual background information and experience or candidate personal and professional educational thoughts and philosophies.

Other criteria, cautions, and questions to be asked and answered in developing the school district's application forms include: Does the application ask for more information than is really needed? Does it ask inappropriate, illegal, or personally offensive questions? Is the form well organized and easily readable? Is its appearance and style pleasing? Does it provide an opportunity to assess a candidate's writing ability? Is there adequate space for candidate responses? Does it still ask the question popular in the fifties for elementary teaching positions, "Do you play the piano?"

The appearance of the application is important, and desktop printing today can produce attractive application forms at minimum costs — although quality paper is worth the small extra expense for the better impression it makes on prospective applicants.

"Wakeups" and "Makeups"

Fairminded employers, and even others who have received governmental "wakeup" calls, don't discriminate against candidates because of race, creed, religion, etc. To the extent reasonably possible, most are willing to make the extra effort to find qualified minority candidates — to "makeup" for the years of inattention to this issue. School districts, especially city districts with concentrations of minority students, have active affirmative action plans that, although enjoying some successes, still have usually left these districts far short of desired numbers of minority teachers and administrators.

One obstacle that districts face carrying out affirmative action plans is the "purification" of applications, so it's impossible to know from them whether or not the person is part of a minority group. However employer mailings and advertising have targeted minorities in appropriate ways to allow better recognition of applications coming from the targeted group.

Obviously, women candidates are usually identifiable by their names, and many superintendents, superintendent search consultants, and boards of education interview a high percentage of women and minority applicants when they can recognize them legitimately. This isn't viewed by its practitioners as reverse discrimination but, by at least giving minorities opportunities to be personally interviewed and judged fairly on their merits, as balancing years of clear discrimination against these groups.

Application forms and other recruiting literature and procedures should avoid discriminatory questions or requests for discriminatory information. Both national and state agencies monitor employment practices, and although such practices should be avoided because of their intrinsic inappropriateness, administrative entanglements with federal and state agencies are also painful, guilty or not, and should be avoided by all but masochists. We shouldn't need these bureaucratic "wakeup calls" to do the right thing anyway.

INTERVIEWING

The Second Great Flood

The eighties were, and the nineties have been, characterized by an abundance of teacher candidates, and in the past few years, it hasn't been unusual to receive two or three hundred applications for two or three elementary teaching positions.

Because of such strong competition among outstanding teacher applicants, undergraduate schools, and maybe even graduate schools, should spend more time discussing preparation of letters of application with their students. Superintendents occasionally receive candidate correspondence for teaching positions and sometimes for administrative posts on yellow, lined tablet paper written in pencil; on scraps of paper; typed letters filled with major grammatical errors and misspellings; and letters with all the holes in vowels, and some consonants, solid with typewriter dirt (word processors have helped here). Materials that accompany letters of application vary widely in content and appearance from over-slick printed resumes to the rag-tag toilet paper varieties.

One secretary or clerk should receive, organize, and file applications. After applications are received, they should be dated and placed in a file specifically for that particular application. There should be a checklist maintained, which shows what part of the application requirements each applicant has met, for example, letter of application, letters of reference, completed application form, placement papers, names of persons to be contacted for direct references, certification information, and any other special district requirements.[151]

Interrogations and Quiz Shows

It is important to broaden the interviewer base when selecting teachers or administrators. Various levels of school personnel should be involved in professional candidate interviews, including central office managers, building-level administrators, secondary school department chairmen, teachers, and often parents and students. When these personnel are involved, it's vital that the superintendent, or other responsible administrator, clarify both participants' roles and their constraints in the search process.

Although there may be superintendents willing to "rubber stamp" majority decisions of search or screening committees, most make it clear that a committee's role is to share its perceptions with the superintendent to help him or her make a final choice—or to recommend the best candidates to the board of education for further interviews and final board selection. Generally, a superintendent will not, and should not, hire or recommend someone he or she doesn't want for the position, nor will he or she go forward with someone who receives generally negative reviews from a committee. Although reserving the right to make the final choice, the message should be to interview participants that the final selection will come from a meeting of the minds between the superintendent of schools and search committee members.

The various groupings and sequencing of interviews depends upon circumstances; two or more interviews involving smaller numbers of people generally are more productive than one interview with greater numbers of people. Sometimes, key interviewers should see candidates more than once—possibly at second or third interviews with other interviewing groups. Similarly, in hiring noninstructional staff, other suport staff should be involved; for example, secretaries should be involved in secretarial interviews, custodians in custodial interviews, etc.

In all interviews, the objectives are similar. The interviewer is attempting to learn the candidate's knowledge, experiences, opinions, beliefs, and attitudes and to develop a valid impression of the candidate as a person and as a professional. There are as many different styles of interviews as there are different interviewers. Some superintendents

---

[151]See also, this chapter, "It Hasn't Always Been This Way," p. 223 and "Do You Play the Piano?" p. 227.

conduct interviews in a relatively informal setting and attempt to make those interviewed as comfortable as possible. Others, especially for administrative positions, prefer stress interviews where the candidate is placed under emotional strains from the questions asked – and sometimes from the interviewer's attitudes. Some vary the style of interview throughout the interview and from interview to interview.

Interestingly, most interviewers in a given search tend to agree on the best candidates, regardless of professional positions or previous experiences in interviewing. For example, although there will be variations in rankings, it is quite common for a dozen interviewers (including superintendent, central office staff, building-level administrators, classroom teachers and specialists, parents, and students) to end up with the same handful of top choices from a large number of candidates interviewed.

Although there are certainly exceptions, more often than not, similar conclusions are reached by different interviewers – highlighting the importance of personal, visceral reactions to candidates. Assessments of the technical and professional soundness of applicants' responses vary, depending upon the interviewer's experience and position; however, the personal reactions tend to be similar. In balance, the personal judgments may outweigh professional reactions – with the equivocation that better candidates must still perform within reasonably acceptable professional limits.

In other words, from a large and varied group of interviewers, it would be rare to find consensual all-American candidates who also didn't display the expected range of professional competencies; but, in the final analysis, their personal impact on interviewers is the deciding factor. If interviewers like people as people, they also tend to like their answers as well. This doesn't mean interviewers forgive candidates' significant professional deficits; it does mean they are prepared to rationalize away a few minor imperfections or shortcomings – or maybe even more than that if they like the applicant enough.

Again, the final choice, made more viscerally than cerebrally, will be from among candidates, all of whom have the requisite experience, professional knowledge, personal abilities, and skills. More important, however, than the latest acceptable answers to interview questions and more important than a demonstration of great professional knowledge, candidates must somehow make the interviewers like them personally – not through ingratiating attempts to please, which don't work anyway, but by making it clear, every way they can naturally, that they also respect and like their interviewers. Most professionals around the table are themselves likable and worthy of candidate efforts to let them know in subtle ways that they like their interviewers, too. Interviewers will return a candidate's feelings when they are perceived as genuine and honest.

A major advantage of group interviews, for a superintendent or principal is the immediate check of one's own perceptions; also, there is a real advantage in figuratively stepping outside of the interview for a minute or two and observing the candidate as he or she interacts with questioners.

Once the field is reduced to a smaller number, follow-ups on written references should be made for each survivor. Although experience gives good interviewers valuable help interpreting written references, it is still crucial to speak directly with those providing letters of reference. On occasion, for very important positions, interviewers visit the candidate's current place of employment or previous places of employment to gain more direct impressions of the candidate's performance.[152]

SELECTING

Choose the Best Available Athlete

Some interviewers and search consultants work too hard at, or at least claim to work very hard at, matching the right candidate with the right school district, and within school districts, superintendents, personnel directors, and principals may also attempt to match the right candidate with the right position in the right school with the right needs in the right grade and place them next door to just the right teacher. This all sounds good and is a legitimate district goal, but interviewers and decision makers shouldn't lose sight of the gestalt through an excessive focus on each candidate's specific attributes.

Sometimes, you will hear National Football League coaches speak about an upcoming draft of college players, and, usually, when asked what their team's specific needs are from the draft, they have a few positions in mind—unless they finished last the previous year, in which case, they might cite eleven positions they need to bolster. But when it comes down to choice time, they may still choose the best available athlete, regardless of position. Often, that's a good choice for educational leaders as well.

---

[152]See also, Chapter 2, "A Baker's Dozen of Interview Suggestions," p. 49.

To drag a "straw man"[153] into this discussion and then demolish him to prevent someone else from doing the same thing, superintendents wouldn't choose an outstanding high school principal who is suddenly on the job market and who also holds primary certification for a kindergarten position over an outstanding, experienced kindergarten teacher. To the other extreme, it would be counterproductive to let the consensual all-American candidate for an elementary principalship, who had the healthiest professional personality and the whitest teeth you've ever seen, get away in favor of a lesser light who had a bit more experience in, for example, whole language—the district's most recent cause du jour—than did the all-American applicant.

Candidate screening and final selection are two among an extensive list of leadership activities in which administrators need to search for the Aristotelian Golden Mean[154]—in this instance, between specific attributes and overall attributes. In hiring top-quality educational personnel, the golden mean is usually found closer to overall personal attributes and professional qualifications than to specific ones. If you choose the best and the brightest, within reasonable parameters of desirable experience, they will learn the rest of what they need to know in short order, but, more importantly, as long as they are with your district, they will provide more effective leadership or instruction or both than will those who aren't as intelligent, committed, charismatic, etc.

Although particular demands of a particular position are important, the best overall personal and professional qualities available among the candidates are even more important.

Grabbing the Brass Ring

Depending upon the size of the school district and other variables, the superintendent of schools will be involved in the filling of vacancies in their earliest stages or somewhere in the middle or at the final step. In all but the largest districts, superintendents should interview each candidate before appointment or before recommendation to the board of education for appointment. With experienced and trusted assistants, it may be appropriate to depart from this procedure when on vacation—or in other rare instances.

Nothing is more important to the school district's success than selecting the right people, and the superintendent must ensure that

---

[153]See also, Chapter 4, "Ray Bolger and Other Straw Persons," p. 161.
[154]See also, Chapter 1, "In Search of Gold," p. 7.

recruiting, interviewing, and selection are thorough and effective. A good selection process involves as many people as reasonably possible and takes as much time as reasonably available to make correct personnel choices.

Once selected, a warm, welcoming, personal letter to the successful candidate from the superintendent of schools is an outstanding way for a new teacher or administrator to begin his or her years in a school or school district.

Close, but No Cigar

Courtesy dictates that each applicant be notified when someone else is selected for a particular position for which the particular applicants have applied. Sometimes, however, people apply because they are looking for a job, any job, in a district and it's unrelated to a particular position availability. In these instances, acknowledgement of the original application with a message, no matter how gently phrased, that says, "Don't call us, we'll call you," will suffice.

However, the district should notify anyone who has been interviewed and was unsuccessful that the job has been filled. When it's true, it's also nice to add that they will be considered for another position, another time, and that their applications will be filed and reexamined as other vacancies occur. If the unsuccessful candidate was particularly strong, an additional personalized note will be greatly appreciated, and the person may be happier to return for another interview in the future.

With word processing, it is much easier to personalize candidate correspondence, and it's a nice touch to add a handwritten note on the bottom of form letters, even those that appear to be individually typed, especially if you can say something either reassuring or comforting to particular candidates. Interviewers see many more good people than there are positions, and not being chosen often is just the happenstance of personal chemistry, or the lack thereof, with particular interviewers.

Human variables often work against even strong candidates, and there is no immunity against an interviewing group preferring someone else. Occasionally, interviewers are asked by unsuccessful candidates to help them understand why they weren't chosen. If this question is confrontational, the usual response is that we just liked someone else better—case closed. If the inquiry is to learn from an experience and avoid repeating any interview mistakes, most administrators try to be helpful—but, often, especially with good candidates, the answer is simply that somebody else made a slightly better impression on the interviewers or that the interviewers just liked someone else more; it's often difficult to identify more specific reasons why this is true.

Unfortunately, sometimes the reasons for an applicant's lack of success are obvious, and they are realities over which the candidate has little control. For example, some people exude indecision; while it might be possible to give them a two-day cram course in assertiveness training, it wouldn't change that person significantly. It's at least awkward to tell someone they are weak, insecure, not too bright, personally offensive, or any of the other real reasons that sometimes cause candidates to be rejected by the interviewers. Most people don't try to convince others that they are victims of crippling, personal defects.

However, if there are one or two things that might have hurt candidates in particular interviews, it's easier to help them avoid similar mistakes in the future — much different from situations wherein the general perception is that "what you see is what you get" and what you saw was unappetizing. Under those circumstances, there isn't a hell of a lot you can say without being unnecessarily hurtful.

A magazine cartoon of many years ago pictured a patient on the couch with his psychiatrist saying, "You have an inferiority complex, Mr. Jones, but I can't help you because you really are inferior."

Once in a great while, an interviewer may occasionally level with people after they have interviewed them a number of times, and it seems only fair to tell them that, if they applied for the next hundred years, they won't be selected for a principalship or a superintendency.

We should couch that awful message as gently as we can and stress that the job they have is also important and that only a select few can do the work they do and that, similarly, they shouldn't aspire to some jobs and not to feel bad about that. Rejection is always painful, and being told that you're unacceptable for any position, for any reason, is a tough message to accept. Because we aren't personally responsible for each person's career, these critiques should be limited to the rarest of circumstances, especially because personal judgments are fallible and therefore often better unspoken.

PRACTICE MAKES PERFECT/SIMULATED INTERVIEW

Using questions selected from the list below, conduct a number of simulated interviews with associates, alternating the role of interviewers and interviewee. Answering ten or so questions, with responses of reasonable duration, will normally require forty-five minutes to an hour. Sample questions are phrased for principal, director, or other administrative positions, but changes to make them suitable for teacher applicants are easily discerned.

(*1*) We've read your application and other papers, but it would be helpful for us to have you review your educational and other experiences that you believe are pertinent to your interest in our position.

(*2*) When did you first become interested in teaching and why? in administration and why?

(*3*) As someone interested in public education, what have been the most worthwhile changes in it? Have there been changes with which you disagree? Tell us about those please.

(*4*) In terms of its value in preparation for a career in administration, what has been your most important professional or educational experience?

(*5*) What aspects of administration do you expect to find most appealing? least appealing?

(*6*) How would you manage or balance your responsibility to improve a teacher's performance with his or her personal and social needs to grow and be fulfilled as individual human beings?

(*7*) Tell us about an administrator in your career who had a major influence on your professional life and why.

(*8*) Discuss both significant positive and negative leadership behaviors you have encountered in your educational career.

(*9*) How would you handle a personal or professional conflict with your superintendent, for example, if you believed his approach to staff management and leadership was not appropriate? What are your own views on personnel leadership?

(*10*) What do you believe is the appropriate role of parents in schools and in their children's education?

(*11*) As a prospective administrator in our system, identify your educational priorities for students.

(*12*) What is the most humorous school incident you can recall?

(*13*) Public relations with the community is always a concern and especially so today. What can you do as a principal to improve the community's attitude toward public relations?

(*14*) How would you describe your leadership style with particular reference to staff motivation?

(15) As you recall your own school years, what are major differences that you see now compared to then?

(16) What kind of inadequacies would, in your judgment, require termination of a teacher's contract?

(17) What has been your greatest educational accomplishment and greatest disappointment as a teacher?

(18) Is there a trend today away from teachers working harmoniously with parents and the community to more adversarial positions? Explain your answer.

(19) Describe your major strengths as a teacher. What are your shortcomings, if any? How do you compensate for any professional imperfections?

(20) As a principal, what would your work day be?

(21) Please identify two or three national educational issues and give us your thoughts on them.

(22) Give us a half dozen adjectives that best describe you as a person; now the same number characteristic of you as a professional educator.

(23) Recall for us a professional crisis from your past, and tell us how you dealt with it.

(24) How would you characterize your interpersonal relationships?

(25) What should teachers' roles be in curriculum development?

(26) What perceptions do you have of this school system from any information you have obtained?

(27) Give us your very brief understandings of and reactions to the following: educational restructuring, teacher empowerment, the effective schools movement, outcome-based education, the public's perception of a decline in teaching skills and abilities, teacher accountability for student results, standardized and mastery testing, site-based management, mainstreaming of special education students, regular education initiatives, computers and other instructional technology, whole-language instruction, math manipulatives, and cultural and ethnic diversity in public education.

(28) Do you have any apprehensions about beginning an administrative career?

(29) How do you see the relationship of special education and regular classroom instruction?

(*30*) What is the role of extra-class activities and athletics in public education?

(*31*) Who has had the greatest impact on your personal life? on your professional life?

(*32*) What qualities do you bring to this position that you feel will be of major benefit to our system?

(*33*) Please summarize for us why we should consider you a particularly strong candidate for our position.

(*34*) What questions should we have asked you, but did not?

(*35*) What questions do you have for us?

CHAPTER 8

Personnel Attitudes and Relationships

A CHEST FULL OF RIBBONS

MOST PEOPLE DON'T spend a great deal of time reflecting on sea-going warships and don't dwell on, understand, or care about the concept of floating gun or missile platforms or that a destroyer, its crew, its machinery, and its provisions collectively exist for one purpose – to move five-inch guns or missiles close enough to enemy targets so this armament can be placed on hostile positions. Today's submarines are only mobile missile platforms or torpedo launching pads, and the peripatetic city that is an aircraft carrier has as its single purpose the ocean transport of aircraft and aircrews to locations within flight range of enemy personnel, ships, aircraft, or installations. Because of that reality, it's the pilots and aircrews who should and do receive most of the medals from grateful governments and also the greatest amount of public recognition. They are the people who accomplish what the ship exists to accomplish.

Similarly, boards of education, superintendents of schools, central office staffs, and to some extent, even principals who are in regular contact with students have one real educational purpose – to help create and maintain conditions within which teachers can deliver instruction and guidance to students. To the extent that all other district personnel facilitate classroom and other teachers' direct work with their charges, they fulfill their roles effectively. To the extent they don't, district personnel have no true educational importance.

This concept, that all other positions exist for their potential service to teachers, is difficult for some educational egos to accept, but it's true nevertheless. Believing it doesn't imply other people are unimportant to district success, but it does mean their success should be measured in terms of how they individually contribute to teacher achievement.

For leadership to focus on what they can do to help teachers do their jobs doesn't require concessions to each teacher's, or faculty's, thoughts, wants, whims, or needs—or agreement with every teacher negotiator's demands. It only means what it says: "That all board members, administrators, and support staff have only a single educational *raison d'etre*—to help create and maintain conditions within which teachers can do their jobs educating public school students." For their good efforts to achieve that which the school district exists to achieve, teachers rightfully receive the plaudits from school leadership, from parents, and from the general public.

Teachers wear the medals in school districts.

BEAT IT TO DEATH WITH A STICK

Early in a principal's administrative career, he had to dismiss a teacher for a variety of reasons; for a few weeks prior to her departure, the district's curriculum supervisor spent quite a bit of time in her classroom observing. Shortly after the teacher with the problems "retired," the curriculum supervisor paid a few routine, observational visits to a new first-grade teacher's classroom.

The first-grade teacher, alert to clues in her professional environment, had made a recent connection between supervisory visits and teacher termination, without fully realizing the two events weren't always in a passionate cause-and-effect embrace. So she stopped to see the principal one morning to ask if the recent visits by the supervisor indicated her job was also in jeopardy.

It was a Monday morning; the principal had spent the weekend with a submarine reserve unit; he knew she knew he knew she was a fine beginning teacher, and he had a headache from smoking too much over the weekend. So he said something like, "You're nuts, get outta here with that nonsense!" The young teacher understood that the principal was telling her she didn't have anything to be concerned about, and she left smiling.

A week later, the school's administrative gadfly, a superb seventh- and eighth-grade teacher, and a wonderful person in her own right, came to see the principal for one of her periodic emotional release sessions. On this occasion, she enumerated her typical long list of complaints, criticisms, and recommendations on how the principal could improve his performance and persona, ending with, "Furthermore, you threw poor Marie out of your office when she was really concerned that she had a major problem because of Kay's visits, and you gave her no reassurance at all, and you're an insensitive, mean, rotten person."

The principal asked who in the world told her that, and the teacher said Marie did. The principal knew when Marie came to see him with her worry that she had understood the real meaning of his overtly unsympathetic reaction—regardless of its packaging. So after his administrative conscience left the office, like a dummy, he went to see Marie and asked her if it was true she had told the gadfly he'd thrown her out of his office without allaying her concerns. She denied doing so, saying she had understood his uncouth message completely, and she didn't understand from whence the incorrect notions had cometh.

So, like a bigger dummy, the principal went back to the upper grade teacher and told her that Marie said she hadn't felt mistreated and that she denied saying anything to justify that interpretation.

Guess what? The seventh- and eighth-grade teacher then returned to see Marie, and they began World War III about what Marie had or hadn't said to her and what each had said to the principal and what he'd said to whomever. All this created tender feelings between the two teachers that took some time to go away.

Then Marie returned, upset with the principal for telling the other teacher about Marie's most recent conversation with him, in which she had denied saying what the other teacher said she'd said.

By now, it's difficult to imagine a principal dumb enough to prolong this travesty on administrative acumen, and even our protagonist wasn't that obtuse.[155] After a lingering, festering illness, this entire subject finally was allowed to die its miserable death and was buried without further ceremony.

Remembering this one series of absurd incidents that never needed to happen was helpful to him over the next three decades of school administration. This experience reinforced what he already should have known—which was to let issues expire peacefully unless something more important than his ego was involved.

Unfortunately, throughout his career he witnessed hundreds of situations where other people couldn't leave well enough alone, and their sometimes heroic, but often dumb, behaviors prolonged and sometimes even brought back to life controversies that then lived far beyond their natural life spans—to the discomfort of all concerned.

When minor issues seem to have died, don't resuscitate them. If they even twitch, beat them to death with clubs carved from benign indifference.

---

[155]Detractors will argue this point, but what do they know?

CAUSE AND EFFECT—A ONE-ITEM INTELLIGENCE TEST OR "MY GRANDFATHER SMOKED A PACK A DAY AND LIVED TO BE NINETY"

Problems from misunderstanding cause-and-effect relationships infest administrative lives as fleas flock to homeless dogs—and dogs with good homes for that matter. Determination of the actual cause, or causes, of important effects is generally a very complex task, but it's seen as simple by people who are themselves simple.

Variations on cause-and-effect confusions include (1) citing an exception to the rule as the rule itself. To these misguided persons, the reason their grandfather lived as long as he did was because he smoked as much as he did, instead of in spite of smoking as much as he did. School leadership must survive such aberrant reasoning among staff occasionally, among the public often, and among some board members frequently to almost always. (2) Assigning a specific cause to an effect, which, although possible, is only one of a number of possible causes and not likely the most reasonable cause. Consider the example of two serious injuries on a playground within a month when there haven't been others like them in five years. Many may assume inadequate supervision, which is always a reasonable possibilty, but, by this also often incorrect assumption, they rule out much too quickly "happenstance"; or two random, unforeseeable, or unpreventable reckless behaviors; or defective equipment; or many other unknown possibilities as well. (3) Identifying a cause that probably didn't produce the particular effect. For example, a parent of a child new to a district blames an outstanding experienced teacher for her child's suddenly inappropriate behavior. The behavior could be the result of the particular classroom, but, considering the teacher's qualifications and ability, it's more likely that the behavior was triggered by the change of schools or by something in the home resulting from or related to the move or by some factor yet unidentified. (4) Specifying a cause that couldn't have created the effect; for example, the high school has a new principal this year, and two months after he arrives, SAT scores decline significantly; the superintendent can reassure worriers that the new person's few months as principal aren't the cause of lower SAT scores. (5) Not recognizing the original cause when a perceived cause is itself an effect of the unrecognized true cause, for example, blaming bad student test results on a particular classroom teacher who, although sharing responsibility for the scores, was incorrectly placed in an assignment for which he or she clearly was unqualified. In this instance, the root cause was the administrator's assignment of the teacher, and the effect of that assignment was inadequate teaching, which, in turn, was at least partially the cause of poor educational results. (6) In the worst cases, a complete reversal of cause and effect; for example, a principal is clinically depressed, and the board believes his illness to be the effect of his recently poor professional performance. The reverse is more likely true, and his illness is probably the cause of his poor administrative performance.

Determining cause and effect correctly is an effective, one-item, intelligence test, and the ultimate mistake, cause-and-effect reversal, should render people ineligible even to walk through a room in which intelligence tests might someday be administered.

CONSENSUS VERSUS THE RIGHT TO DIFFER AND TO BE DIFFERENT

Most educational "line officers," superintendents and principals, in making important decisions, proclaim their eagerness to hear differing views from those with whom they work. Prototypical superintendents can live with administrative differences at administrative councils, and principals can usually accept teacher differences at teachers' meetings, but once decisions are reached after full discussion of the issues, leadership usually expects everyone to support decisions fully. Sometimes, administrators lose sleep and, sometimes, the respect of staff because they can't live comfortably with dissent—not just until a decision has been made, but indefinitely.

Sometimes, decisions are made by a majority of one—a principal or superintendent deciding alone on courses of action against group preferences; in these instances, continued differences should be expected, not suppressed.

Individual support of group decisions is a desirable outcome of educational decision making and is a legitimate "expectation" of group leaders—but it is an unworkable "requirement." It's fine to hope administrators or teachers support group consensus, but it's self-defeating to demand it unequivocally. Individual conformity can't be enforced, no matter how desirable it is seen to be, and it's generally poor management to place leadership effectiveness on the line through futile attempts to require particular behaviors that can't be controlled in any event.

If conflict and dissent on particular decisions can be tempered or prevented during implementation of educational decisions or while preliminary decisions are being discussed further to gain board of education approval on a recommended course of action, maybe the conflict should be muted, but at other times, it probably shouldn't be—but that's moot anyway because people are and will always be free to differ with individual and group decisions. The first amendment unequivocally protects legitimate dissent in educational circles as in other settings.

Leaders should work to create an expectation of group solidarity accompanied by a clear understanding of individual freedoms to differ beyond the level of initial decisions. The good leader's attitude should be, "Take your best shot, and if I can't convince the board (or the superintendent) that my recommendation, however it was arrived at, isn't the best course of action, so be it."

However, superintendents and principals can preempt many retaliatory strikes by making it clear to the troops that, as a matter of routine, the superintendent will always convey, openly and fairly, to the board (or the principal to the superintendent) dissenting views and the reasons for them.

When a superintendent is comfortable enough with himself or herself and his or her professional leadership, all the players in the game should know he or she will always inform boards of education that recommendations are being made for these particular reasons, acknowledge the existence of contrary views, state those differing views accurately, and explain reasons for different opinions fairly.

Superintendents of schools display the personal and professional security characteristic of effective leadership when they make it known to their communities, boards of education, and staffs that, if people feel strongly about a group decision, they are free to express their differences without fear of negative consequences.

That leadership approach, followed faithfully, will diffuse negative aspects of disagreements and raise pedagogical children whose cheerful dispositions are the polar opposite from the temperaments of educational offspring fathered by dissent and conceived in insecurity.

DIVERGENCE AND CONVERGENCE

Superintendents, principals, directors, and other administrative leaders look divergently outward and see around them all the educators and other staff for whom they hold supervisory responsibility. Superintendents look out at hundreds of district employees. After working with colleagues for a time, leaders know their minor human and professional frailties—and sometimes their major flaws. With their broad bases of comparison, superintendents appropriately accept human imperfection as long as it's offset by greater personal and professional strengths. Other central office administrators also have a relatively "global" view of school district personnel. Principals typically work with dozens of certified professionals in their buildings, and they also can identify, in each staff, the usual spectrum of personal and professional weaknesses and strengths.

Staff members, to the contrary, perceive administrative leadership convergently, with all eyes from the circumferences of varying sized circles focused on the leaders in the center of those educational circles, whether they are principals or superintendents or others in administrative posts. When the entire staff scrutinizes one person closely over long periods of time, every human leadership blemish is identified, collected, categorized, analyzed, magnified, linked with other faults, dissected in isolation, shared, discussed, rediscussed, even enjoyed, and, thankfully, often forgiven, at least by many on the staff, because the problems aren't really that great, especially compared to the leader's positive attributes.

Many staff members join in "boss bashing" only to be companionable and really aren't as critical of the principal or superintendent as they may appear to their luncheon or faculty room companions. Other times, reminiscent of squirrels storing away nuts for the winter, staff members will deposit their boss's human imperfections safely away in memory banks for conversational withdrawals at a later time. Occasionally, these discussions result in the target administrator being "done to death by slanderous tongues" [55]. Fortunately, this only happens in the worst situations.

This divergent/convergent concept also can be applied to relationships between boards of education and their one superintendent of schools; this particular species of divergence/convergence theory often is even more intense and complicated, because many board members have known only that superintendent—while their superintendent will have worked previously with dozens, sometimes scores, and occasionally even hundreds of board members.

Broadened further, the public looks convergently inward at school leaders and school leaders divergently outward back at the public—this, possibly, giving rise to the concept expressed by arguably the greatest English satirist[156] that "censure is the tax a man pays to the public for being eminent" [56].

Although it's easier said than done, school leaders need to accept the inevitability of being the center of not so gentle lunchtime discussions. In their direct contacts with district leadership, most participants in critical discussions will manage to be friendly and civilized with the principal or superintendent, and effective leaders accept what is said directly to them by staff members and don't worry about what may be said outside of their hearing. If superintendents and principals can't manage to do this, their personal and professional lives will be much more difficult than they otherwise need to be.[157]

Accept the realities of leadership arising from diverging and converging views with objectivity and equanimity; you can't change them no matter how hard you try.

FREQUENTLY UNDERSTANDABLE, OFTEN FORGIVABLE, NEVER ACCEPTABLE

Almost everyone understands the general proposition that mistakes are a part of leadership life, as well as life generally, but too many times, errors are forgiven and accepted as inevitable when particular mistakes could have been prevented with reasonable forethought and attention to detail. As possibly another example of creative schizophrenia,[158] understanding the inevitability of human error as a general concept doesn't mean either that the specific reasons for mistakes are automatically understood or that they should be accepted as inevitable. Instead, each mistake of any consequence should be examined and dissected in detail, depending upon the relative importance of issues involved, to find out exactly how it occurred and thereby to prevent it from happening again.

Yes, we understand that people, including ourselves, inevitably err, but we should frequently spend the time needed to understand why particular mistakes occurred; we should often even forgive ourselves and others for all but the most egregious mistakes, practicing the philoso-

---

[156]Jonathan Swift was a contemporary and friend of Addison, Steele, Halifax, and Congreve. He was a Whig until he became disenchanted with their policies, at which point he became a Tory in 1710 and the party's leading writer and editor.
[157]See also, this chapter, "If You Didn't Hear It Directly, You Didn't Hear It," p. 251.
[158]See also, Chapter 3, "Creative Schizophrenia," p. 66.

phy of, "I hate the sin, but I love the sinner" [57] — but mistakes of consequence and many lesser errors should really never be acceptable.

If educational leaders don't hold themselves and others to this high standard of performance, education will be the worse for our excessive kindness.[159]

"FRUERE DIE!"

The Latin poet Horace[160] suggests in his eleventh ode that we should "avoid far reaching hopes," because we don't know what tomorrow will bring — and ends with the advice, "Carpe Diem!" [58] or "Seize the Day!" Yeah, I know you may be thinking, "Get outta here! It wasn't some dufus named Horace said that — it was Robin Williams." You're right. In the movie *Dead Poets Society,* Robin Williams, as Professor Keating, did use the poet's quote to remind his students of their mortality and stressed the urgency of Horace's "Carpe Diem!"

A more cheerful imperative to each school administrator and teacher as we go about each day at work would be "Fruere Die!" or "Enjoy the Day!" "Carpe Diem!" exhorts us to grab each day by the scruff of the neck and shake the most out of it. "Fruere Die!" suggests we should enjoy each day fully, as well as seizing and shaking it thoroughly. Enjoying the day is not inconsistent with deferral of gratification or working hard to make a better future or planning for the future; those worthy behaviors don't require that we miss legitimate pleasures from each available moment at work and at home.

Much too frequently, educators, as do others, put today's enjoyment on hold and wait for the weekend, the holidays, summer, or for when we can find our first principalship or superintendency — or until whatever phase of life comes next. Unfortunately, this bad habit usually worsens through middle age. When we always wait until tomorrow to enjoy ourselves, we lose the potential pleasures of each minute, of each hour, of each day, of each week, of each month, of each year, of each decade — and all too sadly, of each lifetime.

Educators, as well as their students, need to be both sensitive and

[159]See also, Chapter 1, "The Devil Is in the Details," p. 18.
[160]Quintus Horatius Flaccus seized the wrong day when he joined Brutus's and Cassius's army against Octavian and Mark Antony. It was only after that choice didn't work out at Philippi that he took to writing odes. He probably wrote his eleventh ode about seizing at his meeting, arranged by his buddy Virgil, with Maecenas who became his patron. (Maecenas was the Sam Walton of his time and supported Horace, in a manner to which Horace quickly became accustomed, for the rest of the poet's life on his estate.)

open to the many honest pleasures each sunrise offers—and not invest emotional capital only in organized, planned chunks of the future. Reinforcing that point arithmetically, let's say, beginning at age forty, your life seems empty until you acquire your first superintendency—when you attain it, you hold on to it and all succeeding new positions for five to ten years before moving on. When you wake up the day after accepting your sixth superintendency, you'll be somewhere between sixty-five and ninety years old. Beginning a superintendency at age forty and negotiating fifteen three-year teacher contracts will make you eighty-five years old—maybe even older than that in dog years.

Accepting, albeit grudgingly, that life inevitably gives each of us our special portion of professional disappointment and personal sadness, to the fullest extent we can manage, we should recognize each moment of our lives as "quality time" and cherish each minute between now and our first elderhostel—and all the minutes, days, and years beyond that as well.[161]

IT'S WHAT YOU DO THAT GETS ME IN TROUBLE

A veteran superintendent said frequently to his principals that he never did anything that got him into any trouble with boards of education; he claimed it was principals' decisions and actions that caused him problems. Principals countered that it wasn't what they did, but what teachers did that got both the principals and the superintendent into trouble and caused his difficulties with the board. Teachers said it was what the students did; the kids blamed everything on their parents, and parents blamed each other for genetic deficiencies from each spouse's half of the family unit.

Passing the buck is a well-worn, even shopworn, practice with which all school administrators are familiar—and a practice that some even may have used more than once themselves. Of course, there's some truth in the point that most of educational leadership's problems originate in actions or decisions of those for whom leadership is responsible, but leaders remain responsible for mistakes, for correcting them when they happen, and for preventing them from happening again.[162]

The important idea embedded unseen in blame-passing maneuvers is that among a school leader's greatest contributions to education is mak-

[161]See also, Chapter 11, "Educational Colleagues and Friends," p. 366.
[162]See also, Chapter 1, "The Devil Is in the Details," p. 18 and this chapter, "Frequently Understandable, Often Forgivable, Never Acceptable," p. 246.

ing him or herself unnecessary or as close to that as possible. It should be a primary leadership goal to help professional colleagues acquire sufficient knowledge and ability to function successfully without direction, supervision, or guidance. Although this organizational end may rarely, if ever, be reached, it's the correct goal. Unfortunately, strong egos often keep leaders from accepting this valid concept.

To achieve the goal of working themselves out of a job, school leaders must trust those who work with them through giving them frequent opportunities for leadership and decision making. That part is relatively easy, but allowing true responsibility and freedom, including opportunities to fail as long as the failure isn't catastrophic, is much more difficult. It requires continuous efforts with boards and communities to develop the requisite level of understanding of this leadership approach, while still remaining accountable for all colleagues' work on delegated tasks, which provides the superintendent support as he or she allows approriate freedom to leadership colleagues.[163]

Site-based management includes elements of this worthwhile approach, but it can also diffuse and confuse responsibilities for local education. As desirable as it may be to encourage individual school freedom, for a school district to remain an intact, functional district, it must also retain an appropriate degree of districtwide unity—in both its purposes and its practices. Otherwise, the district is really only a collection of ducal castles, each with its own drawbridge, moat, and parent army that rides into town occasionally to do battle with wicked King John in the central office.

I WENT TO COLLEGE AND YOU DIDN'T

Most suburban and many rural school districts are blends of various socioeconomic strata, from well-off families to families with modest or low incomes; although city districts also include disparate socioeconomic circumstances, they also contain concentrations of poverty and associated problems much more prevalent than in most American school systems. Many districts lack the extremes of either great wealth or dire poverty.[164]

To prospective homeowners, relatively affluent suburban school dis-

---

[163]See also, Chapter 3, "Efficient or Effective—Choose Any Two," p. 73.
[164]My own professional experience has ranged from a large city of well over a million residents, Houston, Texas, to rural, emerging suburban, and suburban districts in New York and Connecticut.

tricts often emit educational pheromones characteristic of communities that have remained immune from unwanted social assaults from the less affluent.[165] Unfortunately, many people erroneously judge a school district's educational quality based on the relative affluence of its community—to many, including some professional staff members, less wealthy communities don't project the staff's preferred educational aura of success.

One of the most invidious phenomena encountered at times in public education is the negative, self-fulfilling prophecy that crawls occasionally out from under rocks in faculty rooms or in conversations between or among teachers or between and among teachers and principals. At one time or another, most school leaders have heard staff members express skepticism about their particular student clientele's learning abilities based on their biases toward children of less educated parents—a caste-based example of first generation college graduates being critical of communities not heavily populated with Harvard and Yale alumni.

Most teachers are fairer and more perceptive than that and don't judge student potential on the basis of their socioeconomic backgrounds; however, it does happen. Much has been written about the harm teachers do minority students by not expecting them to achieve, but minor league versions of that atrocity can occur in almost any district, including ordinary suburban, or quasi-suburban, school districts that don't enjoy the affluence of the "best" residential communities.

It's ironic that the patronizing attitude exhibited in the old "I went to college and you didn't, ha, ha!" syndrome can even come from educators, most of whom themselves aren't descended from landed gentry. Most of us are, instead, decent representatives of sturdy peasant stock from a myriad of ethnic groups populating farms, suburbs, towns, and cities. Many of us were the first generation in our families to attend a college or university and to change our collars from blue to white, or to pink or striped, and maybe back to a pastel blue. As educators teach today's children, those fortunate enough not to have been judged harshly by our own teachers, just because our parents weren't rich, well educated, or particularly good looking, shouldn't forget our own humble to modest origins.

We need to remember who we are and from whence we came. Some of us may have inherited superintendent behaviors naturally; for example, my grandfather's uncle was Abe Frisby, "the only justice of the

---

[165]Often through various zoning machinations and/or housing costs in those particular towns.

peace in the history of Texas to sentence a man directly to the penitentiary" [59]. Later, some of his unorthodox doings were 'being investigated by an unfriendly grand jury. . . . The justice of the peace reportedly had taken some of his records home. About this time, the . . . office caught on fire. When Judge Frisby heard about the fire, he went home and got the records that were there and brought them down and threw them into the fire. That ended the investigation" [59].

A bit draconian, but with luck, that approach might even work today.

IF YOU DIDN'T HEAR IT DIRECTLY, YOU DIDN'T HEAR IT

Many times in each career, indirectly from others, leaders will hear about unflattering, critical, or otherwise negative comments about himself or herself, and for a variety of good reasons, it's a huge mistake to react to such secondhand discoveries.

It's quite possible nothing like what you were told was ever really said; it's also quite possible that, in its original context, the remark wasn't nearly as unpleasant as it appeared in the version you finally heard. You don't know the tone of voice, the facial expressions, the body language, and the entire context of what you heard. It's possibly true that what you were told was repeated by someone who has his or her own agenda totally unrelated to the alleged statement or statements and that he or she is attempting to use your leadership office to further his or her own causes; maybe what you heard was absolutely correct and taken from testimony of the world's purest and most reliable person—but so what?

The last reason for remaining relaxed about alleged comments, the "but so what?" rationale, is the most powerful. Who among leaders has never made an unkind comment about somebody else? Most of us would be horrified if our critical remarks ever reached their ears—not out of fear of retribution but from concern about gratuitously hurting someone else's feelings. Most people who say terrible things about leaders never intend for them to hear what was said, and regardless of how unfair their comments may be, if heard indirectly, they should be ignored or promptly forgotten—unless you recognize that the statement about you is true. In that case, modify the criticized behavior or attitude.

Even assuming what you heard was said was truly said exactly as it was repeated to you, it may have come from momentary anger or frustration and doesn't really accurately reflect a critic's true attitude about the superintendent or principal; or it may have been a coldly reasoned, intentional cruelty.

Whichever of the two preceding options may be true, the "but so what?" concept should be reinvoked. When people allegedly have said something leaders would rather not hear, they will either say it again directly to the administrator or they won't, with the odds being approximately a million to one that they won't. And if they really don't want leadership to hear what they said directly, hearing it secondhand shouldn't be acknowledged in any way.

Don't react to individuals on the basis of something that was allegedly said. Both the question, "Did you say such and such about me?" or the accusation that "I heard you said this or that about me!" illustrates weak, counterproductive leadership, which should be avoided because it exhibits personal insecurity anathema to effective leadership; it also involves the person who told you, and it keeps the issue alive when it should be allowed to die and receive a proper burial.[166] If people are pleasant to you face to face, whatever they may have said elsewhere isn't important, and finally, if you can't stand the heat. . . .

KITCHEN CABINETS AND ASSOCIATED HARDWARE

In addition to dispensing sound counsel and prescribing solutions to complex problems, superintendents and other administrators are also expected to listen to and hear ideas and suggestions from a variety of people with whom they interact on a regular basis. Superintendents' advisory groups may include administrative councils (or administrative cabinets, or maybe just principals' or administrative meetings), teacher advisory groups, parent advisory groups, and sometimes student groups. Principals, in addition to regular faculty meetings, typically work with both teacher and parent groups and also student councils or other student organizations.

Administrative Councils, Superintendent's Cabinet, Principal's Meetings

Commonly, councils or cabinets meet regularly once or twice each month and on special issues or problems as necessary in addition to the

[166]See also, this chapter, "Beat It to Death with a Stick," p. 240.

regular sessions. Superintendents' councils or cabinets are key bodies in school district administrative leadership, offering (1) regular opportunities for superintendents to cover their professional agendas with other district educational leaders and (2) similar opportunities for other administrators to raise important issues for discussion with the superintendent and administrative colleagues.

Quite often, these meetings are filled with a long list of superintendent informational items and, occasionally, even an action item or two to leaven the loaf, leaving few opportunities for principals to originate discussions on pressing concerns they may have. Leadership meeting time is used more effectively when superintendents cover administrivia in memoranda instead of at meetings—after ensuring that principals and other administrators understand this approach and have committed themselves to careful reading of superintendent correspondence.

When correspondence, electronic or written, is used for routine informational items, council or cabinet meetings should focus on one or two issues of common professional interest. Although flexibility should be the rule when scheduling primary discussion topics or meeting themes, a tentative yearly schedule, which spells out mutually approved topics for council or cabinet discussion and action, should be developed cooperatively by superintendents and council members.

Teacher Advisory Groups

These groups, called "Superintendents' Advisory Committees" or "Teacher Advisory Committees," or other names, offer two-way communication between superintendents and teachers and between principals and teachers. From a teacher's perspective, they can introduce topics for discussion or questions to be answered, by either the superintendent of schools or the building principal, reflecting interests of staff members whom they represent—either districtwide or in a given school.

Superintendents and principals have similar opportunities with teachers or other staff to disseminate[167] information or discussion items important to them. These advisory groups also offer leadership opportunities to resolve differences informally, rather than always through the grievance process.

---

[167]I've always been fascinated with the consistent use of "disseminate" by *New York Times* writers whenever they speak of birth control—as in "dissemination of birth control information"—but they probably know what they're doing.

In responding to teacher issues, superintendents and principals usually classify staff interests in one of three categories and respond accordingly:

(*1*) Questions, issues, problems, suggestions, complaints, concerns that can be addressed appropriately either within the framework of the advisory group or by the superintendent or principal working with other administrators outside of the advisory group and returning to it with the solution or response. Examples of issues in this category might include teacher inquiries about makeup days in the calendar because of school days lost because of inclement weather. The administrator may be able to respond directly based on board of education policy or on the basis of a recent board decision, or the superintendent may need to confer with the board and bring its response back to the group. A principal may need to confer with the superintendent to answer the question raised by the staff. Teacher requests for a change in meeting times or days for a particular advisory group—this should be addressed at the session in which it was brought up, although sometimes conflicting activities might require a delay until schedule conflicts could be resolved.

(*2*) Questions, issues, problems, suggestions, complaints, or concerns that properly should be referred back to particular schools or departmental administrators for discussion and resolution or that should be referred to the board of education for answers or to a school district attorney for legal clarification or to town officials or to state education departments or to some other governmental bodies. In these instances, there may be preliminary discussions to clarify the particular questions, issues, problems, suggestions, complaints, or concerns or to explore staff feelings even when the problem's ultimate resolution must come from elsewhere.

This kind of question, or issue, also encourages superintendents to inform principals or directors of concerns brought to their attention, both to hear their preliminary reactions to the issues and also to let them know a problem will be referred to them for resolution. Or the administrator may assume the responsibility for raising the issue with the appropriate body or person and bringing an answer back to the advisory group.

These are often typical of situations where superintendents forestall grievances by prompt, decisive action, even if they must involve other administrators; principals prevent grievances by similar conversations with themselves.[168] Examples of issues in this category might include:

- When brought before the superintendent, teacher concerns about equity in lunch duty assignments at particular schools. If this issue is raised at a principal's advisory group, the principal should address it and resolve it when possible.
- Teachers asking for a change in next year's calendar; if this request is to a principal, he or she would refer it to the administrative council and the superintendent of schools for review, and, if the review of the suggestion is favorable, probably then to the board of education for final decision and action. If the issue were raised with the superintendent, he or she probably would need to confer with the board of education before responding to the advisory council.

(3) Questions, issues, problems, suggestions, complaints, or concerns that can't properly be addressed by the particular advisory group:
- personnel issues—those that intrude upon someone's rights to privacy or confidentiality
- questions or discussions about pending litigation—not appropriate for advisory committee discussions

Parent Advisory Groups

These groups, known by various names, and often PTA- or PTO-related, also offer two-way communication between superintendents and parents and between principals and parents. Parents may introduce topics for discussion or questions to be answered, by either the superintendent of schools or the building principal, reflecting parental interests districtwide or at a given school. Superintendents and principals have similar opportunities to bring up informational or discussion items important to them. Administrators can usually classify parental interests into one of the same three categories used to describe classifying staff topics for advisory group discussions.

---

[168]Assuming they are sufficiently persuasive to win arguments with themselves.

Student Advisory Groups

These are normally principals' groups, although superintendents sometimes participate or meet directly with representative students on items of mutual concern. Often, these groups are student council affiliated, and they also provide the same two-way flow of ideas that characterize other advisory groups discussed. Principals' reactions to topics introduced also parallel administrative categorizations of the issues raised in other advisory groups.

The common themes interwoven through all advisory groups are opportunities for two-way communication and exchange of ideas; building stronger personal and professional relationships between administrators and staff; and resolving staff, parent, or student concerns early to prevent them from escalating into major problems.

Each of these varied groups offers an invaluable opportunity for open communication and for establishing and cementing personal and professional relationships—or opportunities to lecture, hector, and bore. Your call.[169]

LET'S DO IT AGAIN SOON

Education's cyclical schedule is a major benefit of the profession. Only professional athletes share a similar excitement to that of beginning a new year, closing it out, and resting for a time until it all begins again. And each teacher, school, and district can be a winner each year—unlike professional sports, where only a few teams win divisional championships, and only one group can win the Superbowl, or the World Series, or the Stanley Cup, or the NBA Championship. All but one team in each sport is unfulfilled each year and is disappointed that it wasn't ultimately successful; the off seasons of team members are filled with "might have beens." Each educator, though, has the opportunity to enjoy each summer, basking in reflections of a successful school year.

This holds true for administrators who work year 'round also. Even though summers are busy enough, the emotional highs occur as school opens in the fall and as it ends in June. School leaders need to capitalize on both the opening of school emotions and the potential satisfaction of completing another successful school year through school opening let-

[169]See also, Chapter 3. "Fireside and Other Chats and Communications—I–V," pp. 75, 78, 79, 80, 81.

ters to staff, opening day remarks, staff letters marking the end of the school year, and any other opportunities that become available.

Educational leaders should highlight the very real advantage of annual educational rebirths, which are always followed by periods of rest and reflection (or at least a change of pace for those who choose to or must work during summer vacations) after productive instructional and administrative years; and help teachers and others recognize and appreciate, even more than they may now, one of the special advantages of their chosen profession.

An educational adaptation of a famous quote from Shakespeare's *Henry V* [60] might serve as the basis of an appropriate welcome back letter to teachers and administrators:

Drums and Colours. Flourishes.

Once more unto the breach, dear friends, once more . . . ;
In summer there's nothing so becomes a teacher
As modest stillness and repose;
But when the blast of September blows in our ears,
Then imitate the action of the tiger;
Stiffen the sinews, summon up the blood,
Disguise fair nature with hard favour'd rage;
Now set the teeth, and stretch the nostril wide;
Hold hard the breath, and bend up every spirit
To his full height!
I see you stand like greyhounds in the slips,
Straining upon the start. The year's afoot:
Follow your Superintendent, and, upon this charge, cry:
God for (insert town/school district here), our schools, and each of us.

On, on you noblest pedagogues,
Fly the course; teach all in your path; let none escape
Your dedication and resolve.

Alarums and Excursions. Exeunt.

MANAGING CONFLICT [61]

"Arms on Armour Clashing Brayed Discord" [34]

Conflict, both constructive and destructive, is prevalent within and between organizations and systems. In addition to traditional sources, such as human nature that at times can make momentary cycnics of us all,[170] there is greater insistence on individual and group rights; an increased awareness of the finite nature of all kinds of resources; more emphasis on and expectations of perfect public and corporate morality; easier and faster access to information; and an accelerated rate of world, national, state, and local change. Each of these precipitates differences about decisions that must be made, including who should make decisions about personnel issues such as promotions, terminations, assignments and reassignments, fiscal matters, and implementing decisions once made.

Because conflict is increasingly present in all public and private leadership, it's important to accept that it is inevitable and that, generally, although not always, it can be either productive or damaging, depending upon how it is handled.

"Blood, Toil, Sweat, and Tears" [62]

Conflict arises from attempts to structure the future differently, which argues that significant change and growth are impossible without it—although it's often exhausting, annoying, and costly, conflict is a prerequisite for significant breakthroughs and organizational growth. There are many conflicts that produce bad results, but leadership initially should assume that conflicts are both inevitable and include choices among reasonable, though divergent, alternatives. Sometimes, it may not be between or among reasonable people or reasonable alternatives, and at some point, you may need to change your initial premise.

No group can be totally without conflict, and degrees of and potential for conflict infest human relationships. Depending upon how it's handled, conflict can contribute to personal and organizational growth or can be destructive. An absence of conflict can actually be harmful to school districts, but the public typically views educational conflict negatively. People most often associate with conflict words such as "troubles, problems, harmful, damaging, difficult, painful, stressful"; conversely, "peaceful, harmonious, calm, tranquil" carry positive associations. Not too many educators recognize conflict as challenging, interesting, exciting, and essential to progress.

Organizations and school districts in conflict are apt to be criticized for it even when conflicting parties believe their struggles are important

---

[170]See also, Chapter 11, "Some Days You Might Think Tom Hobbes Had It Right, p. 355."

and will eventually lead to educational improvement; that's usually not understood by those not part of the conflict. When it's misunderstood, conflict often creates unnecessary problems: (1) When it's viewed as a bad and dirty business, people may also believe it justifies doing anything necessary to win. Once people become engaged in a conflict, some of them may abandon normal restraints and observances of their usual civilized conduct—or if you are already in the gutter, why worry about a little more dirt? (2) Negative views of conflict also cause people to avoid situations they should face; because conflict can be so stressful, they avoid it, regardless of the organizational cost of such avoidance and even when avoidance requires more energy than would the conflict itself. Examples are principals who tackle particular tasks themselves, rather than assigning them to appropriate staff members and monitoring their achievement.

Damage Control

When conflicts are seen in terms of "win" or "lose," winners will be seen as better than losers and having better intellectual and personal qualities than losers. Winners are inflated by their victories and often take themselves and their achievements too seriously. Winning may also make them less likely to listen to other people—especially to the losers.

Losing isn't pleasant for the losers, and often they also lose faith in themselves and believe other people see them as less important than winners—and often they are so viewed. In education, losers may become emotional dropouts and avoid taking part in resolving succeeding issues; they may even leave the school district. Losers not only feel defeated, they often become angry. A "win-lose" approach to problem solving restricts the number of potential solutions considered to either "mine or yours," and not much time or effort is devoted to discovering other possible answers.

Adversarial conflicts polarize organizations, pressure people to choose sides, and greatly increase organizational costs regardless of which side "wins." For example, two teachers may each appeal to their department chairman for support when they have a disagreement. The department chairman may then approach the principal, and the principal may involve the superintendent of schools. All devote time and emotional energy to an issue that would have been resolved between the original parties if their approach had been other than "win-lose."

To avoid the negative side effects of conflict, conflict should be depersonalized and transformed into issues to be resolved, rather than contests to be won.

How to Get There from Here

Techniques employed in problem solving affect participants' communications style, their agendas, and their motives. Problem solving requires agreement among its participants that they will be supportive, rather than critical; clarifying, rather than argumentative; and objective, rather than personal. Participants' ideas should be protected and "win-lose" behaviors discouraged. It's difficult to change old communications patterns, and especially when judgmental communications have been the norm, change requires effective leadership.

The goal is achievement of excellence with the best possible solution; the focus is on what everyone needs, what the organization needs, and what is best for the long and short term. Another way to describe this approach is "win-win."

Valid assessment inventories are available, with norms and computer scoring that measure schools' and school districts' organizational and interpersonal climates and the openness and effectiveness of communications up, down, and laterally. When costs preclude the use of commercial inventories, simpler, locally prepared assessments are also worthwhile. To be as effective as they should be, organizational assessments require the full support and participation of building and central administration and of staff.

"Much Might Be Said on Both Sides" [63][171]

The benefits of a problem-solving approach to resolving educational conflict include the following: (1) The process makes staff meetings desirable, rather than activities to be avoided, and the faculty is more concerned with the quality of outcomes than with personal agendas. (2) Discussions may be focused and intense but without the personal tensions characteristic of "win-lose" struggles; humor is a natural part of staff work sessions. (3) Staff differences of opinion are accepted as normal, instead of provoking anger between and among faculty members with different points of view, and all ideas are respected, regardless of the hierarchical status of an idea's originator. (4) The faculty works

[171]Joseph Addison was a late seventeenth and early eighteenth century English essayist, poet, and statesman, and contributor to Steele's *Tattler* and wrote an equal portion of the *Spectator* — Steele's other well-known vehicle for their shared social satire and literary criticism.

toward the best solutions to the issues before them, instead of attempting to impose one faction's preferred outcome or outcomes, allowing considerations of solutions that otherwise may not have been either proposed or discussed. (5) Staff decisions are provisional until their implications to the school or school district can be fully explored, and the faculty is not adverse to changing tentative conclusions based on new information.

TELEPHONE—II: ONE RINGY DINGY, TWO RINGY DINGIES . . .

You wouldn't think superintendents of schools and school principals would need to discuss proper telephone manners with secretaries and receptionists, but, empirically, it is necessary. There are a number in inappropriate telephone habits in many districts, even where Lily Tomlin isn't the switchboard operator, and three among the many occur with regularity—two relatively small and easily correctable, although they still are important in conveying district interest to its constituents, and one larger, and somewhat more difficult to banish, bureaucratic habit inimical to a district's best interests.

(*1*) *Secretaries and receptionists answering calls without identifying themselves to callers:* It's annoying not to know with whom you are speaking, even when it's only a person's name that isn't even connectable to a familiar face—when such connections can be made, that's even better.

When the person answering the telephone gives his or her name, it makes the call a bit warmer and more personal. It's such as easy pattern to instill that it should be required unequivocally of all whose duties involve receiving calls. If clerical or secretarial personnel are, for whatever reason, anxious about using their names, give them a choice of first names, last names, nicknames, or aliases—as long as callers can identify the person on your end of the line by name.

(2) *Secretaries and receptionists keeping callers on the line without acknowledging them as they complete an office conversation, all of which is clearly audible to callers:* Sure, the office staff is busy, but this is a vile habit that should make superintendents' and principals' mustaches quiver.[172]

---

[172]If they are of a gender and inclination to favor decorative facial hair.

(3) *The thoughtless bureaucratic habit of requiring callers who don't know exactly with whom they should address problems, questions, or concerns to call another district number for assistance, where they may well be asked to call another district number for assistance, where they may be asked to call another district number for assistance, where they may be asked to call another district number for assistance, where they may be asked to call another district number for assistance:* Callers eventually begin to feel as if their ancient RCA Victor phonograph needle is stuck in a 78 RPM record groove or that they are in a time warp reliving the Kingston Trio's rendition of "Charlie on the MTA," doomed to wait forever for the right person on the telephone as "the man who never returned" rode forever through the streets of Boston on the Metropolitan Transit Authority.

Unless the caller knows with whom to speak *and* the school employee receiving the call is sure that person, or his or her secretary, is available to take the call, school district secretaries and receptionists should take the caller's name and number, note the issue or issues involved, and tell the caller the appropriate school official will call them back as soon as possible with a response to their questions, issues, or concerns.

Observing this practice means callers make one call only, not a series of calls, and don't experience the common phenomenon of alternating "muzak" and dead air as they are routed, ad nauseam, through labyrinths rivaling the Minotaur's mythological habitat[173] on the Island of Crete.

Even though the third bureaucratic habit is the most difficult to eradicate, all can be managed, and eliminating or modifying them makes a major difference in the public's perception of a school district. It's worth the administrative time and effort required to instill effective telephone practices in all employees, even if surgical implantation becomes necessary. Use some of that Blue Cross coverage.

---

[173]Daedalus, an early prison architect, didn't have anything on a few superintendents who preside over telephone bureaucracies more formidable than King Minos's maze. The Minoan king had the labyrinth built to confuse his favorite monster in the same way that some school districts' telephone switchboard procedures are designed to bewilder parents and other callers who are foolhardy enough to call a school or the central office in search of information. And the callers don't even have access to Ariadne's ball of thread to help them find their way out of their educational maze.

THE CAPTAIN MADE ME DO IT

Among the first concepts instilled in aspiring military officers is personal acceptance of responsibility for directives to others regardless of how uncomfortable the orders may be to their recipients. A typical example of junior officer behavior, both correct and incorrect, might involve a deck officer on a minesweeper who has been told by his captain that, because the ship had been placed on a four-hour standby for leaving port as part of an important mine removal operation, there won't be liberty for a particular group of deck hands until repairs are completed on minesweep gear critical to the ship's mission readiness. There are basically two ways the ensign could handle this order from the captain.

He may return to his department and say to the affected crew members, "Captain says you can't go ashore until the acoustic hammer and the magnetic tail are operational." He could even make his behavior worse by adding, "You know I wouldn't be this tough about this, but what can I do? The captain made me do it." Or he may return to his department and say to the crew, "The ship has been placed on a four-hour standby to leave port on an important sweep mission, so there won't be liberty for the department until we repair the acoustic hammer and the magnetic tail. We'll work in three-hour shifts until the job is done; I'll take the first shift with half of you, and Chief Bosuns Mate Nutsanbolts will work alternate shifts with the other half."

The parallel between this shipboard scenario and daily school district situations should be obvious. It is weak teacher leadership, after there has been a decision by the principal to require more homework of students, for teachers to say to students and their parents, "Gee, guys, I wouldn't ask you to do this myself, but I was told I had to." It is weak administrative leadership for principals, after receiving particular directions from superintendents requiring extra work of teachers, to say to faculty, "Gee, guys, I wouldn't ask you to do this myself, but I was told I had to." It is similarly weak administrative leadership for superintendents, after receiving an assignment from boards of education requiring extra work from principals, to say to them, "Gee, guys, I wouldn't ask you to do this myself, but I was told I had to."

All of these leadership behaviors are even more pathetic when there has been open administrative and/or faculty and/or board discussion and consideration of all appropriate staff ideas and points of view on the particular issue.

These are special variations on the concept that divergent administrative and other staff views should be both permitted and encouraged.[174] As long as issues are being discussed at less than the final decision-making level, administrators or staff should be strong enough to accept dissenting opinions from those with whom they work. But at the point that a decision has been made at the highest level, administrators and teachers shouldn't play the blame game with whomever they can play it.

If a leader can't support a directive from his or her boss, he or she should advance reasons for feeling that way as articulately and forcefully as possible to the originator of the message. If they aren't persuasive, the person in the middle should either find another place to work if the issue is that important to him or her or present the point of view adopted to others in the circuit as if it were their own. Nobody, or almost nobody, can carry this off without exception, but we should do the best we can with this concept.

Superintendents should remember that passing along unpleasant messages through others, and avoiding direct contact with the people most affected, lessens the chances of educational change occurring as expected.

As directives move further away from their origins, they grow weaker—the educational results of indirect instructions reflect this inevitable attenuation of the directive's or request's original purpose. It's also, unfortunately, not uncommon for anger, frustration, or hurt feelings to be transmitted from group to group within the educational enterprise; it's crucial for both superintendents and principals to change the tone of an angry directive recently received as we enlist the help of others to carry it out. Otherwise, it is often transmitted the same way to classroom teachers, with an eventual loss of student learning.

THE STRANGE CASE OF THE GIGANTIC, NEARSIGHTED, ENGLISH BULLDOG

For a number of years during Christmas vacations, a college student in Houston, Texas, worked as a post office extra, delivering seasonal mail, and for two or three years he walked a particular route in a rundown city neighborhood. In his brief experience as a letter carrier, he met (and got to know better than he wanted to) a gigantic, nearsighted, English bulldog with a nasty disposition and the largest teeth you've

---

[174]See also, this chapter, "Consensus versus the Right to Differ and to Be Different," p. 243.

ever seen.[175] The dog was on a chain shackled to the family clothesline, which only allowed him to waddle back and forth along the line. His primary function in life appeared to be terrorizing the college student disguised as a mailman, and it appeared fortunate that, each time the bulldog tried to eat the mailman, his chain kept him from it. Seemingly frustrated, he would lunge repeatedly, barking, snarling, foaming, and ravening, forelegs in the air, restrained only by his chain. Or at least that was the story he kept trying to sell the temporary postman.

On a particular day, the shackle that usually connected bulldog chain to bulldog clothesline had broken, and when the carrier's bulldog nemesis commenced his usual bullbog barking, snarling, foaming, and ravening routine, he soon became totally bulldog disoriented because he wasn't pulled up short upon reaching the end of the bulldog clothesline. As he took an additional tentative step or two unchecked, realized he was now free to digest whomever he chose, but also that he was simultaneously vulnerable to whatever his tiny brain thought the student might be able to do to him, he looked absolutely stricken. Turning his curly bulldog tail in my direction, he broke into his swiftest bulldog waddle, not stopping until he had crawled far under the old house—where he crouched howling piteously until the part-time postman had delivered the mail and departed.

We often see principals, and superintendents of schools, and teachers, and board members who resemble that bulldog—not in appearance, although that happens, too, but in their administrative, leadership, pedagogical, or oversight behaviors. Over and over, again and again, they whine and moan, bark and growl, foam and rave that if only someone, please God somehow, would remove the onerous constraints placed on them by bosses and/or cruel fate, which keep them from instructional supervision, or principal evaluation, or helping students, or board of education policy for board members who love to micromanage and dabble in administrivia, that they would hurl themselves recklessly at all those important tasks they really should be addressing.

The sad truth, more often than not, is these folks spend their time doing exactly what they like to do and what they feel comfortable doing. If they were finally freed from their self-perceived "educational or administrative or board of education shackles," they also would run under their desks or tables and howl piteously.

---

[175]See also, Chapter 6, "Taming the 450-Pound Media Gorilla—A One-Act Morality Play," p. 212, for information about the bulldog's midwestern brother and the origin of that Chapter 6 essay.

When teachers really want to teach, they can do that; when principals really want to be instructional leaders in their schools, they can do that; when superintendents want to work directly with staff to improve district education, they can do that; when board of education members want to be ferocious policymakers, they can do that. All we need do is give up a reasonable amount of what we like to do and are comfortable doing, and then we can do more of what we should be doing.

WHO IS THIS PERSON?—II

At least once, probably every superintendent in a district of any size has overheard a student ask another student or a teacher or the principal who he or she is. If a teacher asks a student that question, the superintendent is in real trouble; if a teacher asks a student the same question about the principal, the situation is even worse. There may be a number of explanations for that innocent question, some more legitimate than others, such as, in spite of regular administrative visits to the school, the particular kid just got mixed up—this is the best face that can be put on the situation. After all, everyone of the same sex over twenty-five years of age looks about the same to children—and, sometimes, kids don't even notice gender differences among people from twenty-five to ninety-five years old. They see each of us as indistinguishable molecules in the elderly staff compound that surrounds them each day of their school careers.

A variant of the first rationale, also acceptable to us, is that young people are simply so wrapped up in their own lives that "old" people don't even register on their consciousness—or said another way, superintendents cause a child's "tabula" to remain "rasa" or the kid's Polaroid® film to remain undeveloped or his optic nerve impulses to drown in an unmarked open synapse. Or, for whatever legitimate reason, the kid just doesn't remember the superintendent; unfortunately, that's not a felony—it's not even a misdemeanor.

The least acceptable cause of this phenomenon is that the superintendent rarely sets foot in the school, and there's no reasonable way kids should be expected to recognize him or her, even if all the youngster's circuits are "go," functioning perfectly, and he or she has the unusual ability to discriminate among relatively mature people.

Often, superintendents of schools complain of the onerous constraints placed on them by boards, and/or cruel fate, which keep them from getting out amongst the troops in the trenches. Unfortunately, they probably are spending their time doing what they like to do and what they are more comfortable doing. If superintendents truly want to spend more time in schools, they can do that. All they need do is give up a reasonable amount of what they now like to do and are comfortable doing; then they can spend more time in the schools, which is what they should do.[176]

Among recurring reasons and/or opportunities for superintendents to visit schools are (1) classroom observations—to monitor district instructional programs and to become knowledgeable about individual teacher's instructional abilities; (2) faculty meetings—opportunities to see principals and teachers working together and to discuss important districtwide activities and events directly with staff; (3) observations of building principals—although it's never exactly the same atmosphere with superintendents in the buildings, there are still valid indications of principal/staff relationships, principal/parent relationships, and principal/student relationships; (4) becoming better acquainted with students—except in the smallest systems, it's unlikely superintendents will ever know every child by name, but increasing the time superintendents spend in schools increases the number of students known by the superintendent, and it's guaranteed to increase the number of students who recognize the superintendent at special programs and school events such as concerts, assemblies, field days, awards ceremonies, plays, and other student performances; (5) school open houses—although normally only annual events, it's important for the superintendent to attend these evenings; (6) parent/teacher conferences—while not expected to participate in the actual conferences, it's good public relations with both staff and parents to be visible in the schools on these days; (7) Parent/Teacher Organization or Association meetings, dinners, and other events—good opportunities for superintendents to meet and speak with both parents and teachers, observe principals in these circumstances, and present themselves and their educational ideas to receptive audiences; (8) special school days—the first days teachers return in preparation for the new school year offer good opportunities for informal contacts with staff; the first day of school for students is another good day for superintendents to be in school buildings saying hello to kids; days before and after holiday weeks and, especially, days immediately prior to the close of school provide superintendents opportunities to assess school atmosphere and if instruction continues as

[176]See also, this chapter, "The Strange Case of the Gigantic, Nearsighted, English Bulldog," p. 264.

vigorously as it should—regardless of holiday or vacation proximity; or (9) any time at all.

In all community and staff interviews preceding superintendent searches, consultants always, always, always, always, always receive strong, clear messages from participants that it's crucial for the superintendent of schools to be regularly visible in the schools and at school and community events.

YOU CAN'T TELL ANYBODY WHERE YOU HEARD THIS, BUT . . .[177]

Throughout their careers, school leadership is approached by a teacher, another administrator, parent, board of education member, town official, or someone else, who says it's necessary to share something important with the educational leader. When ushered into the inner sanctum and given a cup of coffee, the visitors say they have something really important to tell you, but they will only say it if they are guaranteed no one will ever know the source of the information they are peddling.

Because this kind of approach logically involves someone besides the visitor,[178] the only appropriate leadership response is to explain very carefully and clearly that, even before hearing what he or she has to say, you can understand someone's reluctance to become involved in certain kinds of issues; unfortunately, you can't guarantee the requested assurance of anonymity; after hearing what your visitor has to say, if in good conscience you can preserve their confidentiality, you will do so. Further, as soon as you've heard what the person has to say, you will either confer the requested anonymity or tell them they may eventually need to stand up and testify because you must follow up what you've just been told.

If after that explanation, the teacher, administrator, parent, board of education member, town official, or someone else isn't willing to share the information with you, so be it; you will just have to live without the information unless you can acquire it another way—and you may never know what the person was willing to share with you.

Any immediate guarantee of confidentiality would erode the value of

[176]See also, this chapter, "The Strange Case of the Gigantic, Nearsighted, English Bulldog," p. 264.

[177]See also, Chapter 3, "Whom Did You Say Is Calling?" p. 105.

the information to be shared, because you can't, in good conscience, act against someone with information from what is to them an anonymous source. Guaranteeing witness immunity against further testimony, and anonymity for information given, requires you to either confront the accused without being able to reveal who accused them—a terrible position in which to find yourself and even if you receive an admission from the accused, it's a miserable leadership practice—or do nothing, except possibly monitor an elevated blood pressure from frustration over your inability to act on the information.

Assuming the "informant" agrees to the terms outlined and says whatever he or she came to say, a couple of hypothetical instances that would probably result in different administrative reactions to the "informant" are discussed briefly.

In the first instance, an administrator is told that the visitor witnessed, or has reasonable cause to suspect, child abuse by a parent or a staff member. Under this circumstance, depending upon state laws, the visitor may well be entitled to anonymity under the statutes. School officials, however, are bound by various state laws and/or regulations to report suspected child abuse to the proper state agencies and/or law enforcement officials.

In the second situation, the administrator is told the visitor saw a teacher coming out of an unsavory night club where it is rumored that alcohol is sold openly. In this circumstance, the administrator might be able to guarantee confidentiality because the information has no legal or other significance and can't be used in any meaningful way against a teacher anyway. At this time, administrators should make it clear to the visitor, as nicely as they can manage, that they aren't really interested in such reports of vague, unspecified behaviors by staff members.

In probably the most difficult scenario, an administrator is told that the visitor, who in this instance is a district teacher, witnessed another teacher slap a fourth-grade boy twice in the face because he cursed the teacher, who then slapped him in retaliation. Hearing this, the administrator must be up front with the reporter and tell him or her that the district will investigate the claim and that the witness will, at some point, probably be required to testify against the accused and, further, that you will acknowledge the source of your information with the accused teacher if asked to do so.

Other than suggesting strongly that the first thing you should do , if you are the superintendent, is call your school attorney or call the superintendent if you are a principal or other administrator, we'll skip discussion on each of the many combinations and permutations possible from corroborating testimony from the child or a lack thereof, confession or denial from the accused, deciding whether or not to call parents to let them know and if so when, whether or not to involve the police, the decision on formal charges to dismiss the teacher, potential disciplinary action against the child for swearing at the teacher who slapped him, etc.

The numbers and variety among types of specific information received by administrators from one person accusing another are only about two away from infinite, but the three preceding examples illustrate typical school leadership experiences.

All of these situations illustrate yet another need to balance conflicting rights and needs.

YOU PEOPLE AREN'T AS GOOD AS YOU THINK YOU ARE

As superintendents begin new superintendencies, they have two basic options.

In assertions, actions, and attitudes to and with students, teachers, administrators, parents, citizens, board members, town officials, and others, make it clear to them all that the school district was a good district before the new superintendent arrived, is a good school district now, and will be a good school district after the new superintendent is gone and, further, that every educational system can improve and that the new leader will work cooperatively with them to make their schools even better.

In assertions, actions, and attitudes to and with students, teachers, administrators, parents, citizens, board members, town officials, and others, make it clear to them all that the new leader believes the school district is broken and that, "By God, I am going to fix it if it's the last thing I do!"

Choose the first option, not only because it works and the second approach does not, but because it's also almost always true in spite of the real flaws all districts have. Even if later you discover you overstated slightly or even more than slightly, there's no harm done; you said you wanted to work together with everyone and make things better, and we'll just have further to go before we arrive where we want to arrive.

The second choice will kill new superintendents quickly, at least professionally, along with their chances to bring about needed educational improvements.

YOU ARE ALL SET TO RETIRE—AS YOUR SUPERINTENDENT, I GUARANTEE IT

A young principal worked for a veteran superintendent of schools[179] who served four rural, eastern Connecticut school districts as a state education department employee of the Bureau of Field Services—a division of the state education department responsible for a "remuda" of superintendents furnished free of charge to small districts financially unable to employ their own. Among many pieces of good advice he gave the principal was never to offer advice to teachers or other administrators on two subjects: teacher certification and teacher retirement.

His tripartite reasoning was similar for both circumstances. First, although we can all read statutes and regulations, these particular issues are complicated, and various reasonable interpretations are often possible on particular statutes or regulations and in response to an individual's specific queries; secondly, the only answer that really counts is the answer received directly from the state teacher certification office or the state teacher retirement system; anything else is speculation. Although it may be a very informed speculation, it's still just that; thirdly, and finally, the answers to these questions are too important for anyone to provide, except those people with statutory and regulatory responsibility and authority to provide them—and, even more importantly, the same responsibility and authority to back them up.

Throughout twenty-five years as superintendent, the once principal remembered his former boss's advice and acted, or didn't act, accordingly.

A positive corollary to the earlier admonition would be always to pose questions and receive answers on important issues in writing; different bureaucratic functionaries may render different interpretations or provide different answers at different times, and the same bureaucrat may even give different answers at different times. A far distant second

---

[179]Dr. Karl D. Ginand.

best to written questions and responses, especially when dealing with these crucial career issues, are dated summaries of conversations with retirement or certification counselors.[180]

At times, even oracles should keep silent.

PRACTICE MAKES PERFECT—MATCHING THEMES/MAIN IDEAS AND TITLES

Match the themes/main ideas stated below with subhead titles. Answers are provided in Appendix C, p. 478.

A Chest Full of Ribbons _____

Beat It to Death with a Stick _____

Cause and Effect—A One-Item Intelligence Test _____

Consensus versus the Right to Differ and to Be Different _____

Divergence and Convergence _____

Frequently Understandable, Often Forgivable, Never
  Acceptable _____

"Fruere Die!" _____

It's What You Do That Gets Me in Trouble _____

I Went to College and You Didn't _____

If You Didn't Hear It Directly, You Didn't Hear It _____

Kitchen Cabinets and Associated Hardware

Let's Do It Again Soon _____

Managing Conflict _____

Telephone—II: One Ringy Dingy, Two Ringy Dingies . . . _____

The Captain Made Me Do It _____

The Strange Case of the Gigantic, Nearsighted, English
  Bulldog

Who Is This Person?—II _____

You Can't Tell Anybody Where You Heard This, But . . . _____

You People Aren't as Good as You Think You Are _____

You Are All Set to Retire—As Your Superintendent,
  I Guarantee It _____

[180]A year or so ago, mindful of my own advice, I wrote the state teacher retirement bureau, asking for clarification of limitations on post-retirement earnings and setting forth three separate personal interpretations of retirement regulations thinly disguised as questions; the bureau's response to them were "yes," "OK," and "looks right," written in pencil on my original letter, undated, and unsigned—that didn't really provide me with a total sense of security or set my mind at ease.

Themes/Main Ideas

(1) Beginning a job in a positive manner is more productive than focusing on what is wrong in your new position.

(2) People can control their choices of activities far beyond their willingness to admit that.

(3) School district leaders should use effectively the annual educational cycle of rebirth, growth and achievement, and rest and reflection.

(4) There are times when it's better not to give advice.

(5) Except in rare crises situations with legal implications, leadership shouldn't use information from staff or others who aren't willing to be identified as the source of the information.

(6) It's crucial for the superintendent of schools to be regularly visible in schools and at school and community events.

(7) We need to remember who we are and from whence we cometh and, even if we come from the aristocracy, invest students with an equal potential to our own.

(8) If leaders disagree with directives from above, they should express that disagreement as articulately and forcefully as possible, but, if they don't prevail, they should act as if they were their own ideas.

(9) Organizational conflict is inevitable, but effective educational leadership usually can make it productive instead of harmful to the school or school district.

(10) Advisory groups offer invaluable opportunities to school leaders for open communication and for establishing and cementing personal and professional relationships.

(11) Mistakes of consequence should be examined and dissected in detail to find out exactly how they happened to keep them from happening again.

(12) Don't react to individuals on the basis of something allegedly said about you.

(13) Leadership should accept the difference between diverging and converging views with objectivity and equanimity because it is inevitable.

(14) Among a school leader's greatest contributions to education is becoming as unnecessary as it's possible to become.

(*15*) Other people's problems with misunderstanding reasons why events occur are the bane of leadership lives.

(*16*) When issues fade, don't bring them out to be painted again.

(*17*) Educators should recognize each moment of their lives as "quality time" and cherish each minute, day, and year we're given.

(*18*) Leadership should work toward group solidarity accompanied by understanding of individual freedom to disagree before decisions are final.

(*19*) Teachers do almost all of what the school district exists to do and should be recognized for it.

(*20*) Office bureaucracies can do major damage to educational causes through cavalier treatment of a school district's constituents.

CHAPTER 9

Collective Bargaining and Contract Implementation

COLLECTIVE BARGAINING

An Offer You Can't Refuse—I

GOOD NEGOTIATORS KNOW how to work effectively with other people and probably are successful in most professional relationships. Collective bargaining, which does require a modicum of specialized knowledge, is primarily a singular extension of interpersonal relationships. The most highly skilled negotiators can't cloud men's or women's minds and, through their articulateness or arcane negotiations techniques, persuade the other side to surrender cherished goals. The best they can do is give and take where the ground isn't as stony and hope self-interest eventually persuades the other party to abandon unrealistic positions. Although negotiators need to understand good and bad contract language, governing statutes and state regulations, ground rules, etc., basic human qualities define effective negotiators. One possible definition of a perfect negotiator might be "a person with a closed mind, a cast iron backside, and the ability to shake his/her head slowly from side to side."[181]

Clear, easily understood contract wording is crucial to successful administration and implementation of negotiated agreements approved by both parties. Ambiguous contract articles that have precipitated past grievances should be discussed at the bargaining table and clarified — or even better, as soon as the wording of a contract article is recognized to be unclear, it should be rewritten and agreed upon through "memoranda of understanding" or "sidebar agreements" between the parties — not waiting until the next round of formal negotiations to correct problems identified. Any existing contract can be modified by agreement of its parties, and "memoranda of understanding," "letters of

---

[181]An actual description of a board chairman with whom I worked for many years.

clarification," "sidebar agreements," or roses by any name, should be used to correct inappropriate or sloppy contract language. Such modifications, carefully thought out, won't jeopardize other sections of the agreement.

Negotiating teams should restrict discussion at the table to spokespersons only. At times, it makes sense to change spokespersons to give someone else on the team the opportunity to speak on an issue with which he or she is more knowledgeable than the regular spokesperson; this should only be done in a very clear way for a specific session or topic, after which the regular spokesperson should resume his or her former role. The reason for the role rigidity is to prevent the other side from exploiting differences of thought among a negotiating team's membership.

Because there are always these individual team member differences, superintendents should advise the board negotiating team to assign one or more of its nonspeaking members at the table the responsibility for monitoring, or "reading," the other side's nonspeaking members during bargaining sessions. Frowns, wriggles, smiles, moans, groans, snickers, and other such expressions, along with body language, give an experienced negotiating team targets for arguments that may result in eventual agreements favoring the side able to read the signals inadvertently sent by careless, or unperceptive, negotiators across the table.

Also, any member of the negotiating team should have the ability to call a caucus for purposes of discussing the team's position on an issue or to share with the team's spokesperson his or her reading of the other side or to suggest a different approach in the negotiation tactics of the moment or for other good reasons that might occur—either through prearranged signals or simply requesting it of his or her spokesperson.[182]

An Offer You Can't Refuse—II

Public school districts have been involved in collective bargaining with teachers, administrators, and support staff and with the attendant administration of negotiated contracts since the middle sixties. Over almost thirty years of legislative trial and error, there have been signifi-

---

[182]Try to avoid those signals used by third base coaches in major league baseball. They are far too distracting, and some of them are obscene.

cant refinements in the process, as well as substantive changes in governing statutes, but the major improvement in public sector bargaining has emerged from an increased understanding of collective bargaining and what contracts can and should do—and a greater effectiveness and efficiency from that greater understanding. That's not so different from the natural evolution in other human endeavors such as marriage and in other personal relationships; after a while, unrealistic expectations are tempered by experience and wisdom, and people adjust to their new realities.

In a number of states, changes have included "final last offer binding arbitration" and imposition of fixed negotiations time schedules based upon district budget submission dates. In spite of occasional rough spots, collective bargaining gives teachers and administrators an appropriate measure of self-determination and involvement with decisions in which they should have been involved anyway—most educators agree its pluses are greater than its minuses. Although usually a civilized process, collective bargaining is also inherently adversarial, and particularly in its infancy, there was polarization of teachers and management; while that's still a way of life in certain districts, over the years, most participants have mellowed and have accepted the need to control negative side effects from negotiations. When bargaining is concluded and contracts are approved, the parties are more willing to leave their differences at the bargaining table. In many school districts, outside professional negotiators have also contributed to less traumatic employment/management relationships.

Support staff unions, in various combinations and affiliations with different national, state, and local unions, represent secretaries and clerks, custodians and maintenance workers, paraprofessionals and teachers' aides, and food service workers in collective bargaining—often governed by separate state statutes specifically for municipal employees. Bus drivers and other transportation personnel are also represented in districts operating their own bus fleets.[183]

Support staff are vital to school district operations, and boards of education and superintendents of schools should give the same close attention to collective bargaining with their representatives that they do with certified staff groups. It's often necessary to recognize and diffuse support staff feelings that they aren't considered worthy of serious board and superintendent attention in bargaining or don't receive the

---

[183]In Connecticut, for example, municipal bargaining procedures follow different timelines than teacher and administrative negotiations and differ in other minor ways from certified staff collective bargaining.

same day-to-day managerial respect as certified employees—sort of a "Mom always liked teachers best" syndrome. Unfortunately, they are often correct, and management needs to honor daily contributions of these important educational personnel every way it can.

Adversarial roles in collective bargaining are real, but once the process ends, they need to be wrapped carefully and stored away in closets until the onset of negotiations for successive contracts. When board members or administrators view teachers as the enemy or when teachers see board members or administrators as the bad guys opposed to teachers' welfare, education suffers. No matter how difficult teacher groups may be at the bargaining table, management should remember that teachers are the only people in the entire school system who educate children. It's also important for superintendents to help assuage psychic injuries, on either side of the negotiating table, which may result from collective bargaining.

Oversimplified to make the point, typical boards of education negotiation philosophies maintain that their discretion to manage school districts, within their authority from state statutes, is untrammeled, except as limited by specific provisions in employee contracts. Oversimplified to make the other point, teacher associations/unions assert that boards can only do those things specifically allowed in negotiated agreements. As is usually the case with polar positions, neither is totally correct. The board's position is closer to correct, especially with "management rights clauses" included in agreements, but the "past practice" concept, as enforced by state labor relations boards, does restrict board behavior beyond specific contract restraints. The extreme association/union position that the board can act only as spelled out in employee contracts can't be defended successfully in legal challenges to it.

However, as previously mentioned, past practice theory often makes it advisable for boards to include contract language authorizing administrative or management rights that require particular teacher or administrator behaviors and actions—particularly if that behavior is a departure from past practice. Otherwise, bargaining units can bring a successful violation of "past practices" charge before a state labor board, and the board of education probably will be enjoined to hold the new practice in abeyance and forced to negotiate with representatives of the teacher association/union to reinstate it. This section applies equally to noncertified staff negotiations. Differences have been and are further highlighted as applicable.

Contract Body Parts

In the ice age of collective bargaining, state teachers associations/ unions, with help from their national parent bodies, developed prototypical employee demands and contract clauses. Almost thirty years later, through the science of cryogenics, employee agreements still contain many of these generic building blocks of accumulated association/union contractual wisdom and experiences that have survived collective bargaining's antediluvian era frozen and stored in article banks until thawed for use by affiliated employee groups—and that still, in their original wording, assert, identify, list, set forth, prohibit, limit, spell out, provide, afford, require, assure, or establish employee rights, freedoms, privileges, or abilities.

Many of the most common are listed in this section with brief explanations of their intent and contents. Although some clauses are self-explanatory from the specificity of their titles, except in the miscellaneous clause roundup at the end of the listing, explanations are given for each anyway. Titles used are among the most common contractual descriptions of the articles. Single asterisks indicate clauses that board of education negotiators should try to have included in contracts, although they are often mutually beneficial to employee bargaining units as well; double asterisks are those that should generally be avoided by board of education negotiators, and triple asterisks identify proposals that should be resisted until the end of the world and even beyond. The absence of asterisks means "ho hum, routine item."[184]

When labeling proposed articles, management is "wise to 'euphemize' " and to remember grandmotherly aphorisms such as, "A little honey makes the medicine go down!" or some other such rustic folk wisdom—or to consider tucking provisions away amidst clauses with titles not so obviously related to management interests.

Teachers will agree to an article called "Board of Education Responsibilities" more easily than they would the exact same clause identified as "Board of Education Management Rights to Do Whatever We Damn Well Please Whether Employees Like It or Not—So There!" They may also react more favorably to an untitled management rights article placed in the middle of a "Recognition" clause instead of set apart and labeled clearly as "Board of Education Prerogatives."

Employee negotiators play the same tunes, and management

---

[184]Because I've been so described, "half asterisks" aren't used.

negotiators need to remain alert for such concepts as "Maintenance of Standards," which may be otherwise titled or buried in another article, requiring employers to maintain all current employee working conditions and educational standards as they now exist; these provisions are open invitations for grievances, which employees will often win in arbitration, based on almost any conceivable, perceived departure from past practices—*por ejemplo*, "The principal frowned at me this morning, and he usually smiles at me."

(*1*) Zipper Clause*—neither party is obligated to discuss additional contract provisions during the life of the existing contract, and the contract contains all existing agreements between boards and associations/unions.

(*2*) Board Prerogatives or Management Prerogatives*—boards of education's overall statutory responsibility for school district management except as limited by specific provisions of negotiated agreements

(*3*) Severability Clause*—if one part of the contract is subsequently found to be illegal, the rest of it remains in effect.

(*4*) Maintenance of Standards***—all current working conditions and educational standards must be maintained as they have been previously (there are many possible titles for this, and, often, employees try to hide the words in other articles, particularly under general working conditions).

(*5*) Contract Duration*—effective life of negotiated agreements

(*6*) Recognition Agreement*—identifies employees covered by contracts and their bargaining representatives

(*7*) Grievances*—procedures to resolve employee differences with administrators or boards of education; from management's perspective, effective grievance procedures limit the scope of grievances to "alleged misapplications or misinterpretations of specific contract articles."

(*8*) Dues Checkoff or Salary Deductions—provisions for deductions of association/union membership dues (or sometimes also agency fees—see #10 below) from paychecks and transmittal of dues collected to associations/unions

(*9*) No Strike Clause*—prohibits illegal job actions: strikes, slowdowns, or other forms of withholding services; because in many states strikes are already illegal, it may seem gratuitous to include such articles; however, they give boards another remedy against illegal actions through state labor relations boards and "prohibited practices" or "improper labor practices" statutes administered and enforced by such state boards.

(*10*) Agency Shop or Agency Fee**– requires all employees, as a condition of their continued employment, to contribute specific amounts in support of their bargaining unit's efforts, on behalf of all employees (whether association/union members or not) in collective bargaining and contract implementation, including grievance processing and representation; applies only to employees who have chosen not to join their association or union and pay requisite dues (covered in #8, "Dues Checkoff or Salary Deductions")

An "agency shop" (as distinct from a "closed shop," which forces employees to join their associations/unions *and* pay dues) was illegal in many states for years and still may be in some. Recently, agency shops have been permitted through statutory changes; good arguments exist in support of agency fees, but most superintendents would probably prefer to respect the wishes of employees who are philosophically opposed to professional associations/unions. Their preferences are of no consequence when state laws require agency shops but may be a negotiations issue in states that have made agency shops legal but not mandatory; even in these states, arbitrators tend to favor employees in this instance.

(*11*) Reduction in Force (RIF) or Layoffs**– procedures and rationales for decisions on teacher layoffs if or when the board of education cuts teaching positions; also usually provide, for a specified number of years, recall procedures for employees who lose jobs through reductions in force (including such factors as seniority, past performance, certification, qualifications, and school district's requirements and needs)

(*12*) Class Size**– maximum numbers of students permitted in classes, usually varying according to grade levels in elementary schools and according to subjects in secondary schools; because budget implications are so great, many boards of education have managed to keep these clauses out of contracts – or have diluted them until they become advisory or philosophical guidelines, rather than prescriptions or controls.

(*13*) Assignments and Transfers**–administrative procedures and/or limitations and teachers' rights in school assignments, involuntary transfers, and postings of position vacancies

(*14*) Calendar, Work Day, or Work Year–employees' work year and/or work day

(*15*) Fringe Benefits, Benefits, or Employee Benefits–employee benefits other than salaries and supplemental pay schedules (often leaves with pay are included here, but it's common for them also to be elsewhere in contracts)

(*16*) Absences with Pay–conditions under which employees receive pay for time off; when this clause is included, most often there are subdivisions under this article for personal days, professional days, etc.

(*17*) Association/Union Leave**–days off with pay for organizational leadership in association/union business during school time (sometimes a category of Personal Leave or Leave with Pay clauses)

(*18*) Academic Freedom or Controversial Issues–faculty rights to teach controversial issues; boards should insist on contract wording requiring teachers to present balanced and even treatment of both sides of issues.

(*19*) Professional Issues**–professional employees' rights to participate in educational decisions, including rights to be heard on board of education policies or administrative regulations; double asterisks don't mean employees shouldn't have these rights, but because such rights are more safely granted through board of education policy where staff misunderstandings can't be grieved and arbitrators can't render horrendous decisions (many possible titles for this, and often the concept is placed strategically in other articles).

(*20*) Employee Working Conditions**–specific working conditions that the board of education must provide for employees

(*21*) Reimbursement for Graduate Courses–conditions for reimbursement of staff for educational course work toward master's degrees, sixth-year certificates of advanced graduate study, and doctorates (often found in professional employee supplemental pay schedules, and they often only cover graduate study after a staff member has met state requirements for permanent certification–usually a master's degree or equivalent).

(22) Conference and Travel Reimbursement—reimbursement for conference and/or travel expenses (often under Professional Days clauses)

(23) Sick Leave or Temporary Disability—absences with pay for childbirth and associated conditions

(24) Sick Leave Bank**—a communal pool of sick days, contributed to by all members of bargaining units for use by individuals who exhaust their personal allotment; most districts already afford teachers ten to fifteen sick days yearly, which often can be accumulated without limit; as unfeeling as it may sound to staff, there comes a time when employees shouldn't be paid unless they work; sick leave banks should be resisted by boards of education.

(25) Leaves (Child Rearing, Child Care, or Parenthood Leaves; for Restoration of Health; Graduate Study; etc.)—leaves, almost always without pay, for one or more school years to allow employees to care for infants, including adopted children; men and women are equally eligible for such leaves; beyond accumulated sick leave, leaves of absence may be granted for restoration of employee health; there are also leaves without pay for graduate study for employees not eligible for, or not awarded, sabbaticals; the federal Family Leave Act should be examined alongside contractual leave provisions to avoid any conflicting requirements.

(26) Sabbatical Leaves—Leaves with pay, usually half to three-quarters of regular pay, for advanced graduate study and less commonly for travel or other approved educational reasons; boards often restrict the number of sabbaticals granted in a given year and also usually retain the right to award none at all; conditions are normally placed on staff eligibility for sabbaticals, including length of district service, provisions for maintaining insurance, credit on salary schedules for time spent on leave, guarantees on employees' rights to return to the district and in what positions, employees' obligations to return to the district and serve a specified number of years, restrictions on employment while on leave, etc.

(27) Retirement Incentives—monetary payments to employees meeting eligibility requirements, which can include length of district service, length of total educational service, provisions for maintenance of health insurance benefits (sometimes with the board sharing part of the costs), etc.; these provisions have often saved

districts money overall through replacement of teachers at the top of salary schedules with new teachers at the bottom of the schedules; this savings can't be guaranteed, and districts must be careful about federal and state regulatory agencies and charges of age discrimination in choosing new teachers to replace veteran teachers; often, with the employment market as good as it is for employers, new teacher applicants are superb, but if they are always chosen over better qualified, experienced teachers with equivalently high personal qualities, claims alleging age discrimination can be made effectively and sometimes are.

(28) A hodgepodge of other contract articles with various titles (or found within other contract clauses) that assert, identify, list, set forth, prohibit, limit, spell out, provide, afford, require, assure, or establish employee and management rights, freedoms, privileges, or abilities, including this dozen among others: (1) provision of contract copies to employees, (2) salary schedules and attendant conditions for moving from one category of remuneration to another, (3) prohibition of discriminatory practices, (4) employee benefits upon termination of employment, (5) stipends for coaches and class and club advisors, (6) limitations on after-school staff meetings, (7) staff evaluation procedures, (8) existing contract continuing in full effect until a new agreement is negotiated (strict timelines in some states have rendered this provision obsolete), (9) procedures for amending negotiated contracts, (9) staff members' access to personnel files and administrative procedures in maintaining files, (10) employment contracts, (11) negotiations ground rules, and (12) teachers' responsibilities for collecting student funds.

Don't Run Up the Score—Crushing the Opposition Is Bad Form

Continuity among and between bargaining teams is difficult—especially for boards of education unless they use outside professional negotiators. But continuity contributes to successful negotiations, as well as to stability in local collective bargaining. When negotiators change often, mutual understandings and respect that may have existed between people who shared previous experiences are lost and must be reestablished; this requires ritual dances resplendent with strange posturings and vocalizations, all of which are better avoided. Stability at the bargaining table increases when competent, outside representatives for both sides negotiate—another good reason to consider them.

Negotiators learn quickly that when one side "wins" too big, both sides lose. If one or the other parties suffers humiliating contract losses, their efforts redouble in the next round of negotiations. Sometimes, employee bargaining units change union/association affiliations because of a big time defeat, and the newly crowned replacement bargainers try to compensate for their predecessor's losses and establish themselves and the new representative organization as the true champions of the oppressed and downtrodden. When this happens, reason takes a holiday.

Many experienced negotiators argue that successful negotiations are characterized by both parties being mildly unhappy with the results—said more positively, both parties are allowed to feel modestly successful, but not quite satisfied, with collective bargaining outcomes. Less than euphoric feelings on both sides or mild satisfaction on both sides indicate that an appropriate balance between winning and losing has been achieved.

It's Not My Job

Although the adversarial mentality, which in its earlier years characterized collective bargaining, is not as prevalent today, superintendents of schools should avoid spending too much time at the negotiations table when good alternatives are available—and should be careful not to be seen as opposed to legitimate teacher or administrator interests. That's pushing professional good nature and sophistication too far and can interfere with superintendents' day-to-day staff leadership. If boards of education don't understand the risks of a superintendent's presence at the bargaining table, he or she should explain them to the board. Central office representation (assistant superintendents, personnel directors, business managers) on board negotiating teams is, however, important, regardless of whether board members or outside negotiators represent management.

In small districts with limited funds, board members often negotiate directly with staff, but even when they're personally well suited for this role, it's usually wiser for boards to consider professional negotiators—if competent mercenaries are available and the board can afford them; not because the "pros" are automatically so much better (although often they are and also save the district much more than their fees), but because they can diffuse the more intense feelings that may still be generated from negotiations.

When both sides employ professional negotiators, everyone at the table knows the game and plays it with much less emotional wear and tear on district education—and board negotiators probably will produce better results, keep catastrophic contract articles out of contracts, and, in the final analysis, save school districts money. If educational budgets won't allow paid negotiators for all bargaining units, central office assistants and business managers are especially good alternatives, particularly with support staff unions.

Superintendents of schools are key advisors to whomever negotiates for boards. They sometimes also provide unofficial, behind the scenes, assistance to employees in collective bargaining through personal persuasion in leadership relationships to diffuse inappropriate staff expectations from negotiations—being careful to avoid being perceived as, in any way, disloyal to their boards of education. Principals' practical experience and their support of superintendents' efforts are key to superintendents' success as collective bargaining advisors to boards of education.

School chiefs, with appropriate involvement of building principals and central office assistants, usually have the greatest understanding of day-to-day effects of contract provisions and should, at a minimum, analyze employee proposals and provide recommendations on district positions and responses to board negotiators. Prior to such recommendations, superintendents should review proposals with principals and other key administrative assistants unless they happen to be parties to administrative negotiations.

Also, prior to commencement of collective bargaining, superintendents should advise boards of current contract articles requiring modification—or which should be removed from current agreements. Organizing recommended responses to staff proposals, with reasons therefor, into categories such as (1) "No problem," (2) "Maybe in return for concessions on other issues important to the board," and (3) "Not until hell freezes over and beyond" help board negotiators keep bad things from happening contractually.

In spite of the earlier caution against superintendents at the bargaining table and depending on the size of the district, in mediation or arbitration superintendents may need to be more involved with direct assistance to board negotiators. In resolving negotiations conflicts, especially concerning articles involving public control of local education, superintendents should help boards understand employee positions but, on the other side of arguments, also clarify for board members the potential effects from surrendering or weakening management control of any aspect of district governance.

A cartoon from somewhere in my negotiating history showed Moses, having just returned from a second trip up and down Mount Sinai with the stone tablets, speaking to an anxious assemblage of Israelites at the foot of the mountain. His opening statement about his recent trip to the theistic negotiations table was, "It was hard bargaining—we get the milk and honey, but the anti-adultery clause stays in." Apparently, God wasn't willing to relinquish or weaken management control of certain behaviors.

Quid Pro Quo and All That . . .

Some management negotiators feel obliged, either because of bad advice or intrinsic ignorance of bargaining realities, to prepare extensive lists of demands to balance those advanced by employees—or "If there are five pounds of employee demands, we must submit five pounds of management demands." *Not!* Although negotiations are, to a limited degree, two-way streets and often result in employee concessions to board of education proposals, there are more lanes on the employees' side than on the board's. It's a mistake to believe that there must be, or even can be, a quid pro quo from employees for each management concession in negotiations.

Boards of education have more of what the other side can take from collective bargaining—money, benefits, control, etc. Bargaining can't gain increased teacher dedication, competence, quality of instruction, etc. Boards may negotiate additional teacher in-school time or increased teacher service on committees, and these often are positive achievements, but the quality of employee service is not contractually available. You can contractually drive a teacher to a seminar, but you can't make him think.

Although management should begin employee negotiations with a few important but realistic proposals on behalf of improving district education, overworking "quid pro quo" is a time-consuming, silly, unproductive habit that should be avoided.

The Wisdom of Solomon—I

In most states, mediation and arbitration are dispute resolution procedures for boards of education and employee associations/unions that have reached negotiations impasses. Mediation is the first step, with a single mediator chosen by mutual agreement of the parties, often from a panel of state-approved mediators. Although the parties may, in many jurisdictions, choose anyone upon whom they can agree as their mediator (someone's Uncle Fred, for example), it's unusual for them to go outside the state panel of approved mediators. Usually, the parties share mediation costs, including mediator's fees and associated expenses.

Parties typically present in mediation are the mediator; regular negotiations teams for both sides; possibly a legal advisor for either, or both, boards and associations/unions; association/union state or area representatives; and superintendents or their designees for board negotiations teams.

Aspects of mediation can be formal, but compared to arbitration, it's a relatively casual process. Mediators are highly skilled amoral beings in their special roles working between the parties who often are ensconced in different rooms after mediators' initial statements; sometimes, mediators pass go immediately and begin discussions with each party separately, attempting to move either or both sides as far as necessary to secure contract agreement.

Although mediators don't have any authority to compel the parties to make further concessions or to agree, they usually tell each side it should compromise as necessary and use the other party's most effective data and arguments to help achieve contract agreement. Even when privately holding strong views on who's right and who's wrong, mediators will argue both sides as effectively as they can while trying to make each party believe the mediator is interested in that party's welfare *uber alles*; as soon as mediators begin their discussion with the other party, they reverse their arguments without the slightest twinges of guilt.

Good mediators are often very effective in resolving differences that appeared insurmountable as sessions began. In addition to a variety of other mediators' approaches—their interpersonal skills, their special experiences, their professional knowledge and wisdom, and their personal insights into the process—one of their most effective techniques is keeping the parties working toward settlements until fatigue kicks in; agreement can then be reached just so participants can get the hell out of the room, go home, and have a couple of martinis.

Mediators can be partially successful, as well as totally successful, or completely unsuccessful. Often, although not managing complete agreement on each disputed article, they manage to bring both sides together on many unresolved items—leaving fewer contested issues still on the table for arbitration. Mediators may also adjourn to second (and, even rarely, to third) sessions, and parties are sometimes encouraged to continue meetings on their own between the initial mediation and any follow-up sessions. When mediators aren't completely successful and contract resolutions aren't reached between the parties, arbitration begins.

The Wisdom of Solomon—II

Arbitration, if binding instead of advisory, is normally the ultimate step in collective bargaining impasse procedures, but it may be the penultimate step in exceptional situations when one of the parties files for a judicial review of an arbitration decision. Aspects of arbitration can be informal, but compared to mediation, it's a relatively formal process.

Arbitration typically employs a single arbitrator or a panel of three arbitrators chosen from an approved list of state arbitrators. If the parties decide on a tripartite arbitration panel, which is common, boards choose one arbitrator to represent their interests as do employee groups, and the two so chosen select the third, or neutral, arbitrator—neutral arbitrators control arbitration awards, and the roles of the two interest arbitrators, in addition to voting the politically correct way at the conclusion of the process to make their employers happy, are to be persuasive with neutral arbitrators and affect their thinking and their final decisions on arbitrated issues. Customarily, the parties pay their own "interest arbitrator's" fees and associated expenses and share fees and expenses of the "neutral arbitrator." Although the single arbitrator option available in some states saves money and probably results in the same outcomes, three arbitrators appears to be the more popular choice.

Parties customarily in attendance at arbitration sessions are a three-person arbitration panel or single arbitrator; regular negotiations teams for both sides; possibly a legal advisor for either, or both, boards and associations/unions; association/union state or area representatives; superintendents or their designees for board negotiations teams.

Unlike mediators, arbitrators control the outcomes of contract disputes. Generally, representatives for both sides make final presentations to arbitrators and give their ultimate positions for arbitrators to consider before they render arbitration awards binding on the parties—unless arbitration is, by statute, only advisory.

In some jurisdictions, "final last offer binding arbitration" is a special version of arbitration, which forces arbitrators to choose one party's position intact on each item in dispute—with no opportunity for compromise between the parties' positions available in other forms of arbitration. This forced choice is intended to, and generally does, move parties closer together to avoid the possibility of a major loss for either one. For example, both sides are driven to huddle around the going rate for salary increases in the state and area, instead of wandering off too far from the campfire.

Some states provide for court review of arbitrators' decisions, but arbitration awards are upheld unless moving parties can show that arbitrators exceeded their statutory authority or that they acted arbitrarily or capriciously.[185] Recently, some statutes allow town or district legislative bodies to reject arbitration awards; however, initial awards are normally referred back for review to another panel of arbitrators whose decision is binding and who almost always uphold original arbitration awards.[186]

When they believe it will make them more popular at reelection time, politicians are often eager to spend taxpayer funds to run quixotically at each arbitration windmill.

CONTRACT IMPLEMENTATION

Knit One, Purl Two

Weaving negotiated agreements often can be the easier part of producing the overall collective bargaining fabric; the most difficult tasks can involve administration of agreements approved by both sides—sometimes, this aspect of collective bargaining more closely resembles stitching up wounds than weaving cloth. Administering negotiated agreements is a complex business and requires consistency and expertise; it doesn't always cause major personnel problems, and it won't if superintendents of schools, principals, and other administrative staff understand and practice their craft knowledgeably and fairly.

---

[185]Seems strange that "arbitrators" can't act "arbitarily," but they're not supposed to.
[186]But not until after school districts and towns have incurred significant additional expenses and wasted personnel time and effort.

A Not Always Merry Band of Brothers

Among major components in superintendent success are building and maintaining effective working relationships with teacher and administrative unions or associations. The same kind of functional contacts with support staff unions are also important and should be given similar attention, even if it often comes from a business manager or assistant superintendent instead of the superintendent of schools.

Effectiveness with employee organizations requires the same kind of professional skills and personal attributes as does effectiveness with people generally. The triumvirate of honesty, openness, and trustworthiness are essential for superintendents who want to work successfully with association/union leadership. It's also essential for superintendents to respect the role of unions or associations and to recognize their special organizational responsibilities.

There are many common interests between employee groups and administrative leadership in developing and maintaining productive educational environments, programs, and practices; in adequate numbers of well-prepared staff; in educational tools, supplies, and equipment provided; in the public's view of the school district; and in many other areas; however, unions and associations inherently hold employees' salaries, benefits, and welfare uppermost in thought and deed.

No matter how strong the mutual feelings of respect between superintendents and unions or associations may be, in the crunch, employee unions and associations inevitably will support their group's interests above all else. It's futile and counterproductive for superintendents to feel betrayed when union leadership, with whom they have worked closely, oppose administrative positions when they seem not to be in employees' best interests. In these instances, union/association leaders are still good people and can remain professional friends while honoring their primary responsibilities to their staff compatriots.

Practices that contribute to building and maintaining strong working relationships with employee associations and/or unions include: (1) regular work sessions with union/association leadership to discuss matters of mutual interest, (2) frequent communication with union/association leadership to inform them of important district developments in which they might have an interest, and (3) recognition of union/association accomplishments locally and statewide.

The four requirements for an effective working relationship between superintendents and employee unions/associations are (1) communications, (2) communications, (3) communications, and (4) communications. (They could also be the ten requirements, the dozen requirements, the hundred requirements, or the zillion requirements, and each would remain the same.)

Meeting all four, ten, twelve, hundred, or zillion requirements still only improves the odds, instead of guaranteeing success,[187] but better odds are better than the inevitable bad odds from an absence of effective communications between superintendents of schools and the not always merry bands of union/association brothers and sisters.

Trouble, Thy Name Is Interpretation

Negotiating contracts typically requires two or three months and often is less troublesome than administering them, and compared to the two or three months required to build contracts, administering agreements is an unending responsibility for school administrators. Although superintendents are ultimately responsible to boards of education for contract administration, the first line contract interpreters and enforcers are building administrators: principals and assistant principals.

Superintendents should insure that each building administrator knows the effects each contract article can have on daily building operation and understands the superintendent's attitudes toward liberality or "scroogeness" in contract interpretations when contract wording allows some degree of administrative leeway in its interpretations. Variations in contract administration generating differences in staff treatment among district schools always create major school personnel problems; to prevent these problems, superintendents must work with all district administrators to develop consistent contract interpretations and personnel decisions among all school buildings and school departments.

Annually, and more often if necessary to insure administrative understanding of personnel contracts, superintendents should review all employee contracts with building-level administrators, giving special emphasis to important contract articles, such as grievance procedures, and how negotiated articles should be interpreted at the school level.

---

[187]See also, Chapter 4, "Better Odds Are All You Can Expect—In Poker or Leadership Life in General," p. 113.

Sometimes the Darn Thing Doesn't Work Right

Administering negotiated agreements is relatively easy when contracts are tighlty drawn and precisely written. Under those conditions, administrators don't need much more than rudimentary literacy, but perfect contract wording is almost as difficult to find as a perfect set of board policies.

Real-life administration frequently encounters different understandings between and among reasonable teachers and administrators. Differences between employees and supervisors cause grievances, but differences in administrative contract interpretations and grievance decisions create even greater personnel difficulties than grievances themselves.

Occasionally, administrators recognize certain contract articles are unfair to particular teachers in particular circumstances. When contract wording is clear, administrators must abide by the specific contract language, even when their instincts say that mitigating or special conditions make specific articles overly restrictive on, or inappropriate in some way to, particular grievants. Although school superintendents may persuade boards of education to modify contracts through memoranda of understanding, or letters of agreement, with the association/union leadership, until that happens, superintendents and other administrators must interpret contract articles as written—not as administrators wish they had been written. Because negotiated contracts are agreements between boards of education and employee bargaining groups, boards in concert with associations/unions have authority to clarify or change contract interpretations, but superintendents of schools and principals are not empowered to do so.

When contract language is ambiguous, creative administrative contract interpretations to provide more equitable grievance decisions become legitimate possibilities, but administrators who ignore clear and plain language, for whatever humanitarian reasons, are asking for big-time troubles with their bosses. Again, administrators are bound to follow specific contract articles as they are written even when they see them as imperfect or unfair, and subsequently work with superintendents of schools and boards of education to have them modified, retroactively when possible, to accommodate legitimate special concerns of employees.

When administrators are required to decide grievances, they must understand the redress sought by grievants. Sometimes grievances don't specify an administrative action desired; under these circumstances, administrators should refer grievances back to the grievant for clarification, especially if there seem to be important issues lurking within the grievance that require identification and a leadership response. Administrative willingness to consider technically defective grievances on their real merits produces better personnel results than grievance rejections on technical grounds—even when such rejections are contractually defensible.

Administrators may believe particular grievances are specious because claims have no relationship to specific contract articles, as often required in contract definitions of grievances; for example, challenging the substance of teacher evaluations when contracts specifically prohibit grieving supervisory judgment on employee evaluations. Such defective grievances must still be heard administratively before determinations are made on them. Also, even frivolous grievances may be appealed through all hearing levels.

Grievances initiated beyond allowable time limits for grievance submission can be rejected without an administrative hearing on the substance of the allegations, but even in these circumstances, it's often better practice to hear them. In these instances, administrators should be sure the grievance record reflects that the grievance is untimely, and in decisions denying such grievances, this should be the first reason given for their rejection. Acting on the substance of grievances, in addition to rejecting them on the basis of untimeliness, builds better administrative cases if and when grievances reach binding arbitration

Throughout grievance hearings and grievance administration, common sense and practicality should prevent bureaucratic behaviors. Grievances aren't educational versions of television courtroom scenes where each lawyer's single purpose is securing a favorable verdict for his client. School administrators need to hear other parties' feelings and frustrations, rather than winning at any cost through minor technical flaws in grievances. Too many administrators and too many teacher associations/unions turn grievance hearings into win/lose contests.

Although one party or another will always be the official "winner," effective grievance administration minimizes the negative effects of "win/lose" and allows everyone to emerge from the process with something of value—a "win/win" approach to grievance administration.

You Done Me Wrong

Grievance procedures are primary methods of resolving differences between employees and management, and although contract wording varies, all try to do the same thing—provide mechanisms for orderly and civilized resolutions of differing points of view. Grievance procedures are among the most important articles in employee contracts but are not always recognized for their value to school leadership and to staff—or for their potential to create educational mischief. All grievance procedures have a relatively small number of sections in common.

Grievance definitions are the key paragraphs in the grievance procedures, and from an administrator's perspective, good definitions restrict grievances to violations, misapplications, or misinterpretations of specific contract provisions. Although this narrow definition has obvious management advantages, it also offers cleaner, more easily administered employee contracts that discourage ambiguous grievances otherwise impeding association/union pursuit of more important issues. Many states also provide other remedies for alleged management improprieties through state labor relations boards.

Final resolution levels in grievance procedures are second in importance, for both management and employees, only to grievance definitions. Most of today's grievance procedures have provisions for binding arbitration as the last and final grievance stage following board of education rejection of grievances.

Grievances usually require initial informal discussions before initiating formal grievance steps. The first formal grievance level is with immediate supervisors, typically building principals; superintendents of schools, or designees, are the second; boards of education are the third level; and arbitrators are the final step—either advisory or binding. Over the nearly thirty years of public sector collective bargaining, this final step has evolved from a board of education final decision to advisory arbitration and, in most situations in most states, to binding arbitration. Boards of education have been understandably reluctant to give up final control of grievances, but when contracts between two parties are interpreted only by one party, employee benefits from bargaining are more illusory than real. Good contracts imply mutuality and equality and bind both parties—anything less than binding arbitration unfairly skews contract control toward boards of education.

However, there are important contractual restrictions on binding arbitration that management should try to include in grievance procedures: that arbitrators may decide only one grievance in each instance and that arbitrators may not add to or delete from specific contract language. In other words, arbitrators aren't free to interpret creatively if such interpretation adds, deletes, or changes the contract words and intent.

Time limits for grievance stages are important. At each grievance stage, there are prescribed time limits for grievants to appeal an earlier administrative decision to the next higher management level and other time limits for administrative or management respondents to render their decisions on grievances. Times usually range from three working days to as many as fifteen, and sometimes even thirty, work days for boards of education or arbitrators. The most important time limits restrict the initiation of grievances to a finite period—usually five to thirty work days from the time grievants "knew or should have known" of alleged contract violations.

What happens if either party exceeds prescribed time limits? For grievants, their grievance is usually lost when they exceed time limits. When administrators or boards of education exceed limits, there are two likely possibilities: grievances automatically progress to the next higher stage, or grievants win their grievances.

The first option is preferable to management and more common in negotiated agreements. Although it appears one-sided for teachers to lose when they don't meet time limits and for lesser management penalties to be imposed when its representatives exceed time limits, life isn't always fair, and there are defensible explanations of the differences.

In one situation, the moving party fails to act and is appropriately responsible for his or her own fate. On the other hand, errors by any of a few involved school district administrators can have major negative effects on boards of education for many years. Management should try to insure that missing a time limit "fails safe," and the grievance proceeds to the next level, rather than the grievant "winning" the grievance.

Sometimes management and sometimes employees also view grievances as painful procedures or as indications of management failures. This is unfortunate because, although numerous grievances caused by narrow, bureaucratic, contract interpretations are bad administrative omens, grievances provide employees an organized method of dealing with frustrations, as well as revealing imperfections among lower management. When superintendents or boards of education frequently hear grievances resulting from ineffective contract implementation, they gain knowledge necessary to correct errors resulting from poor administrative judgment.

Big Brother Is Watching

Many states provide labor relations boards that are empowered and directed to prevent unfair labor practices by either public employers or public employees.[188]

When complainants allege unfair labor practices, the labor relations board may dispatch an agent to investigate, and in most instances, agents either make a report to labor boards recommending dismissal of complaints or issue written complaints charging unfair labor practices to be heard by the board.

Although it's unusual for boards and their agents to conflict, sometimes they do. When the labor board receives its agent's findings, it may accept or override such recommendations. The board may also hold hearings on its own initiative without receiving field agents' recommendations. It may investigate allegations further even when agents recommend their dismissal. When agents issue written complaints charging unfair labor practices, the board may dismiss charges either before or following the recommended board hearings.

Labor board hearings, although normally not bound by the prevailing courtroom rules of evidence, are formal hearings to take testimony and argument on alleged unfair labor practices, order further investigations of allegations, state findings of fact, dismiss complaints or find unfair labor practices, and issue orders to offenders (usually cease and desist orders).

Labor board findings can compel employers to bargain on the impacts of employer changes in working conditions not covered in employee contracts. In other words, when employers unilaterally change past practices, they may be directed to negotiate with employees on the effects of such changes. State labor relations boards prohibit either side from engaging in unfair labor practices such as coercing, dominating, or interfering with another party's appropriate exercise of collective bargaining rights; these constraints are among the most significant, arising from actions of state labor relations boards under labor relations statutes.

Either party aggrieved by final orders of the labor board's granting or denying the relief sought, in whole or in part, may obtain court reviews of such orders. While court proceedings are pending or underway, labor relations board orders stand.

[188]Although each state's labor statutes will differ to some degree, information in this section is based on Connecticut laws governing its state labor relations board.

The potential for labor relations board's involvement, or interference depending on who's asked, has not been fully explored by most public school associations/unions, and the specter of bureaucratic control of local affairs remains a shadowy figure in a corner of the collective bargaining arena. Arguments have been made on behalf of excluding public school districts from the purview of labor relations acts, but so far, teacher and other employee lobbies have been too strong.

COLLECTIVE BARGAINING AND CONTRACT IMPLEMENTATION DISCUSSION CASES

Determine whether each situation described should be considered a prohibited practice, or in other ways illegal, by any of the parties involved in school district collective bargaining. Reponses should be based on the illustrative state collective bargaining statutes provided in this chapter following the Discussion Cases, p. 304. (Statutes included don't always spell out exactly specific courses of action required, and responses may, in a few instances, need to be deduced from other sections of this chapter, from statutory context, and from as much professional experience as may be brought to bear on the case studies. In many of these real-life circumstances, consultation with district counsel would be appropriate and often essential.) Appendix C, pp. 480–489, provides suggested answers/responses, citations of specific statutes as possible, and reasons for recommended teacher, administrative, board of education, or other positions.

(1) FACTS: You serve as the president of a local bargaining unit affiliated with the American Federation of Teachers (AFT) in a district that also has an active National Educational Association (NEA) teacher minority unit. Your current contract with the board of education prohibits use of personal time for union business. Because you have a good working relationship with the superintendent, you ask and receive approval to attend a statewide union meeting. A union associate questions accepting these personal days. Under the circumstances, are there potential legal consequences from accepting personal days for union business? If so, what are they?

(2) FACTS: As negotiator for your association, in the last three contract negotiations, you have attempted to negotiate a dental plan. Each time, board negotiators rejected it because of its costs. One

of your bargaining team colleagues suggests filing an improper labor practice against the board for its refusal to bargain in good faith. What is the likely labor relations board response?

(3) FACTS: You are an active member of an NEA affiliate in a district facing a representation election between rival teacher factions—the NEA association and an AFT union. In the teachers' room, the building principal is openly critical of the AFT because he says teaching is a profession incompatible with union membership, and he derides people with "union mentalities." What remedies may be available to the AFT affiliate in this situation—both practical and legal?

(4) FACTS: In this same situation, an active AFT (American Federation of Teachers—national teachers union) colleague complains to the superintendent that she is encountering overt hostility in the teachers' room from NEA (National Education Association—national teachers association) supporters. She claims they won't talk to her and that she was not asked to a recent after-school social by other teachers in her grade. Does either the teacher or her organization have a successful legal remedy? If so, what should it be?

(5) FACTS: As a new superintendent of schools, you are discussing negotiations with your board chairman who questions the appropriateness of your business manager belonging to the district's administrative bargaining unit. Are there legitimate grounds for this concern.

(6) FACTS: As board of education spokesman in negotiations with the teacher bargaining unit, you receive a proposal from the teachers' bargaining representatives spelling out the teachers' responsibilities for evaluating the work of paraprofessional teachers' aides. Included with teachers' rights to evaluate aides are a chain of command for aides to observe and establishment of teachers' jurisdictional superiority over aides in the classroom. Is this a legally appropriate teacher proposal and, if not, why not?

(7) FACTS: As a building principal in a district that has not heretofore had an administrative bargaining unit, your fellow principals are considering forming such a unit. The superintendent of schools prepares a memorandum to administrators in which he makes the following points:
   • He cites the correct current annual membership costs for administrators if the unit is formed.

- The board and superintendent of schools have previously enjoyed good working relationships with administrators, and the previously informal working relationships might change if administrators form a bargaining unit.
- He asks each administrator to weigh carefully the relative advantages and disadvantages of forming an administrative bargaining unit, including financial costs to administrators and possible changes in working relationships among the management team.

Is the superintendent legally or procedurally in error, and if so, what recourse, if any, is available to your group?

(8) FACTS: As chief teacher negotiator, you and the board of education's chief negotiator have mutually agreed on three dates to begin collective bargaining. On all three occasions, board representatives did not appear or even call beforehand to cancel and reschedule the meetings. Your team is understandably angry about this and discusses possible remedies available to you. What charges could you levy against the board and to whom?

(9) FACTS: As superintendent of schools, you are reviewing the status of teacher negotiations with your board chairperson who also heads the board's negotiating team at the table. She is angry about a teacher proposal for an "agency shop" and has strong feelings about forcing all staff members to support financially an organization they may otherwise prefer not to support. She is prepared to refuse to discuss the teacher proposal with their bargaining representatives. What should your advice be to her?

(10) FACTS: As a district teacher, your bargaining unit is discussing the possibility of adding a particular nontenured teacher to your group. You are aware that the teacher has had serious classroom problems with a son of the board of education chairman who also chairs the board's bargaining team and that the chairman has expressed strong feelings against the teacher. Are there any statutory prohibitions against the teacher serving on your team? From a teacher's perspective, can you think of any practical reasons to put a teacher on a bargaining team when the board chairman, and possibly other board members, seem "out to get" that particular nontenured teacher?

(11) FACTS: As chief negotiator for the board of education, you receive a proposal from teachers on class size. In a caucus with your team, a member suggests rejection on the grounds that class

size is nonnegotiable. Is that a proper position for you to take? Could it be advantageous to take this position? What's the worst legal outcome of your team's adopting that bargaining position?

(*12*) FACTS: As a member of your administrative bargaining team, you are entering arbitration over next year's salaries. You're convinced that the board will maintain a final offer of zero increase. Recent area settlements in districts of similar financial ability have been about three percent. For "last best offer arbitration," what would your recommended final salary offer be and why?

(*13*) FACTS: As superintendent of schools, you are contacted by Ebeneezer Scrooge, chairman of the town fiscal body, who informs you he was appointed by the board of finance to represent that board in teacher negotiations, and he plans to attend teacher negotiations sessions. In discussing this with the board of education chairman, he expresses strong reservations about Scrooge's participation, on the grounds that his presence would affect the outcome of the process. What advice would you give the chairman on whether or not to encourage or allow Ebenezer's involvement in teacher negotiations? Are there any limits the board of education might place on his participation?

(*14*) FACTS: As personnel director of a school district, you are approached by the representative from your custodial bargaining unit. The district's current contract with his union doesn't contain provisions for payroll deductions of union dues; however, the district is deducting dues for secretaries' and bus drivers' unions under specific articles in their contracts. The custodial representative asks that his group receive similar treatment, and he points out that the previous representative union for custodians had such a provision in their contract and that his union inadvertently left out a dues deduction proposal during the recently concluded negotiations. Legally, what rights, if any, do you have to refuse his request? Other than the legalities of his request, what else might be considered?

(*15*) FACTS: As personnel director, you are the spokesperson for the board of education and have received a teacher proposal on reduction in force (RIF). A member of your team wants to place a counterproposal before the teachers, asserting that when a husband and wife are both employed the RIF (or layoff) article in the contract makes the female spouse more vulnerable to position loss. What would your advice to him be?

(*16*) FACTS: As the union spokesperson in negotiations, after three separate and lengthy discussions of your proposal for an "agency fee" provision, the board negotiator refuses to agree to it and says further that it's a dead issue unless later resolved in mediation or arbitration. Your team members are pushing you to file a prohibited practice complaint against the board for not negotiating in good faith.

(*17*) FACTS: You are a principal opposed to agency shops, and the board of education has agreed with the administrative bargaining representatives on an agency fee provision in the new contract, including a five percent surcharge over association dues for administrators not belonging to the association. The provision is clearly designed to increase association membership in addition to ensuring financial support from all administrators. Do you have any recourse under these circumstances?

(*18*) FACTS: As superintendent of schools, one of your assistant superintendents appears at the bargaining table as the new spokesperson for the administrative association; he requests that the next scheduled administrative negotiations session be changed to another date because he has a previous commitment as the board's representative in secretarial negotiations. Anything amiss here?

(*19*) FACTS: Teachers walk out of the initial bargaining session with the board of education representatives, refusing to negotiate as long as the attorney selected as the board's spokesperson is in that role. Their state association had listed him, in an organizational newsletter rating professional management negotiators, as the worst, most arbitrary, least respectful of the teaching profession it had encountered over ten years of statewide negotiations.

(*20*) FACTS: As a board of finance member, the board negotiating team during the initial negotiations session with administrators refuses to allow you to address them on the need to hold salary increases in the next contract to less than the cost of living.

(*21*) FACTS: As the board of education's chief negotiator, you distrust the finance board representative's ability to keep board positions confidential and want to exclude him from a particularly sensitive board of education negotiators' caucus on a final salary offer to the district's administrators. Is this legally appropriate? Why or why not?

(*22*) FACTS: As superintendent, your board of education successfully completed contract negotiations with district teachers; the legislative body in your town rejected the contract and sent it to the second arbitration permitted by state statutes. The teachers' group has submitted a written response to the legislative body with a copy to the commissioner of education.

The board of education disagrees with the town's rejection of the contract and believes the second arbitration is probably pro forma and will result in upholding their original agreement with teachers. In discussing this position, some board members ask the superintendent to contact the board's negotiator, an outside attorney, and ask him to prepare a written response to the second arbitration panel; others are unwilling to incur the additional expense this would entail. As a result of this belief, both sides on the board turn to you and ask who is legally correct. What is your response?

(*23*) FACTS: As teacher negotiator, you are arguing a vehement staff position on the school calendar, restoring the February midwinter vacation week, which the board of education, for the first time ever, has omitted from this year's school calendar. You submit a proposal to establish three week-long vacations during each school year; one in December, one in February, and one in April. The assistant superintendent serving as the board of education's spokesperson in negotiations flatly refuses to negotiate on your proposal. What recourse do you and your association have in this instance?

(*24*) FACTS: As superintendent of schools, one of your board negotiators, citing public anger against sizable numbers of district teachers who are paid from the proceeds of local taxation but don't pay town taxes themselves, wants to include a proposal in negotiations that requires teachers to maintain residence in town as a condition of employment. She is willing to grandfather all existing teachers but insists the article must apply to all teachers employed after the effective date of the new teacher contract. What is your advice to her?

(*25*) FACTS: Teacher negotiators are angered by your board negotiator's absolute refusal to discuss, or even to hear, the teachers' point of view on a teacher proposal suggesting changes in a current contract article that is clearly a mandatory subject for negotiations. However, the board spokesperson claims the teacher proposal is unbecoming and even demeaning to professional educators. Following this meeting, union leadership openly calls for teachers to call in sick, in accordance with a schedule prepared and promulgated by the union president, until such time as the board will listen "in good faith and with an open mind" to the teachers' request. As superintendent, what is your advice to the board of education negotiating team?

COLLECTIVE BARGAINING STATUTES FOR DISCUSSION CASES[189]

Discrimination because of Marital Status [64]

"No local or regional board of education shall discriminate on the basis of sex or marital status in the employment of teachers in the public schools or in the determination of the compensation to be paid to such teachers."

Rights Concerning Professional Organization and Negotiations. Annual Service Fees Negotiable Item [65]

(a) Members of the teaching profession shall have and shall be protected in the exercise of the right to form, join, or assist or refuse to form, join, or assist any organization for professional or economic improvement and to negotiate in good faith through representatives of their own choosing with respect to salaries, hours, and other conditions of employment free from interference, restraint, coercion, or discriminatory practices by any employing board of education or administrative agents or representatives thereof in derogation of the rights guaranteed by this Section and Sections 10-153b to 10-153n inclusive.

(b) Nothing in this section or in any other section of the general statutes shall preclude a local or regional board of education from making an agreement with an exclusive bargaining representative to require as a condition of employment that all employees in a bargaining unit pay to the exclusive bargaining representative of such employees an annual

---

[189]You may assume that any words omitted and indicated by an ellipse . . . have no bearing on your response.

service fee, not greater than the amount of dues uniformly required of members of the exclusive bargaining representative organization, which represents the costs of collective bargaining, contract administration, and grievance adjustment, and that such service fee be collected by means of a payroll deduction from each employee in the bargaining unit.

Selection of Teachers' Representatives [66]

(a) . . . (1) The "administrators' unit" means the certified professional employee or employees in a school district not excluded from the purview of Sections 10-153a to 10-153n, inclusive, employed in positions requiring an intermediate administrator or supervisor certificate, or the equivalent thereof, and whose administrative or supervisory duties . . . shall equal at least fifty percent of the assigned time of such employee. . . . (2) The "teachers' unit" means the group of certified professional employees who are employed by a local or regional board of education in positions requiring a teaching or other certificate and are not included in the administrators' unit or excluded from the purview of Sections 10-153a to 10-153n, inclusive. "Commissioner" means the commissioner of education. (4) "To post a notice" means to post a copy of the indicated material on each bulletin board for teachers of every school in the school district . . . or to give a copy of such information to each employee in the unit affected by such notice. (5) "Budget submission date" means the date on which a school district is to submit its itemized estimate of the cost of maintenance of public schools for the next following year to the board of finance in each town having a board of finance, to the board of selectmen in each town having no board of finance, and, in each city having a board of finance, to said board and otherwise to the authority making appropriations therein. (6) "Days" means calendar days.

(b) The superintendent of schools, assistant superintendents, certified professional employees who act for the board of education in negotiations with certified professional personnel or are directly responsible to the board of education for personnel relations or budget preparation, temporary substitutes, and all noncertified employees of the board of education are excluded from the purview of this section and Sections 10-153c to 10-153n, inclusive.

(c) The employees in either unit defined in this section may designate any organization of certified professional employees to represent them in negotiations with respect to salaries, hours, and other conditions of employment with the local or regional board of education that employs them by filing . . . with the board of education a petition that requests recognition of such organization for purposes of negotiations under this section . . . and is signed by a majority of the employees in such unit.

(d) Twenty percent or more of the personnel . . . may file . . . with the commissioner a petition request that a representation election be held to elect an organization to represent such a unit.

Meeting between Board of Education and Fiscal Authority Required. Duty to Negotiate. Procedure If Legislative Body Rejects Contract [67]

(a) Within thirty days prior to the date on which the local or regional board of education is to commence negotiations pursuant to this section, such board of education shall meet and confer with the board of finance in each town or city having a board of finance, with the board of selectmen in each town having no board of finance and otherwise with the authority making appropriations therein. A member of such board of finance, such board of selectmen, or such other authority making appropriations shall be permitted to be present during negotiations pursuant to this section and shall provide such fiscal information as may be requested by the board of education.

(b) The local or regional board of education and the organization designated or elected as the exclusive representative for the appropriate unit, through designated officials or their representatives, shall have the duty to negotiate with respect to salaries, hours, and other conditions of employment about which either party wishes to negotiate. For purposes of this subsection . . . (1) "hours" shall not include the length of the student school year; the scheduling of the student school year; the length of the student school day; the length and number of parent teacher conferences; and the scheduling of the student school day, except for the length and the scheduling of teacher lunch periods and teacher preparation periods. . . . Such negotiations shall commence not less than 210 days prior to the budget submission date. . . . All organizations seeking to represent members of the teaching profession shall be accorded equal treatment with respect to access to teachers, principals, members of the board of education, records, mailboxes, and school facilities. . . .

**Strikes Prohibited. Interference with the
Exercise of Employees' Rights Prohibited. Hearing
before State Board of Labor Relation. Appeal.
Penalty [68]**

(a) No certified professional employee shall, in an effort to effect a settlement of any disagreement with the employing board of education, engage in any strike or concerted refusal to render services. This provision may be enforced in the superior court for any judicial district in which said board of education is located by an injunction issued by said court or a judge thereof. . . .

(b) The local or regional board of education or its representatives or agents are prohibited from: (1) interfering, restraining, or coercing certified professional employees in the exercise of the rights guaranteed . . . (by statute); (2) dominating or interfering with the formation, existence, or administration of any employees' bargaining agent or representative; (3) discharging or otherwise discriminating against or for any certified professional employee because such employee has signed or filed any affidavit, petition, or complaint under said sections; (4) refusing to negotiate in good faith with the employee's bargaining agent or representative . . .; or (5) refusing to participate in good faith in mediation or arbitration. A prohibited practice committed by a board of education, its representatives, or agents shall not be a defense to an illegal strike or concerted refusal to render services.

(c) An organization of certified professional employees or its agents is prohibited from: (1) interfering, restraining, or coercing (A) certified professional employees in the exercise of the rights guaranteed . . . (by statute), providing that this shall not impair the right of an employee's bargaining agent or representative to prescribe its own rules with respect to acquisition or retention of membership provided such rules are not discriminatory and (B) a board of education in the selection of its representatives or agents; (2) discriminating against or for any certified professional employee because such employee has signed or filed any affidavit, petition, or complaint under said sections; (3) refusing to negotiate in good faith with the employing board of education, if such organization has been designated or elected as the exclusive representation in any appropriate unit; bargaining agent or representative . . .; (4) refusing to participate in good faith in mediation or arbitration; or (5) soliciting or advocating support from public schools students for activities of certified professional employees or organizations of such employees. A prohibited practice committed by a board of education, its representatives, or agents shall not be a defense to an illegal strike or concerted refusal to render services.

(d) As used in this section, Sections 10-153a to 10-153c, inclusive, and Section 10-153g, "to negotiate in good faith" is the performance of the mutual obligation of the board of education or its representatives or agents and the organization designated or elected as the exclusive representative for the appropriate unit to meet at reasonable times, including meetings appropriately related to the budget-making process, and to participate actively so as to indicate a present intention to reach agreement with respect to salaries, hours, and other conditions of employment, or the negotiation of an agreement, or any question arising thereunder and the execution of a written contract incorporating any agreement reached if requested by either party, but such obligation shall not compel either party to agree to a proposal or require the making of a concession.

(e) Whenever a board of education or employees' representative organization has reason to believe that a prohibited practice . . . has been or is being committed, such board of education or representative shall file a written complaint with the state board of labor relations and shall mail a copy of such complaint to the party that is the subject of the complaint. Upon receipt of a properly filed complaint, said board shall refer such complaint to the agent who shall, after investigation and within ninety days after the date of such referral, either (1) make a report to said board recommending dismissal of the complaint or (2) issue a written complaint charging prohibited practices. If no such report is made and no such written complaint issued, the board of labor relations, in its discretion, may proceed to a hearing upon the party's original complaint . . . which shall in such case be treated . . . as a complaint issued by the agent. Upon receiving a report from the agent recommending dismissal of a complaint, said board of labor relations may issue an order dismissing the complaint or may order further investigation or a hearing thereon. . . . If, upon all the testimony, said board determines that the party complained of has engaged in or is engaging in any prohibited practice, it shall state its finding of fact and shall issue and cause to be served on such party an order requiring it to cease and desist from such prohibited practice. . . .

Mediation and Arbitration of Disagreements [69]

(c) (4) . . . In arriving at a decision, the arbitrators or the single arbitrator shall give priority to the public interest and the financial capability of the town or towns in the school district, including consideration of other demands on the financial capability of the town or towns in the school's district. The arbitrators or the single arbitrator shall further consider, in light of such financial capability, the following factors:

(A) The negotiations between the parties prior to arbitration, including the offers and the range of discussion of the issues; (B) the interests and welfare of the employee group; (C) changes in the cost of living averaged over the preceding three years; (D) the existing conditions of employment of the employee group and those of similar groups; and (E) the salaries, fringe benefits, and other conditions of employment prevailing in the state labor market, including the terms of recent contract settlements or awards in collective bargaining for other municipal employee organizations and developments in private sector wages and benefits.

(c)(7) . . . Within ten days after receipt of such notice *(legislative body rejection of an initial arbitration award)*, the exclusive representative of the teachers' or administrators' unit shall prepare, and the board of education may prepare, a written response to such rejection and shall submit it to the legislative body or legislative bodies, as appropriate, and the commissioner. . . . The review conducted *(of the legislative body's rejection of the initial arbitration award)* pursuant to this subdivision shall be limited to the record and briefs of the hearing pursuant to subdivision (2) of this subsection, the written explanation of the reasons for the vote, and a written response by either party. . . .

Residency Requirement Prohibited [70]

No municipality or school district shall require that an individual reside within the municipality or school district as a condition for appointment or continued employment as a school teacher.

GRIEVANCE SIMULATIONS

Using the teacher contract (WFCT) or the administrator contract (WASA), as appropriate, in Appendix A, provide written administrative decisions on the following Grievance Simulations. Suggested administrative responses are provided in Appendix C, pp. 490–496. For purposes of these exercises, unless otherwise stated, you are a building principal who has held the informal discussion required in Step 1 of the grievance procedure and could not resolve the issue at that point. Reading grievance procedures in each contract before beginning the exercise is recommended. (In the WFCT contract, although the contract wording isn't as clear as it should be, Step 1 is the informal discussion with the teacher's immediate supervisor, and Step 2 is the formal meeting with the supervisor.)

The Administrative Hearing Officer

Your choices as the administrator hearing the grievance are either to grant the redress sought by the grievant, at which point the grievance ends, or you may reject the grievance, and the grievant must then make a decision whether or not to proceed formally to the next step of the grievance procedure. It's wise for administrators faced with a grievance to have discussed it with their superintendent prior to making a decision at their level—this is neither inappropriate nor prejudicial to a later decision when grievances reach a higher level. It's a normal and expected part of the grievance process.

(1) GRIEVANCE: A teacher grieves her assignment as a lunchroom monitor because it is an alleged violation of past practice. The teacher is given the duty-free lunch period required by statute and by contract; her complaint is that she has never been made to do this before and that because it is a violation of past practice, she shouldn't have to do it now. There is no contract article cited in the grievance.

(2) GRIEVANCE: The same conditions apply, with the exception that Article 36 of the contract is cited as the article that has been allegedly violated by the building principal.

(3) GRIEVANCE: You receive a grievance from a teacher in a given school alleging violation of Article 37 on class size. It is her contention that her fifth-grade class of twenty-seven students violates the contract.

(4) GRIEVANCE: The same situation exists as in #3, except the grievant is a physical education teacher who has been assigned forty-five students per period.

(5) GRIEVANCE: For this grievance, you are the superintendent of schools. You receive a grievance from a fifth-grade teacher, challenging your involuntary transfer of her from one school to another. Because she was senior to a number of other teachers

who were not transferred, she claims her transfer is a violation of Article 41.

(*6*) GRIEVANCE: You receive a grievance from a teacher complaining about your practice, as a building principal, of maintaining your own copies of each personnel file for teachers who work with you. She alleges a violation of Article 42.

(*7*) GRIEVANCE: As superintendent of schools, you receive a grievance from a principal claiming that, upon initial employment, he was misplaced on the salary schedule and not granted credit for three years as a private school principal in Virginia, which is in violation of Section IV-1 of the Wayward Administrators and Supervisors Association Contract.

(*8*) GRIEVANCE: As superintendent of schools, you receive a grievance from a teacher alleging violation of Article 8. The teacher had received longevity payments for each of the previous four years, but in June 1994, the business manager did not include the amount in her paycheck. The teacher files the grievance on July 1, 1994.

(*9*) GRIEVANCE: As superintendent of schools, you receive a grievance, similar to the one in #8, from a teacher who, in the fall of 1994, begins her twentieth year of teaching in the district, alleging violation of Article 8. It is her contention that she received an incorrect $400 longevity payment in June 1994. The grievance was filed on September 1, 1994.

(*10*) GRIEVANCE: As superintendent of schools, you receive a principal's grievance on a deduction under the agency shop provision of the identical amount paid as dues by members of WASA, Section X-1, when the principal isn't an Association member. Furthermore, he cites current figures from WASA that show "71% of the amount paid as dues by Association members is used in support of the Association's costs for collective bargaining and grievance administration."

(*11*) GRIEVANCE: As superintendent of schools, you receive a grievance from a teacher in her last year of teaching prior to retirement. She claims the director of personnel has denied her the increase in pay (which she requested in writing on September 1 of her last year) provided under Article 12, because her fifteen years of service were broken into two segments — one of eight years and one of seven years.

(*12*) GRIEVANCE: As superintendent of schools, you receive a grievance from a principal whose family had the unfortunate experience of a major medical problem, running up bills covered by major medical insurance of over $700,000, asking the board of education for payment of that amount. Under Article 5-1 in the administrators' and supervisors' contract, the board must provide $1,000,000 in major medical insurance; because of business office error, the principal was not enrolled in the major medical plan until a month after the major illness began. The insurance company won't pay his medical bills over and above BC/CMS payments because, in its contract with the board, employees must be covered prior to the onset of particular illnesses.

(*13*) GRIEVANCE: While on sabbatical leave, a principal completed a graduate course that had previously been approved by you as superintendent of schools. You receive a grievance from her because the director of personnel had denied course reimbursement, claiming that a principal on leave is not eligible for such reimbursement. The principal, who has returned to the district and is working in her regular position during the current academic year, claims violation of Section VI-2 of the WASA agreement.

(*14*) GRIEVANCE: As superintendent of schools, you receive a teacher grievance because he has not been given credit for a partial year of teaching prior to a leave of absence for health reasons. He cites Article 21 of the agreement. It is his assertion that, because he taught September through January, those five months constituted one-half of a school year. His placement on the salary schedule does not reflect credit for that year because the personnel director said that teaching eighty-eight days from September through the end of January was less than half a school year.

(*15*) GRIEVANCE: A teacher who has taught in your school district for ten consecutive years applied for a sabbatical leave of absence; it was not granted. In the year she applied, the board awarded no sabbaticals. She cites Article 25 as the article allegedly violated.

(*16*) GRIEVANCE: A teacher grieves the initiation of a new spelling curriculum, citing Article 31. She claims she was not sufficiently involved in the development of the curriculum, that she had volunteered to serve on the committee that developed the curriculum, but that she was not given that opportunity.

(*17*) GRIEVANCE: A teacher grieves her perceived insufficiency of teaching materials, citing Article 32.

(*18*) GRIEVANCE: As superintendent of schools, you receive a grievance from a teacher who claims the building principal chastised him for nonattendance at PTO meetings. He had not attended any during the year, with the exception of the "back-to-school night." The principal admits discussing the teacher's nonattendance with him but says all he did was point out a general professional obligation to participate in those meetings.

(*19*) GRIEVANCE: As superintendent of schools, you receive a grievance from a teacher who claims the local bargaining affiliate was not allowed to meet in accordance with Article 34. The WFCT had arranged a meeting to discuss a new board of education policy; the principal insisted on being present and attended the WFCT meeting in spite of protests by union leadership.

(*20*) GRIEVANCE: You receive a grievance from one of your teachers who claims that you did not enforce discipline properly. She had recommended pupil suspension, and you had not followed her advice. No specific contract violation is cited.

(*21*) GRIEVANCE: You receive a grievance from a teacher who alleges your violation of Article 38 by requiring her to collect funds for the *Weekly Reader Magazine*.

(*22*) GRIEVANCE: A teacher pursues, at the board of education level, the superintendent's refusal to overturn an earlier principal's refusal to grant him personal leave covering the two days immediately preceding the February vacation for his planned family ski trip. He cites a violation of Article 18e. As a board member, how should you vote on this grievance appeal? How vulnerable do you believe the district will be if the teacher takes his grievance to binding grievance arbitration upon the board of education's rejection of it?

(*23*) GRIEVANCE: Between the first and second pay periods in June, a teacher submitted his resignation for retirement purposes to the board of education, and now, in early July, is grieving the business manager's refusal to pay him for the accumulated sick leave provided for in Article 22.

(*24*) GRIEVANCE: As superintendent, you hear a grievance from a principal who is grieving the districts refusal to cover her extended illness from the "sick leave bank" under Section VI-5 after she had exhausted her accumulated sick time. The business manager points out that she hasn't participated in the sick leave bank, until now, through voluntary contributions of sick days to the bank.

(25) GRIEVANCE: A teacher, citing Article 28, grieves her teaching assignment, which allows her only two planning periods per week.

CONTRACT ANALYSIS EXERCISE

There are a number of generic, standard, or prototypical clauses in teacher and administrator contracts, many of which are described below. Examine your own district's teacher and administrator contracts and the WFCT and WASA contracts in Appendix A to identify similar articles as they exist, and list the titles of the articles that say, assert, identify, list, set forth, prohibit, limit, spell out, provide, afford, require, assure, or establish the following (you probably won't find them all, and many will exist in a variety of different configurations):

(1) . . . Agreements in this contract are all that exist between the board and the association/federation, and neither party is obligated to discuss other articles during the life of the contract; (2) . . . the board's overall responsibility for management of the school district; (3) . . . if one part of the contract is found to be illegal, the rest of it is still in effect; (4) . . . the duration of the contract; (5) . . . the group of employees covered by the contract; (6) . . . procedures to resolve an employee's difference of opinion with administrators or the BOE; (7) . . . collection of membership dues or fees for the association/union; (8) . . . illegal job actions; (9) . . . steps to reduce the number of staff employed; (10) . . . maximum number of students allowed in classes; (11) . . . assignment/transfer; (12) . . . employees work year and/or work day; (13) . . . benefits other than salary; (14) . . . conditions under which employees can receive pay for time off; (15) . . . union or association business on school time; (16) . . . a faculty's right to teach controversial issues; (17) . . . rights to participate in educational decisions; (18) . . . specific working conditions to be provided; (19) . . . maintenance of all previous working conditions; (20) . . . staff reimbursement for educational coursework; (21) . . . reimbursement for conference expenses; (22) . . . leaves with pay for certain other educational purposes; (23) . . . leave connected with childbirth; (24) . . . leave for child-rearing; (25) . . . provision of contract copies to employees; (26) . . . compensation and conditions for various levels of compensation; (27) . . . discriminatory practices;

(28) . . . early retirement benefits or incentives; (29) . . . benefits upon termination of employment; (30) . . . posting of job vacancies; (31) . . . stipends for coaching and advisory positions; (32) . . . administrative authority to conduct after-school meetings; (33) . . . staff evaluation; (34) . . . rights to express staff opinions on board of education policies or administrative regulations; (35) . . . communal pool of sick days for use by teachers; (36) . . . existing contract continues in full effect until a new agreement is negotiated; (37) . . . contract amendment procedures; (38) . . . access by teachers to their own personnel files; (39) . . . employment contracts to be used; and (40) . . . negotiations ground rules.

CHAPTER 10

Planning

THE WELL SEEMS DRY

THROUGHOUT MOST OF the eighties, many public school systems across the nation received strong financial support reflective of the overall national economy and the economic optimism characteristic of that decade—misplaced though it was. Some states, possibly wanting to get a head start on the national economic deterioration, began experiencing financial problems earlier than the rest of the nation. Beginning in the late eighties and persisting at least into the mid-nineties, national economic woes have been paralleled by similarly difficult conditions in many states and localities.

This unfortunate combination of events has continued to freeze school district budgets to late eighties or early nineties levels—in spite of continuing increases in salaries, albeit small percentages most recently, and with modest inflation in costs of educational goods and other services. The national mood is to hold taxation at fixed levels, or even to cut taxes, and many school districts are really hurting financially and, therefore, educationally.

The synergistic effects of static budgets, combined with gradually higher prices for the same services, has had deleterious effects on class sizes; on the quantity and quality of educational supplies, equipment, and textbooks; and on the already significant problems with thousands of school facilities. Originally, many buildings were cheaply constructed and have been poorly maintained over the years, and because of construction shortcuts and deferred maintenance, these facilities have aged badly. For many years, they have required health and safety improvements, including asbestos removal, as well as major renovations to improve their educational adequacy—few of which have been accomplished. In many locales, especially cities, school facilities are characterized by leaky roofs, inadequate ventilation, erratic heating systems, impure drinking water heavily laden with lead and other nondigestibles, and a general air of decrepitude.

Because of the public's inability or unwillingness to spend more on education, the preponderance of educational gains in the future must come primarily from improved staff performance, from stronger pupil motivation, from greater parental support of educational goals, and from existing resource reallocation to meet higher academic priorities. Because most teachers and administrators are already doing their best and because social turnarounds don't happen easily, rearranging existing expenditures is almost the only arrow remaining in education's quiver. Many, if not most, school districts have been traveling the "reallocation path" for too many years already—California districts live with abysmal class sizes, and, as a result of Proposition 2-1/2, Massachusetts schools have shifted funds among accounts until there is nothing left to reallocate.

Although increased expenditures result in educational benefits for students, gains cannot be directly proportional to higher expenditures, and if educational spending were to double, student output would not. But if American public education is to maintain its best educational programs, improve those that badly need improvement, and rehabilitate its buildings, educational costs must inevitably rise, even in the face of a fierce national inclination to hold the line. Increases will take place much more gradually than in previous decades, regardless of the pent-up need for such educational spending increases.

MAKING DO WITH LESS WATER

The fiscal realities confronting American public education require continuous and effective long-range planning to develop school district consensus on educational priorities, to impose effective internal expenditure controls, and to develop and maintain public financial support of public education. Community support, reflected in budgetary allocations, affects a board of education's ability to provide sufficient staff and thereby maintain reasonable class sizes; modern facilities; up-to-date textbooks and library books; adequate instructional supplies; equipment, especially technological; appropriate special education programs; building maintenance and upkeep; heat, lights, and telephones; insurances; pupil transportation; and various other needed educational goods and services.

Long-range planning helps school districts use available personnel, financial, and facilities resources more efficiently and effectively, regardless of a given district's relative affluence.

Effective educational planning requires data collection, assumptions, estimates, inferences, projections, analyses, insights, organizations, syntheses, judgments, conclusions, guesses, recommendations, and decisions by people not graced with infallibility. Educational planners can't guarantee correct courses of action for all circumstances and will never know what alternative courses of action might have produced, but long-range planning provides information and guidelines essential to board/administrative efforts to maintain consistent educational progress and to make significant improvements in student programs.

It's always easier to identify needs than to meet them and easier to recognize problems than to solve them, but long-range planning remains the foundation for necessary discussions, decisions, and actions to meet district educational needs and to solve related problems. However, plans can neither be prescriptions to cure all present and future school district ills nor immunizations against bad economic things happening in the first place.

Recommendations in long-range plans may not be accepted – some because funding is not available and others because boards of education or communities disagree with them. Although existing programs are often automatically assumed to be worthy of continuation, they are neither sacred nor immutable, and they may be eliminated or modified from necessity – or because of philosophical choices by boards of education. Regardless of fiscal climates, long-range planning is integral to a school district's effective use of available resources to clearly identify educational priorities; to project, for five or more years, detailed budgetary costs of maintaining existing high-priority personnel, programs, and facilities; and, within the context of realistic funding, to calculate future costs, over the next five or more years, of the improvements recommended in long-range plans.

STRATEGIC PLANNING

"Strategic planning" is a special varietal of long-range planning, involving community, town government personnel, boards of education, school administration, teachers, other staff, and, often, students in retreats, workshops, and committees to establish school district mission statements, goals and objectives, and to develop action teams and action plans to determine in detail how to achieve missions, goals, and objectives. The American Association of School Administrators (AASA) has an effective model of strategic planning, and a number of state and national consulting groups are well prepared to facilitate districts' strategic planning efforts.

Strategic plans are outstanding preludes to specific long-range budget planning when they bring community consensus on educational goals and objectives—and if they set forth specifically the means of achieving them. However, if strategic planning stops short of translating mission statements, goals, objectives, and action plans into specific budgetary expenditures, it's likely the effort won't achieve its intent.

As a continuation of strategic planning, districts still must (1) consider recommendations with cost implications in the context of all the ordinary, fixed budgetary needs, as well as computing estimated costs of conceptual programmatic changes suggested in strategic plans, and (2) incorporate strategic plans into specific long-range budget documents with good projections of *total* educational costs for five or more years.

Without complete long-range budget projections, program improvement decisions are made in fiscal vacuums, and, eventually, the ensuing disappointments will generate cynicism about the planning process. Too often, school district planners don't take this last step effectively, and good ideas languish unfulfilled.

HOW MUCH WILL A NEW WELL COST?

Although dramatic increases in educational expenditures would benefit public education greatly, they don't appear likely in the last years of this century; however, if schools are to maintain quality educational programs and improve those programs requiring improvement, educational costs will rise—even if much more slowly than in the previous decade.

Projecting budgetary expenditures for five to ten years is reminiscent of a scene from *Raiders of the Lost Ark*. Indiana Jones is suddenly confronted by a giant, scimitar-wielding, Middle Eastern gentleman intent on doing him terminal injury, and the movie audience is convinced Jones is really in deep stuff. Indiana shrugs resignedly, says, "Oh, expletive deleted," draws a large pistol from his belt (which the audience has totally forgotten he had), and drops the villain in his tracks.

The big guy with the sword is analogous to long-range budget projections, which, similarly, can be wasted by fiscal or legislative "Indiana Joneses," by changes in local and state economies, and by numerous other unforeseen circumstances; however, the uncertainty of the future makes it more, rather than less, critical to look into the future, project overall expenditures carefully and in detail, and then be prepared to modify long-range plans to cope with unexpected conditions and problems. We should ascertain what the well will cost before starting to dig, and long-range planning will help us determine future costs necessary to meet district goals and objectives.

SO HERE'S MY PLAN . . .

There's a great old cartoon picturing two pathetic, bearded men, shackled hand and foot, high up on a dungeon wall. The length of their beards indicates they have obviously been there for decades. One is leaning toward the other saying, "So here's my plan!" Although it's true that life's vagaries sometimes make an educational plan equally useless, long-range planning still remains a necessary activity.

Whether preceded by strategic planning or not, thorough long-range plans contain varied information and cost estimates; some cost projections are relatively simple based upon historical precedents; others provide data that is analytical, judgmental, or both. Financial histories of budgetary expenditures, by functions or objects for periods of three to five years, are essential foundations of long-range budget projections.

Long-range plans provide educational conclusions and make recommendations that, although often subjective, are based upon experience and sound practice. Examples of contents characteristic of a complete long-range budget and other planning are provided under the following sample table of contents:

TABLE OF CONTENTS

[190]A complete staffing plan, including certified and noncertified or support staff, is included as shown in Appendix D.

List of Tables

List of Plans

Long-Range Plan Appendices

A. Summary of Staff Comments and/or Suggestions
B. Equipment Requests
C. Floor Plans Including New Facilities at
    J. William Couillard Middle School, R. E. L.
    Frisby, and Ernest Burns Epperson Elementary
    Schools
D. Unscheduled Special Projects
E. Annual Building Inspection Checklists—
    Bob Alexander High School
F. Annual Building Inspection Checklists—
    J. William Couillard Middle School
G. Annual Building Inspection Checklists—
    Ronald Walling Elementary School
H. Annual Building Inspection Checklists—
    R. E. L. Frisby Elementary School
I. Annual Building Inspection Checklists—
    Ernest B. Epperson Elementary School
J. Annual Building Inspection Checklists—
    Mary Olivia Elementary School

K. Annual Building Inspection Checklists—
Marie Fontanella Elementary School

WHAT DO WE DO IF WE DON'T HIT WATER?

Any long-range plan is an unfinished document. Long-range plans, as board of education policies, may be reminiscent of the indigent professor in *McSorley's Wonderful Saloon* and the professor's *Unfinished History of the World* [44].

Before approval by boards of education, proposed long-range plans should be given final reviews with administrative and teaching staffs who previously should have been involved closely in their development. Following necessary changes in a superintendent's recommended long-range plans, boards of education should formally adopt specific planning documents for further review with parent-teacher organizations and town agencies, including fiscal authorities and legislative bodies. Acknowledging that long-range plans are always unfinished chronicles of school district life and times, they should be put to regular use, even if always under close scrutiny and revision and never finally completed.

Adopted plans should be reviewed by superintendents of schools and boards of education annually and maintained current through periodic inclusion of additional years to the plan—and by planning modifications to accommodate changes in district direction or priorities. More intensive plan analyses should be made at their midpoints and more often as necessary. Board members, school staffs, students, local governmental bodies, and the general public should be afforded regular opportunities to make suggestions for modifications of long-range plans.

Recommendations in effective long-range plans will generate healthy and predictable controversy. Analyses of inevitably strong differences on desirable school district goals and objectives and how to achieve them make it at least possible for boards of education to reach consensus on educational direction for five or ten years—and maybe even beyond.

HARK, IS THAT A CANNON I HEAR?

Sometimes even the best laid plans. . . .
A superintendent of schools in the Midwest retired to Las Vegas,

Nevada, and began a second career dealing blackjack in one of the city's largest casinos. His retirement, while not exactly forced, was the result of a free-wheeling, off-the-cuff style, which had caused him to be caught unprepared on a number of important occasions. In addition to dealing cards, he also fulfilled another lifelong ambition by joining a community theater group and playing small roles in local amateur productions while longing for greater opportunities in professional theater.

Even though his new employment wasn't nearly as complex as the superintendency, he had learned from his previous public school experiences and from his earlier shortcomings, and he vowed never to be taken unawares again.

As a result, he applied himself completely to becoming the best blackjack dealer in Las Vegas, and his work ethic quickly caught the attention of his casino superiors. They were impressed with his thoroughness, and he was made a pit boss. Here, too, he learned all there was to learn about being a world-class gaming supervisor. Although the promotion made scheduling his avocational activities more difficult, he continued with the community players, totally dedicated to preparing himself as an actor to be able to handle any larger roles life might offer him.

One day, while overseeing his blackjack dealers, a friend rushed up to him and asked if he'd be interested in a suddenly available part in the professional theater production opening in town that very afternoon. The former superintendent said, "Of course, I would, tell me about the part."

"Well, the good news is that it's a speaking role in a play that is set in the early nineteenth century; the bad news is there's only one line, and because the actor scheduled to play the part suddenly took ill, the play began without him. Your part is in the third act, but you only have twenty minutes to learn the part, get to the Globe Theater, have yourself made up and costumed, and stand by for your cue."

"No problem," said the ex-superintendent. "The Globe's only five minutes from here, and I'd love a crack at even the smallest professional opportunity. What's my line?"

"Your line is, 'Hark, is that a cannon I hear?' "

"Great, 'Hark, is that a cannon I hear?' I got it!"

Quickly making arrangements with the casino boss to cover his job, he rushed out to hail a taxi—all the while giving his line various readings and inflections: "Hark, is *that* a cannon I hear?"

"Hark, is that a *cannon* I hear?"

"Hark, is that a cannon *I* hear?"

"Hark, is that a cannon I *hear*?"

Quickly settling on the second reading, stressing *cannon* as most appropriate, he caught his cab, gave the driver directions to the theater, and remembering past problems from his previously casual approach to presentations as a superintendent of schools and his vow never again to be caught unprepared, he continued practicing his line, driving himself mercilessly to ensure perfect delivery of his small part. "Hark, is that a *cannon* I hear?" "Hark, is that a *cannon* I hear?" "Hark, is that a *cannon* I hear?" "Hark, is that a *cannon* I hear?" "Hark, is that a *cannon* I hear?" "Hark, is that a *cannon* I hear?" "Hark, is that a *cannon* I hear?" "Hark, is that a *cannon* I hear?" "Hark, is that a *cannon* I hear?"

The cab driver thought the superintendent surely had escaped from somewhere, but he took the aspiring thespian to the Globe. Paying the driver, the would-be actor was met at the curb by the director's assistant who rushed him inside, had him made up and costumed as a French soldier, and introduced him to the director.

"Pivotal third act," said the director. "Your reading of its opening line sets the tone for the act, and the success of the entire play depends on how well the third act is received by the audience. Can you handle it?"

"Absolutely! Hark, is that a *cannon* I hear? Hark, is that a *cannon* I hear? Hark, is that a *cannon* I hear? How's that? OK?"

"Wonderful," said the director. "Stand by. Alright now!"—and with that, the director pushes the superintendent/pit boss through the curtains, where he stands squinting into the glare of the footlights, waiting to emote; a second later, there is a thunderous sound from off-stage. Completely startled by the terrific explosion, the former superintendent blurts out, loudly and clearly, "Whaaaaat the (insert favorite Anglo-Saxon expletive here) was that?"

As every experienced superintendent of schools knows, bad fortune sometimes triumphs over even a combination of the most thorough preparation and the best of intentions.

LONG-RANGE PLANNING EXERCISE

Locate the elements of a complete long-range plan that are now available in your school district. For those planning items that are not available, why do you believe they aren't available? Use the space provided for comments for items that cannot be found.

Enrollment Projections and Analysis   Yes   No

Comments _____

Staffing Plans   Yes   No

Comments _____

Staff Development Plan   Yes   No

Comments _____

Districtwide Educational Philosophy   Yes   No

Comments _____

Professional Development Plan   Yes   No

Comments _____

Plans and Procedures—
   Curriculum Development and Revision   Yes   No

Comments _____

Current Curriculum—Not More Than Five Years Old

Social Studies   Yes   No

Comments _____

Art   Yes   No

Comments _____

Language Arts   Yes   No

Comments _____

Health and Physical Education   Yes   No

Comments _____

Science   Yes   No

Comments _____

Music   Yes   No

Comments _____

Foreign Languages   Yes   No

Comments _____

Industrial Arts   Yes   No

Comments _____

Home Economics   Yes   No

Comments _____

Mathematics   Yes   No

Comments _____

Business and Career Education   Yes   No

Comments _____

Computer Education   Yes   No

Comments _____

Guidelines for Textbook Selection   Yes   No

Comments _____

Schedule of Textbook Adoptions   Yes   No

Comments _____

Capital Equipment Expenditure Plan   Yes   No

Comments _____

Technology Plan   Yes   No

Comments _____

Facilities Inventory and Building Capacities   Yes   No

Comments _____

Preventative Maintenance Plan and/or Checklists Yes   No

Comments _____

CHAPTER 11

Reflections

A CONFEDERACY OF DUNCES

ON PARTICULARLY BAD days, it's understandable that a mildly megalomaniacal superintendent might recall another quote from Jonathan Swift: "When a true genius appears in the world, you may know him by this sign, that the dunces are all in confederacy against him" [44].

In spite of the temptation to think that way now and again and in spite of the fact that, in rare instances, it may even be true, there are better reasons not to fall into this particular mental and emotional trap, including the following: (1) Few of us are really geniuses, and even if we belong to MENSA, we still have too much to learn to be proud of that accident of birth that made us eligible. (2) Not everybody who disagrees with us is a dunce—even though many could well be and some definitely are. (3) It might be a precursor of incipient paranoia crawling out from under a rock taking a quick look around and seeing if he likes the neighborhood. (4) It's counterproductive to indulge yourself this way. It comes across clearly to others, even to dunces, and this makes working with them constructively and productively almost impossible.

Nobody ever said public life was devoid of frustrations—or that every member of the general public, all staff, each board of education member, every parent, all town officials, all students, and every other person and groups of persons with whom school leadership is in professional contact will always be intelligent, insightful, open, empathetic, tolerant, emotionally secure, flexible, well motivated, or any other way you'd prefer them to be.

That being the case, it profits us not to categorize those around us as card-carrying members of the "confederacy of dunces" who resent our true administrative genius. But from time to time, everybody's entitled to feel that way—at least momentarily.[191]

---

[191]See also, this chapter, "Some Days You Might Think Tom Hobbes Had It Right," p. 355.

COULD SOCRATES SURVIVE THE SUPERINTENDENCY?

In a 1962 edition of the *Phi Delta Kappan,* a researcher used a modern personnel rating scale to evaluate Socrates as a teacher. Socrates was rated low on "personal qualifications" (1) for dressing in an old sheet; (2) for low self-esteem because he was always asking students questions, instead of the other way around; and (3) because, under pressure, he self-destructed [71]. Old "Soc" wouldn't be well received today as a superintendent of schools either without a Ph.D. in Administrative Sophistry. Even if the public could accept his clothing, it expects definitive answers from superintendents — not hard or unsettling questions. Also, his first board of finance meeting would do him in for good.

Public leadership positions today are more difficult than ever before because of inflated public expectations, an abundance of only semi-solvable problems, and the gaggle of single-issue constituencies infesting all levels of government. With the Socratic evaluation as a guide, it may be instructive to examine other important historical figures to determine whether or not they could be effective as a nineties kind of school superintendent guy or gal — as well as having been successful, or at least well known, in their own special fields and in their own eras. Identified eccentricities, peccadilloes, or other shortcomings would, in most cases, equally lessen their effectiveness today as a school principal, town manager, or any other appointed public leadership post; for elective positions, interestingly enough, aberrant behaviors almost seem to be prerequisites.

(1) Julius Caesar — Jules could never handle Total Quality Management and the participatory leadership style required these days, and there are plenty of Marcus Junius Brutuses and Gaius Cassiuses on boards of education who would do the same things to him that the original Roman duo did. Dr. Caesar certainly wouldn't be sending his famous, *"Veni, vidi, vici"* communiqués anymore about coming, seeing, and conquering anything.

(2) Napoleon Bonaparte — Walking around scratching his chest constantly would inspire merciless staff, student, parent, board, and media comment and criticism. Faculty room conversation would be vicious, and the funny hat wouldn't help either.

(3) Pepin the Short — He may have been a wonderful King of the Franks, but town councils or boards of finance would run him out

of town in a hurry; they just don't like "vertically challenged" guys that much.

(3) Tomas de Torquemeda—Tom's version of Socratic data acquisition probably wouldn't be tolerated well by older district administrators whose pain thresholds have already been exceeded by central office requirements to script teachers' classroom presentations.

(5) Rasputin—Trim that beard, and he'd do fine, although he should work on becoming a little less flamboyant and maybe even a bit "nerdier"—possibly wearing one of those shirt pocket protector "thingies" filled with pens and such, the way engineers do.

(6) Winston Churchill—Sure, if he gave up tobacco. You can't smoke anything today on school grounds, and cigars are prohibited even in the Grand Canyon.

(7) Machiavelli—"Prince" Niccolo probably would do fine—if he could overcome his naivete. Otherwise, board members would gobble him up and spit him out thoroughly chewed.

(8) Robert E. Lee—Marse Robert might do OK in an especially refined Virginia suburb, but he's far too patrician and dignified for most communities today. Aloof and paternal no longer cut it the way they did in his time.

(9) King Kong—Too direct and forceful for today's tastes in leadership, even though a large district might benefit from his personal strengths—if he could stop climbing school buildings to avoid being viewed as a "top-down" gorilla. Also, he might be a bit too intellectual for some aspects of the modern superintendency.

(10) Charles Lutwidge Dodgson (Lewis Carroll)—Charlie would fit right in as a chief school officer with his built-in central office staff of Alice, the Mad Hatter, March Hare, and all their other Wonderland colleagues. They would feel right at home at board of education meetings and blend right in.

As were the random collection of ten notables previously considered, other great historical figures might also be found equally wanting—even without singling out their relatively minor personal or professional imperfections. Sure, these folks could temper their foibles or other inappropriate characteristics that might disqualify them for modern educational leadership. Napoleon could quit tickling himself and put away his funny French three-cornered hat; Winston could give up his coronas and panatelas; and King Kong could join a self-help group to curb his more aggressive behaviors and attend local cultural events for intellectual stimulation.

Regardless of any unfair disqualifications of these well-known historical personages, it remains true that public positions today are not for everyone—only a select few measure up to their rigors and demands. Unlike the superintendent's or other official's divergent view of the world looking outward at hundreds and even thousands of people, he or she is the focus of intensely convergent views from staff, parents and the general public, board members, town officials, and others. Every personal and professional flaw is magnified by this close scrutiny, and only the lucky and the strong can survive it forever.[192]

"DEAD BEFORE TAKEOFF"

A number of years ago, a magazine article recounted circumstances surrounding the pilot of an air force jet who crashed and was killed on takeoff. A post-crash investigation revealed that the combination of runway length, air temperature, relative humidity, fuel and ammunition loading, and other contributing factors made it impossible for the aircraft to take off successfully—the ill-fated pilot was, in effect, "dead before takeoff." That phrase became the sad, but intriguing, title for the magazine article.

On occasion, superintendents (and other administrators) assume professional positions burdened by so many preexisting, adverse circumstances that they are also, figuratively at least, "dead before takeoff." Fortunately, most administrative icons retired years before administrative icons became unfashionable, but following a highly regarded predecessor is, unfortunately, still an effective method of reducing leadership runway length—or of adding weight to leadership efforts to get districts safely off the ground. Other preexisting conditions contributing to shorter than typical leadership tenures that superintendents may discover only coincidentally with their arrivals in new positions might include (1) a major departure of board of education members who had recently elected the new superintendent without any community involvement in the selection process; (2) recent taxpayer revolts and newly formed taxpayers' associations or long-standing taxpayer bitterness and organized citizen efforts against educational spending; (3)

---

[192]See also, Chapter 8, "Divergence and Convergence," p. 244.

philosophically divided boards; a degree of this is always possible and maybe even expected today, but sometimes the divisions are so long-standing, bitter, and deep that the superintendency resembles a minefield to be traversed, rather than a stroll through snowy woods on a quiet morning; (4) excessive influence on or control of board members by political parties, mayors, and councilmen; (5) angry communities divided over curriculum approaches such as outcome-based education; (6) a history of even more than usually difficult teacher and/or administrator bargaining disputes, distrust, and general bad feelings; and (7) conditions existing for decades in any modern American city—or in states with spending caps.

Although effective leadership might ameliorate, or possibly eliminate, some or all of these problems, even the best superintendents may realize shortly after beginning a new superintendency that they must keep their contacts and placement papers current—in spite of what they believed was a thorough preacceptance review of the position. This possibility, although not the norm, dramatically increases the importance of careful prior examination, study, and figurative dissection of a new position before signing the contract. In some cases, and very often in large cities, superintendents begin new positions with full knowledge of exactly what they face and with the attitude exemplified by, "It's a dirty job, but somebody's got to do it."

Somebody does have to do it, and children in the most impossible districts for superintendents are especially in need of effective educational leadership. Going down in flames, after heroic efforts to right the school district, may not be the worst thing that could happen to a career, as long as it doesn't become an administrative habit.

But before superintendents accept new positions, they should understand the choices they are making before they no longer have any choices to make.[193]

DON'T YOU REALIZE HOW DANGEROUS IT IS OUT THERE?

Among the many joys of snow belt superintendents are early morning, frozen precipitation deliberations on closing school or delayed school openings—or similar decisions later that day about early school closings. Not surprisingly, in those parts of the nation where snow falls almost daily from December through February, such decisions aren't as

---

[193]See also, Chapter 3, "Who Is This Person?—I," p. 103.

difficult as they are in communities where significant snowfalls are major meteorological events. Because of oversaturated television coverage of local, state, national, and world weather, even an inch of predicted snow causes electronic hysteria among underworked weatherpersons on local television news programs.

Among the more interesting phenomena after a sudden, intense, unexpected snowfall are mid-morning callers who ask if you're closing school. When told no, they often ask, "Don't you realize how dangerous it is out there?" to which superintendents often reply, "Yes, and that's why the kids are safer in school until the end of the day when the snow plows will have cleaned and sanded the roads."

Except for an easy consensus that the highest priority should be pupil safety, there are no clear guidelines for superintendents to follow, and, although there may be complete conceptual unanimity, there are no practical absolutes with pupil safety issues. To a large degree, each community sets its own safety standards, and, as implied earlier, these standards are different in different sections of the country. Parents in Buffalo, New York, and in other upstate New York districts with lake effect snow, know there aren't reasonable alternatives to buses traveling snow-packed roads, and schools aren't normally closed unless drifts are too deep for plows to break through. Near the other end of that spectrum, in some shoreline Connecticut towns, an inch or two of snow is reasonable cause for parental "alarums and excursions"—not to mention serious deliberations and dissent about whether or not school should open late, if at all, or close early.

Having just returned from a tour in a snowy upstate New York community to a comparatively moderate snow area in Connecticut, a Connecticut superintendent of schools kept school open on a snowy day that in upstate New York would have been a normal winter's day—in Connecticut, it was perceived to be a blizzard. Upon arrival in the office, he was deluged with angry calls from parents questioning his sanity. As the snow continued, he had to attend a meeting out of town, so he empowered his assistant to close early if necessary. An hour or so later, the assistant did call school off, but by the time the children arrived home, the sun shone brightly. On that particular day, the central office was "oh for two," or no hits in two times at bat.

Having acknowledged the lack of definitive school closing guidelines, there are still a few worth a superintendent's serious consideration:

(*1*) The year's first snowfall of any consequence is the most dangerous of the season. Over the spring, summer, and early fall months, automobiles and buses somehow have forgotten how to climb slippery hills and how to stop at intersections. All vehicles require a period of retraining to survive the long winter ahead.

(*2*) Similarly, early spring snows catch cars unawares, and they are prone to seek refuge in ditches and other places they consider more secure than the snowy highway itself. In one of these unscheduled spring snows, as a New York State superintendent was returning to his school district in the west, cars were scattered alongside the New York Thruway as if Rip Van Winkle had had a good bowling day. A month before, the same conditions wouldn't have fazed anybody or their automobiles.

(*3*) Early closings are often more dangerous than holding students until the end of the day when road crews have plowed and sanded; some blizzard conditions counterbalance this advice, but generally it's sound. Also, in spite of a district's best efforts, many students will be returning to empty homes because both parents work—and both parents who live next door also work.

(*4*) School delays of an hour or so are sensible options when there's freezing rain and temperatures are rising or when town crews need a bit more time to clean up last night's snowfall that has recently ended. Delays are much more questionable if the snow is continuing and if the superintendent is either hoping it will stop or just isn't sure what to do. An hour or two delay followed by a closing is a minor disaster, aggravating parents and staff considerably more than would an early and decisive school cancellation.

Closing school before snow actually begins to fall is always an unpleasant choice for superintendents who have been listening to guaranteed radio predictions of heavy snow arriving shortly in their area. If, however, there is a predictable pattern of weather front movement and if it's snowing heavily an hour or two away and moving in your direction, close. You may look silly if the storm veers out to sea, but it's better than sending the kids in with snow falling heavily as they arrive at school—or worse, as they are being picked up by their buses.

(*5*) Predecision telephone discussions among area superintendents is the norm; even when one person may be right and everyone else wrong, hanging out there alone against the prevailing wisdom of that day is uncomfortable—unless the superintendent's hide is even thicker than usual. Some superintendents have difficulty bringing themselves to share this decision because of a perverse sense of infallibility, but most are secretly glad when other superintendents check with them, and they find out what their caller is thinking before deciding themselves.

(6) If any one of most superintendents' normal sources of information on road conditions (usually public works, police, and bus company) advises that conditions are unsafe, two out of three isn't good enough, and the superintendent should probably close or possibly delay.

(7) Although many conscientious superintendents arise even earlier than usual on bad mornings to check the roads themselves, this is risky. Even with car phones, you can be difficult to reach, and, generally, it's better to remain in your "command bunker," usually your home at that hour, and rely on a synthesis of reports on road conditions. If there's no phone in the car, it's almost foolhardy to be out and away from a telephone—being stuck somewhere out of touch at a critical time is to be avoided whenever possible.

A quick summary of all these suggestions would be to close school if there are any reasonable doubts about the safety of doing otherwise.[194] A superintendent may make a sound decision against canceling school and still have a bus accident; but if schools are closed, it's also possible children could be injured at home because of inadequate or nonexistent supervision. If, under less than desirable conditions, superintendents decide to keep schools open, they should go to the office early to be readily available in case of bus or other problems.

Although when schools are shut down because of inclement weather kids will be safe from bad road hazards, superintendents will be criticized by a number of parents whose lives they've inconvenienced and by those school board members who love to second-guess administrative decisions. We can live with that.

To hell with listening to the radio to find out who did what throughout your geographic area, how many agreed with your decision, and how many didn't. A month from now, absent the always present specter

[194]See also, Chapter 4, "Better Odds Are All You Can Expect—In Poker or Leadership Life in General," p. 113.

of a bus accident, nobody will remember what you did anyway. Go back to bed, and sleep well.

HOLIDAY NUTS TO STAFF

When John Milton wrote, "When I consider how my light is spent . . ." [72], he was, among other things, reminding some of us to keep our eyeglasses close by. A few years ago, a superintendent was reading a list of his superintendent chores prepared by his administrative assistant. One item said, or he thought it did," "Send holiday nuts to staff."

Because he had left his reading glasses in his car that morning, he wasn't sure whether he had also forgotten to send an insulting memorandum to the staff or to prepare bid documents for a carload of pistachios. Fortunately, before he sprang into action to tackle either of those inappropriate alternatives, he took a trip downstairs and retrieved his twelve-dollar drugstore special prescription glasses from the front seat of his automobile.

Upon his return to the office, he discovered that he could read the list of work to be done much more easily than without the specs. What he thought had said "Send holiday nuts to staff" really was "Send holiday note to staff"—a much simpler assignment and one that he handled easily enough.

This can be considered as just another reminder about the importance of frequent staff communications at various times of the year.[195]

JUST A RED ANT IN THE NOONDAY SUN

As a boy, an incipient superintendent of schools used a magnifying glass, combined with the Texas sun, to kill ants on his great grandmother's concrete driveway. He'd cast a quarter-sized circle of light and heat over the ants, and they'd begin to sweat, stagger, and give out little ant screams. He would narrow the circle, and they'd fall over with their tiny little tongues hanging out. Then he'd focus the light to a pinpoint and crisp them—snap, crackle, and pop. In retrospect, he feels bad about that practice, but then it seemed like fun; if reincarnation exists,

---

[195]See also, Chapter 3, "Fireside and Other Chats and Communications," pp. 75–81 and Appendix B, "Administrative Correspondence."

he suspects he already knows in which insect form he will return, and it's probably only fair.[196]

The superintendent didn't fully empathize with ants until he became a superintendent of schools and had to endure state education department bureaucracies with their circles of heat generated by too many dangerously enthusiastic middle management chiefs. Many of these energetic men and women, unfortunately, have nothing better to do than crisp superintendents the way he did his boyhood ant victims. Experiences with state education department functionaries made him further regret the way he had treated his little red ant buddies.

Over their careers, many superintendents may have experienced sea changes in their attitudes toward educational governance. As young principals, many see a few ineffective boards of education up close and, at that point, would prefer control of public education to be centered in state education departments—at least state departments of education are populated by other educators. As they become more experienced, leaders begin to identify bureaucratic ineffectiveness and inefficiency that are characteristic of many state education departments and often swing back to the side of local control—working with good boards of education helps also.

A great example of a state education department contemplating its own navel is found in a 1971 state department of education memorandum to school district administrators in a large Middle Atlantic state:

May 10, 1971

TO: School District Administrators

FROM: (Name omitted to protect the guilty)

SUBJECT: Education Department Organizational Change

The April issue of the School District Administrator's newsletter mentioned several problems which resulted from budgetary considerations. These problems have not only involved staff reductions, but they have made clear the necessity for organizational changes which will sustain and hopefully strengthen services to the schools. Those major changes which concern Elementary, Secondary and Continuing Education are described below. (More detailed explanations will be forthcoming from the offices involved.)

Office of Research and Evaluation. The Office of Research and Evaluation, exclusive of the Information Center on Education, is transferred to

---

[196]I was always kind to dogs, cats, birds, and younger siblings. I just didn't care much for red ants—a minor failing at worst.

Elementary, Secondary and Continuing Education. The Associate Commissioner for Research and Evaluation will report to the Deputy Commissioner for Elementary, Secondary and Continuing Education.

The Information Center on Education is transferred to the Office of Long-Range Planning but will report to the Executive Deputy Commissioner until such time as the position of Assistant Commissioner for Long-Range Planning is filled.

Division of Educational Communications. The Classroom Communications Unit and the School Television Unit of the Bureau of Mass Communications, both formerly components of the former Division of Educational Communications, are transferred to the Division of Research and Educational Communications in the Office of Research and Evaluation.

The Bureau of Mass Communications, with the exception of the School Television Unit, will remain in Cultural Education and will report to the Associate Commissioner for Cultural Education.

Division of Curriculum Development. The functions of the Division of Curriculum Development have been assigned temporarily to the Division of School Supervision. The Bureaus of Elementary Curriculum Development, Secondary Curriculum Development, and Continuing Education Curriculum Development are assigned to the Division.

Civil Defense in Schools. The . . . State Department of Civil Defense has been abolished and, since the Office of Civil Defense in Schools was funded through that agency, the position of Coordinator has been eliminated. We have been encouraged by the U.S. Office of Civil Defense to submit a proposal for funding of Civil Defense Education as it relates to Strand V of the Health Education materials. Results of that proposal will be reported at a later date.

It's probably difficult for anyone who wasn't there to imagine how excited superintendents in small upstate districts became about these changes and how they awaited the "more detailed explanations . . . forthcoming from the offices involved." Their eyes even uncrossed and refocused within just a few days of reading about those crucial state department rearrangements.

Throughout administrative careers, when state education department functionaries appear at the office door, inevitably their opening words are, "I'm here to help you," or something close to that. Although it doesn't always ring true, surprisingly enough, many of them actually do help.

The best of all worlds includes competent superintendents; strong, well-motivated boards of education; and state education employees who recognize their responsibility to assist districts—not to impede their efforts with excessive bureaucratic requirements and reports.

By the time they retire, many superintendents probably believe that, in the best of all superintendent worlds, they would have untrammeled authority to do whatever they damn well please without foolish and unnecessary constraints from either boards of education or state education departments—but then we also know the best of all worlds doesn't exist.

LANTERNS IN THE WINDOW

Administrative spouses, with or without careers of their own, deserve special credit for their personal support and patience with and understanding of a superintendent's untold evenings away from home at school or district meetings—although sometimes a superintendent's return home in the early morning hours after a particularly late meeting can be dangerous. Fortunately, for reasons to be explained shortly, superintendents and other school administrators have primitive, although well-adapted, nervous systems designed to ignore all but the most serious warnings of trouble.

Physiologically, the way this works is that the little electrical couriers who live and work in administrators' bodies wear tiny lead boots. As they bound merrily along from neuron to neuron on their way to the brain, they inevitably splash into a deep synapse and drown. Only the strongest of warning messengers leap all the chasms or swim out of the synaptic pools into which they may fall. This may seem cruel, but imagine superintendents' lives if every indication of danger got through to administrative brains. This would totally overload their personal "flight or fight circuitry," and their entire nervous system would seize-up into an inert mass of charred insulation and twisted wires.

After a pressure-filled board of education meeting, a superintendent of schools, in this example male, has been known to relax for a time amid congenial companions and surroundings. He arrives home at 2:15 A.M. to the only house on his block with a lantern in the window and a wide awake, already angry wife. An aura of cigars and bourbon march boldly ahead, stroll alongside, and lurch in his wake. If he's really unlucky, a female board member's perfume intermingles with the other scents because she sat close to him earlier in the evening. The smiling (what else can he do) superintendent approaches his wife in her armchair, unaware that his entire persona is telling a story he'd rather not have told.

The ensuing ambush and massacre have already been best described in English verse [34][197]:

> *Now storming fury rose,*
> *And clamour such as heard in Heaven till now*
> *was never.*
> *Arms on armour clashing brayed discord.*
> *Dire was the noise of conflict;*
> *Overhead the dismal hiss of fiery darts in*
> *flaming volleys flew,*
> *All air seemed then conflicting fire.*

Except in the rare instance just described, administrative spouses provide support, patience, wisdom, fortitude, character, charm (or a more masculine version with spouses of distaff superintendents) and are specially deserving of "The Lantern in the Window Award" for sharing fully the spousal successes, failures, pleasures, pains, friendships, hostilities, exhilarations, boredom, and all the myriad other experiences and emotions that are the common lot of school leadership.[198]

MAY I HAVE THE ENVELOPE PLEASE?

Former recipients of the "Julius Caesar Leadership Award" for "arbitrary and absolute exercise of power"[199] and presenters of that and other awards to superintendents, principals, teachers, board members, secretaries, bus drivers, custodians, students, and parents strongly recom-

---

[197]This quote recounts a small portion of the first of three major battles wherein Archangels Michael and Gabriel were sent by God to vanquish Satan and his crew; the first two fights were inconclusive, but in the third, God sends his Son, Messiah, into the fray, and Messiah drives Satan and his legions into the place of punishment prepared for them in the Deep.

[198]See also, Chapter 2, "Golden Shovels," p. 56 and this chapter, "May I Have the Envelope Please?" p. 349.

[199]I was much younger when I received the first ever "Julius Caesar Award" and hadn't yet learned the virtues and values of participatory management—the general ignorance of the times allowed me to survive my autocratic predilections until I grew wiser.

mend them as potential bright spots in otherwise uneventful days, weeks, months—or maybe, if lucky, uneventful years.

A partial listing of original awards presented to administrative and board colleagues includes

(*1*) The "Mohammed Ali Rope-a-Dope Award" for superintendents' impregnable defenses at board of education meetings—also suitable for principals' and other administrators' behavior at administrative council meetings

(*2*) The "Ali Shuffle" or the "Sugar Ray Leonard Two-Step Award," obviously companion pieces to the "Rope-a-Dope Award," presented for exceptional footwork in a variety of administrative settings

(*3*) The "Al Capp, Mr. MXYZPTLK Literary Award" for the murkiest administrative prose in staff, student, or parent newsletters

(*4*) The "John Updike Award for Creative Fiction" to superintendents for imaginative annual reports to boards of education and the state education department

(*5*) The "National Academy of Old Testament Thespians Award" to long-suffering administrators for their creative public interpretations of the Book of Job and Lamentations.

(*6*) The "Al Pacino/Godfather Award" to superintendents, principals, or board members for their contributions to employee relations during contract negotiations

(*7*) The "Sosigenes/Pope Gregory/Julius Caesar Award" to superintendents or board members for the most creative school calendars each year

(*8*) The "Billy Mitchell/Curtis Lemay/Michael J. Fox/Back to the Future/Time Warp Award" to superintendents for their effective strategies and initiatives in effectively returning state education departments back to the stone age

The previous listing of potential awards to administrators, teachers, and board members contains only a fraction of the potentially powerful presentations that might be made in a given school year.

Superintendent and other administrative groups may present these awards at meetings, conferences, workshops, or major awards assemblies—similar to those award presentations for graduating high school seniors or the annual "Oscar" ceremonies in Hollywood. They or variations thereon are joys to give, and recipients will treasure them forever—or at least a few weeks.[200]

OLD DOGS, NEW TRICKS

A Gary Larson *Far Side* pictured an especially hazardous circus act—a dog riding the unicycle on a high wire with all sorts of juggling apparatus in her paws and between her teeth and no safety net between her and the concrete floor far below. The expression on her doggy face reflects her precarious position, and the caption says, "Samantha couldn't help thinking that she was an old dog—and that this was a new trick."

There are times in every school leader's career when he or she can empathize with that old dog. However, throughout principalships, superintendencies, and service in other leadership posts, administrators, while retaining the core values that have served them well,[201] have varied opportunities to learn new educational and administrative tricks; growing and changing professionally are required if school leaders are to remain effective.

One significant administrative opportunity to adjust or modify personal and professional behaviors occurs when superintendents, principals, assistant superintendents, and other administrators change positions—from one superintendency to another; from one principalship to another; from a principalship to an assistant superintendency, a superintendency, or some other central office position; from an assistant superintendency to a superintendency; or from any administrative position to another administrative position. At these special times, the leader isn't working against strong, preconceived perceptions of him or her, and all personal and professional leadership changes have a much better chance of being recognized and appreciated. Also, there is a lack of self-consciousness when leaders interact with new colleagues who accept their new and possibly improved behaviors without puzzling over them because they are new.[202]

Although not always easy to master, old administrative dogs can learn new tricks and continually need to do so.

[200]See also, this chapter, "Lanterns in the Window," p. 348 and Chapter 2, "Golden Shovels," p. 56.
[201]See also, Chapter 3, "Dance with the One Who 'Brung' You," p. 68.
[202]See also, Chapter 3, "Who Is This Person?—I," p. 103.

RABBIS—II[203]

One of the most gratifying activities for school superintendents is teaching assistant superintendents, principals, and other district staff aspiring to educational leadership how to be effective leaders – and, in turn, learning from them. This mentoring takes place primarily by example, but there are frequent opportunities for conversations and discussions on why this approach or that one is used in a particular situation. Demonstrating the proper leadership ethics and behavior may be far more important than teaching the techniques of leadership – and even with the best of mentors, it's also true that those with whom we work often learn much of what they shouldn't do, as well as what they should, by observing our peculiar frailties and imperfections.

Interviewers often ask administrative aspirants, whether for the superintendency or a principalship or a director's position, what qualities they have admired in those for whom they have worked and what qualities those same people exhibited that the candidate would not want to emulate. It's a revealing question, not only of the strengths and weaknesses of the applicant's former bosses, but of candidates themselves and of their professional and personal insights and values.

Probably no aspect of the superintendency is any more satisfying than mentoring outstanding beginning administrators who show great promise for being better than you ever have been in the job you care so much about. Experienced superintendents have the good fortune of seeing former principals and assistant superintendents move on to superintendencies in school districts and serve successfully in them. Cynics would say it's an overstatement, but each of these professionals carries a bit of you with them throughout their careers – sometimes possibly a mixed blessing for them.[204]

SCHOOL CALENDARS—I

If administrators could write an educational ballad that included all reasons why it's difficult to teach children this month, or this week, or this day, here's how that song would be sung.

[203]In police novels, policemen and detectives often have "rabbis." In police circles, as in religious institutions, "rabbi" means "teacher" or "mentor."
[204]See also, Chapter 2, "Rabbis – I," p. 33 and this chapter, "Educational Colleagues and Friends," p. 366.

September and June are lost causes because it takes at least the month of September before children settle down to learning, and excitement generated by the impending summer rules out June as meaningful learning time.

The typically beautiful fall weather in October and November, accompanied by the dramatic colors of the seasonal foliage, along with Halloween and Thanksgiving parties, pre-party planning, and post-party depressions, preoccupy and overwhelm students—these months are sure educational losers.

Obviously, December is a total wipeout, what with Christmas and Hanukkah and all their attendant fun, games, and gifts—not to mention fewer available teaching days because of the holiday week and a half.

After the December seasonal break, there's a major student letdown from all the previous month's excitement, and the terrible winter weather in January and February is only suitable for funerals; colds and flu bugs have hitched a ride into town via Amtrak, and everybody's sick. Kids can't get out to play, and their pent-up energy hurts their concentration.

March is a real bummer with winds, rain, and eternal mud. School corridors and classrooms are a mess, and custodians keep the entire faculty upset with constant grumbling about students tracking playground mud into the school and onto previously clean, shiny floors.

Naturally, the warmth of a May springtime with its new leaves, other growth, and changes, both botanical and human, totally distracts students from classroom pursuits; learning doesn't come easily in the midst of seasonal reawakenings.

So far, we've ruled out September, October, November, December, January, February, March, May, and June, although April has, momentarily, survived intact—but even "the cruelest month" won't escape unscathed. After subtracting April vacation, usually the third week of the month, and the final week, which presents the same learning barriers as the month of May, only the first two weeks of the remaining month are still available.

We must add, to all previously enumerated difficulties, the real problem of educating kids on Mondays and Fridays in any week, and we need also to recognize an inevitable mid-week slump on Wednesdays.

Therefore, it's important for educators to be poised, enthusiastic, willing, and able to impart 180 days of wisdom, knowledge, attitudes, facts, and skills on Tuesdays and Thursdays during those two available April weeks.

OK, I exaggerate because, collectively, the list of learning impediments makes great lyrics, but if someone hangs around long enough, he or she will hear all of them at least once—and many of them much more often.

The overriding truth in this unsung song is, however, that ninety-nine point four percent (from one of Dave Barry's scientific surveys) of teachers and administrators work hard each day of their careers, clearing a myriad of seasonal and other student learning hurdles. Those who grumble occasionally about external learning distractions do so from legitimate frustrations—and from dedication to their profession.

SCHOOL CALENDARS—II
(OR SON OF SCHOOL CALENDARS—I)

Although each section of the country has its own peculiarities and special considerations, wherever you find yourself, as a principal or superintendent of schools, you will experience annual hassles that arouse passions beggaring description and live through futile efforts to establish the perfect school calendar. Talk about single-issue constituencies.

(1) There's the back before Labor Day faction, which insists "summers already are too long, and if we don't get the kids back in school before Labor Day, they will have forgotten everything they ever learned during that unnecessary, additional week of vacation."

and

The post Labor Day groupies whose plea is that unless we wait until after Labor Day, family vacation plans are ruined—and merchants and others who depend upon summer trade will all file Chapter Eleven unless we delay opening school an additional week.

(2) Families and staff who must have a week in February for their annual winter ski vacation and their nonskiing compatriots who, with absolute conviction, argue that without a February break colds, flu, and other rhinovirus plagues will strike down their firstborn children with indescribable contagions and attendant sufferings—along with their second-, third-, and fourthborn children.

How they discover exactly when the germs are due in town from other regions of the country on Amtrak, or by bicycle, or possibly driving rental vehicles, we don't know; somehow people are convinced it's during that February vacation week.

and

Their equally passionate nonskiing opponents of this wasted vacation just six weeks or so after the December holiday hiatus. "If our kids don't stay in school for some serious uninterrupted stretches of time, how are they to achieve educational excellence? We don't need to subsidize ski bums at the expense of our children's future economic success—and the kids have the presidents' birthdays off anyway."

(*3*) The proponents of a week off in March coincidental with college and university schedules; have you noticed how higher education is becoming more like candy bars? Students pay more, but colleges operate fewer and fewer days each year.

and

Supporters of an April vacation when the weather is good enough to enjoy, instead of the winds and mud of March.

and

Our friends, the nemeses of February breaks in school schedules, who are equally passionate against lost learning opportunities from additional educational interruptions in either March or April.

(*4*) Fortunately, from Maine to Texas, from Virginia to California, we all seem to agree on the December holiday vacation—although, in Maine, you have the potato picking crowd, and, during the annual West Coast migrations of the whales, the whale watchers and counters who want even different school schedules, and maybe ice fisherpersons in Minnesota, and . . .

SOME DAYS YOU MIGHT THINK TOM HOBBES HAD IT RIGHT

Thomas Hobbes, a seventeenth century English philosopher, believed that people are moved chiefly by desire for power and by fear of others and that "without a common power to keep them all in awe" (read superintendent of schools), human life is "solitary, poor, nasty, brutish, and short" [73]. If you think those views shocked his contemporaries, contemplate for a moment the reaction those words would generate today from avid proponents of total quality management.

On any kind of normal day, superintendents and other leaders in public education wouldn't subscribe to Hobbes's manifesto, and modern educational leadership is participatory and democratic, but consider the day when a superintendent who has, throughout his career, subscribed to modern leadership theories, decentralized decision making, and shared authority arrives at work to discover: (1) An elementary school has no water because the custodian forgot to repair a broken water pump. (2) There was a bus accident that morning because the bus supervisor ignored an obviously frayed tire; fortunately, nobody was injured, but parents are hysterical. (3) Following an executive session, to which he wasn't invited after last night's board of education meeting, board members voted five to four to freeze his salary for the second straight year on the basis that he already earns more than any of the board members. (4) The teachers' association has held a press conference about a principal's breach of teacher confidentiality in a dismissal case; the principal allegedly told his drinking buddies at a local pub every detail of the charges against the teacher. (5) A teacher filed a grievance against the superintendent for not speaking to her in the hall the week before; she is supposedly emotionally distraught and unable to work because of his insensitive administrative behavior. (6) The business manager, in whom the superintendent has reposed complete trust, reports a projected budget overrun of over a million dollars in a twenty-million dollar budget—he had forgotten to include expenditures for a major roof repair in his earlier budget projections. It's only a week and a half before the close of the fiscal year, and the superintendent had recently reassured the board that the annual budget was in fine shape. (7) A story has appeared in the morning paper about a high school English teacher who is threatening to fail his entire class of senior honor students, making it impossible for them to graduate in ten days, because they misunderstood his ambiguous directions for their term papers. All twelve parents, eight of nine board members (one is out of town), the high school principal, the English department coordinator, the tyrannical English teacher, the mayor, six town council members, and the new reporter covering district news are awaiting the superintendent's return calls. (8) A middle school teacher, sneaking a smoke in the men's room, inadvertently set fire to a wastebasket, which brought the volunteer fire department to the school; the fire chief wants to speak with the superintendent immediately about the school's allegedly "smoke-free environment." (9) The mayor is angry because district interviewers didn't recommend his daughter for an open position in the school system, choosing a board member's son instead; the board member also is angry because she wants her son to go to law school and then join the family law firm—not to be a teacher. (10) The superintendent's administrative assistant has called in sick with the mumps. The superintendent never had mumps as a child and has feared the potential side effects of "ooh, ooh, orchitis" all his adult life; to make matters worse, yesterday, while ecstatic over her raise for next year, the assistant gave the superintendent a sisterly peck on the corner of his mouth, and his doctor is away on vacation until next week.

And the day has just begun. . . .

At times such as these, a superintendent might be justified in believing, at least fleetingly, that old Tom Hobbes had it right after all and that people are just no damn good.

THE BEST LACK ALL CONVICTION . . .

Although I'm sure you already have, take a close look at the crowd at your next budget or town meeting when an issue has heated up the political climate. Too many of those present are wild-eyed, foam-flecked angries living lives of "noisy desperation"; the town or district's comparatively well-adjusted people are at home watching a TV ball game with a beer or a sherry in one hand, patting his or her spouse on his or her backside with the other. An Irish poet, who undoubtedly had attended many such meetings, captured this school district dilemma when he wrote, "The best lack all conviction while the worst are full of passionate intensity" [14].

This phenomenon can also be identified frequently among faculties, teachers' unions or associations, board of education candidates, and boards of education. Empirically, it appears emotionally easier and more satisfying to fight against causes perceived to be evil than to support those believed to be good. Nut cases remain eternally poised to leap out against something—anything—while rational folks take forever to become excited enough to involve themselves in the fray.

"Aginners" always have a pool of ready reservists, or "minutepersons," who can be mustered in a twinkling to march on town hall against any issue, especially any issue with cost implications. Except for parent-teacher organizations, unfortunately moribund in most school districts because two-job parents appear to have too much else on their plates already, there is no ready cadre of supportive citizens upon which school leadership can draw.

The obvious lesson for school leaders is not to wait until crises appear to do everything that reasonably can be done to develop supportive groups for local educational causes. It's tough enough to manage under any circumstances today, and it's almost impossible to assemble supporters at the last minute. The only effective way to develop support is to use every available means through daily leadership and staff efforts; even then, the chances for success only get better, and failure isn't precluded in spite of the best of leadership efforts.

THE CONSCIENCE OF A SHELLFISH

A grain of sand,
the conscience of a shellfish,
though irritating to the oyster
is responsible for the pearl.
If men were like mollusks
and mollusks like men,
we'd have some damn small pearls
and a whole lot of oysters fooling around with other oysters' girls![205]

Some may believe I digress, but this original verse conceptually embodies forces that often shape and reshape educators' lives just as they do other lives in other professions—occasionally, even on school grounds during the school day.

Experienced superintendents tell their other administrators about student activity funds and how many leadership careers have been blighted by mishandling or misappropriating these funds, but in education, nobody will even whisper "*S E X*" or quietly acknowledge it's potential for ending promising careers. Small consciences produce small human pearls, which, in turn, may be causative factors in mishandled professional relationships and/or misappropriating someone else's oyster—which, in the history of administrative flight, has, in

---

[205] I considered a gender neutral version of this but rejected it as inappropriate.

turn, caused more professional and personal lives to crash than clear air turbulence and thunderstorms combined.

A few decades ago, in a small New England town, a prominent church figure resigned his position in the congregation when caught in a relationship with a member of the choir—both being married to others at the time of their dalliance. In his emotional resignation statement, he announced he was going off to a mental health facility for a psychiatric cure; being a young part-time cynic, a young teacher told friends that if the churchman wanted to guarantee future behavior he should visit a veterinarian, not a psychiatrist.

Although much private behavior is tolerated today, which would not have been accepted a few decades ago, school leaders still hold public positions. Heightened public awareness of sexual harassment and the consequences of it should cause educational leaders to be much more careful about avoiding inadvertent misunderstandings and attendant consequences. That's supremely appropriate, because, especially today, the first inappropriate, illicit, or unwanted overture can ground administrative flight indefinitely—and, even in today's relatively free atmosphere, inappropriate or illicit advances made and accepted can increase professional hazards dramatically.

Administrators fooling around with other oysters' friends may run their leadership careers smack into sheer mountain walls.

Ah, well . . .

"THIS IS TO REMEMBER . . ."

At Connecticut's Stonington Point, there is a magnificent view of the harbor and an impressive marble monument honoring a local contribution to American history. The carved message on the stone begins, "This is to remember. . . ." Quite a classy and beautiful opening, and the words continue, "Here the brave men of Stonington defeated a landing force from His Majesty's Ship Ramillies bent on burning the town and its shipping, August 10, 1814."

One sunny afternoon years ago, as a number of visitors to "The Point" lazed cozily in post-martini euphorias, enjoying the outstanding view from their automobiles over Stonington Harbor, a pair of carrier-based seagulls swooped low out of the sun searching for targets of opportunity—they found some beauties.

The wingman did what many superintendents would like to do, but which few can afford to do; he made a sizable deposit on a new Mercedes. The flight leader simultaneously devastated the monument, thereby accomplishing what few superintendents intend to do, but which many do well even if accidentally—he obfuscated the message.

In a perfect microcosm of administrative life, the seagulls also brought reality back into a previously idyllic day. One minute you're watching a gorgeous sunset or rocking along enjoying an unusually peaceful board of education meeting. The next thing you know, you're covered with seagull splatter—it's important to remember always the vagaries of public school leadership and how you earn your living.

A VAST ARMADA OF SMALL BOATS

A few years ago, at the *Conference for the Exchange of Educational Opinion,* an annual, New England rite of convocation and educational conversation each October, superintendents in attendance heard an analogy verging on a parable from a featured morning speaker [74]. Although the following paragraphs have had many yards of embroidery added to the original telling, its essence springs from the professor's story.

Imagine if you will, American public education as a vast armada of small boats, with little freeboard, held together only with thin, easily parted lines. Each school district comprises a division of this great fleet, all of which stretches from horizon to horizon. Through legend, folklore, and informal oral histories, these nautical educators have a dim sense of where they've been during their long migration, but there are no navigators, or even prophets, who can tell them where they're headed. The career of an individual teacher, principal, or superintendent of schools is only an infinitesimal part of the eternal educational voyage. Large troop transports regularly deliver fresh oarspeople and, in exchange, haul away haggard and exhausted veterans to island retirement communities.

In a given hypothetical nautical district, there's a relatively large High School Galley divided into different working sections, or departments—in addition to primary responsibilities teaching their particular subjects, almost all have a secondary assignment for galley propulsion, and a few have other auxiliary functions. Various educational specialties are easily identified by their behaviors:

- Usually, the Mathematics oarsfolk (a concrete/sequential bunch) pull hard to help reach their flotilla's ultimate destination, although, unfortunately, they don't know what that is. Being compulsive about numbers, they count oarstrokes ad nauseam. They're a notoriously unmusical collection, and their off-key voices can be heard throughout the boat as they sing, "Three billion bottles of beer on the wall, three billion bottles of beer . . ."

- In striking contrast, Social Studies Department troops, in unholy alliance with a few demonic spirits from the Business Department, hardly ever row. These swashbucklers spend their free time indiscriminately whacking other crew members and each other with their oars and/or plotting a takeover of the ship—and, of course, buckling their swashes. When their planned mutiny takes place, the Captain of the Galley, or the high school principal, is "outta there."

- Guidance Counselors don't row much either, but they don't have to. They have records documenting everything and everybody, including where the bodies went over the side and who pushed them. They also have a whole shipload[206] of free advice for everyone about everything. All in all, important people to have on your side whenever there's dissension and trouble in the family (or whenever "the fit hits the clan").

- The Poetry, Punctuation, and Pronunciation Popinjays (reading teachers are included) pull together now and again, but, more often, they debate heatedly the philosophical origins of semicolons, especially their relationship to life and to the endless sea journey. Frequently, fierce hostilities erupt from strong opposing viewpoints, and English Department oarspeople have been mysteriously lost over the side for heretical beliefs on such controversial issues as the comma splice or the meaning of particular Elizabethan love sonnets. Generally, the department enjoys both the fighting and the journey.

- The Physical Education contingent doesn't even know it's on a trip, but that's OK. Its members are strong, vigorous, clean of limb, morally semi-pure, and all can row forever—a useful

---

[206]If you read this aloud, enunciate clearly. It's whole "shipload."

skill if they would only stop with the katzenjammer jai alai using oars as cestas. And without an onboard fronton, they frequently bounce their pelotas off the Captain's "cabeza" and the cabezas of assistant principals as well.[207]

- Art Gallery dilettantes naturally have the prettiest part of the galley—colorfully painted and decorated by its aesthetic crew with flowers, oceanscapes, and statuary. Their artistic temperament makes it hard for them to focus on mundane issues, such as rowing or survival, but, engrossed in their art, they're a happy bunch in spite of physical discomforts and the chaos that surrounds them. Sometimes, the entire department seems so laid back its members appear to be posing for a group portrait on *Family Feud*—but they're probably just envisioning their next project.

- The Music Ensemble's percussion section sets the tempo for anyone on the galley who chooses to row at any given moment. One department functionary, much more interested in concert bands and reacting reluctantly to orders from on high, is organizing a marching band, including flags and wooden rifles, for competition among nearby high school boats.

- Energetic engineers from Industrial Arts remain focused on the development of nuclear powered oars, although with only modest success to date. Their work spaces are generally cluttered and oil stained, but, overall, their messiness is accepted because they work hard and remain in their own end of the boat. Acting upon a confidential request from the Social Studies and Business Department buccaneers, they have crafted a beautiful, three-by-twelve foot plank of the finest teak for some unspecified shipboard ritual involving the Captain.

- When they're not in class, Home Economics teachers stay busy preparing nutritious and delicious meals for the crew and mending torn garments with fishbone needles and frayed pieces of old mooring line. They hate the frequent shipboard conflicts, and, as was true of "schoolmarms" in the Old West, they can't understand why there must always be so much violence on the boat. They're a pleasant counterbalance to some of the surlier groups on board.

[207]I taught PE and coached for a time, so there's no malice in my characterization of former compatriots.

- And, finally, on behalf of otherwise understandably confused crew members, Foreign Language dandies are laboriously translating administrative correspondence, especially the superintendent's memos to staff. Work progresses slowly because most department members are usually on sabbatical in Paris or Madrid. The ship's linguists are eager to arrive somewhere, anywhere, so they can teach Latin, or possibly the morphology of principals' newsletters, to the ignorant natives of that unknown shore.

All in all, High School Boats, with their varied and colorful personnel, have been inspirations to both Gilbert and Sullivan in composing their lighthearted operatic romps.

The ship's company on the Junior High, or Middle School Galley is typically embroiled in a neverending, onboard, reorganization hassle and arguing over the name of their medium-sized craft. They're never sure what kind of boat they're supposed to be. Should they row close to the larger high school flagship or among the smaller elementary vessels? Are they papa bears, momma bears, or baby bears? They can't seem to get their porridge "just right." This controversial craft is often crewed by teachers thrown out of the other boats for various reasons, including aberrant views on the aforementioned comma splice or on long division using three-figure divisors. Because of their checkered and troubled pasts, they are a piratical and mutinous lot, and their Commanders live exciting and hazardous lives aboard this educational halfway house.

As a refreshing contrast, Elementary Skiffs are generally filled with contented, cheerful oarspeople who pull cooperatively and happily together. Occasional recess or lunchroom duties seem to be the only clouds in their otherwise sunny sky. Most willingly follow the stroke requested by their leader, the Principal Coxswain or Coxswainess, but there are many individualistic, and even a few downright eccentric, crew members on these small craft who will row only to their own beat. Their Coxswain or Coxswainess approaches them at great risk to his own life, liberty, and continued pursuit of sexual fulfillment. Once in a while, too many of these volatile crew members end up on the same boat, and there's really hell to pay.

Last, but very important, the special education aggregation, or "aggravation" as they're often known, are being towed along in their unusual Oceangoing Barge, engaged in their customary quarrelsome and inconclusive PPT meeting (PPT stands for professional protesters team). They talk loudly and simultaneously in a strange tongue called "mystery-speak," filled with initials and acronyms, and, like Lamont Cranston in his radio role as "The Shadow," their conversations "cloud men's and women's minds." As directed by the Commodore of their peculiar vessel, each has prepared an extensive, personalized IEP— that's an "individualized excuse program"—to explain why he or she is always in a PPT instead of rowing.[208]

But regardless of, and maybe even because of, the range of human strengths and frailties among its crews, our unique flotilla and the entire armada move on forever—propelled painstakingly toward an unknown and never-reached landfall by the steady efforts of dedicated teachers who somehow keep their boats headed in roughly the same direction and the thin lines that bind them together intact.

Periodically, during their eternal voyage, frightening storms develop with howling winds and seas that rise to monstrous force and heights. When this happens, powerful command ships carrying superintendents of schools grudgingly haul in their sea anchors and roar busily around their particular flotillas. Their luxurious yachts also carry great numbers of specialists who operate these high-powered "love boats" smoothly and comfortably in the worst of weather, as teachers, up to their armpits in often frigid water, fight to avoid capsizing their tiny craft amidst the angry seas.

Superintendents stand imperially on their bridges with stern, yet benevolent, expressions and issue instructions over loudspeakers— sometimes with a number of special assistants alongside them. Depending upon the voyage's decade, their confused and even contradictory directives to beleaguered teachers might have included or do include: "Forget the old math. Shift your course smartly to modern mathematics!" "Make your curriculum more relevant to students!" Develop mini-courses!" "Try sharing open classrooms without walls!" "Write behavioral objectives for students!" "Educational television is the answer!" "Use more phonics! or less phonics! or throw phonics over the side and use whole language and process writing!" "Set your course to return to basics!" and the ever popular, "Dammit, do something, the board of education is on my 'bleep.' "

And, each time, the winds roar and the waves nearly swamp the

[208]My wife is a special education teacher, so, obviously, I say these things also with only love and affection.

small boats and superintendents issue their stentorian orders, all the teachers (and sometimes their Captains, Commodores, Coxswains and Coxswainesses, and their Cousins and Their Aunts) rise precariously to their feet, balancing against the pitching and rolling, and appear to shout something in unison. But because of the storm's fury, superintendents can never hear the voices and can never understand the message that teachers try in vain to share with them.

This phenomenon both fascinates and confuses school executives. When they repair to island retreats (while teachers continue their daily rowing) and ponder high-level issues that only executives are allowed to ponder, one inevitable discussion centers around the unheard voices. Theories abound: most believe it's simply a matter of teachers cheering their chief school officer's insightful suggestions; a minority think that it's an aerobic breathing exercise, but no firm conclusion can ever be reached. In part, this is because superintendents typically react to colleagues' suggestions, and for that matter almost everybody else's, much the same way chimpanzees approach a bright orange ball—growling suspiciously, touching it tentatively, rolling it over cautiously, marking it with scent, and finally fleeing from it as if it carried a plague.

Often, at these high-level affairs, airplanes fly overhead, and Madeline Hunter or Lamar Alexander or Public Education's Savior du Jour parachutes down to tell superintendents more things they should do to teachers, or have teachers do for them. Then, following lively discussions on more expensive perquisites and benefits in professional contracts, superintendents return to their well-appointed quarters aboard their palatial craft, on the periphery of their flotillas, armed with a gaggle of new and recycled concepts to help teachers reach their true potential—and many new programs for them to juggle as they row.

And so it came to pass, after two and a half decades as a wholesale distributor of educational wisdom, a prototypical superintendent was steaming about his flotilla, in the midst of a really bad oceanographic event, strewing executive pearls of wisdom like rose petals amongst the storm-tossed crews struggling to survive. The brilliant bits and pieces of advice freely shared involved such nostrums as "educational accountability," "restructuring," "privatization," "technology/computers/ distance learning," "clinical supervision," "strategic and long-range planning," "total quality management," "math manipulatives," "portfolio and other alternative student assessments," the satanic and much feared, "outcome-based education," and many others of at least equal import.

During this most violent tempest in the superintendent's twenty-five years of shepherding nautical flocks, God intervened and sent a powerful meteorological message. In just seconds, the winds disappeared; the waves lessened to ripples, and the seas became as calm and as quiet as a stagnant pond. It was a miracle. For the first time, the superintendent could hear clearly what each teacher had been trying so hard to tell him for so long. They stood in their boats, and over the waters, all together, distinctly and unmistakably, their voices spoke to him—as they had so many times before when he didn't understand.

And the voices said, "(mysteryword) you!" (I couldn't say it—at least in written form. Insert your own favorite Anglo-Saxon expletive here or send $.32 and a self-addressed, stamped envelope for a complete transcript of this story with the missing word included.)

EDUCATIONAL COLLEAGUES AND FRIENDS

"Irish Heartbeat" [75], a song written and performed by Van Morrison, although hardly composed and sung especially for school administrators, captures the essence of careers spent working alongside educational colleagues striving together toward achievement of worthwhile goals. In the song, Morrison suggests that "because this old world is so cold and don't care nothin' for your soul" that we not stray too far from our "own ones."

After spending a major part of your professional life in the precarious, challenging, frustrating, enervating, and sometimes exhilarating role of educational leadership shared by superintendents of schools and other school leaders, your "own ones," the teachers, principals, superintendents, and others with whom you have striven together in a worthwhile cause, will mean a great deal to you. And opportunities to "talk awhile with your own ones" will always remain among life's great pleasures.

Yeah, the whole notion may be a little reminiscent of the territorial behavior exhibited by educational musk-oxen standing rump to rump in a circle defending themselves against the world—but so what! A little paranoia makes good glue to hold a group together.

After almost four decades of walking the walk alongside some of the most dedicated, competent, selfless people in the world, I wouldn't have had it any other way.

PRACTICE MAKES PERFECT—EXCERPTS

Match the following titles with the correct extract(s); some titles have more than one excerpt. Answers are provided in Appendix C, pp. 496–497.

A Confederacy of Dunces	——
Could Socrates Survive the Superintendency?	——
"Dead before Takeoff"	——
Don't You Realize How Dangerous It Is Out There?	——
Holiday Nuts to Staff	——
Just a Red Ant in the Noonday Sun	——
Lanterns in the Window	——
May I Have the Envelope Please?	——
Old Dogs, New Tricks	——
Rabbis—II	——
School Calendars—I	——
School Calendars—II	——
Some Days You Might Think Tom Hobbes Had It Right	——
The Best Lack All Conviction . . .	——
The Conscience of a Shellfish	——
"This Is to Remember . . ."	——
A Vast Armada of Small Boats	——
Educational Colleagues and Friends	——

Excerpts

(*1*) Although I'm sure you already have, take a close look at the crowd at your next budget or town meeting when an issue has heated up the political climate. Too many of those present are wild-eyed, foam-flecked angries living lives of "noisy desperation"; too many of the town or district's comparatively well-adjusted people are at home watching a TV ball game with a beer or a sherry in one hand, patting their spouse on his or her backside with the other. An Irish poet, who undoubtedly had attended many such meetings, captured this school district dilemma . . .

(*2*) Therefore, it's important for educators to be poised, enthusiastic, willing, and able to impart 180 days of wisdom, knowledge, attitudes, facts, and skills on Tuesdays and Thursdays during those two available April weeks.

(*3*) But before superintendents accept new positions, they should understand the choices they are making before they no longer have any choices to make.

(*4*) Interviewers often ask administrative aspirants, whether for the superintendency or a principalship or a director's position, what qualities they have admired in those for whom they have worked and what qualities those same people exhibited that the candidate would not want to emulate. It's a revealing question, not only of the strengths and weaknesses of the applicant's former bosses, but of the candidate him or herself and of his or her professional and personal insights and values.

(*5*) When John Milton wrote, "When I consider how my light is spent . . ." [72], he was, among other things, reminding some of us to keep our eyeglasses close by.

(*6*) Nobody ever said public life was devoid of frustrations—or that every member of the general public, all staff, each board of education member, every parent, all town officials, all students, and every other person and groups of persons with whom school leadership is in professional contact will always be intelligent, insightful, open, empathetic, tolerant, emotionally secure, flexible, well motivated, or any other way you'd prefer them to be.

(*7*) One significant administrative opportunity to adjust or modify personal and professional behaviors occurs when superintendents, principals, assistant superintendents, and other administrators change positions—from one superintendency to another; from one principalship to another; from a principalship to an assistant superintendency, a superintendency, or some other central office position; from an assistant superintendency to a superintendency; or from any administrative position to another administrative position. At these special times, the leader isn't working against strong, preconceived perceptions of him or her, and all personal and professional leadership changes have a much better chance of being recognized and appreciated. Also, there is a lack of self-consciousness when leaders work with new colleagues who accept their new and possibly improved behaviors without puzzling over them because they are new.

(8) The superintendent didn't fully empathize with ants until he became a superintendent of schools and had to endure state education department bureaucracies with their circles of heat generated by too many dangerously enthusiastic middle management chiefs. Many of these energetic men and women, unfortunately, have nothing better to do than crisp superintendents the way he did his boyhood ant victims. Experiences with state education department functionaries made him further regret the way he had treated his little red ant buddies.

(9) The year's first snowfall of any consequence is the most dangerous of the season. Over the spring, summer, and early fall months, automobiles and buses somehow forget how to climb slippery hills and how to stop at intersections; vehicles require a period of retraining for the long winter ahead.

(10) The ensuing ambush and massacre have already been best described in English verse.

(11) Regardless of any unfair disqualifications of these well-known historical personages, it remains true that public positions today are not for everyone—only a select few measure up to their rigors and demands. Unlike the superintendent's or other official's divergent view of the world looking outward at hundreds and even thousands of people, he or she is the focus of intensely convergent views from staff, parents and the general public, board members, town officials, and others. Every personal and professional flaw is magnified by this close scrutiny, and only the strong and the lucky can survive it forever.

(12) One sunny afternoon years ago, as a number of visitors to "The Point" lazed cozily in post-martini euphorias, enjoying the outstanding view from their automobiles over Stonington Harbor, a pair of carrier-based seagulls swooped low out of the sun, searching for targets of opportunity—they found some beauties. The wingman did what many superintendents would like to do, but that few can afford to do; he made a sizable deposit on a new Mercedes. The flight leader simultaneously devastated the monument, thereby accomplishing what few superintendents intend to do, but many do well even if accidentally—he obfuscated the message.

(13) Ah, well . . .

(*14*) It's counterproductive to indulge yourself this way. It comes across clearly to others, even to dunces, and this makes working with them constructively and productively almost impossible.

(*15*) He'd cast a quarter-sized circle of light and heat over the ants, and they'd begin to sweat, stagger, and give out little ant screams. He would narrow the circle, and they'd fall over with their tiny little tongues hanging out. Then he'd focus the light to a pinpoint and crisp them — snap, crackle, and pop. In retrospect, he feels bad about that practice, but then it was fun; if reincarnation exists, he suspects he already knows in which insect form he will return, and it's probably only fair.

(*16*) . . . public leadership positions today are more difficult than ever before because of inflated public expectations, an abundance of only semi-solvable problems, and the gaggle of single-issue constituencies infesting all levels of government. With the . . . evaluation as a guide, it may be instructive to examine other important historical figures to determine whether or not they could be effective as a nineties kind of school superintendent guy or gal — as well as having been successful, or at least well known, in their own special fields and in their own eras. Identified eccentricities, peccadilloes, or other shortcomings would, in most cases, equally lessen their effectiveness today as a school principal, town manager, or any other appointed public leadership post; for elective positions, interestingly enough, aberrant behaviors almost seem to be prerequisites.

(*17*) "We don't need to subsidize ski bums at the expense of our children's future economic success — and the kids have the presidents' birthdays off anyway."

(*18*) Often, at these high-level affairs, airplanes fly overhead, and Madeline Hunter or Lamar Alexander or Public Education's Savior du Jour parachutes down to tell superintendents more things they should do to teachers, or have teachers do for them.

(*19*) . . . believed that people are moved chiefly by desire for power and by fear of others and that "without a common power to keep them all in awe" (read superintendent of schools), human life is "solitary, poor, nasty, brutish, and short" [73]. If you think those views shocked his contemporaries, contemplate for a moment the reaction those words would generate today from avid proponents of total quality management.

(*20*) This phenomenon can also be identified frequently among faculties, teachers' unions or associations, board of education candidates, and boards of education. Empirically, it appears emotionally easier and more satisfying to fight against causes perceived to be evil than to fight in support of those believed to be good. Nut cases remain eternally poised to leap out against something—anything—while rational people take forever to become excited enough to involve themselves in the fray.

(*21*) Demonstrating the proper leadership ethics and behavior may be far more important than teaching the techniques of leadership, and even with the best of mentors, it's also true that those with whom we work often learn much of what they shouldn't do, as well as what they should, by observing our peculiar frailties and imperfections.

(*22*)   *A grain of sand,*
        the conscience of a shellfish,
        though irritating to the oyster
        is responsible for the pearl.
        If men were like mollusks
        and mollusks like men,
        we'd have some damn small pearls
        and a whole lot of oysters fooling around with other oysters' girls!

(*23*) After spending a major part of your professional life in the precarious, challenging, frustrating, enervating, and sometimes exhilarating role of educational leadership shared by superintendents of schools and other school leaders, your "own ones," the teachers, principals, superintendents, and others with whom you have striven toward worthwhile causes, will mean a great deal to you. And opportunities to "talk awhile with your own ones" will always remain among life's great pleasures.

(*24*) Superintendent and other administrative groups may present these awards at meetings, conferences, workshops, or major awards assemblies—similar to those award presentations for graduating high school seniors or the annual "Oscar" ceremonies in Hollywood. They or variations thereon are joys to give, and recipients will treasure them forever—or at least a few weeks.

(*25*) In a perfect microcosm of administrative life, the seagulls also brought reality back into a previously idyllic day. One minute you're watching a gorgeous sunset or rocking along enjoying an unusually peaceful board of education meeting. The next thing you know, you're covered with seagull splatter—it's important to remember always the vagaries of public school leadership and how you earn your living.

Negotiated Agreements—WFCT and WASA

WFCT (WAYWARD FEDERATION OF CLASSROOM TEACHERS)

I
PREAMBLE

1. This Agreement shall be effective from September 1, (year), through August 31, (year). In cases where the school calendar begins prior to September 1, annual changes to this agreement shall be effective on the first work day.

II
NEGOTIATIONS

2. Recognition. The Board of Education (hereinafter referred to as the "Board") recognizes the Federation of Classroom Teachers (hereinafter referred to as the "Federation") for the purpose of negotiations as the exclusive representative for all certified professional employees who are employed by the Board in positions requiring a teaching certificate and who are not included in the Administrators and Supervisors Association unit or excluded from the purview of teacher negotiations pursuant to Connecticut General Statutes, §§10-153b through 10-153d.

3. Scope of Agreement. This Agreement contains the full and complete agreement between the Board and the Federation on all negotiable issues, and neither party shall be required during the term hereof to "negotiate" (within the meaning of Connecticut General Statutes, §10-153d) upon any issue.

4. Teacher Contract. Teachers shall have an initial contract upon hire and an annual salary notice thereafter. Contract dates shall terminate on August 31.

III
RECOGNITION OF RESPONSIBILITIES OF THE BOARD

5. Conflicts with This Agreement. When Board policy and/or administra-

373

tion regulations and conditions of this Agreement conflict, the conditions of this Agreement shall prevail.

6. <u>Board Rights, Responsibilities, and Prerogatives.</u> It is recognized by both the Board and the Federation that the Board has and will continue to retain, whether exercised or not, the sole right, responsibility, and prerogative to direct the operation of the public schools in the Town in all its aspects, including, but not limited to the following: to maintain good public elementary and secondary schools and provide such other educational activities as in its judgment will best serve the interests of the Town to give the children of the Town as nearly equal advantages as may be practicable; to decide the need for school facilities; to determine the care, maintenance, and operation of buildings, lands, apparatus, and other property used for school purposes; to determine the number, age, and qualifications of the pupils to be admitted into each school; to employ, assign, and transfer employees; to suspend or dismiss the employees of the schools in the manner provided by statute; to designate the schools that shall be attended by the various children within the Town; to make such provisions as will enable each child of school age residing in the Town to attend school for the period required by law and provide for the transportation of children wherever it is reasonable and desirable; to prescribe rules for the management, studies, classification, and discipline for the public schools; to decide the textbooks to be used; to make rules for the arrangement, use, and safekeeping of the school libraries and to approve the books selected therefor; to approve plans for school buildings, and to prepare and submit budgets and, in its sole discretion, expend monies appropriated by the Town for the maintenance of the schools and to make such transfers of funds within the appropriated budget as it shall deem desirable. These rights, responsibilities, and prerogatives are not subject to delegation in whole or in part, except that the same shall not be exercised in a manner inconsistent with or in violation of any of the specific terms and provisions of this Agreement. No action taken by the Board with respect to such rights, responsibilities, and prerogatives, other than as there are specific provisions herein elsewhere contained, shall be subject to the grievance and arbitration provisions of this Agreement. Subject to the provisions of this Agreement, the Board and the Superintendent of Schools reserve and retain full rights, authority, and discretion, in the proper discharge of their duties and responsibilities, to control, supervise, and manage the Department of Education and its professional staff under governing laws, ordinances, rules, and regulations—municipal, state and federal.

IV
SALARIES

7. <u>Placement on Salary Schedule.</u> Teachers shall be placed on the appro-

priate step of the salary schedule based on the following criteria: full credit for previous experience in private schools accredited by the State of Connecticut, public schools, accredited colleges, and military dependency schools provided that such experience for any one (1) year shall have been continuous service for at least one-half (1/2) of the school year. A school year should be defined as the minimum number of days required for a school year under Connecticut state law. Credit for part-time teaching shall be granted provided the teaching assignment is equal to or more than one-half of a full teaching assignment as established by the institution.

8. Salaries. Teacher salaries shall be determined in accordance with the foregoing paragraph based on the teacher salary schedules, which follow:

Salary Schedule—First Contract Year

Step	Bachelor Salary	BA+30/MA Salary	BA+45/MA+15 Salary	MA+30/6th Salary
0	28,314	31,570	31,825	32,051
1	29,602	33,920	34,232	34,529
2	30,891	36,270	36,638	37,006
3	32,179	38,620	39,045	39,484
4	33,467	40,970	41,452	41,961
5	34,755	43,320	43,858	44,439
6	36,044	45,670	46,265	46,916
7	37,332	48,021	48,672	49,394
8	38,620	50,371	51,078	51,871
9	39,909	52,721	53,485	54,349
10	41,197	55,071	55,892	56,826

Step	MA+45/6th+15 Salary	MA+60 Salary	Ph.D. Salary
0	31,995	32,420	33,127
1	34,571	35,067	35,846
2	37,148	37,714	38,564
3	39,725	40,362	41,282
4	42,301	43,009	44,000
5	44,878	45,656	46,718
6	47,454	48,304	49,436
7	50,031	50,951	52,154
8	52,607	53,598	54,873
9	55,184	56,246	57,591
10	57,761	58,893	60,309

Note: Everyone will advance one (1) step from the current salary schedule.

Salary Schedule—Second Contract Year

Step	Bachelor Salary	BA+30/MA Salary	BA+45/MA+15 Salary	MA+30/6th Salary
0	29,017	32,354	32,499	32,644
1	30,300	34,762	34,965	35,183
2	31,582	37,171	37,432	37,722
3	32,865	39,579	39,898	40,261
4	34,147	41,988	42,365	42,800
5	35,430	44,396	44,831	45,339
6	36,712	46,804	47,298	47,878
7	37,995	49,213	49,764	50,417
8	39,277	51,621	52,231	52,956
9	40,560	54,030	54,697	55,495
10	41,843	56,438	57,163	58,034

Step	MA+45/6th+15 Salary	MA+60 Salary	Ph.D. Salary
0	32,731	33,224	33,950
1	35,372	35,938	36,736
2	38,012	38,651	39,521
3	40,653	41,364	42,307
4	43,293	44,077	45,092
5	45,934	46,790	47,878
6	48,574	49,503	50,664
7	51,215	52,216	53,449
8	53,856	54,929	56,235
9	56,496	57,642	59,021
10	59,137	60,355	61,806

Note: Everyone will advance one (1) step from the first contract year schedule.

Salary Schedule—Third Contract Year

Step	Bachelor Salary	BA+30/MA Salary	BA+45/MA+15 Salary	MA+30/6th Salary
0	29,767	33,190	33,339	33,488
1	31,083	35,661	35,869	36,092
2	32,398	38,132	38,399	38,697
3	33,714	40,602	40,930	41,302
4	35,030	43,073	43,460	43,906
5	36,346	45,544	45,990	46,511
6	37,661	48,014	48,520	49,116
7	38,977	50,485	51,050	51,720

8	40,293	52,955	53,581	54,325
9	41,608	55,426	56,111	56,929
10	42,924	57,897	58,641	59,534

Step	MA + 45/6th + 15 Salary	MA + 60 Salary	Ph.D. Salary
0	33,577	34,083	34,827
1	36,286	36,886	37,685
2	38,995	39,650	40,543
3	41,704	42,433	43,400
4	44,412	45,216	46,258
5	47,121	47,999	49,116
6	49,830	50,783	51,973
7	52,539	53,566	54,831
8	55,248	56,349	57,688
9	57,956	59,132	60,546
10	60,665	61,915	63,404

Note: Everyone will advance one (1) step from the second contract year schedule.

For placement on the BA + 30/MA salary schedule, thirty semester hours must be earned in a planned program approved by the Superintendent or the Director of Instruction and Personnel Services and taken at an accredited institution and must fulfill Connecticut State Department of Education educational requirements for the professional educator's certificate.

All credits for placement on other salary schedules must be earned in courses approved by the Superintendent or Director of Instruction and Personnel Services and taken at an accredited institution. Such approval must be sought at least fifteen days prior to the start of any course, if possible.

Salary track placement shall be granted for the next pay period following receipt of an official transcript and/or official grade report.

The social worker shall be placed on the MA + 30 schedule.

Salaries are based upon a one hundred eighty-two (182)–day teaching year plus one (1) day prior to the start of the school year. In those positions requiring more or less time than the one hundred eighty-three (183)–day base, the salary shall be prorated on a per-diem basis.

LONGEVITY. Commencing with the fifteenth (15th) year of teaching in the school system, a teacher will receive Four Hundred Dollars ($400) in June of that year and in each subsequent year of teaching in the school system until his/her twentieth (20th) year, whereupon he/she shall receive Fourteen Hundred Dollars ($1,400) per each subsequent year of teaching in the school system, such sum payable in June of each year.

9. <u>Salary Payment Schedule.</u>
   a. Each professional employee covered by this Agreement shall be paid his or her annual salary in twenty-six (26) equal installments; in twenty-one (21) installments, each equal to 1/26 of the applicable annual salary, and the twenty-second (22nd) installment equal to 5/26 of the applicable annual salary; or in twenty-two (22) equal installments.
   b. Election of method of payment must be made by the last school day of the prior school year, except in the case of newly hired teachers, who shall elect their method of payment within the first full week of employment.
   c. If no election is made, the prior method of payment will continue in effect, or, if no election has ever been made, payment will be made in twenty-six (26) equal installments.
   d. The first payday shall be the first Thursday following the opening of school.
   e. Paydays shall be every other Thursday.
   f. In the event of a scheduled payday falling during the Christmas, winter, spring, or summer vacation, the payroll shall be distributed on the last day of school prior to the beginning of the vacation.
   g. When mailed, paychecks shall be sent only to the teacher's address, as shown on the official staff list, not later than the Wednesday prior to the scheduled payday.

10. <u>Adjustments in Pay.</u> Adjustments in pay due to absence without pay will be computed on the basis of school days worked. The daily rate of pay for each school day will be computed by dividing the annual salary by 183.

11. a. <u>Salary Deductions.</u> Teacher authorized payroll deductions shall be made for the following:
   (*1*) Tax-sheltered annuities through a bonded annuity distribution agent selected by the board
   (*2*) Wayward Teachers' Federal Credit Union
   (*3*) Blue Shield
   (*4*) Blue Cross
   (*5*) Increased retirement
   (*6*) United Fund
   (*7*) Dental insurance
   (*8*) Disability insurance
   Changes in payroll deductions for the above shall not be made for units less than Five Dollars ($5.00), except Blue Shield, Blue Cross, and dental. Teacher-authorized payroll deductions shall be made for WFCT and WEA dues in not more than eight (8) consecutive monthly installments per school year and in amounts of not less than Six Dollars ($6.00) per installment, except for the final installment.

11. b. <u>Agency Shop.</u>

(*1*) All teachers shall, as a condition of continued employment, join the Federation or pay the Federation a service representation fee as determined annually by the Federation. The Federation shall provide each nonmember with a statement of the major categories of expenditures for such purposes made in the prior fiscal year at least thirty (30) days before the commencement of the succeeding contract year, said statement verified by an independent auditor.

(*2*) The Federation shall establish and notify the Board in writing of the amount of Federation dues and representation fee.

(*3*) The Board agrees to deduct the service fee from the salaries of all nonmembers.

(*4*) The Federation shall hold the Board and the Town harmless against all claims, demands, liabilities, lawsuits, counsel fees, or other costs that may arise out of, or be by reason of, action taken against the Board as a result of compliance with the provisions of subsection b.

12. Salary Adjustment. Teachers shall receive during the last year prior to retirement, after ten (10) years or more service in the district, an increase in pay of Eight Hundred Twenty-Five Dollars ($825) for that year. Application for such increase in pay must be made to the superintendent of schools by September 15 of the year prior to the school year in which retirement is planned for the increase to be paid in that final year of teaching—otherwise, the increase shall be paid in the school year following retirement.

13. Supplemental Pay. Supplemental pay positions shall be paid according to salary indicated for the applicable year as described in Appendix A.

14. Supplemental Pay—Hourly. The following supplementary positions shall be paid at the rate of $24 per hour:
   * adult education and summer school teachers
   * summer scheduling
   * curriculum planning and summer workshop attendance
   * homebound and special education tutoring as approved by the Superintendent
   * presentation of professional development activities as approved by the Superintendent
   * Summer school teachers and professional development presenters shall be paid for one preparation hour per two clock hours of instruction.

15. Supplementary Pay—Positions. Supplementary pay positions shall be created upon the recommendation of the Superintendent. The Board shall place the new supplementary pay position in the appropriate category.

V
FRINGE BENEFITS

16. <u>Insurance.</u> The Board will provide each teacher the following insurance or equivalent.
    a. One Million Dollars ($1,000,000.00) family major medical insurance.
    b. Fifty Thousand Dollars ($50,000.00) employee life insurance.
    c. Eighty-five Percent (85%) of the cost of participation in individual or family semiprivate Blue Cross, including individual or family copay prescription drug rider and semiprivate maternity care rider.
    d. Eighty-five Percent (85%) of the cost of individual or family Blue Shield Century 96 contract. The home and office rider shall be a maximum of $300 per individual and $1,200 per family.
    e. Eighty-five Percent (85%) of the cost of individual or family full-service dental plan (equivalent to Blue Cross full-service dental plan) as selected by the Board.
    f. Eighty-five Percent (85%) of the cost of dental riders for additional basic benefits, periodontics, and orthodontics equivalent to Blue Cross A, C, and D riders.

The Board and the Federation may mutually agree to choose to provide different coverage regulations equivalent to that provided by the present carrier.

Any teacher who terminates service at the end of a complete school year, may, if the teacher elects, continue to receive the benefits in this paragraph for the remainder of that Agreement year.

Section 125 Plan

No later than the effective date of this Agreement, the Board shall implement and maintain a Section 125 Salary Reduction Agreement, which will be designed to permit exclusion from taxable income the employee's share of health insurance premiums. The Board makes no representations or guarantees as to the initial or continued viability of such a salary reduction agreement and shall incur no obligation to engage in any form of impact bargaining in the event that a change in law reduces or eliminates the tax-exempt status of employee insurance premium contributions. So long as the Board makes a good faith effort to comply with this paragraph, neither the Federation or any teacher covered by this Agreement shall make any claim or demand, nor maintain any action against the Board or any of its members or agents for taxes, penalties, interest, or other cost of loss arising from a flaw or defect in the salary reduction agreement or from a change in law that may reduce or eliminate the employee tax benefits to be derived therefrom.

Notwithstanding the above, should a change in the law or a disallowance of the plan reduce or eliminate the tax-exempt status of employee insurance premium contributions, the Board shall reinstate the 90%/10% premium sharing plan to the extent of such reduction or elimination.

The Board and the Federation recognize that escalating healthcare costs are a problem for both employer and employee and thereby agree to create a joint health insurance study committee comprised of two members appointed by the Superintendent of Schools and two members appointed by the President of the Federation. The health insurance study committee will study alternative insurance coverage, self-insurance, waivers, programs that may reduce costs while maintaining or improving coverage provided to employees, the establishment of an employees' wellness program, and positive changes that will help contain health insurance costs.

17. <u>Insurance While on Leave.</u> Election to have group health, life, and/or major medical insurance continued in force for the duration of such leave, on the then current basis, shall be allowed, provided arrangements for the payment of the premium therefore are made by the teacher concerned in advance of the date of leave and provided that the foregoing is acceptable to the insurance company involved.

VI
PROFESSIONAL BENEFITS

18. <u>Absence with Pay.</u>
    a. Up to six (6) days each year of personal absence with pay may be granted for the following:
       (*1*) Personal [three (3) days maximum]. Personal leave shall not be used to extend holidays or vacation periods. Reasons for personal absences shall be discussed orally with the principal. The Request for Absence with Pay form for personal absence shall be used and shall require twenty-four (24)-hours' notice and prior approval of the immediate supervisor if possible.
       (*2*) Legal
       (*3*) Religious
       (*4*) Family (birth, death, marriage, illness, graduation)
       (*5*) College or university conferences [one (1) maximum per year]
       Absence with pay under items 1, 2, 3 and 5 above may be approved only when it is not reasonable for the required activity to have been scheduled during other hours.
    b. Officers of the Federation may be granted five (5) days' absence with pay for Federation business. For extenuating circumstances, an additional five (5) days may be granted.
    c. The Request for Absence with Pay form for other than personal business shall be used and shall require twenty-four (24) hours' notice and the approval of the immediate supervisor. Immediate supervisor

means the building principal or the supervisor of Special Services.

d. The Federation shall submit a report on the use of absence with pay to the Superintendent in June of each school year.

e. The Superintendent may waive requirements in this article if, in his or her judgment, there are extenuating circumstances that justify such action.

19. Professional Days. (Conventions, conferences, and observations). Subject to prior approval by the immediate supervisor, a teacher may attend conventions, conferences, or the observation of an activity in another school building or school system. Approved attendance shall be without loss of pay. Reimbursement for reasonable costs incurred in connection with professional days must have prior approval by the immediate supervisor. A written report shall be submitted to the Superintendent or his/her designee within two (2) weeks of the termination of the convention, conference, or observation. Upon request, the Superintendent shall have the right to waive the written report at his/her discretion.

20. Graduate Study Reimbursement. When in the judgment of the Superintendent the course for which reimbursement is requested will make a meaningful contribution to a more effective performance of the duties to which the professional staff member is assigned, then such reimbursement may be granted. Courses must be completed with a grade of B or higher. If a lesser mark is received and the teacher desires, extenuating circumstances may be explained to the Superintendent for his/her consideration. All nontenured teachers and teachers holding TEP certification shall discuss graduate study courses with their building principal prior to submittal to the Superintendent. Courses and institutions must have prior approval of the Superintendent at least fifteen (15) days prior to the start of the course, if possible. The Board of Education will provide an annual account of Thirty Thousand Dollars ($30,000.00) and prorate the amount per semester hour in the event that more courses are completed than are budgeted.

Graduate study reimbursement is payable in one lump sum in the second December check of the school year following the school year in which the academic study was completed. Teachers must submit an official grade report or an official transcript of the approved course(s) and a copy of the bill for tuition and fees. The amount of the reimbursement shall be equal to the cost of tuition and fees (excluding books) incurred for the course.

21. Leave of Absence. This section shall apply to tenured teachers in the school system. A leave of absence without pay may be granted for illness, graduate study, or other reasons such as child-rearing leave. The leave of absence may extend only for eighteen (18) months or less, and the date of return must be the first day of a student marking period or at a

time mutually agreed upon by the Superintendent and the teacher. A teacher on leave of absence must notify the Superintendent in writing, prior to January 1, of his/her intention to return or not to return for the following school year. In the event the teacher wishes to return to the system, he/she will be returned to his/her former position or a similar position for which he/she is certified and qualified, if one so exists, subject to Reduction in Force policy. Qualified shall mean having the proper certification and having taught in a similar assignment in the district. Teachers taking leave of absence are not eligible for salary or for step credit unless they have taught for more than one-half (1/2) of a school year. Teachers shall be allowed to buy Blue Cross, Blue Shield, dental insurance, and major medical as provided in paragraph 17.

22. Sick Leave. Teachers shall be granted annually fifteen (15) days of sick leave with full pay. The accumulation of sick leave shall be unlimited. Each teacher shall be notified in September of the amount of his/her accumulated sick leave. Teachers returning from any leave shall retain prior accumulated unused sick leave. Teachers, upon retirement in accordance with the State Teacher Retirement Act or death, after ten (10) years of service in the district, the last five (5) of which must be consecutive, shall receive payment of up to forty-three (43) school days of unused sick leave. In case of a death, payment of unused sick leave shall be made to the teacher's beneficiary as designated on the life insurance policy provided to the Superintendent's office by September 15 of the year of retirement for the pay to be made in the final year.

The payment shall be made in the first pay period of June of the year of retirement. If notification is not given by that date, sick pay shall be made payable in the first pay period in the fiscal year following retirement.

When a teacher is absent from school as a result of a personal injury caused by an accident arising out of or during the course of his/her employment, the Board shall pay his/her full salary, less workers' compensation payments, while recuperating, without deducting from the teacher's accumulated sick leave to a maximum of one hundred eighty-three (183) days or to the date of maximum recovery, whichever is sooner.

23. Assault.
   a. When a teacher is assaulted as a result of his/her employment, the Board will pay his/her full salary, less workers' compensation payments, while recuperating, without deducting from the teacher's accumulated sick leave.
   b. The Board of Education shall have the right to have the teacher examined by its physician to determine, together with the teacher's physician, when the teacher should return to work.
   c. The Board of Education shall be responsible for teacher losses as a result of an assault as follows:

(*1*) Clothing or other personal property damaged, stolen, or destroyed in the course of an assault

(*2*) The cost of medical, surgical, or hospital services beyond those covered by workers' compensation and/or any insurance provided by the Board

24. Sick Leave Bank.
    a. Membership in the sick leave bank is voluntary on the part of employees.
    b. The Board of Education will cooperate in the establishment of a sick leave bank on a voluntary basis.
    c. Each new employee enrolling in the bank will donate one (1) day of his/her sick leave to the bank. Days will be added when the bank is depleted to three hundred (300) days. Each member will then donate one day of sick leave.
    d. A person withdrawing from membership in the bank will not be able to withdraw the contributed days.
    e. Persons withdrawing sick leave days from the bank will not have to replace these days, except as a regular contributing member to the bank.
    f. The sick leave pool shall be administered by a five (5)-member board, two (2) members chosen by the Board of Education and two members chosen by the Federation, and these four members shall choose a physician as the fifth member. Each request for aid, as certified by a doctor's certificate, for the sick leave pool shall be decided by the board on the merits of the individual request. Action of the board shall be by the majority vote.
    g. Not more that Thirty-One Thousand Dollars ($31,000.00) shall be expended from this fund during any one (1) year. No more than Eleven Thousand Dollars ($11,000.00) shall be expended upon any one (1) employee during any one (1) year.
    h. Those employees not contributing to the sick leave bank shall not participate in it.

25. Sabbatical Leave.
    a. Purpose: Sabbatical leave of not less than one (1) semester and not more than one (1) year in duration may be granted to a teacher by the Board of Education upon recommendation of the Superintendent, the building principal, and the department chairperson, if applicable, to:
       (*1*) Improve the educational program of the school system
       (*2*) Stimulate professional growth of personnel
    b. Eligibility: Seven (7) years of consecutive teaching service in the district prior to the start of the sabbatical year. In computing years of service in the district, approved leaves of absence for illness shall not be counted as years of teaching service, but shall not be considered as breaching the requirement of "consecutive" years of service. Other approved leaves of absence which do not involve full-time employ-

ment outside the school system, shall not be counted as years of teaching service, but shall not be considered as breaching the requirement of "consecutive" years of service, except that no more than nine (9) calendar years can include both such leaves and actual teaching services in the district.

c. Criteria for Selection:
   (*1*) Value of leave to school system
   (*2*) Quality of service
   (*3*) Type of planned college credits, type of planned research project, or type of activity planned
   (*4*) Number of years' service
   (*5*) Allocation of leaves among divisions of the school system

d. Quota: A maximum of two percent (2%) of the professional staff may be on sabbatical leave at one time; not more than five percent (5%) of any division: elementary, middle school, senior high school, or special services.

e. Compensation: Compensation during the leave shall be seventy-five percent (75%) of the teacher's salary for the sabbatical leave and shall not include supplementary pay. In the event of employment during the sabbatical leave by a commercial agency, an adjustment shall be made so that the total amount of remuneration received during the sabbatical leave shall not exceed the salary that the teacher would have received had he/she been employed by the district during the school year; however, the amount of any noncommercial educational grant shall not be taken into consideration. Regular increments shall be granted for the sabbatical year.

f. Application: Sabbatical leave application shall be submitted between February 1–15 of the school year preceding the leave. The application shall be accompanied by sufficient information to establish the nature and value of the leave. Application is to be made on the form available in the office of the Superintendent. The Board shall take action on all applications at the first April meeting. Later applications shall be considered through May 31 if, in the Board's discretion, additional grants of sabbaticals are consistent with this contract and would not, because of the lateness in filing, have a negative impact on the educational program for the following year.

g. Obligations: A teacher granted sabbatical leave is obligated to return to the school system for three (3) years of service. If the teacher does not return, he/she shall, within two (2) years from the commencement of the school year immediately following the sabbatical leave, repay to the Board the amount received during the sabbatical leave. If a teacher leaves the school system without remaining for the full three (3) years of service, he/she shall, within two (2) years after leaving the school system, repay to the Board the amount of money having the same ratio to the amount granted as the unexpired period of service ratio is to three (3) years. This condition may be waived by the Board.

h. Guarantees: A teacher returning from leave is guaranteed:
   (1) Reappointment to the former or a mutually acceptable position
   (2) The regular salary increment for the leave
   (3) Recognition of course credits earned
   A teacher while on leave is guaranteed:
   (1) Continued coverage by any group health or insurance program
   (2) Retention of sick leave accumulated prior to the commencement of the sabbatical leave

i. Reports: A teacher on sabbatical leave shall submit to the Superintendent of Schools for transmittal to the Board of Education an interim and a final report with the following information, where applicable: courses taken, credits earned, travel itinerary, project completed, leave benefits, and other pertinent aids for evaluating the leave program.

26. Retirement Incentive. (This provision shall expire one day prior to the expiration of this contract.)
   a. Eligibility: Teachers shall be eligible for a retirement incentive under the following terms and conditions:
      (1) The teacher must be at least fifty-five (55) years old on June 30 of his/her last working year prior to retirement.
      (2) A teacher with twenty (20) to twenty-nine (29) years of credited service in the Connecticut Teacher Retirement System, ten (10) of which are in this district, who meets the fifty-five (55)-year-old age requirement, shall be entitled to a $5,000 payment upon retirement by one of the methods described below.
      (3) A teacher with thirty (30) to thirty-four (34) years of credited service in the Connecticut Teacher Retirement System, ten (10) of which are in this district, who meets the fifty-five (55)-year-old age requirement, shall be entitled to a $4,000 payment upon retirement by one of the methods described below.
      (4) A teacher with thirty-five (35) to thirty-nine (39) years of credited service in the Connecticut Teacher Retirement System, ten (10) of which are in this district, who meets the fifty-five (55)-year-old age requirement, shall be entitled to a $3,000 payment upon retirement by one of the methods below.
      (5) A teacher with at least forty (40) years of credited service in the Connecticut Teacher Retirement System, ten (10) of which are in this district, who meets the fifty-five (55)-year-old age requirement, shall be entitled to a $2,000 payment upon retirement by one of the methods described below.

b. Notification: Notification of intention must be given to the business office before December 1 of the last year of service. Final confirmation must be given to the business office before January 1 of the last year of service.

c. Method of Payment: Those who meet the above requirements are eligible for payment in one (1) of the following ways:

(*1*) Lump sum payable the first pay period of the next school year after retirement

(*2*) Two (2) equal payments the first pay period in the first and second school years following retirement

(*3*) Four (4) equal payments payable the first pay period in the first through fourth school years following retirement

(*4*) Six (6) equal payments payable the first pay period in the first through sixth school years following retirement. Selection of the method of payment must be made by January 1 of the last year of service.

d. Insurance:

(*1*) Any teacher with twenty-five (25) years of teaching experience, the last ten (10) of which must be in the school system, and who is eligible to collect Connecticut Teacher Retirement Benefits, will be given the option of continuing group insurance coverage after retirement to age sixty-five (65), providing the insurance carrier allows. The net cost of extended coverage is to be divided equally between the retiring teacher and the Board of Education.

(*2*) At age sixty-five (65), or subsequent to retirement from the Public Schools, a retiree may, at his/her option and provided this is allowable by the insurance carrier, purchase the health insurance package or a portion thereof on a yearly basis for life.

e. Waiver: All applicants for the retirement incentive must sign a waiver before being eligible for payment under the Plan. A form waiver is attached at the end of the Agreement.

VII
WORKING CONDITIONS

27. Teacher's Responsibilities—General. Teachers have an obligation to satisfy teaching responsibilities that maintain the quality of the educational process.

28. Preparation and Planning Periods.

a. Five (5) preparation periods per week are regarded as desirable for teachers.

b. Teachers shall be assigned classes requiring as few different preparations as reasonable.

29. <u>Staff Assignments</u>. Board Policy 4114 regarding equitable assignments among the staff shall only be changed with the agreement of the Federation.

30. <u>Department Chairperson Responsibilities</u>. Each department chairperson shall submit to his/her principal, prior to May 1, a report on recommendations for improvement and implementation of curriculum. A copy shall be forwarded to the Superintendent.

31. <u>Curriculum Revision</u>. Teachers shall play an active role in the preparation and evaluation of curricula, are urged and expected to make recommendations concerning revisions of any existing curriculum, and shall be an integral part of any committee established for curriculum study.

32. <u>Teaching Materials Requests</u>. Upon request, a teacher shall be informed at which level a budget item has been cut.

33. <u>Meetings and Extra Work Scheduled by Administration</u>.
    a. The principal may schedule each teacher to function for two (2) after-school hours per week from September through May in extra help to students and/or curriculum planning, departmental meetings, teachers' meetings, and exchange of ideas. Two (2) one-session days for curriculum review and planning may be scheduled.
    b. Faculty or department meetings may be called no more than once a month in each category. Exceptions may be made by the administration for situations necessitating immediate action or when a group recognizes the need for more than one (1) meeting in a given month. Teachers are expected to attend parent-teacher conferences and pupil evaluation conferences. Attendance at parent-teacher association/organization meetings is considered to be a professional obligation for all teachers for the back-to-school night and any night the teacher is part of the program. In the event of a time conflict between a parent-teacher association/organization meeting and a college or university course, the teacher shall be excused by the immediate supervisor at his/her discretion from the parent-teacher association/organization meeting.

34. <u>Special Faculty Meetings</u>. The Federation may schedule meetings during times after school hours when no other meetings conflict.

35. <u>Interviews.</u> Whenever practical, the department chairperson in secondary schools and elementary teachers may participate in interviews of candidates for teaching positions in their respective schools.

36. <u>Paraprofessionals</u>. Duties such as playground, cafeteria, bus supervision, and clerical tasks shall be performed by paraprofessionals whenever practicable. The Board shall furnish two (2) paraprofessionals at each elementary school for one-half (1/2) hour per day for outside morning duty. All

teachers shall have an uninterrupted, duty-free lunch period of at least thirty (30) minutes.

37. Class Size. Desirable enrollment for classrooms in the school district is as follows:

Grade Level	Number of Pupils
K–1	23
2–3	24
4–6	25
7–8	26

a. Exceptions to the above desirable maximums shall be acceptable in music 7–8, physical education, chorus, band, study halls, and library classes.

b. Student enrollment should not exceed by more than five (5) the maximum established.

c. Enrollment for grade levels shall be arrived at by using the average number of students in a particular grade level in each individual school.

d. During the course of a school year, if class size enrollment exceeds the maximum established, the Board should endeavor to correct the situation by the employment of one (1) of the following, whichever is most practicable:

   (*1*) Hiring a new teacher

   (*2*) Hiring a paraprofessional

   (*3*) Reassignment of students

   (*4*) Transfer of students

   The use of classroom paraprofessionals should be a measure only for the remainder of any one (1) school year. The following school year, a balance should be reached by the opening of a new class at the appropriate grade level or by one of the alternatives stated above.

e. The Board shall furnish monthly enrollment figures to the president of the Federation.

f. The number of students should not exceed the number of student stations in special areas such as in fine arts and industrial arts.

38. Classroom Collections. Teachers shall be responsible for such collections as assigned by the principal but shall not be responsible for the purpose of collections for school pictures, lunch, dental, or pupil insurance programs.

39. New Board Policies. The Federation shall be notified by the superintendent prior to major policy changes contemplated by the Board and shall, upon request, have the opportunity to present its views to the

Superintendent and to the Board at least ten (10) calendar days prior to final adoption or rejection of the aforementioned policy change.

40. Principal's Absence. Only a certified teacher who agrees shall be appointed to act in the place of the principal in an elementary school during a known prolonged absence of the principal. Only a certified teacher who agrees shall be appointed to act in the place of the administrators in a secondary school during known prolonged absences of all administrators.

41. Assignment and Transfer. Involuntary transfers and assignments shall be made by the Superintendent of Schools in the best interest of students. When two (2) or more employees are being considered for transfer, the junior person shall be transferred unless, in the judgment of the Superintendent of Schools, such a transfer would be detrimental to the best interests of students.

    Staff vacancies shall be posted in each school. Although transfers and assignments remain the responsibility of the Superintendent of Schools, the Superintendent will consider the following when two (2) or more qualified and certified staff members request the same assignment:
    a. Seniority—length of service in the district; if two (2) or more teachers requesting transfer to the same position have identical service, continuous service in the district shall be used; if two or more teachers are still tied in seniority, total length of teaching service will be considered.
    b. Qualifications

42. Personnel Files. No material derogatory to a teacher's conduct, service, character, or personality shall be placed in a teacher's personnel file unless it has first been shown to and discussed with the teacher by the immediate supervisor. The teacher shall initial and date the actual copy to be filed. The initials shall signify merely that the teacher has examined the material.

    The teacher may submit a written notation regarding any material placed in his/her personnel file, and the same shall be attached to the file copy of the material in question. If the teacher believes that material to be placed in his/her file is inappropriate or in error, he/she may request adjustments provided cause is shown through the grievance procedure, whereupon the material will be corrected or expunged from the file.

    There shall be only one official personnel file per teacher to be kept in the central office. Information not contained in the above official file shall not be used in any way against the teacher at any hearing, disciplinary action, or meeting concerning the teacher.

43. Grievance Procedure. To secure, at the lowest possible level of employer-employee relationships, solutions to problems that may arise concerning the interpretations of any provisions of this Agreement and all

disputes between either a teacher and the Board or between the Federation and the Board concerning the interpretation of any provisions of this Agreement shall be dealt with as follows:

a. Definitions:

    (*1*) A grievance shall mean a complaint by a party in interest that his/her rights under the specific language of this Agreement have been violated or that as to him/her there has been a misapplication or misinterpretation of the specific provisions of this Agreement.

    (2) A "party in interest" is a teacher or the Federation.

b. Grievance Procedure:

Step 1: A party in interest having a grievance shall first notify his/her principal within thirty (30) calendar days of when he/she knew or should have known of the incident. If a solution is not reached within five (5) calendar days after its submission, then the teacher shall discuss the grievance with the officers of the Federation before initiating the grievance procedure and proceeding to Step 2.

Step 2: A party in interest with a grievance shall, within five (5) calendar days of the denial of the grievance by the principal, make a written statement and then discuss it with his/her principal and the Federation's representative. If the grievance is not resolved within five (5) calendar days, a written statement shall be given within five (5) calendar days by the principal for use in Step 3.

Step 3: The grievance shall be discussed by the Superintendent and the party in interest. If the grievance is not resolved within five (5) calendar days after submission, a written statement shall be given within five (5) calendar days for use in Step 4.

Step 4: The grievance shall be discussed by the Board and the parties in interest within thirty (30) calendar days. The Board shall make a written statement of the action taken within thirty (30) calendar days of its submission.

Step 5: If the grievance is not solved under the above grievance procedure, the party in interest may, within five (5) school days after the written statement by the Board of Education, submit the matter to the American Arbitration Association for binding arbitration. Any charges by the arbitration board shall be shared one-half (1/2) by the Federation and/or the teacher and one-half (1/2) by the Board.

    The arbitrator shall hear and decide only one (1) grievance in each case. Such arbitration shall be binding upon both parties.

c. General Provisions:

(*1*) Parties in interest may participate in grievance procedures without jeopardizing their standing in the school community.

(*2*) Parties in interest may be represented by counsel, the Federation, or any representative of their choosing beginning at Step 2.

(*3*) All documents, communications, and records germane to the processing of a grievance shall be filed separately from the permanent file of any party in interest.

(*4*) The sole and exclusive remedy for a teacher who wishes to challenge a termination pursuant to the Reduction in Force policy shall be Connecticut General Statute Section 10-151.

VIII
OTHER PROVISIONS

44. Termination Notice. Whenever practicable, a teacher shall give sixty (60) days' notice of resignation. A sample is provided at the end of the Agreement.

45. Calendar. The school calendar shall be set by the Board after consulting with the Federation. It shall define the number of teacher working days.

46. Severability. In the event that any provision or portion of this Agreement is ruled invalid for any reason, the balance and remainder of this Agreement shall remain in full force and effect.

47. Part-time Teachers. Teachers who work fewer than one hundred eighty-three (183) days will be paid on a per-diem basis using 1/183 of base salary for each day worked. Teachers who work part of each day shall be paid a salary proportional to the number of hours worked of seven hours. Additionally, the following special provisions apply to part-time teachers.

   a. Article 9, Salary Payments Schedule, shall apply to part-time teachers.

   b. Teachers employed half-time or more shall receive the same insurance benefits as full-time teachers. Teachers employed less than half-time shall receive no insurance benefits.

   c. Benefits under Article 18, Absence with Pay, shall be proportional to the percentage of employment rounded to the nearest tenth (1/10).

   d. Sick leave lengths shall be proportional to the percentage of employment rounded to the nearest tenth (1/10).

   e. Graduate study reimbursement shall be the same as for full-time teachers.

   f. Under Article 25, Sabbatical Leave, salary payment while on leave shall be proportional to the percentage of employment rounded to the nearest tenth (1/10).

g. Under Article 28, <u>Preparation and Planning Periods,</u> these periods shall be proportional to the percentage of employment rounded to the nearest tenth (1/10).

48. <u>Instructional Day</u>. Any increase in the instructional day for students shall not require any corresponding increase in current requirements for the teachers' usual obligation of seven (7) hours at school exclusive of special requirements set forth in Article 33 of this Agreement.

49. <u>Professional Issues Committee</u>. The professional issues committee will be composed of four (4) members appointed by the Superintendent and four (4) members appointed by the President of the Union. Regulations and guidelines for its operation must be approved by the Superintendent and the Board.

The Committee shall develop regulations and guidelines for its operation to be approved by the Superintendent and the Board.

The Committee may opt to select personnel to work on particular projects at full pay as recommended by the Superintendent of Schools and approved by the Board. It is assumed that such special projects and opportunities should be announced to all interested staff. The number of persons involved in such assignments at any given time will not be deducted from the number of persons eligible to apply for consideration for sabbatical. The Committee might choose to invite a particular staff member to pursue special study or research, which would make him/her of special value to the school district.

The Professional Issues Committee shall have at its disposal reasonable resources as approved by the Superintendent of Schools within budgetary limitations.

<u>Types of Assignments</u>. Applications will usually encompass a wide variety of purposes, including experimental projects involving development of teaching methods and materials, curriculum improvements, teacher-student relationships, subject matter research in one's field or specialization, and other professional activities.

BOARD OF EDUCATION

<u>APPLICATION FOR THE EARLY RETIREMENT INCENTIVE PLAN</u>

Name _____ School _____

Age as of June 30, 19____ : _____

Length of Service as a teacher in

the district as of June 30, 19____ : _____ years

W̲A̲I̲V̲E̲R̲

By my application to participate in the Early Retirement Incentive Plan, I agree to waive my right to file any claim against the school district ("Board") and/or the Federation of Classroom Teachers ("Federation") that in the establishment or implementation of this Plan either party (or both parties) has discriminated against me on the basis of my age in violation of state or federal law, including the Age Discrimination in Employment Act, or has violated any of my other rights, including those arising under state or federal constitutional provisions, statutes, regulations or case law. Furthermore, I waive my right upon application to file any grievances relating to the matter of this Plan under the existing collective bargaining agreement.

I understand that I have had a period of at least forty-five (45) days to consider the Board's offer of early retirement benefits under this Plan as set forth in the collective bargaining agreement between the Board and the Federation. I further understand that this Waiver is revocable for a period of seven (7) days following the date upon which I sign it, but that this waiver shall thereafter be irrevocable. Finally, I have been advised to consult an attorney prior to signing this application.

Signature _____   Date _____

R̲E̲S̲I̲G̲N̲A̲T̲I̲O̲N̲

I hereby submit my resignation as a teacher in the school district effective August 31, 19____ , contingent upon the approval of my application of this Plan by the Board.

Signature _____   Date _____

THE TERMS OF THE EARLY RETIREMENT INCENTIVE PLAN ARE FOUND IN THE TEACHERS' CONTRACT AND SHOULD BE READ CAREFULLY BEFORE SIGNING. THIS FORM SHOULD BE PREPARED IN TRIPLICATE WITH ONE COPY TO THE TEACHER, THE SECOND COPY TO THE BOARD AND THE THIRD COPY TO THE FEDERATION.

SIGNATURE PAGE

FOR THE WAYWARD BOARD OF EDUCATION

By: _____   Date: _____

By: _____   Date: _____

By: _____   Date: _____

FOR THE WAYWARD FEDERATION OF CLASSROOM TEACHERS

By: _____   Date: _____

By: _____   Date: _____

By: _____   Date: _____

WASA (WAYWARD ADMINISTRATORS' AND SUPERVISORS' ASSOCIATION)

I
PREAMBLE

1. This Agreement shall be effective from September 1, (year) through August 31, (year).
2. Successor Agreement. Negotiations for the successor agreement shall begin in conformity with the timetables provided in §10-153d of the Connecticut General Statutes.

II
NEGOTIATIONS

1. Proposals Not Covered by This Agreement. Proposals not covered by this Agreement may be submitted to the Superintendent in writing, and the Superintendent shall forward such proposals with his/her recommendations to the Board within fifteen (15) days. The Board shall meet with rep-

resentatives of WASA to discuss such proposals. Any agreement reached by the Board and WASA shall be reduced to writing and shall be signed by the Board and WASA and shall be appended to the existing Agreement.

2. Recognition. The Board recognizes WASA as the exclusive representative of all certified professional employees who are employed in positions requiring an intermediate administrator or supervisor certificate and whose administrative or supervisor duties shall equal at least fifty percent of the assigned time of such employee and who are not otherwise excluded from the purview of Sections 10-153a to 10-153n, inclusive.

3. Scope of Agreement. This Agreement contains the full and complete agreement between the Board and WASA on all negotiable issues, and neither party shall be required during the term thereof to "negotiate" (within the meaning of Connecticut General Statutes §§10-153d and 10-153n) upon any issue, except as required by law.

4. Severability. This Agreement is deemed to be in compliance with all state and federal laws (including the Constitution of the United States and the constitution of the State of Connecticut), and the Board and WASA shall comply with all applicable state and federal laws. If a provision or provisions of this Agreement are unlawful, then that provision or those provisions shall be automatically stricken from this Agreement, and the balance of this Agreement shall continue in full force and effect.

5. Gender Blind. Whenever in this Agreement "he" or "him" is used, it shall refer as well to "she" and "her" as if fully provided herein.

III
RECOGNITION OF RESPONSIBILITIES OF THE BOARD

Board Rights, Responsibilities, and Prerogatives. Subject to the provisions of this Agreement, the Board and the Superintendent of Schools reserve and retain full rights, authority, and discretion, in the proper discharge of their duties and responsibilities, to control, supervise, and manage the Department of Education and its professional staff under governing laws, ordinances, rules, and regulations—municipal, state, and federal.

IV
SALARIES

1. Administrators' Salary Schedule. Administrators shall be placed on a step equivalent to years of experience as a public school administrator in the position or a substantially equivalent position for which the administrator is hired. Full credit for previous experience in the position or substantially equivalent position for which the administrator was hired will be granted,

provided that such experience for any one (1) year shall have been continuous service of at least one-half (1/2) of that school year and provided further that the Board shall have the right to place a new administrator [one who has been employed less than sixty (60) days] at a higher step on the appropriate salary schedule. Thereafter, each administrator shall be advanced one (1) step on the appropriate salary schedule at the beginning of each successive work year.

2. Salary.

First Contract Year

	Step 0	Step 1	Step 2	Step 3	Step 4
Assistant Principal MS/ Dean of Students HS— Masters	63,185	64,538	65,891	67,244	68,599
(10 Months; 192 days)— M+30/6th	65,742	67,095	68,452	69,804	71,157
Asst. Dir. Spec. Serv.—Masters	64,835	66,189	67,541	68,894	70,249
(11 Months; 212 days)— M+30/6th	67,392	68,745	70,103	71,454	72,808
High School Assistant— Masters	63,858	65,142	66,495	67,845	69,203
(10 Months; 192 days*)— M+30/6th	66,342	67,698	69,048	70,409	71,758
Elementary Principal— Masters	66,944	68,299	69,652	71,005	72,360
(10 Months; 192 days)— M+30/6th	69,499	70,857	72,208	73,565	74,915
Supervisor Special Services—Masters	74,897	75,699	76,409	77,166	77,923
(11 Months; 212 days)— M+30/6th	77,742	78,499	79,257	80,014	80,768
Middle School Principal— Masters	75,911	77,264	78,614	79,975	81,325
(11 Months; 212 days)— M+30/6th	78,471	79,823	81,178	82,530	83,882
High School Principal— Masters	78,919	80,275	81,628	82,981	84,335
(11 Months; 212 days)— M+30/6th	81,477	82,833	84,186	85,538	86,894

Second Contract Year

	Step 0	Step 1	Step 2	Step 3	Step 4
Assistant Principal MS/ Dean of Students HS—					
Masters	64,449	65,829	67,209	68,588	69,971
(10 Months; 192 days)—					
M+30/6th	67,057	68,436	69,821	71,200	72,580
Asst. Dir. Spec.					
Serv.—Masters	66,132	67,513	68,892	70,272	71,654
(11 Months; 212 days)—					
M+30/6th	68,740	70,120	71,505	72,883	74,264
High School Assistant—					
Masters	65,135	66,445	67,825	69,202	70,587
(10 Months; 192 days*)—					
M+30/6th	67,669	69,052	70,429	71,817	73,193
Elementary Principal—					
Masters	68,282	69,665	71,045	72,425	73,807
(10 Months; 192 days)—					
M+30/6th	70,889	72,275	73,652	75,037	76,413
Supervisor Special					
Services—Masters	76,394	77,213	77,937	78,709	79,481
(11 Months; 212 days)—					
M+30/6th	79,297	80,069	80,842	81,614	82,383
Middle School Principal—					
Masters	77,430	78,809	80,187	81,575	82,951
(11 Months; 212 days)—					
M+30/6th	80,040	81,420	82,801	84,181	85,559
High School Principal—					
Masters	80,498	81,881	83,260	84,641	86,021
(11 Months; 212 days)—					
M+30/6th	83,106	84,490	85,869	87,249	88,632

Third Contract Year

	Step 0	Step 1	Step 2	Step 3	Step 4
Assistant Principal MS/ Dean of Students HS—					
Masters	65,738	67,146	68,553	69,960	71,370
(10 Months; 192 days)—					
M+30/6th	68,398	69,805	71,218	72,624	74,032

Asst. Dir. Spec. Serv.— Masters	67,455	68,863	70,270	71,677	73,088
(11 Months; 212 days)— M+30/6th	70,115	71,522	72,935	74,341	75,749
High School Assistant— Masters	66,438	67,774	69,181	70,586	71,999
(10 Months; 192 days*)— M+30/6th	69,022	70,433	71,837	73,253	74,657
Elementary Principal— Masters	69,648	71,058	72,466	73,874	75,283
(10 Months; 192 days)— M+30/6th	72,306	73,720	75,125	76,538	77,941
Supervisor Special Services—Masters	77,922	78,758	79,496	80,284	81,071
(11 Months; 212 days)— M+30/6th	80,883	81,671	82,459	83,246	84,031
Middle School Principal— Masters	78,978	80,385	81,790	83,206	84,610
(11 Months; 212 days)— M+30/6th	81,641	83,048	84,457	85,864	87,271
High School Principal— Masters	82,108	83,518	84,925	86,334	87,742
(11 Months; 212 days)— M+30/6th	84,768	86,180	87,587	88,994	90,404

Additional salary provisions—all contract years: Administrators having a doctorate shall receive $4,000 more than the comparable step of the Masters+30/Sixth Year column. *At the senior high school, there will be twenty (20) additional days of work, payable at a per-diem rate, available to be divided between the Assistant Principal and Dean of Students at the discretion of the Superintendent.

3. Salary Payment Schedule. Each professional covered by this Agreement shall be paid his or her annual salary in twenty-six (26) installments.

4. Adjustments in Pay. Absences other than those covered by this Agreement shall require a deduction in pay of 1/200 of the administrator's annual salary per school day for those with ten (10)-month contracts, and 1/220 for those with eleven (11)-month contracts.

5. Salary Deducations. Administrator-authorized payroll deductions shall be made for the following:
   a. Washington National Insurance
   b. Tax-sheltered annuities
   c. Wayward Teachers' Federal Credit Union
   d. C.M.S.

e. Blue Cross and dental plan
f. Increased retirement
g. United Fund
h. WASA dues
i. EMSPAC dues
j. NAESP dues
k. NASSP dues

Changes in payroll deductions for the above shall not be made for units of less than Five Dollars ($5.00), except C.M.S. and Blue Cross. Administrator-authorized payroll deductions shall be made for professional dues in not more than eight (8) consecutive monthly installments per school year and in amounts not less than Six Dollars ($6.00) per installment, except for the final installment.

6. Salary Adjustment. Administrators, upon retirement or death, after ten (10) years of service in the district, the last five (5) of which must be consecutive, shall receive payment as follows:

   a. Administrators shall receive payment for fifty (50) days or fifty percent (50%) of the unused sick leave, whichever is less, in either case based on a per-diem rate of the last annual salary earned.

   b. After ten (10) years in the system and upon retirement in accordance with the State Teacher Retirement Act, administrators shall receive a terminal stipend of $1,500 subject to the following conditions: written application for such stipend must be made to the Superintendent's office ten months prior to retirement for the stipend to be paid. The stipend shall be paid no later than October 15 of the school year after retirement.

7. Supplemental Pay. The following supplementary pay positions shall be paid as listed below:

Position	Pay
Director of Secondary Summer School	$4,049
Director of Elementary Summer School	$3,811
Director of Enrichment Summer School	$4,049

Nonbargaining unit employees may continue to hold any supplemental pay position they are currently holding. Members of WASA who are certified and qualified shall be given first preference for supplemental pay positions in the bargaining unit.

8. Salary/Change in Working Condition. If an administrator is designated by the Superintendent to work in an administrative position in a higher salary group than his or her regular group and said administrator works in the designated administrative position for more than thirty (30) consecutive work days, then he/she shall receive the pay of the higher salary

group in which he/she is working commencing after the thirtieth (30th) consecutive work day.

V
FRINGE BENEFITS

1. Insurance. The Board will provide for each administrator the following insurance or its equivalent:
   a. At least One Million Dollars ($1,000,000) family major medical
   b. Employee life insurance in the amount of double the employee's annual salary
   c. Eighty-five percent (85%) of the cost of participation in individual or family semiprivate Blue Cross, including individual or family copay prescription drug rider and semiprivate maternity care rider
   d. Eighty-five percent (85%) of the cost of individual or family or C.M.S. Century 96 Contract; the home and office rider shall be a maximum of $300 per individual and $1,200 per family.
   e. Eighty-five percent (85%) of the cost of individual or family full-service dental plan (equivalent to Blue Cross full-service dental plan) as selected by the Board
   f. Eighty-five percent (85%) of the cost of dental riders for additional basic benefits, periodontics, and orthodontics equivalent to Blue Cross A, C, and D riders.
   g. Any administrator who terminates service at the end of a complete school year may, if the administrator elects, continue to receive the benefits in this paragraph for the remainder of that agreement year.
   h. No later than the effective date of this Agreement, the Board shall implement and maintain a Section 125 Salary Reduction Agreement, which will be designed to permit exclusion from taxable income the employee's share of health insurance premiums. The Board makes no representations or guarantees as to the initial or continued viability of such a salary reduction agreement and shall incur no obligation to engage in any form of impact bargaining in the event that a change in law reduces or eliminates the tax-exempt status of employee insurance premium contributions. So long as the Board makes a good faith effort to comply with this paragraph, neither the Association or any administrator covered by this Agreement shall make any claim or demand, nor maintain any action against the Board or any of its members or agents for taxes, penalties, interest, or other costs of loss arising from a flaw or defect in the salary reduction agreement or from a change in law that may reduce or eliminate the employee tax benefits to be derived therefrom.

2. Travel Reimbursement.
   a. Administrators shall be reimbursed for travel between respective

schools and the Board office while performing the business of the public schools and for any school activity to which an administrator has been assigned or is in attendance as part of his or her administrative duties. Reimbursement shall be at the mileage rate established by the Board for all employees.

b. The Board encourages administrators to participate in professional development activities. To that end, it will, within budgetary constraints, continue to provide funds for WASA members for local and regional professional development activities, including major national conventions or conferences each contract year.

VI
ADMINISTRATORS' WELFARE PROVISIONS

1. <u>Absence with Pay</u>. Up to six (6) days of personal absence with pay may be granted. No more than six (6) days' absence with pay shall be granted for any one (1) year, except that the Superintendent of Schools may, at his sole discretion, grant compensatory time for additional days of personal absence. The privilege of absence with pay shall not be cumulative from year to year. The Request for Absence with Pay Form shall be used and shall require 24 hours' notice and the prior approval of the Superintendent. This requirement may be waived by the Superintendent at his/her discretion.

2. <u>Graduate Study Reimbursement.</u> When, in the judgment of the Superintendent, the course for which reimbursement is requested will make a meaningful contribution to a more effective performance of the duties to which the administrator is assigned, then such reimbursement shall be granted.

   Courses must be completed with a grade B or higher. If a lesser mark is received and the administrator desires, extenuating circumstances may be explained to the Superintendent for his/her consideration. Courses and institutions must have prior approval of the Superintendent at least fifteen (15) days prior to the start of the course, if possible. Graduate study reimbursement is payable in one lump sum on either the second payday in September or the second payday in March, whichever most closely follows the completion of the course. Administrators must submit an official grade report or an official transcript of the approved course(s) and a copy of the bill for tuition and fees. The amount of the reimbursement shall be equal to the cost of tuition and fees (excluding books) incurred for the course. It is mandatory that an administrator be on the staff at the time of payment in order to receive any of the above reimbursements.

3. <u>Personal Leave.</u> A personal leave of absence may be granted by the Board for illness or other personal reasons. The leave shall extend only for one (1) school year or less. The administrator shall return to the

school district upon expiration of the personal leave. The administrator shall be given his/her previously held administrative position or another administrative position that is mutually agreed upon by the administrator and the Board.

If the administrator and the Board are unable to agree upon another administrative position as aforesaid, then the administrator shall be given his/her previously held administrative position or an administrative position for which he/she is certified and qualified substantially equivalent in status and pay to his/her previously held administrative position. Personal leave of absence shall be taken without pay or credit for salary increments and will terminate at the end of the approved period of time. An administrator on personal leave shall retain the sick leave accumulated prior to the commencement of leave.

4. <u>Sick Leave.</u> Administrators whose work year is 192 days shall be granted annually sixteen (16) days of sick leave with full pay, except while on leave. Administrators whose work year is more than 192 days shall be granted seventeen (17) days of sick leave with full pay, except while on leave. The accumulation of sick leave shall be unlimited. Each administrator shall be notified in September of the amount of his/her accumulated sick leave.

5. <u>Sick Leave Bank.</u>
   a. Membership in the administrators' sick leave bank is voluntary on the part of the administrators after five (5) years of service in the school system. Each participating administrator contributes from one (1) to five (5) days of sick leave per year at his/her discretion.
   b. The Board of Education will cooperate in the establishment of a sick leave bank on a voluntary basis.
   c. Each employee enrolling in the bank will donate from one (1) to five (5) days of his/her sick leave to the bank each year until the bank is built up to one hundred fifty (150) days. No more days will be added until the bank is depleted to ninety (90) days. The bank will then be built up to one hundred fifty (150) days again and the process repeated.
   d. Additions will be made to the bank in October of each school year, according to the above limitations.
   e. A person withdrawing from membership in the bank will not be able to withdraw the contributed days.
   f. Persons withdrawing sick leave days from the bank will not be able to replace these days, except as a regular contributing member to the bank.
   g. The sick leave pool shall be administered by a five (5)-member board, two (2) members chosen by the Board of Education and two (2) members chosen by the Association, and these four (4) members shall choose a physician as the fifth member. Each request for aid, as certified by a doctor's certificate, from the sick leave pool shall be decided

by the board on the merits of the individual request. Action of the board shall be by the majority vote.

h. Not more than Twenty-Five Thousand Five Hundred Dollars ($25,500) shall be expended from this fund during any one (1) school year. No more than Eight Thousand Five Hundred Dollars ($8,500) shall be expended upon any one (1) employee during any one (1) year. (Exceptions to these limitations may be made only upon specific administrative requests and Board of Education approvals.)

i. Those employees not contributing to the sick leave bank may not participate in it.

6. Sabbatical Leave.

 a. Purpose: Sabbatical leave may be granted to a member of the administrative staff by the Board upon recommendation of the Superintendent and building principal, when applicable, to

 (1) Improve the educational program of the school system
 (2) Stimulate professional growth of personnel

 b. Eligibility. Seven (7) years of consecutive administrative service in the district prior to the start of the sabbatical leave. In computing years of consecutive service in the district, unpaid leave of absence shall not be counted.

 c. Criteria: The following criteria will be used for selection:

 (1) Value of leave to the school
 (2) Quality of service
 (3) Number of years' service
 (4) Availability of a certified and qualified person to serve as an interim administrator

 d. Quota: A maximum of one (1) administrator may be on sabbatical leave at one time.

 e. Compensation: Compensation during the leave shall be seventy-five percent (75%) of the administrator's monthly salary during his/her sabbatical leave. In the event of employment during the sabbatical leave by a commercial agency, an adjustment shall be made so that the total amount of remuneration received during the sabbatical leave shall not exceed the salary that the administrator would have received had he/she been employed by the School System during the school year; however, the amount of any noncommercial educational grant shall not be taken into consideration.

 f. Application: Sabbatical leave application shall be submitted prior to February 1 of the school year preceding the leave. The application shall be accompanied by sufficient information to establish the nature and value of the leave. Application is to be made on the form available in the office of the Superintendent.

 g. Obligations: An administrator granted sabbatical leave is obligated to return to the school system for three (3) years of administrative service. If the administrator does not return, he/she shall, within two (2) years from commencement of the school year immediately following the sabbatical leave, repay to the Board the amount received during the sabbatical leave. If an administrator leaves the School System without remaining for three (3) years of administrative service, he/she shall, within two (2) years after leaving the school system, repay to the Board the amount of money having the same ratio to the amount granted as the unexpired period of administrative service ratio is to three (3) years. This does not apply if the administrator becomes incapacitated or the condition is waived by the Board.

When the administrator returns to the school system, he/she shall be reappointed to his/her original position or to a mutually acceptable administrative position of comparable status and pay.

h. Guarantees: An administrator while on leave is guaranteed:
    (*1*) Continued coverage by any group health or insurance program
    (*2*) Retention of sick leave accumulated prior to the commencement of the sabbatical leave
    (*3*) An additional year of seniority

i. Reports: An administrator on sabbatical leave shall submit to the Superintendent for transmittal to the Board an interim and a final report with the following information where applicable: courses taken, credits earned, travel itinerary, projects completed, leave benefits, and other pertinent data for evaluating the leave program.

7. Graduate Study Leave of Absence. A graduate study leave of absence may be granted for one (1) school year or less upon recommendation of the Superintendent and approval of the Board. An interim administrator will be appointed during the absence of the administrator on graduate study leave of absence. An administrator on graduate study leave of absence must notify the Superintendent in writing prior to March 1 if he/she intends to return to the school system the following year. In the event the administrator so indicates his/her intention to return, he/she shall be reappointed to his/her original position or to a mutually acceptable position. Criteria for graduate study leave of absence shall be

a. Value of leave to the school system
b. Quality of service
c. Number of years' service
d. Availability of a certified and qualified person to serve as an interim administrator

Graduate study leave of absence shall be taken without pay or credit for salary increments and will terminate at the end of the approved period of time. An administrator on graduate study leave shall retain the sick leave accumulated prior to the commencement of the leave.

8. Maternity, Military, Peace Corps, and Vista Leaves. Maternity, military, Peace Corps, and Vista leaves may be granted by the Board under terms and conditions approved by the Board.

9. Professional Development. The Board agrees that professional development activities such as conferences, workshops, institutes, etc., are in the best interests of the school system. The Board encourages such activities and shall fund such activities within its budgetary constraints.

10. Evaluations. A copy of any written evaluation shall be placed in the administrator's file and a copy forwarded to said administrator. Materials placed in an administrator's file after appointment shall be reasonably available for inspection by the administrator.

11. Personnel Files. No material derogatory to an administrator's conduct, service, character, or personality shall be placed in an administrator's personnel file unless it has first been shown to and discussed with the administrator by the immediate supervisor. The administrator shall initial and date the actual copy to be filed. The initials shall signify merely that the administrator has examined the material.

    The administrator may submit a written notation regarding any material placed in his/her personnel file, and the same shall be attached to the file copy of the material in question. There shall be only one official personnel file per administrator to be kept in the central office.

VII
WORKING CONDITIONS

1. Administrators' Responsibilities—General. The Board and WASA recognize the importance of responsible participation of the entire administrative staff in the educational process.

2. Supervision. Each administrator shall supervise the performance and professional development of the staff for which he/she is responsible. Such supervision shall be in accordance with the district system of staff evaluation and staff development.

3. After-School Meetings. The administration of each school shall schedule meetings as deemed necessary or as directed by the Superintendent. Meetings during teacher instructional time shall be held only when no other time is practicable.

4. School Administration. The principal shall administer his/her school according to established administrative regulations and shall assign teachers to various duties as necessary for the proper management of the school. The principal shall periodically evaluate the efficiency of each teacher in terms of his/her assigned duty.

5. Scheduling of Teachers. Secondary school administrators shall assign teachers in order that a maximum efficiency of a teacher's time is used for

the teaching of pupils, with a minimum assignment for such things as study halls and planning periods.

6. Curriculum Revision. Curriculum shall be periodically reviewed, and administrators shall pay an active role in the organization, implementation, and evaluation of curriculum.

7. Policies and Directives. Administrators shall carry out all policies of the Board and the directives of the Superintendent of Schools, when not in conflict with this Agreement.

8. Budget Requests. Administrators shall prepare budget requests as outlined by the Superintendent.

9. Substitute Teachers. Administrators shall prepare materials and conduct informational sessions for substitute teachers as directed by the Superintendent.

10. Staff Personal Day. The administrator shall evaluate the reason for a staff member's request for a personal day in determining whether or not to grant the request.

11. Staff Absences. The administrator shall periodically review staff members' absences and arrange conferences with any staff member suspected of abusing the privilege.

12. Assignment and Transfer. Under state statutes (as exercised through its policies), the Board of Education has the sole right to employ, assign, and transfer administrators and empoyees. In carrying out those responsibilities,

   a. The Board may transfer administrators when it determines that such transfers are in the best interests of the school district. Administrators shall not lose salary as a consequence of involuntary transfers; they shall be paid their prior salary until pay for the new position exceeds it, at which time they will be paid the rate for the new position.

   b. For reasons of professional growth, two or more administrators may request transfers agreeable to those involved. If such requests are granted, administrators shall be paid at the rate for the new positions.

   c. Administrative staff vacancies shall be published in each school as soon as possible. Administrators who apply for and are transferred to new assignments shall be paid at the rate set for the new position.

13. Work Year.

   a. The work year of ten (10)-month administrators shall be the regular school year (currently 182 days), plus ten (10) work days, no more than six of which may be assigned within two weeks immediately preceding the opening day of school or within two weeks immediately following the last official day of school. The assigned days must be continuous work days. The Superintendent shall give thirty (30) days' notice to the administrators of the schedule of the before and after school year work days.

b. The work year of eleven (11)-month administrators shall be the same work year as ten (10)-month administrators, plus twenty (20) additional work days during July and/or August or as approved by the Superintendent of Schools.

c. All administrators shall be required to work three (3) days during the Christmas/New Year school break, if directed by the Superintendent.

d. The Superintendent shall notify the administrators one (1) month in advance of the dates during the Christmas/New Year school break on which he/she wishes the administrators to work.

To the extent that the Superintendent has the authority and exercises it to require any administrator to work beyond the work year, the administrator shall be paid as follows:

(*1*) Administrators whose work year is 192 days shall be paid 1/192 of their annual salary for each day worked beyond 192 days.

(*2*) Administrators whose work year is 212 days shall be paid 1/212 of their annual salary for each day worked beyond 212 days.

(*3*) If administrators are required to work for less than four (4) hours in a given day, such work time shall be calculated as one-half day. If they are required to work four (4) or more hours, such time shall be calculated as a full day for purposes of computing payment for work beyond the work year.

VIII
GRIEVANCES

1. Grievance Procedure. To secure, at the lowest possible level of the employer-employee relationship, solutions to problems that may arise concerning the interpretation of any provisions of this Agreement, all disputes between either an administrator and the Board or between WASA and the Board concerning the interpretation of any provision of this Agreement shall be dealt with as follows:

a. Definitions:

(*1*) A grievance shall mean a violation of a specific term or terms of this contract to the detriment of an administrator or group of administrators.

(*2*) "Administrator" shall mean any member of the bargaining unit.

(*3*) A "grievant" shall mean the person or persons making the claim or WASA.

b. Procedure:

Step 1: A grievant shall first notify his/her Superintendent. If a solution is not reached in two (2) school days, then the administrator shall discuss the grievance with the officers of WASA before initiating the grievance procedure. In the case of an assistant principal, he/she will notify his/her principal first.

Step 2: A grievant shall first make a written statement and then shall discuss it with the Superintendent and WASA's representative. WASA's representative shall be a chairperson or representative of WASA. If the grievance is not resolved within two (2) school days, a written statement shall be given within three (3) school days by the Superintendent for use in Step 3.

Step 3: The grievance shall be discussed by the Board, or committee thereof, and the party in interest within fifteen (15) days. The Board, or committee thereof, shall make a written statement of the action taken within three (3) school days.

Step 4: If the grievant and WASA are not satisfied with the disposition of the grievance at Level Three, they may, within ten (10) days after the decision of the Board, or committee thereof, or within ten (10) days after the meeting with the Board, or committee, submit the grievance to arbitration by notifying the Superintendent of their intent to do so. If WASA and the Superintendent cannot mutually agree upon a single arbitrator to hear the grievance within three (3) days of the notice of intent to submit to arbitration, then the grievant and WASA may submit the grievance to arbitration by filing a demand for arbitration under the Voluntary Labor Arbitration Rule of the American Arbitration Association. The American Arbitration Association shall then act as the administrator of the procedures.

The arbitrator selected shall confer promptly with the representatives of the Board and the grievant, shall review the record of prior hearings, and shall hold such further hearings as he shall deem requisite.

The arbitrator shall be bound by the Voluntary Labor Arbitration Rules. He shall hear only one grievance at a time. He shall have no power to add to, delete from, or modify the agreement. The decision of the arbitrator shall be submitted to the Board and to the Association and, subject to law, shall be final and binding.

The costs of the services of the arbitrator shall be borne equally by the Board and the Association.

c. General Provisions:

(*1*) No reprisals of any kind shall be taken by the Board or by any member of the administration against anyone by reason of participation in the grievance procedure or support of any participant thereto.

(*2*) The grievant may be represented by Counsel, WASA, or any representative of his own choosing so long as WASA has the opportunity to be present at any meetings or hearings on the grievance and has the opportunity to present its views.

(*3*) All documents, communications, and records generated by the filing of the grievance shall be filed separately from the permanent file of the grievant.

(*4*) "Days" shall mean business days from June 1st until the start of the next school year.

IX
OTHER PROVISIONS

1. Termination Notice. Whenever practicable, an administrator or supervisor shall give sixty (60) days' notice of intent to terminate. The earliest possible termination notice is desirable.

2. WASA Nonstrike Clause. WASA shall not call, authorize, instigate, sanction, or condone any strike, slowdown, work stoppage, refusal to render services, or any action against the Board, which would impede the proper functioning of the school system at any time.

3. Administrator Nonstrike Clause. No administrator shall, in an effort to effect a settlement of any disagreement with the Board, engage in any strike or refusal to render services.

4. Administrative Council. The Superintendent is responsible for the organization, scheduling, and conducting of the administrative council. Administrators may submit suggestions for the agenda for administrative council meetings to the Superintendent. Such suggestions may be made up to the day of the meeting and their inclusion on the agenda will not be unreasonably withheld.

5. Reduction in Staff.

    a. It is recognized that, under §§10-220 and 10-4a of the Connecticut General Statutes, the Board of Education has the responsibility to maintain good public elementary and secondary schools and to implement the educational interest of the state. However, recognizing also that it may become necessary to eliminate certified staff positions in certain circumstances, this procedure is adopted to provide a fair and orderly process should such eliminations become necessary.

    b. In order to promote an orderly reduction in the administrative personnel, the following procedure will be used:

        (*1*) Any administrator relieved of his duties because of reduction of staff or elimination of position shall be offered an administrative position if an opening exists in his classification for which he is certified.

        (*2*) If there is no existing administrative opening in his classification, the displaced administrator shall be offered the position of the administrator who has the least seniority in the classification of the displaced administrator.

(*3*) If there is no opening in the classification of the displaced administrator and the displaced administrator has the least seniority in his classification, he will be offered any vacant position in an administrative classification below the classification of the displaced administrator, for which he is certified and qualified.

(*4*) Any administrator whose contract of employment has been terminated due to the elimination of an administrative position shall be placed on a reappointment list for a period of twenty-four (24) months. When the Board determines that an administrative vacancy exists, administrators on the reappointment list shall be offered any such position for which they are certified and in which such administrators have previous Wayward experience, in the inverse order of placement on the reappointment list. Administrators shall remain on the reappointment list for twenty-four (24) months or until offered a certified position in the school system.

(*5*) For purposes of this Article and for all relevant provisions in this Agreement, seniority shall be defined as the length of continuous service as an administrator in the school system, beginning on the first day of actual service and ending on the date for which such determination is made. Continuous service shall be deemed to be unbroken during periods on the recall list and during authorized leave. In the event of a tie, continuous nonadministrative certified employment with the Wayward Board of Education, immediately preceding service as an administrator, shall be considered.

(*6*) The classifications referred to in this Article are as follows, in descending order:

   a. High School Principal

   b. Special Services Supervisor

   c. Middle School Principal

   d. Elementary School Principal

   e. Special Services Assistant Supervisor

   f. Assistant Principal/High School Dean of Students

6. Retirement Incentive.

  a. Eligibility: Administrators shall be eligible for a retirement incentive under the following terms and conditions:

    (*1*) The administrator must be at least fifty-five (55) years old on June 30 of his/her last working year prior to retirement.

    (2) An administrator with at least twenty (20) years of credited service in the Connecticut Teacher Retirement System, ten (10) of which are in the district, who meets the fifty-five (55)-year-old age requirement, shall be entitled to a $5,000 payment upon retirement by one of the methods described below.

    (*3*) An administrator with at least twenty-five (25) years of credited service in the Connecticut Teacher Retirement System, ten (10) of which are in the district, who meets the fifty-five (55)-year-old age requirement, shall be entitled to a $4,000 payment upon retirement by one of the methods described below.

(4) An administrator with at least thirty (30) years of credited service in the Connecticut Teacher Retirement System, ten (10) of which are in the district, who meets the fifty-five (55)-year-old age requirement, shall be entitled to a $3,000 payment upon retirement by one of the methods described below.

(5) An administrator with at least thirty-five (35) years of credited service in the Connecticut Teacher Retirement System, ten (10) of which are in the district, who meets the fifty-five (55)-year-old age requirement, shall be entitled to a $2,000 payment upon retirement by one of the methods described below.

b. Notification: Notification of intention must be given to the business office before December 1 of the last year of service. Final confirmation must be given to the business office before January 1 of the last year of service.

c. Method of Payment: Those who meet the above requirements are eligible for payment in one (1) of the following ways:

(1) Lump sum payable the first pay period of the next school year after retirement

(2) Two (2) equal payments the first pay period in the first and second school years following retirement

(3) Four (4) equal payments payable the first pay period in the first through fourth school years following retirement

(4) Six (6) equal payments payable the first pay period in the first through sixth school years following retirement

Selection of the method of payment must be made by January 1 of the last year of service.

(1) Any administrator with twenty-five (25) years of teaching/administrative experience, the last ten (10) of which must be in the school system, and who is eligible to collect Connecticut Teacher Retirement Benefits, will be given the option of continuing group insurance coverage after retirement to age sixty-five (65), providing the insurance carrier allows. The net cost of extended coverage is to be divided equally between the retiring administrator and the Board of Education.

(2) At age sixty-five (65), or subsequent to retirement from the public schools, a retiree may, at his/her option and provided this is allowable by the insurance carrier, purchase the health insurance package or a portion thereof on a yearly basis for life.

d. <u>Waiver:</u> All applicants for the retirement incentive must sign a waiver before being eligible for payment under the Plan. A form waiver is attached to this contract.

X
AGENCY FEE

1. <u>Conditions of Continued Employment.</u> All members of the bargaining unit employed by the Board shall, as a condition of continued employment, join WASA or pay WASA a service fee. Said service fee shall be equal to the proportion of WASA dues uniformly required of members to underwrite the costs of collective bargaining, contract administration, and grievance adjustment.

2. <u>Members.</u> All members of the bargaining unit who elect to join WASA shall sign and deliver to WASA, if they have not already done so, an authorization for the payroll deduction of membership dues. Employee authorization for dues deduction will be in writing.

   Said authorization shall continue in effect from year to year unless such administrator shall notify the Board and WASA in writing not later than thirty (30) days prior to the commencement of the school year. If said notice is timely delivered, it shall mean that, in the coming school year, said administrator shall pay the service fee as described in Paragraph 1 above, and paid in accordance with Paragraph 3 below.

3. <u>Nonmembers.</u> For those members of the bargaining unit who have not joined WASA and delivered said authorization card by October 1st of the first year of this Contract, the Board agrees to deduct the annual service fee from their salaries through payroll deduction. The amount of said service fee, equal in amount to underwrite the costs of collective bargaining, contract administration, and grievance adjustment, shall be certified by WASA to the Board.

4. <u>Subsequent Employment.</u> Those members of the bargaining unit commencing employment after the date of execution of this Contract shall, within thirty (30) days of such commencement, sign and deliver to the Board an authorization card as described in Paragraph 2 of this Article or fall under the provisions of Paragraph 3 of this Article after thirty (30) such days.

5. <u>Forwarding of Monies.</u> The Board agrees to forward to WASA each month all monies deducted during that month for local dues and local service fee deductions.

6. No later than the first paycheck in October of each school year, the Board shall provide WASA with a list of all bargaining unit members employed by

the Board and the administrative positions held by said employees. The Board shall notify WASA of any changes in said list.

7. The right to refund the employees' monies deducted from their salaries under such authorization shall lie solely with WASA. WASA agrees to reimburse any employee for the amount of any dues deducted by the Board and paid to WASA, which deduction is by error in excess of the proper deduction, and agrees to hold the Board harmless from any claims of excessive deduction.

8. WASA agrees to indemnify and save the Board harmless from all claims, demands, lawsuits, or other forms of liability arising from the Board's fulfillment of its obligations under this Article. The Board agrees that WASA shall assume the exclusive legal defense of any such claim or lawsuit. In assuming such defense on the Board's behalf, WASA will hire and compensate legal counsel. Legal counsel hired by WASA shall confer with the Board or its representatives concerning the defense of claims and lawsuits against the Board. WASA shall have the right to compromise or settle any claim or lawsuit against the Board under this Article but shall not do so without Board approval, such approval not to be unreasonably withheld.

BOARD OF EDUCATION

APPLICATION FOR THE EARLY RETIREMENT INCENTIVE PLAN

Name _____ School _____

Age as of June 30, (year)____: _____

Length of Service as an administrator in

the district as of June 30, (year)____: _____

Length of Service as a teacher in

the district as of June 30, (year)____: _____

W A I V E R

By my application to participate in the Early Retirement Incentive Plan, I agree to waive my right to file any claim against the school district ("Board") and/or the Administrators' and Supervisors' Association ("Association") that in the establishment or implementation of this Plan either party (or both parties) has discriminated against me on the basis of my age in violation of state or federal law, including the Age Discrimination in Employment Act, or has violated any of my other rights, including those arising under state or federal constitutional provisions, statutes, regulations, or case law. Furthermore, I waive my right upon application to file any grievances relating to the matter of this Plan under the existing collective bargaining agreement.

I understand that I have had a period of at least forty-five (45) days to consider the Board's offer of early retirement benefits under this Plan as set forth in the collective bargaining agreement between the Board and the Association. I further understand that this Waiver is revocable for a period of seven (7) days following the date upon which I sign it, but that this waiver shall thereafter be irrevocable. Finally, I have been advised to consult an attorney prior to signing this application.

Signature _____ Date _____

R E S I G N A T I O N

I hereby submit my resignation as an administrator in the school district

effective _____, contingent upon the approval of my

application of this Plan by the Board.

Signature _____ Date _____

THE TERMS OF THE EARLY RETIREMENT INCENTIVE PLAN ARE FOUND IN THE ADMINISTRATORS' CONTRACT AND SHOULD BE READ CAREFULLY BEFORE SIGNING. THIS FORM SHOULD BE PREPARED IN TRIPLICATE WITH ONE COPY TO THE ADMINISTRATOR, THE SECOND COPY TO THE BOARD AND THE THIRD COPY TO THE ASSOCIATION.

SIGNATURE BLOCK

_____

Chairman
Wayward Board of Education

_____

President
Wayward Administrators' and
Supervisors' Association

_____

Date

_____

Date

Administrative Correspondence

PRINCIPAL'S MEMOS—STAFF

Regional School District #24
Lemon Hill Consolidated School
Route 156
Lemon Hill, Connecticut 06731
Telephone 444-4233

September 14

To: Lemon Hill Teachers

From: DLC

Subj: Principalgram (Important Miscellany—as distinguished from the
unimportant miscellany in some previous notes)

Fire Drill. Heads up for an otherwise unannounced fire drill in the near
future.

Staff Observations and Evaluations. Although I won't be doing formal observations and evaluations (as your interim principal), I do need to meet with
each K–5 classroom teacher and special teachers to establish their goals for
the year. Each of you please see me to schedule a meeting—conferences are
possible during a special class, planning periods, or other times during the
regular school day when you are free or at 3:00 P.M. or thereabouts. As those
of you who have been in the system already know, it's possible for experienced
teachers to be placed into the alternative evaluation cycle; if you're interested
in this possiblity, we will talk about it at the goal-setting conference.

Fire Prevention Program. I spoke with Lee Warren this morning about
the annual fire prevention visit, and we agreed on Thursday, October 7th, as
the day with K–1 from 8:30–9:30, grades 2–3 from 9:30–10:30, and grades

417

4–5 from 10:30–11:30. (*Note for Tim and Darren—Lois and Connie have agreed to switch PE periods to make this schedule work.*)

Principal's Classroom Visits. I will be stopping in with my class lists to get to know children by name. I'm also available to read to your group or perform other educational chores of a semidignified nature. (*FYI, I will be out of the school district all day next Thursday, September 23rd.*) Yesterday, I read to both kindergarten classes having selected the philosophical treatise *The Boogey Man* for that purpose. Remembering my almost normal school training about introducing stories, I asked the children if anyone could tell me what a "boogey man" was. One enthusiastic boy in the P.M. session said, "It's the man who picks the stuff out of your nose." The kid was obviously confusing "boogey man" with "booger man," but even with the current bad economy and employment picture, it's probably almost impossible to find anyone for that kind of work today anyway. Remaining reasonably calm, I just said his theory, although a creative effort, wasn't quite correct and moved on to other eager respondents.

October Lemon Hill School Newsletter. As I mentioned briefly at our September faculty meeting, we are planning an October edition of the newsletter, and we need your contributions. Feel free to leave them with either Dot or me. Thanks to Lois Drucker's fourth grade for their outstanding creative compositions for the *Main Street News'* forthcoming Lemon Hill special.

Superintendent's Reception. Last night's welcome for George Partridge at the high school was well arranged and well attended. I had the chance to speak with quite a few board of education members, and a couple of them expressed interest in visiting Lemon Hill School. I encouraged them to do that, and maybe they will soon.

Revised Special Class Schedule and Crisis Team Information. (Attachments) To be continued . . .

Regional School District #24
Lemon Hill Consolidated School
Route 156
Lemon Hill, Connecticut 06731
Telephone 444-4233

September 28

To: Lemon Hill Teachers

From: DLC

Subj: Principalgram (This neverending flow of P-grams may remind you of the children's story about the mill that couldn't stop grinding salt at the bottom of the sea—but things keep happening about which we need some communications, and teachers have too many meetings as it is.)

Open House, Tuesday, October 5th, 7:00 P.M. As I said in my note to parents, which is being sent home today, we will follow past procedures and assemble at 7:00 P.M. in the library for parents to meet PTO chairpersons, the Lemon Hill staff, and Superintendent George Partridge who will be with us for a time. Individual classroom visits are scheduled as follows:

7:15 Morning Kdgn., Grade 1, and Grade 2 classroom presentations
7:30 Afternoon Kdgn., Grades 3, 4, and 5 classroom presentations

My parental epistle said you would be in your classrooms, offices, or teaching spaces from 7:15–8:00, and I said the usual about open house not being intended for individual parent/teacher meetings and that conferences should be scheduled for another time. If we need to talk about anything special before the open house, someone please tell me; otherwise, I'll figure your vast experience with these evenings has prepared you completely for this one.

Fairly Important Stuff. In the past few playground duties, I've noticed a few strains among kids, which, unfortunately, often appear when human nature (maybe we'll never change that completely) catches up with the euphoria usually characteristic of the first few weeks of school; nothing dramatic, but little outbreaks of gratuitous shin kicking during a soccer game (allegedly provoked by some irritating comments by the kickee). There have been other minor problems with kids doing kid things with pencils, grabbing or pushing each other, tearing clothing, lunchboxes somehow orbiting the building and ending up on the roof, and other behaviors we've all seen before but that cause greater problems if not curbed. It would be a good idea (in addition to keeping a sharp eye out for it in classrooms, on the playground, and in the lunchroom) to speak with kids about this kind of behavior and integrate your discussion and the school's theme for the year of "respect"—respecting each other, regardless of gender, age, size, or whatever other differences children may have.

Another less significant part of respect, but still worthy of mention, has to do with students taking better care of Lemon Hill School's buildings and grounds. Lately, I have seen too many discarded bits of flotsam and jetsam (not the old vaudeville act, but food wrappers and such), which came from our kids—as well as some that may have been left after school hours by nonstudents. Although it's not a major problem, I'll talk to Bob and Walt about vigilance in cleaning up the grounds regularly, and you can help by reviewing this issue with your class. To be continued . . .

Regional School District #24
Lemon Hill Consolidated School
Route 156
Lemon Hill, Connecticut 06731
Telephone 444-4233

September 28

To: Lemon Hill Teachers

From: DLC

Subj: Principalgram

<u>Golden Coaches and Pumpkins</u>. In my last note, I complained that my golden coach seemed to have turned into a pumpkin because of the little disciplinary issues that seemed to be showing up here and there. Maybe if I do this principal thing again sometime, somewhere, I'll specify that my availability ends after the fourth week of school — sort of "when the going gets tough (or at least less than perfect), the no longer tough enough run for their lives." Regardless of those plaints, in the wider world of education, any principal of this school should count his/her blessings — which include, among others, the friendly school atmosphere and generally outstanding student behavior, the abundance of parental support, and especially the stellar quality of the Lemon Hill staff. (Maybe I should have saved this for a Thanksgiving note.)

<u>Open House Tuesday, October 5th, 7:00 P.M.</u> The closer it gets, the more convinced I become that we're really going to do it. To be continued . . .

Regional School District #24
Lemon Hill Consolidated School
Route 156
Lemon Hill, Connecticut 06731
Telephone 444-4233

October 18

To: Lemon Hill Teachers

From: DLC

Subj: Principalgram

<u>Photocopcopier.</u> As you know from my Friday note, the copier was in critical

condition, but emergency surgery seems to have saved it; temporary internal repairs have partially restored it to close to normal living, but it requires a major transplant (a drum), and it's on the waiting list for one. Drums are normally expensive organs to replace (approximately five hudred dollars), but the district has a service contract that will take care of it this time.

The best available medical diagnosis is that the machine ingested one or more staples, which overwhelmed its gastric system. If we repeat such an inappropriate diet, it's likely that the company will refuse to cover costs of a second drum transplant. Also, unless we keep the repairman handcuffed to the machine, the downtime will also be extensive. *Please, make sure that all staples, or paper clips, or any such indigestibles are kept far away from the creature's maw.*

November Newsletter: OK, we did a good job with October, but what have you done for me lately? Let's point toward the first week in November (ending November 5th) for contributions for our Thanksgiving edition. Dot should have the October version for student take home either today or tomorrow. To be continued . . .

Regional School District #24
Lemon Hill Consolidated School
Route 156
Lemon Hill, Connecticut 06731
Telephone 444-4233

October 18

To: Lemon Hill Teachers

From: DLC

Subj: Principalgram

Hurtman Park. A couple of weeks ago, I prepared a brochure for park manager Bob Kayak about Lemon Hill's Hurtman Park (located on Grungy Road off Bevis). I worked from Bob's handwritten notes about the park. On page 2, under "The Park," I typed the following from my understanding of Bob's notes (quotes and italic type added):

> Trail maps, available from the park manager and on a display board at the park entrance, show the 8.6 miles of trails in the park, as well as connecting trails in the adjacent Cohanzie State Forest. The area has a diverse wildlife habitat consisting of open fields, wetlands, streams, bogs, ridge tops, and more. The gen-

eral public, students, individuals, and community groups are encouraged to use the park for jogging, hiking, cross country skiing, *"birching,"* nature studies, picnicking, photography, and similar activities.

Not being a rough tough outdoor type, I wasn't familiar with *"birching"* but figured innocently enough that it was some kind of Eastern Connecticut version of Finnish folk flagellation using birch twigs—sort of a woodsy health frolic but sans sauna. You'll see in the final product, after Bob's editing, that what I read as *"birching"* was really *"birding"*. That I understand—even if I don't spend any more time birding than I do birching. In spite of my minor embarrassment, the editorial change was a break, because I hadn't been able to find an acceptable "click art graphic" for "birching."

Regional School District #24
Lemon Hill Consolidated School
Route 156
Lemon Hill, Connecticut 06731
Telephone 444-4233

December 20

To: Lemon Hill Teachers

From: DLC

Subj: Principalgram

My initial retirement was planned a year in advance, and each recurring or seasonal activity became special because it was the last time I'd be part of it—twelve months of that wrings you out emotionally. Here, on the other hand, the first time for most events was also the last and only time for me, so almost everything was noteworthy. All this is my devious way of sneaking up on the reality that this is the last in the series of PG's (picture an arthritic cat stalking a bird)—eleven and a half in all, if you count #5.5—plus multitudes of mixed memoranda.

I've really appreciated this serendipitous rebirth and service at Lemon Hill School until Maigret O'Doul was chosen, finished up her other obligations, and reported for duty. You're an outstanding staff, with just the right number and degree of personal and professional idiosyncrasies—they keep you from being too perfect for an experienced sinner to bear. My relative closeness to kids and faculty at Lemon Hill School (contrasted with twenty-five years as a superintendent without this kind of proximity) has been the best part of this tour and made it one of the most enjoyable periods of my three and a half decades in education. Daily student and faculty interactions have made almost every day a singular joy. (*If this note appears smudged, I'll deny it's tear stained until hell freezes over—for the same reason I couldn't eat quiche in the faculty room. In case you don't already recognize this ageless leadership verity, personal insecurities are the bases for most of our administrative short-comings.*)

All of us know what that good ol' boy T. Clayton Wolfe meant when he wrote *You Can't Go Home Again,* but, that understanding notwithstanding, I will visit with you on occasion. Although eased because I know how good Maigret will be with and for you all, I'll still miss being part of your daily lives. Have a relaxing and enjoyable Christmas holiday and a great new year. To be continued . . . (by Ms. O'Doul)

SUPERINTENDENT'S CORRESPONDENCE—BOARD OF EDUCATION AGENDA NOTES

Bath Public Schools
45 Westminster Road
Bath, Connecticut 06331-0028
Telephone (203) 546-7950
Fax (203) 547-9887

General. We agreed to keep the agenda for this meeting as brief as reasonably possible to allow some time for dealing with preparations for interviews of the superintendent of school's candidates.

Superintendent's Reports.

A. Staff: Although we almost landed a good candidate recently, we're still stuggling to locate a middle school speech "clinician, therapist, correctionist, pathologist"; that good applicant got away from us and swam out of sight upstream of Bath and to the west. We've advertised on at least three occasions, and I've talked to colleagues and the state education department and received, along with heartfelt sympathy, the knowledge that these people are difficult to find today. We're working on an arrangement to share Blaise Mondale, along with a new teaching assistant who will work under Blaise's direction to provide assistance to the least needy children in both schools while Blaise addresses the more involved students; this is an acceptable arrangement, under the circumstances, to the state education department. We'll keep on looking, however, for a speech person.

We were very fortunate to find Joan Montovani, a school psychologist, who was in Putnam. She gave that district the month of September and reported to us at the beginning of October. We're very glad to have Joan with us. We still are looking for one more intern, but otherwise the staff is complete.

B. Goals 2000 Consortium Grant Application: The feds have made some funding available to Connecticut under the Goals 2000 Act, and along with NFA and feeder towns, we're applying for a $25,000 competitive grant to provide staff development symposia at NFA both during the year and during the summer months. There's no financial commitment for us, and if we're lucky, the grant will come through.

C. Superintendent Applicants: I've enclosed a confidential report to you identifying the best candidates in my judgment from the fifty who completed all application requirements – the other twenty have been filed away as also-rans. We'll review this list in executive session if you choose. Also, I'll have suggested questions for candidates, which we can review and divvy up amongst you.

I've asked the Bath Education Association for the name of a teacher to serve with you on the Superintendent Search Committee. (Enclosed for the Board are the names of two citizens/parents who have so far volunteered to serve also.)

Mandi will have copied applications from the asterisked candidates by the time this board meeting takes place, and they will be available in my office on October 12th; when you select the candidates you want to interview, we'll duplicate each of their applications for the search committee members.

D. Gifted and Talented Identification Procedures: It's taken too long, but enclosed are proposed Canterbury procedures – along with correspondence to SDE Consultant Alan Black.

Old Business.

A. Discussion of Board of Education Evaluation and possible scheduling of work sessions on this topic. Vic Veilleux asked that this item be placed on the agenda.

B. and C. Self-explanatory with enclosures.

David Cattanach

September 14

Bath Public Schools
45 Westminster Road
Bath, Connecticut 06331-0028
Telephone (203) 546-7950
Fax (203) 547-9887

General. The agenda is long, and I'm hoping to keep the meeting time reasonable through covering as much of the necessary information as I can to the board of education in these notes and their associated enclosures.

Superintendent's Reports.

A. Strategic School Profile Reports (enclosures Board of Education): School principals will summarize profile information from each school, and I'll do the same for the district; however, since you will have the actual documents well in advance, most of the meeting time on this topic should be used for responding to board members' questions.

B. Revised Language Arts Curriculum (enclosure Board of Education): There appears to be some ambiguity about procedures for board of education approval of districtwide curriculum changes. Good practice says the board should approve them, and the section 6000 policy on curriculum development and approval will reflect this approach when it is presented for your review and consideration.

This language arts curriculum is on the agenda as an informational item to let you know of the new curriculum's development. Also, the math curriculum revision is, or will be soon, ready for presentation to the board of education. In the very near future, we will combine both of these on the agenda for the second board meeting of a given month.

C. 1994/95 Personnel Update: We are still searching for our second speech clinician, but, in the interim, until one of these elusive people can be found, we are examining case loads and making arrangements to provide necessary services from our existing speech clinician with assistance from other special education personnel under her direct supervision; it's not the best of all possible worlds, but it is acceptable to the SDE while we proceed with a further search, and we have no other good alternative at present. We will continue to advertise the position directly to graduate schools, as well as in area newspapers and national publications aimed at this specialty.

D. Budget Projection, Budget Freezes, and Associated Procedures (enclosures): I've developed a procedure with the business manager to monitor budget expenditures, including monthly projections of budget status.

The first of those projections is included, showing an expected deficit of $15,211—attributable overall to unanticipated special education placements ($136,529 in total) that have occurred with some regularity since the budget was approved. Fortunately, most of this overexpenditure is balanced by some good fortune in regular tuition accounts (almost $95,000 in regular tuition savings for students who were shifted to high school special education tuitions), along with a few other positive budget changes. Unfortunately, I don't believe this projected fifteen thousand dollar problem will self-correct through good fortune later in the year, and we certainly can't count on such good luck to prevent a budget overexpenditure.

At our administrative meeting on November 3rd, we will freeze $15,211 in various accounts to protect against overexpending the budget—we hope we'll be able to thaw these freezes at a later time and expend funds as originally budgeted.

As an added safeguard to ensure frozen funds aren't touched, I've asked Joanne to set up a special account, the "Freeze Account," into which we'll transfer frozen funds through a regular budget transfer form; principals, other site directors, and the entire staff will then see an adjusted budget amount within which they must operate at any given time.

I considered moving the entire $104,000 in the ill-fated vocational grant funds to the Freeze Account. Second thoughts suggested it might be better to leave it as a second frozen account right where it is to avoid any public misunderstandings about our motives in moving the funds anywhere. The subject is sensitive enough without aggravating any of its exposed nerve endings through well-intentioned but misunderstood action. The next chapter of the Vocational Grant story is covered under "L" below.

E. 1995/96 Budget: The business manager, principals, other site directors, and I have begun preliminary budget development for next year. We hope to improve the organization and quantity of supportive data for budget requests and leave the new superintendent a workable organization with which to complete his proposed educational budget for the 95/96 school year.

F. Identification Procedures for Gifted and Talented Students (enclosures): Although the enclosures should speak for themselves, we now have in place a workable identification plan, which is currently being implemented as approved by the Commissioner of Education. While we don't have an existing Gifted and Talented program following student identification, it's my expectation that appropriate program adjustments can and will be made within regular classroom programs with specific programming adjustments for each of these students identified as is true for other exceptional children.

G. Professional Development and Evaluation Plan: Professional development committees in each school are working on a new professional development plan, which must be oriented toward student achievement of districtwide student goals and objectives and which includes a staff evaluation component (focused also on student achievement of districtwide student goals and objectives) as an integral part of the staff development plan instead of as a separate set of procedures. More on this later from the staff as the process proceeds.

H. Maintenance Issues: building repairs, custodial assignments, repair schedules, and procedures; Dr. Helena Balkoni Middle School water problem and air quality testing; Bath Elementary School radon testing.

Building repairs, custodial assignments, repair schedules, and procedures—In recent discussions with the property services director, I indicated that it wasn't likely that Bath could provide an additional maintenance position for the foreseeable future. I asked him to group the list of needed repairs developed by the building principals according to type of repair (electrical, plumbing, roofing, carpentry, other), and when that was done, we reviewed the list and who should do what.

The property services director, building principals, and I met on October 19th and discussed shifting custodial supervision to principals so Mike Richards could devote more time to needed building repairs, and we made the custodial shift effective the next day. In the foreseeable future, Mr. Richards will spend a week in each school, alternately, from 7:30 until noon each day on necessary building repairs, meeting on Monday morning with building principals to review the week's priorities. It's understood this change is provisional and will be reviewed by the new superintendent who will decide if it continues.

With some repairs, we will obtain competitive quotes from electrical, plumbing, and carpentry contractors, and depending upon prices and budget status, we will consider assigning some jobs to contractors. The remainder of them will be addressed personally by Mike Richards—and some less technical tasks by custodians to the extent principals decide the custodians' cleaning responsibilities permit.

DHBMS water problem and air quality testing. The bad news is that on Monday morning, we discovered that someone had turned on an outside water valve, and left it on, draining the water tanks filled by the well serving the upper grade section of the building. For a good portion of Monday, we operated without water in that part of the building until we could cross-connect the well serving the 4th and 5th part of the building to the other end. Normally, this is a simple process, but problems developed in the cross-connecting, necessitating check valve and other connecting water line repairs, which Mike corrected on Monday and Tuesday. Also, once the two large 20,000- and 15,000-gallon water storage tanks in that part of the school are emptied, it takes a day or two to bring them back to full, and, according to Mr. Richards, that process must be monitored closely to prevent overtaxing the associated water pumps.

Also, because of repeated concerns over a number of years from middle school staff on perceived problems with air quality at the school, we obtained a couple of price and scope of work quotes for air testing in that building; Mystic Air Company gave us the lower price. I've done business with Charles Eiderdown in the past and was glad to have his company conduct the testing. The tests have been performed, and we are awaiting results of spore cultures, which are important in the overall Mystic report to identify any problems we have and in their recommendations for correcting them.

Bath Elementary School radon testing: The good news is that on Monday morning, we received a letter from the state health department telling us that BES had passed its radon alpha track procedures with readings of 1.2 pCi/L in the two test locations—well under the U.S. Environmental Protection Agency's guidelines of 4.0 picoCuries per liter.

I. BES Nature Trail (enclosure), Playscape: The BES Parent/Teacher Organization has been working on a nature trail and plans to continue these efforts as described in the enclosure. The PTO also is investigating a possible playscape installation, and I've explained to the BES principal that such installation requires board approval, as will any fund-raising efforts for the playscape (under the policy in the 3000 series to be approved on November 8th).

J. Welcome for DHBMS Principal and Arts Fair—December 19 (enclosure): In case you missed the notice in *Bath Blurbs,* I've reprinted it for you as a reminder to save the evening.

K. American Red Cross Use of Facilities (enclosure): Although this appears routine, before I approve it, I wanted to review it with you; I will approve it unless there are some issues about which I'm not familiar.

L. Vocational Equipment Grant Information (enclosures): The letter from Leslie M. Avila, Acting Associate Commissioner, Division of Educational Programs and Services, notifies us of this year's Vocational Equipment Grant. I've given the application forms to Mary Dunsinane to work with Mike Fortier and John Raven to complete. We'll get it done and submitted well before the deadline and send you copies of the grant application letter of transmittal.

Old Business.

A. Change of Date for Board Self-Evaluation Session: Because of a superintendent finalist interview that conflicts with the originally scheduled November 15th date, the session must be rescheduled to another date.

B. Second Reading and Adoption of Series 3000 Policies (enclosures): I hope we can get these in place; to save Mandi's time, some of them reflect board suggestions in longhand if the proposed changes were simple enough; others that required more extensive revision have been redone.

New Business.

A. Search Consultant Report on Schedules for Superintendent Finalists' Interviews on November 14, 15, 16 (enclosures): The short form is that we will have each finalist meet with teachers in each school during the noon hour and an after-school hour for any staff members not able to meet over lunch, a meeting from 2 P.M. to 3 P.M. for members of the public, a working dinner in the BES cafeteria with the board of education and search committee members, and a two- or three-hour interview following dinner. (*After thinking further about the candidate's public sessions I'd mentioned to you, it seemed unlikely we'd get people to come out three consecutive evenings to meet the candidates individually, so it seemed more sensible to combine all three into one event. All three final candidates will be together in the BES cafeteria from 6–7 P.M. on Tuesday, November 15th for a public reception and informal discussion with the prospective Bath superintendents. I've been in these group situations as a candidate more than once, and these public events will be weathered by experienced finalists with no observable psychological damage.*)

B. Review and Action on Teacher Contract: Your negotiators will review the changes in contract language agreed upon by both parties in negotiations for the final two years of the contract.

C. Approval of Fund-Raisers (enclosure): Consistent with the proposed policy on fund-raisers, I asked Mary Dunsinane to prepare a list of them for your review and, we hope, your approval. BES isn't into fund-raisers, unless it's something the PTO does, as discussed earlier in these notes.

D. November WESTCONN Hearing on Local Quality and Diversity Plans for Connecticut Region #14: Your representatives to the state's Region #14 quality and diversity planning process will report on the scheduled WESTCONN hearing and any local hearing that may be scheduled prior to the November 30th deadline.

E. Appointment of Board Member to Serve on Teachers' Tax-Sheltered Annuity Committee: Assuming for the moment board approval of proposed contract changes, one change requires this appointment. Doug, Rich, and

Carole can explain any details of this appointment, which need further clarification.

David Cattanach

November 2

SUPERINTENDENT'S MEMOS AND LETTERS—STAFF

Thank-You Notes

Wayward Public Schools

David L. Cattanach, Superintendent of Schools

David G. Tiddle,
   Assistant Superintendent of Schools

Rosa P. Parks,
   Administrative Assistant to the Superintendent

Edward M. Clerk, Business Manager

J. William Cunyard,
   Director of Buildings and Grounds

25 Rope Ferry Road
Wayward, CT 06385-1907
Telephone (203) 444-7890
Fax (203) 444-5555

November 19

Dear Wayward Staff,

For my son-in-law, Robert Dewey, and the entire family, our deep thanks for your many recent acts of caring and generosity. Your warmth and support, at the wake and the funeral; in telephone calls, cards, letters, and visits; in the plants and flowers; in the fruit baskets, baked goods, and other food sent to us; and in thoughts and prayers, all sustained us more than we can say. Beyond your inestimable worth as teachers, administrators, and other school staff members, American Education Week reinforced my long-standing conviction that school people are among the world's most decent human beings.

At the risk of practicing philosophy without a license, I want to share some personal thoughts with you. (Yes, a Ph.D. is a rudimentary philosophical credential, but possibly closer to Pogo than Plato.) Even with the pain it causes, death adds value and meaning to life in ways nothing else can approximate. If I could, I would be tempted to change that, and that's probably why I'm only a school superintendent. But I can't, and we have no legitimate options beyond acceptance, endurance, and gratitude for whatever time has been granted to our loved ones or to us.

A statement that the minister read at the funeral says as well as I can say what I think and feel about my daughter, her death, and her life, but those words only touch the depths of feeling and love her husband and the family have for her. Writing that tribute was like painting a sunrise in black and white. The morning sun can be outlined and shaded with those restrictions, but the sketch can't convey the brilliance, the vividness, the intensity, the warmth, and the beauty of the living sunrise — or of my daughter.

The joy Mary Jeanne's life brought to me and to so many others makes it possible, without personal pain, to wish each of you a warm and happy Thanksgiving and the same joy in your family and friends with which I have been so blessed.

My sincere appreciation for your friendship throughout my time in Wayward.

Sincerely,

David L. Cattanach

P.S. Please forgive the generic response. Without it, I couldn't say what I wanted to say to all of you before June, and we have important things to do together.

Wayward Public Schools

David L. Cattanach, Superintendent of Schools
David G. Tiddle,
   Assistant Superintendent of Schools
Rosa P. Parks,
   Administrative Assistant to the Superintendent
Edward M. Clerk, Business Manager
J. William Cunyard,
   Director of Buildings and Grounds

25 Rope Ferry Road
Wayward, CT 06385-1907
Telephone (203) 444-7890
Fax (203) 444-5555

November 19

To: Wayward Staff

Date: June 25

It doesn't seem as if I've been here for such a short time; your acceptance and support have made me feel at home. I am impressed with Wayward students, teachers, principals, and support staff. Our schools are good schools; each is different, but all are alike in their dedication to students. Our biggest challenge is convincing everyone we are as good as we really are.

One of my responsibilities in telling Wayward's educational story is to articulate beliefs I know you all have. A major theme that emerges from what you have told me is a strong desire to have the Wayward Public Schools become and/or be recognized as an outstanding school system. As one small step on that journey, I ask you to join me in a public "Commitment to Educational and Personal Excellence" in the Wayward Public Schools. Although we need actions more than maxims, that phrase can help focus attention on our commitment.

Historically, too many school districts have been hesitant to honor scholastic achievement. Sure, life has blessed some people (and students are people too) with more intellectual ability than others. That is just as true with talent in athletics or the arts, and yet schools and society handle those inequities easily. We should not apologize for recognizing and rewarding academic talent but, instead, should accept educational attainment as the primary goal of each school and of each classroom. If we will not honor intellectual accomplishment and ability, then who will? Certainly, we have an equal responsibility to all students, including those less equipped to excel scholastically; that's why we stress commitment to personal excellence, as well as academic excellence. Personal excellence is using to the fullest the abilities we are given. Personal excellence in any endeavor is worthy of respect, and it can be realized through athletics or in many other nonacademic pursuits. Personal excellence is civilized and considerate behavior, and every student (and each of us) is capable of personal excellence.

If we also demand educational excellence of our young people, and of ourselves, we will not be treating anyone unfairly; instead, we will be restoring scholastic achievement to the prominent place it deserves in public education. It's important to identify ways our schools can embody the ideas expressed in "Commitment to Educational and Personal Excellence" and put those words into everyday practice.

Have an outstanding holiday season and new year.

Wayward Public Schools

David L. Cattanach, Superintendent of Schools   25 Rope Ferry Road

David G. Tiddle,
  Assistant Superintendent of Schools
Rosa P. Parks,
  Administrative Assistant to the Superintendent
Edward M. Clerk, Business Manager
J. William Cunyard,
  Director of Buildings and Grounds

Wayward, CT 06385-1907
Telephone (203) 444-7890
Fax (203) 444-5555

To: Wayward High School Staff

From: David L. Cattanach

Date: October 31

I appreciate being paid for working in Wayward, but a superintendent can get a paycheck anywhere; the reason this job is so special is that the people are. The cake and the card made not only a sunny Friday sunnier, but the entire year brighter. It doesn't seem as if it's been three years, but that's to be expected if you're having fun.

Thanks for your thoughtfulness.

Wayward Public Schools

David L. Cattanach, Superintendent of Schools
David G. Tiddle,
  Assistant Superintendent of Schools
Rosa P. Parks,
  Administrative Assistant to the Superintendent
Edward M. Clerk, Business Manager
J. William Cunyard,
  Director of Buildings and Grounds

25 Rope Ferry Road
Wayward, CT 06385-1907
Telephone (203) 444-7890
Fax (203) 444-5555

To: Wayward Staff

From: David L. Cattanach

Date: June 19

Thanks for making my first year in the district so rewarding and for the cooperation, generosity, and patience afforded me as I became part of the district and of the town. My decisions may be debatable, but my good fortune is not. To serve as superintendent with such a fine staff and in a town with our resources is proof of the admonition, "If you can't be perfect, be lucky." Most of us can use the luck, and I appreciate mine.

All of us in the schools are important whether support personnel, teachers, principals, other administrators, or the superintendent of schools, but sometimes an individual is assigned too much responsibility for organizational successes or disappointments. I don't underestimate what I give to public education, but the life and vitality of any district is in its classrooms with teachers and pupils. As the superintendency contributes to the work of those directly involved with young people, the position is important—otherwise it is not. I want to support your efforts with my own.

In Wayward, I've found atomic gold and a staff that can combine talents and energies with those of students, parents, board of education, and the community to build the best school district in Connecticut. I look forward to working with you to do that and have every confidence that together we can make it happen. We have made a good beginning.

Have a good summer. I know it will pass quickly, but by September, most of us will be recharged and ready to go again. Again, thanks for my most memorable professional experience among a sizable collection of experiences.

P.S. I have followed up on your concerns and comments from this summer/fall; we have addressed some issues successfully, some partially, but others remain unresolved. I'll continue to pursue the unanswered questions, plus any new or different areas of staff interest. Enclosed is a page for you to tell me what is on your mind as we end this school year and look forward to next year.

Wayward Public Schools

David L. Cattanach, Superintendent of Schools	25 Rope Ferry Road
David G. Tiddle,	Wayward, CT 06385-1907
Assistant Superintendent of Schools	Telephone (203) 444-7890
Rosa P. Parks,	Fax (203) 444-5555
Administrative Assistant to the Superintendent	
Edward M. Clerk, Business Manager	
J. William Cunyard,	
Director of Buildings and Grounds	

To: Wayward Teachers

From: David L. Cattanach

Date: May 6

May 5–11 has been designated National Teacher Appreciation Week, and Wednesday, May 8th, is Teacher Day U.S.A. Teachers are the nuclei of educational atoms; those of us whose professional orbits revolve around teacher centrality especially appreciate your daily contributions to young people and eventually to our town, state, and nation. (I know that's a sleazy metaphor, but this is nuclear country.)

My sincere thanks for all that you do each day of the year.

Wayward Public Schools

David L. Cattanach, Superintendent of Schools
David G. Tiddle,
   Assistant Superintendent of Schools
Rosa P. Parks,
   Administrative Assistant to the Superintendent
Edward M. Clerk, Business Manager
J. William Cunyard,
   Director of Buildings and Grounds

25 Rope Ferry Road
Wayward, CT 06385-1907
Telephone (203) 444-7890
Fax (203) 444-5555

To: Wayward Teachers and Principals

From: David L. Cattanach

Date: November 18

Last week after a late meeting, I watched an unknown sportscaster (no, he didn't have a paper bag over his head, I just don't know his name) interview Jim Tunney, a senior National Football League official. One question asked of Tunney was why he chose a career as an NFL referee. His answer was that it gave him the opportunity to associate with people who are the very best in the world at what they do.

I thought about that for a while and wondered if I could, during American Education Week, say the same thing about being superintendent in Wayward. Although I like the comparison, it is statistically difficult. On all NFL teams, there are fewer than two thousand athletes. In American public education, there are well over three million teachers, only some of whom are employed locally—in spite of contrary perceptions here and there among our fiscal conservatives. But it's my pleasure to work with educators who are among the best at what they do.

Again, my thanks for doing your jobs so well. (Any analogies next year will involve symphony orchestras or ballet companies so I won't seem preoccupied with a sport invented to keep Pennsylvanians out of coal mines and Texans out of jail.)

Wayward Public Schools

David L. Cattanach, Superintendent of Schools   25 Rope Ferry Road
David G. Tiddle,   Wayward, CT 06385-1907
    Assistant Superintendent of Schools   Telephone (203) 444-7890
Rosa P. Parks,   Fax (203) 444-5555
    Administrative Assistant to the Superintendent
Edward M. Clerk, Business Manager
J. William Cunyard,
    Director of Buildings and Grounds

To: Wayward Teachers and Administrators

From: David L. Cattanach

Date: May 6

One problem with a scheduled departure date some time in the future is that every situation becomes "the last time that. . . ." I suspect I will whale the tar out of that notion before my eventual departure, and this is one of the first such instances.

May 6th through 10th is Teacher Appreciation Week (sponsored by the National Parent-Teacher Assocation), and May 7th is National Teacher Day. The current theme is "Teachers Shape the Future." The professional responsibility inherent in that declaration is one that teachers have always accepted—even though your shaping is affected dramatically by major circumstances you don't control.

In spite of the possible exaggeration of educators' ability to move the world, we do have a major effect on the years ahead—one child at a time. In the midst of our daily efforts, it's easy to focus on the immediate crises we face and not recognize the ultimate worth of what we do. But American public education is vital to the health of this nation, and I'm convinced nobody does it better than Wayward classroom teachers and administrators.

One last time during Teacher Appreciation Week, I convey the thanks and appreciation of the entire community for your competence and commitment on behalf of Wayward students.

Wayward Public Schools

David L. Cattanach, Superintendent of Schools   25 Rope Ferry Road
David G. Tiddle,   Wayward, CT 06385-1907
    Assistant Superintendent of Schools   Telephone (203) 444-7890
Rosa P. Parks,   Fax (203) 444-5555
    Administrative Assistant to the Superintendent
Edward M. Clerk, Business Manager
J. William Cunyard,
    Director of Buildings and Grounds

To: Wayward Teachers and Administrators

From: David L. Cattanach

Date: June 13

As I said in a parallel note to parents, if we added a 13th animal to Huang-Ti's calendar, next year will be the school year of the carpenter ant because of all our building projects. Although important, facilities improvements are minor compared to the contributions of staff. As always, you have done an outstanding job, and the children of the town are the beneficiaries of your dedication and expertise.

I wish each of you a pleasant, restful summer vacation and look forward to beginning a new and even more productive school year in September. To those of you who are forsaking us for the rigors of retirement, my best wishes for many happy years—you've earned them. Come back and see us often.

Wayward Public Schools

David L. Cattanach, Superintendent of Schools   25 Rope Ferry Road
David G. Tiddle,   Wayward, CT 06385-1907
    Assistant Superintendent of Schools   Telephone (203) 444-7890

Rosa P. Parks,   Fax (203) 444-5555
   Administrative Assistant to the Superintendent
Edward M. Clerk, Business Manager
J. William Cunyard,
   Director of Buildings and Grounds

To: Wayward Teachers and Administrators

From: David L. Cattanach

Date: May 6

"Holy Six-Year Plan, Batman! The RTM passed the budget last night with no cuts. With the surplus, we won't lose any educational programs. Does this mean no more biff, bam, sock, and pow? Has peace come at last to Wayward?"

"No, Boy Wonder—not until each child can attend Harvard or the college of his choice, has a good job, or is otherwise profitably engaged. We must always be on guard against the forces of evil threatening education. There is no rest until the Penguin, Joker, and all of their ilk are vanquished. You appear puzzled, Robin."

"What can we tell the staff, Batman? So many of them worked so hard to get our budget passed—and it is National Teacher Appreciation Week."

"Well, Boy Wonder, in your message to the staff, just remember the words of our crime-fighting compatriot, Detective Theo Kojak of Gotham City."

"Golly, Batman, what's that?"

"Just ask them, 'Who loves ya baby?' "

Wayward Public Schools

David L. Cattanach, Superintendent of Schools   25 Rope Ferry Road
David G. Tiddle,   Wayward, CT 06385-1907
   Assistant Superintendent of Schools   Telephone (203) 444-7890
Rosa P. Parks,   Fax (203) 444-5555
   Administrative Assistant to the Superintendent
Edward M. Clerk, Business Manager
J. William Cunyard,
   Director of Buildings and Grounds

To: Wayward Teachers and Administrators

From: David L. Cattanach

Date: November 15

Thanks for a memorable evening on November 1st; it will always remain fresh in my memory. The humor was fantastic, and the many warm words were appreciated. Larry Miller, John Gillespie, and David Title, along with all the other speakers (well, almost all), were tremendous, and both Anne and I enjoyed the evening immensely. The citations and awards are on my new office walls at home; the lamp is in use there; the ship's wheel will become a coffee table; and your individual photographs are on my piano (it's a big piano). Chris Galvin's video is a beautiful memento of my Wayward years, and, heeding the words from Irish (or Scottish) Heartbeat, I won't "stray far from my own ones."

I don't know where to begin or how to thank you for the years we shared. Teachers, principals, and other staff members have been great, and together we have made an outstanding school district even better—one of which we can be proud and one that serves well the young people of our town.

My best wishes remain with each of you and with the students, parents, and citizens of Wayward. You have been a big part of my professional and personal life, and I will miss working with you more than I can say.

New School Year Correspondence

Wayward Public Schools

David L. Cattanach, Superintendent of Schools   25 Rope Ferry Road
David G. Tiddle,   Wayward, CT 06385-1907
    Assistant Superintendent of Schools   Telephone (203) 444-7890
Rosa P. Parks,   Fax (203) 444-5555
    Administrative Assistant to the Superintendent
Edward M. Clerk, Business Manager
J. William Cunyard,
    Director of Buildings and Grounds

To: Wayward Teachers and Administrators

From: David L. Cattanach

Date: August 18

A person really has to admire Pope Gregory XIV's ability to build a calendar. You all remember the story of Gregory having astronomers over for a weekend in 1582; together, they deep-sixed Julius Caesar's clunky calendar (which had winter beginning in September and created a much better arrangement for public schools—and the rest of the world as well). Imagine our misery if winter followed August and school opened in a flail of bitter snow. If summer must end, autumn is my choice to succeed it.

It's time again to acknowledge the inexorable erosion of summer vacation and the inevitable beginning of a new year. Although many of you have already begun it in your thoughts and hours spent in voluntary preparation, we begin the new year officially on Monday, August 31st, with a meeting for teachers and administrators at 8:30 A.M. in the Wayward High School Auditorium. Coffee and conversation will be available from 8:00 to 8:30.

I look forward to a new school year with you and your students.

Wayward Public Schools

David L. Cattanach, Superintendent of Schools
David G. Tiddle,
  Assistant Superintendent of Schools
Rosa P. Parks,
  Administrative Assistant to the Superintendent
Edward M. Clerk, Business Manager
J. William Cunyard,
  Director of Buildings and Grounds

25 Rope Ferry Road
Wayward, CT 06385-1907
Telephone (203) 444-7890
Fax (203) 444-5555

To: Wayward Teachers and Administrators

From: David L. Cattanach

Date: August 15

Unfortunately, this isn't an additional paycheck because there was an error in your records. It's a sincere, although financially worthless, welcome to the new year. As has been our practice recently, we will begin with a meeting in the Wayward High School Auditorium on Tuesday, August 29th at 8.30 A.M.—coffee will be available from 8:00.

As always, I can promise 181 days of challenge and opportunity, and I look forward to sharing them with you.

Wayward Public Schools

David L. Cattanach, Superintendent of Schools   25 Rope Ferry Road
David G. Tiddle,   Wayward, CT 06385-1907
  Assistant Superintendent of Schools   Telephone (203) 444-7890
Rosa P. Parks,   Fax (203) 444-5555
  Administrative Assistant to the Superintendent
Edward M. Clerk, Business Manager
J. William Cunyard,
  Director of Buildings and Grounds

To: Wayward Teachers and Administrators

From: David L. Cattanach

Date: August 21

In August, I count swallows on the telephone wires in front of my home as their numbers increase each day. My avian calendar tells me it is now almost time to begin another school year. Even though I enjoy New England's beautiful fall, the most effective cure for my mild melancholy at summer's end is anticipating another school year. Fortunately, that remedy is working again.

As I have said before, the schools and the people were impressive when I began in Wayward, and each day here has reinforced my original perception (well, almost every day). This year should be educationally productive for Wayward students and rewarding for each of us. I look forward to the year and to seeing you again in September.

On Tuesday, September 3rd, an initial meeting is scheduled for teachers and administrators at 8:30 A.M. in the Wayward High School auditorium; coffee and conversation will be available in the lobby from 8–8:30, and I hope the sociability continues even beyond Tuesday morning.

Wayward Public Schools

David L. Cattanach, Superintendent of Schools   25 Rope Ferry Road
David G. Tiddle,   Wayward, CT 06385-1907
  Assistant Superintendent of Schools   Telephone (203) 444-7890
Rosa P. Parks,   Fax (203) 444-5555
  Administrative Assistant to the Superintendent

Edward M. Clerk, Business Manager
J. William Cunyard,
  Director of Buildings and Grounds

To: Wayward Teachers and Administrators

From: David L. Cattanach

Date: August 14

Fallvergnügen—the joy of autumn and a new school year. The Germans have a word for everything. They even have words to describe receiving these back-to-work letters from the Central Office—possibly *Nauseavergnügen,* or worse, depending upon your outlook on life, teaching, and maybe school superintendents. But it's time to welcome you back, and we will begin the new school year on Tuesday, August 28th, at 8:30 A.M. in the Wayward High School auditorium—coffee will be available.

For the few holdouts on staff who still smoke and/or chew tobacco, there is good news if a recent board of education decision helps you abandon either (or both) habit/s. On August 2nd, a policy was approved prohibiting use of tobacco in school buildings at all times and on school grounds between 7:00 A.M. and 5:00 P.M. The policy will be titled either *Nicotineverboten* or-*Coldturkeyvergnügen,* and it applies to staff, students, and school visitors. A copy is enclosed.

I look forward to seeing you soon.

Daily Matters

Wayward Public Schools

David L. Cattanach, Superintendent of Schools
David G. Tiddle,
  Assistant Superintendent of Schools
Rosa P. Parks,
  Administrative Assistant to the Superintendent
Edward M. Clerk, Business Manager
J. William Cunyard,
  Director of Buildings and Grounds

25 Rope Ferry Road
Wayward, CT 06385-1907
Telephone (203) 444-7890
Fax (203) 444-5555

To: Teachers, Administrators, and PTO/A Liaison Council

From: David L. Cattanach

Date: March 22

Attached are drafts of school calendars for the next three years, all of which basically follow this year's calendar. I don't know if the board, staff, or community are interested in a three-year calendar, but it might mean one large pain instead of three medium pains. All three proposals begin with a teacher's work day following Labor Day and student arrivals on Wednesdays. All include a full February and April vacation week, plus a week or more at Christmas—depending on when Christmas occurs. All calendars contain five additional snow days, which will be dropped as possible.

Also attached is an optional form that you may use to communicate calendar preferences and recommendations to me. If you choose to respond, please do so by March 29th, so I might transmit your ideas to the Board.

enclosure

Wayward Public Schools

David L. Cattanach, Superintendent of Schools	25 Rope Ferry Road
David G. Tiddle,	Wayward, CT 06385-1907
Assistant Superintendent of Schools	Telephone (203) 444-7890
Rosa P. Parks,	Fax (203) 444-5555
Administrative Assistant to the Superintendent	
Edward M. Clerk, Business Manager	
J. William Cunyard,	
Director of Buildings and Grounds	

To: Administrators, and Teaching Staff

From: David L. Cattanach

Date: March 26

Some of you probably read the article in the *East London Day* on Friday, March 16. In case you did not, a copy is enclosed. Generally, the article is correct, except for the reference to drafting a reduction in force plan with the advisory council; that is not accurate. Sometimes, I am sensitive to niceties, formalities, and protocols and realize, in this instance at least, that RIF procedures must be developed by the Wayward Board of Education and the Wayward Federation of Classroom Teachers. I can have a role in that process, but I don't control it.

If the Wayward Schools must reduce staff because of school closings or continued enrollment declines, we need two things: 1) an orderly plan for staff reduction, which integrates retirements and other natural attrition. This kind of planning is the responsibility of the Wayward Board of Education, but we will solicit staff participation in the development of such a plan. To some degree, we will need data from the Facilities Study and Long-Range Planning Report for such a plan—the data is scheduled by our University of Connecticut consultants for a June presentation to the board of education. A plan for reducing staff is essential to the mental health of our school district. It is difficult enough to teach without the attendant uncertainties connected with declining enrollments and staff reductions, and it is crucial to make an unpleasant process as fair and as understandable as we can make it. No staff reduction plan is devoid of pain, but a plan can set a more measured pace for the inevitable. To the extent we can integrate reductions with known retirements and other staff changes, it will help. 2) A clear reduction in force (RIF) policy. A staff reduction plan and an RIF policy are connected, and although they can be considered separately, it doesn't make much sense to do that. Through the negotiated agreement, the current RIF policy is locked into place for the next three years; however, it may be changed by mutual agreement of the board and the WFCT. While I hope to see a variety of opinions and concerns considered by an RIF policy, that policy must be agreed upon by the board and the WFCT.

I will help make any process developed as fair as possible.

Wayward Public Schools

David L. Cattanach, Superintendent of Schools	25 Rope Ferry Road
David G. Tiddle,	Wayward, CT 06385-1907
Assistant Superintendent of Schools	Telephone (203) 444-7890
Rosa P. Parks,	Fax (203) 444-5555
Administrative Assistant to the Superintendent	
Edward M. Clerk, Business Manager	
J. William Cunyard,	
Director of Buildings and Grounds	

To: Wayward Teachers, Administrators, and other staff

From: David L. Cattanach

Date: September 11

To keep staff members better informed on topics of district interest, I will provide regularly to each school copies of board of education agendas, superintendent's general notes, agenda notes, and related materials. Although not every teacher has the time, or the desire, to read the volume of information distributed for each meeting, I want you to know what is usually available. Therefore, I am enclosing information for our regular meeting on Thursday, September 13th (except for copies of my opening day remarks, which you heard and which are in the teachers' room notebooks explained below). In the future, general and agenda notes will be placed in notebooks for the teachers' rooms (as they have also been for this meeting) and possibly other places convenient for teachers.

We hope the information contained in notes and agendas is of interest to many or all of you.

Wayward Public Schools

David L. Cattanach, Superintendent of Schools   25 Rope Ferry Road
David G. Tiddle,   Wayward, CT 06385-1907
   Assistant Superintendent of Schools   Telephone (203) 444-7890
Rosa P. Parks,   Fax (203) 444-5555
   Administrative Assistant to the Superintendent
Edward M. Clerk, Business Manager
J. William Cunyard,
   Director of Buildings and Grounds

To: Wayward Teachers

From: David L. Cattanach

Date: October 25

As most of you know, during the school year before last school year and the first half of last year, a committee of teachers from each school worked cooperatively with administrative representatives to revise the teacher evaluation system in Wayward. After I began in Wayward last fall, the process continued and appeared to conclude amiably and effectively. I met with committee members on a number of occasions and was impressed with their cooperation and efforts to improve our teacher evaluation system.

On February 8, of the last school year, the faculty committee unanimously approved the revision (after many drafts and productive attempts to obtain thoughts, perceptions, suggestions, and ideas of whatever variety from each school). At a March 22nd meeting, the board of education also reviewed and approved the revised evaluation procedures. During this past summer, we had the new forms and procedures printed. This fall, the director of instruction worked with principals, and principals with teachers, to acquaint everyone with the new system.

Recently, I was told the teacher bargaining unit wants a vote to approve or disapprove the new evaluation system. There might be a legal argument by WFCT that changes were not made officially with that group; there can also be strong legal and moral argument that what we did was appropriate. Somewhat naively, I have assumed until now that our revision was blessed by all. (Someone once told me never to assume anything in this damn business, mister—obviously, I didn't learn that lesson perfectly.)

I'm particularly concerned that there has been such a long delay between the faculty committee approval and the union desire for a vote on what had earlier seemed settled and acceptable. As a practical matter, any group can vote on whatever it wants to, so I won't throw my body in front of the ballot box. Obviously, even the belated imprimatur of WFCT would be welcome. I'm not sure either what I would do about negative voting results, except complain, but I might think of something—even though I am normally a sweet-tempered person.

Regardless of the outcome of a union vote, I will try to answer questions about the evaluation system and listen to suggestions for improvement. Any evaluation system depends on the integrity and goodwill of the parties involved, and we now have conditions in Wayward conducive to effective staff evaluation, regardless of the particular procedures we use. I hope we can get on with our evaluation process with no hassles or bad feelings, and I'm confident we will.

Wayward Public Schools

David L. Cattanach, Superintendent of Schools	25 Rope Ferry Road
David G. Tiddle,	Wayward, CT 06385-1907
Assistant Superintendent of Schools	Telephone (203) 444-7890
Rosa P. Parks,	Fax (203) 444-5555
Administrative Assistant to the Superintendent	

Edward M. Clerk, Business Manager
J. William Cunyard,
  Director of Buildings and Grounds

To: Wayward Teachers and Administrators

From: David L. Cattanach

Date: April 16

Attached is a revised version of my memorandum dated April 11. Only one word is changed in the corrected and expurgated (especially selected word) edition—physic to psychic—a change that measures the distance between soul and large intestine. When I said teaching takes it out of you, I didn't mean from the digestive tract.

Anyway, I've never been so humiliated in all my life.

Wayward Public Schools

David L. Cattanach, Superintendent of Schools   25 Rope Ferry Road
David G. Tiddle,   Wayward, CT 06385-1907
  Assistant Superintendent of Schools   Telephone (203) 444-7890
Rosa P. Parks,   Fax (203) 444-5555
  Administrative Assistant to the Superintendent
Edward M. Clerk, Business Manager
J. William Cunyard,
  Director of Buildings and Grounds

To: Wayward Staff

From: David L. Cattanach

Date: March 19

Although problems are always easier to identify than solve and plans are easier to make than carry out, long-range planning is essential to a school district. Since last summer, I have worked with staff and the board of education to develop a six-year staffing plan, including support staff. The certified staff has reviewed and helped shape its plan, and support staff members will have an opportunity to review and comment on their plan. The business manager, director of buildings and grounds, and principals have identified major facilities needs for the next six years. All of this will be part of an overall six-year plan for the Wayward Public Schools. The final organization of the proposed long-range plan is not yet developed, but it will include analyses of existing conditions and recommendations to meet identified needs in areas such as 1) staffing, 2) facilities utilization, 3) major textbook adoptions, 4) major equipment purchases, 5) instructional supplies, 6) library and audio-visual materials, 7) major building and grounds repairs and special projects, and 8) curriculum modifications and program directions.

To benefit from your thoughts, I have attached a form on which you may provide your ideas about Wayward's immediate and long-range needs in the areas previously cited and your recommendations to meet those needs. This is an opportunity to share personal notions with me rather than a homework assignment. Although I believe this effort will be productive and provide important insights and recommendations, it is optional. For those who want to reply, please do so by April Fool's Day. (This date is not intended to be of any major significance.)

Wayward Public Schools

David L. Cattanach, Superintendent of Schools	25 Rope Ferry Road
David G. Tiddle,	Wayward, CT 06385-1907
Assistant Superintendent of Schools	Telephone (203) 444-7890
Rosa P. Parks,	Fax (203) 444-5555
Administrative Assistant to the Superintendent	
Edward M. Clerk, Business Manager	
J. William Cunyard,	
Director of Buildings and Grounds	

To: Wayward High School Teachers and Administrators

From: David L. Cattanach

Date: May 28

I have been interested for some time in opening high school classes to adults during the regular school day on a space available basis. This would be in addition to the regular and avocational adult education programs now provided and would probably have a minor effect on class size, especially in the beginning. Opening programs to the community would be a major service to its citizens. Benefits to Wayward High School would include better community understanding of the quality of education at WHS and increased school support because of greater knowledge. We would also benefit younger students through the varied life experiences brought to class by adult students. Imagine students discovering that adults can attend school because they want to learn and for no other reason. Also, if the program is successful, it might require additional teachers beyond those otherwise needed.

I would like to see us begin next year on a space available basis. There are unanswered questions and probably some unasked questions; the program will inevitably have rough edges and awkwardnesses, but I think its advantages far outweigh its disadvantages. We understand the anxiety teachers could feel if this program were forced upon them, and we don't want to do that. Therefore, your principal and department coordinators will discuss possibilities with you, and we will try to begin with volunteer teachers only. We expect that, after some experience with adults in the high school, most teachers will be willing to participate. I would appreciate the faculty's serious consideration of this program. The board of education has authorized me to explore the issue with you and prepare a report with recommendations to the board on it. I ask your cooperation in this effort.

Wayward Public Schools

David L. Cattanach, Superintendent of Schools	25 Rope Ferry Road
David G. Tiddle,	Wayward, CT 06385-1907
Assistant Superintendent of Schools	Telephone (203) 444-7890
Rosa P. Parks,	Fax (203) 444-5555
Administrative Assistant to the Superintendent	
Edward M. Clerk, Business Manager	
J. William Cunyard,	
Director of Buildings and Grounds	

To: Wayward Teachers and Administrators

From: David L. Cattanach

Date: January 13

As most of you know from reading the newspapers, results from Connecticut's first mastery testing are in, and Wayward did very well. Local news articles have been favorable and accurate. I appreciate that, but I appreciate even more the excellent teaching that caused the good test scores. Attached to this memorandum are copies of Wayward test results by school, statewide scores, and some comments on our mastery test results.

You may have noticed that some classy school districts didn't do so well on the test and criticized it as too difficult and also as over-control of curriculum by the state. I don't claim to be an expert on the difficulty of the test, having partially forgotten what it's like to be a fourth grader, but I believe the mastery test measures important basic skills. It should be embarrassing to argue against teaching students to understand what they read, to learn how to write, and to use mathematics. I know it's easier to defend the test when scores are high, but I believe it, regardless of test scores.

Next year, we will assess fourth- and sixth-grade students at the elementary level and eighth graders at the Middle School. I hope our results are at least as good in all three grades as this year's were in one. Again, thanks for what our students have accomplished.

Wayward Public Schools

David L. Cattanach, Superintendent of Schools   25 Rope Ferry Road
David G. Tiddle,   Wayward, CT 06385-1907
   Assistant Superintendent of Schools   Telephone (203) 444-7890
Rosa P. Parks,   Fax (203) 444-5555
   Administrative Assistant to the Superintendent
Edward M. Clerk, Business Manager
J. William Cunyard,
   Director of Buildings and Grounds

To: Wayward Teachers and Administrators

From: David L. Cattanach

Date: September 26

Transcendental indifference may sound like a benign tenet of the Maharishi Mahesh Yogi, but it's really a common administrative approach to problems. Unfortunately, it doesn't always work. At times, I've practiced this doctrine in Wayward, and I tried it on the length of the teachers' work day. Variations from school to school finally nudged me to make some decisions. Most of you have been told what was decided, although possibly some have not been bothered because changes weren't needed at your school.

Although all teachers give far more than is required, we still need staff presence before and after the instructional day for students begins and ends. Administrators retain authority to grant dispensations from our requirements for all sorts of unusual and recurring circumstances, and I support that because I know you give extra time as needed.

It finally became important to insure standardization among our seven schools. Schedule adjustments are relatively minor, and I hope they will be accepted. I will be as generous if I ever disagree with you.

Wayward Public Schools

David L. Cattanach, Superintendent of Schools
David G. Tiddle,
   Assistant Superintendent of Schools
Rosa P. Parks,
   Administrative Assistant to the Superintendent
Edward M. Clerk, Business Manager
J. William Cunyard,
   Director of Buildings and Grounds

25 Rope Ferry Road
Wayward, CT 06385-1907
Telephone (203) 444-7890
Fax (203) 444-5555

To: Wayward High School Teachers and Administrators

From: David L. Cattanach

Date: January 21

I asked each principal to reserve a few minutes at a regular faculty gathering for me to review our proposed budget and attendant problems. Because I teach a graduate course when WHS meetings are held, we arranged a special convocation for January 29th at 2:30 P.M. in the library. We probably won't need more than a half hour or so unless you have a myriad of questions, which I will try to answer.

Attendance is optional. If no one shows up, my feelings might be hurt, but any reasonable attendance will suffice—maybe you can draw straws and short straws have to come to the meeting. I've said before, if superintendents were sensitive, we'd sell aluminum siding door to door because there's less chance of rejection in that work; but then my experience in Wayward has peeled away layers of cynicism acquired in less pleasant circumstances.

If you have a conflict on the 29th, feel free to meet another obligation, or if your interest in the topic is modest or less, do something else and don't worry about a roll call.

Wayward Public Schools

David L. Cattanach, Superintendent of Schools
David G. Tiddle,
   Assistant Superintendent of Schools

25 Rope Ferry Road
Wayward, CT 06385-1907
Telephone (203) 444-7890

Rosa P. Parks,   Fax (203) 444-5555
  Administrative Assistant to the Superintendent
Edward M. Clerk, Business Manager
J. William Cunyard,
  Director of Buildings and Grounds

To: Wayward Teachers and Administrators

From: David L. Cattanach

Date: December 8

At their regular December meetings, the Wayward and East London Boards of
Education approved a program between the two districts, which will link high
schools, junior high schools, and each of our five respective elementary
schools in an informal arrangement to share special school activities. Programs that might be scheduled cooperatively include school visitations, field
trips, special events, and activities (such as student council meetings in
secondary schools, holiday concerts, field days, etc.). We also are considering
cooperative professional staff development efforts and teacher visitations and
exchanges. Aslo, parent-teacher organizations/associations may wish to work
together on particular issues.

All student activities would occur within the normal course of present educational programs. *There are no plans to change, in any way, where children attend school or our existing school district organizations.* Both our goals and
the voluntary activities we will schedule are modest steps to broaden
understanding between neighboring communities – nothing else is being considered.

I will meet with individual faculties after January 1st and review the program.
However, it's important now for you to understand that, while I encourage
your enthusiastic participation with your professional counterparts in East
London, all of this is voluntary. We have no administrative plan to impose on
staff, students, or parents.

SUPERINTENDENT'S CORRESPONDENCE—PARENTS

Wayward Public Schools

David L. Cattanach, Superintendent of Schools   25 Rope Ferry Road
David G. Tiddle,   Wayward, CT 06385-1907
  Assistant Superintendent of Schools   Telephone (203) 444-7890

Rosa P. Parks,
  Administrative Assistant to the Superintendent
Edward M. Clerk, Business Manager
J. William Cunyard,
  Director of Buildings and Grounds

Fax (203) 444-5555

September 14

Mr. and Mrs. Robert D. Wylie
30 West Holland Street
Wayward, CT 06385

Dear Mr. and Mrs. Wylie,

Welcome to Wayward and to the Wayward Public Schools. We are pleased that you and your children have joined us in 1991, and we hope the change has been a comfortable one for your family. Enclosed is information about our schools, and if you have any questions, please call your school principal or me. Our staff is committed to educational and personal excellence and to each student's success. We will work closely with your children to help them achieve their full educational and personal potential.

Again, welcome to the Wayward Public Schools, and I hope to meet you in the near future.

Sincerely,

David L. Cattanach

Wayward Public Schools

David L. Cattanach, Superintendent of Schools
David G. Tiddle,
  Assistant Superintendent of Schools
Rosa P. Parks,
  Administrative Assistant to the Superintendent
Edward M. Clerk, Business Manager
J. William Cunyard,
  Director of Buildings and Grounds

25 Rope Ferry Road
Wayward, CT 06385-1907
Telephone (203) 444-7890
Fax (203) 444-5555

April 10

Ron and Carolyn Beezley
7203 S.E. 15th
Wayward, CT 06385

Dear Mr. and Mrs. Beezley,

Congratulations on the birth of your son. A new child is a major event in any family. Your son is important also to the Wayward Public Schools. We look forward to his joining us in kindergarten. Although that day may seem far off now, time passes quickly, and it will soon be our pleasure to share his childhood with you.

We would also like you to be aware of the "Families in Training Program" sponsored by the Child and Family Agency in New Coventry. This program offers information and assistance, if needed, during the first three years of your child's life. If you are interested, you can reach the agency at 443-2299 for more information.

Wayward Schools are committed to educational and personal excellence and to each child's success. We care about every person, and we will work closely with you over the course of your son's school career to help him achieve his full educational and personal potential.

Again, our congratulations. If we can help you or your child even before he enters school, please call us.

Sincerely,

David L. Cattanach

Wayward Public Schools

David L. Cattanach, Superintendent of Schools   25 Rope Ferry Road
David G. Tiddle,   Wayward, CT 06385-1907
   Assistant Superintendent of Schools   Telephone (203) 444-7890
Rosa P. Parks,   Fax (203) 444-5555
   Administrative Assistant to the Superintendent
Edward M. Clerk, Business Manager

J. William Cunyard,
Director of Buildings and Grounds

January 3

Dear Parents,

It doesn't seem as if I've been here for such a short time; your acceptance and support have made me feel at home. I am impressed with Wayward's students, teachers, principals, support staff, parents, parent organizations, and town government. Our schools are good schools; each is different, but all are alike in their dedication to students. Our biggest challenge is convincing everyone we are as good as we are.

One of my responsibilities in telling Wayward's educational story is to articulate beliefs I know you all have. A major theme that emerges from what you, staff members, and the board of education have told me is a strong desire to have the Wayward Public Schools become and/or be recognized as an outstanding school system. As one small step on that journey, I ask you to join me in a "Commitment to Educational and Personal Excellence" in the Wayward Public Schools. Although we need actions more than maxims, that phrase can help focus attention on our commitment.

Too many school districts have been hesitant to honor scholastic achievement. Sure, life has blessed some people with more intellectual ability than others. That is just as true with talent in athletics or the arts, and yet schools and society handle those inequities easily. We shouldn't apologize for recognizing and rewarding academic talent but, instead, should accept educational attainment as the primary goal of each school and of each classroom. If schools will not honor intellectual accomplishment and ability, then who will?

Certainly, we have an equal responsibility to all students, including those less able to excel scholastically; that's why we stress commitment to personal excellence, as well as academic excellence. Personal excellence is using to the fullest the abilities we are given. Personal excellence is civilized and considerate behavior. Personal excellence in any endeavor is worthy of respect, and it can be realized through athletics or in many other nonacademic pursuits. Every student, and each of us, is capable of personal excellence.

If we also demand educational excellence of our young people and of school staff, we will not be treating anyone unfairly; instead, we will be restoring scholastic achievement to the prominent place it deserves in public education. We should identify ways our schools can embody the principles expressed in a "Commitment to Educational and Personal Excellence" and put those words into everyday practice.

Have an outstanding new year; I look forward to working closely with you on behalf of the Wayward Public Schools.

Sincerely,

David L. Cattanach

SUPERINTENDENT'S CORRESPONDENCE—STUDENTS

Wayward Public Schools

David L. Cattanach, Superintendent of Schools	25 Rope Ferry Road
David G. Tiddle,	Wayward, CT 06385-1907
Assistant Superintendent of Schools	Telephone (203) 444-7890
Rosa P. Parks,	Fax (203) 444-5555
Administrative Assistant to the Superintendent	
Edward M. Clerk, Business Manager	
J. William Cunyard,	
Director of Buildings and Grounds	

December 5

Mr. Benjamin and Mr. Daniel Metz
  c/o Mrs. Lisa Metz
178 Washington Street
Wayward, CT 06385

Dear Ben and Dan,

Welcome to kindergarten and to Frisby School. Your teacher, Mrs. Winters, and your principal Mr. Miner, and all of us in Wayward are glad you are here with us. You will be the only twins in the Frisby School kindergarten class.

We hope you like Frisby School. You will make new friends and learn many new things. We are sending you coloring books about school. Have a good time in kindergarten.

Sincerely,

David L. Cattanach

Wayward Public Schools

David L. Cattanach, Superintendent of Schools	25 Rope Ferry Road
David G. Tiddle,	Wayward, CT 06385-1907
Assistant Superintendent of Schools	Telephone (203) 444-7890
Rosa P. Parks,	Fax (203) 444-5555
Administrative Assistant to the Superintendent	
Edward M. Clerk, Business Manager	
J. William Cunyard,	
Director of Buildings and Grounds	

March 5

Ms. Suzanne Carol
95 Oneco Avenue
Wayward, CT 06385

Dear Suzanne,

Welcome to Wayward and to Wayward High School. We hope you are settled into your new classes and doing well.

We know it's not easy to change schools, but your teachers, your principal, and all of us want you to feel good about being here. Be sure to tell your teachers or your principal if you need any assistance, and they will be glad to help you.

Again, we are pleased you have joined us.

Sincerely,

David L. Cattanach

Wayward Public Schools

David L. Cattanach, Superintendent of Schools	25 Rope Ferry Road
David G. Tiddle,	Wayward, CT 06385-1907
Assistant Superintendent of Schools	Telephone (203) 444-7890
Rosa P. Parks,	Fax (203) 444-5555
Administrative Assistant to the Superintendent	
Edward M. Clerk, Business Manager	
J. William Cunyard,	
Director of Buildings and Grounds	

December 5

Mr. Ernest Hamilton Brown c/o Mary Ann Brown
Althea Drive
Wayward, CT 06385

Dear Ernie,

Congratulations on being named to the Wayward High School Honor Roll for the first marking period. Through your academic achievements you have made a serious commitment to educational and personal excellence. We appreciate the dedication and effort that characterize your school career. Again, our congratulations, and I encourage you to continue your good work.

Sincerely,

David L. Cattanach

Wayward Public Schools

David L. Cattanach, Superintendent of Schools
David G. Tiddle,
  Assistant Superintendent of Schools
Rosa P. Parks,
  Administrative Assistant to the Superintendent
Edward M. Clerk, Business Manager
J. William Cunyard,
  Director of Buildings and Grounds

25 Rope Ferry Road
Wayward, CT 06385-1907
Telephone (203) 444-7890
Fax (203) 444-5555

March 22

Mr. Robert Alexander
14460 Twisted Oak Drive
Wayward, CT 06385

Dear Robert,

Congratulations on being named to the Wayward High School Honor Roll twice this year. I am sure your parents, other relatives, teachers, and friends also recognize this significant achievement. Again, my congratulations, and I encourage you to continue your good work.

Sincerely,

David L. Cattanach

Wayward Public Schools

David L. Cattanach, Superintendent of Schools   25 Rope Ferry Road
David G. Tiddle,   Wayward, CT 06385-1907
   Assistant Superintendent of Schools   Telephone (203) 444-7890
Rosa P. Parks,   Fax (203) 444-5555
   Administrative Assistant to the Superintendent
Edward M. Clerk, Business Manager
J. William Cunyard,
   Director of Buildings and Grounds

May 10

Mr. Michael Boyd Epperson
609 Nancywood Drive
Wayward, CT 06385

Dear Michael,

Congratulations on being named to the Wayward High School Honor Roll three times this year. I am sure your parents, other relatives, teachers, and friends also recognize this significant achievement. Again, my congratulations, and I encourage you to continue your good work.

Sincerely,

David L. Cattanach

Wayward Public Schools

David L. Cattanach, Superintendent of Schools   25 Rope Ferry Road

David G. Tiddle,
  Assistant Superintendent of Schools
Rosa P. Parks,
  Administrative Assistant to the Superintendent
Edward M. Clerk, Business Manager
J. William Cunyard,
  Director of Buildings and Grounds

Wayward, CT 06385-1907
Telephone (203) 444-7890
Fax (203) 444-5555

June 29

Mr. Lee Austin
95 Oneco Drive
Wayward, CT 06385

Dear Lee,

Congratulations on being named to the Wayward High School Honor Roll all four marking periods this year. I am sure your parents, other relatives, teachers and friends also recognize this significant achievement. Our schools are committed to educational and personal excellence, and you have made that commitment as shown by your academic achievements. Again, my congratulations, and I encourage you to continue your good work.

Sincerely,

David L. Cattanach

Wayward Public Schools

David L. Cattanach, Superintendent of Schools
David G. Tiddle,
  Assistant Superintendent of Schools
Rosa P. Parks,
  Administrative Assistant to the Superintendent
Edward M. Clerk, Business Manager
J. William Cunyard,
  Director of Buildings and Grounds

25 Rope Ferry Road
Wayward, CT 06385-1907
Telephone (203) 444-7890
Fax (203) 444-5555

June 29

Ms. Ida Ann Wylie
110 Lakewood Road
Wayward, CT 06385

Dear Ann,

Congratulations on being named to the Wayward High School Honor Roll for the first semester this year, but I missed your name on the Honor Roll for the second semester. Although there are many reasons why a student's name can disappear from an honor roll, they probably can be categorized two ways: (1) You did the best you could, but it just didn't work out. Sometimes it happens that way, and if that's the case in this instance, you have nothing to regret. Instead, you should feel proud of what you have achieved and keep working hard; or (2) You didn't work as hard as you could have, and the results reflected that. If this is the reason your name isn't on the honor roll, I hope you recognize that. Any of us can have a bad day, week, month, or even longer, whether at work or in school; the challenge is for us to work harder and do better next time.

We want each student to achieve in school and experience the satisfaction that comes from doing a worthwhile job well. We hope you continue to have that experience also.

Regardless of whether or not your name reappears on a future honor roll, I wish you the very best at Wayward High School and in your overall educational future.

Sincerely,

David L. Cattanach

Wayward Public Schools

David L. Cattanach, Superintendent of Schools
David G. Tiddle,
    Assistant Superintendent of Schools
Rosa P. Parks,
    Administrative Assistant to the Superintendent
Edward M. Clerk, Business Manager
J. William Cunyard,
    Director of Buildings and Grounds

25 Rope Ferry Road
Wayward, CT 06385-1907
Telephone (203) 444-7890
Fax (203) 444-5555

June 29

William Wylie Wismer
1021 Maple Street
Wayward, CT 06385-1907

Dear Bill,

Congratulations on your recent successes at the Connecticut Special Olympics. Winning a gold and a bronze medal is a major achievement, and we are proud of your efforts there. Enjoy the remainder of this school year, and, in the near future, I will stop by your classroom and congratulate you personally on your recent accomplishments at Special Olympics.

Sincerely,

David L. Cattanach

Answers/Responses to Chapter Exercises

CHAPTER 3

Practice Makes Perfect—Matching Themes/Main Ideas and Titles

Place the number of the theme/main idea of the topics following the titles in the blank to the right of the correct titles.

Ankle Bone Connected to the Foot Bone . . .	4
"Closers"	16
Creative Schizophrenia	2
Dance with the One Who "Brung" You	3
Disclaimers Make the World Go 'Round	1
Dreaming Dreams	5
Efficient or Effective—Choose Any Two	9
Finishing the Run	6
I Always Knew This Would Happen Someday, and It Finally Did	11
"If You Can Keep Your Head When All About You . . ."	8
Puritans and Bears	7
Say Hello to People at Least	13
Sit Down Turkey!—Or a Rose by Another Name Doesn't Smell as Good	10
"Strutting and Fretting Your Hours upon the Stage"	17
Telephone—I: It's Not Alright Unless You Hear from Me	12
"The Emperor's New Clothes"	19
The Lady or the Tiger?	14
Thorns in Administrative Flesh	20
There Aren't Any Cracks in My Facade	22
This Isn't the First Time It's Happened to Me Either	23
"Vox Populi, Vox Dei"—I	24
We Never Did It That Way in My Old District	18
Who Is This Person?—I	15
Whom Did You Say Is Calling?	21

Themes/Main Ideas

(*1*) Leadership survival sometimes requires explanations of our simplest assertions. Although they are only tools, such explanations are important tools.

Disclaimers Make the World Go 'Round

(2) If leaders aren't comfortable holding divergent points of view simultaneously in their thoughts and appreciating the value of each, they probably won't be successful leaders.

Creative Schizophrenia

(3) Leaders should avail themselves of opportunities for personal and professional growth and change while retaining the best basic personal elements that have defined them as individual human beings and as leaders throughout their lives.

Dance with the One Who "Brung" You

(4) Educational leaders must be suspicious of coincidences between similar or related events and should recognize and understand existing connections between and among seemingly disconnected events, visualize overall patterns from apparently independent events, use connections and identified patterns to investigate existing relationships between or among them, develop connections and patterns from relationships, correct existing problems before they worsen, and prevent new problems from spinning off old ones.

Ankle Bone Connected to the Foot Bone . . .

(5) Leadership should articulate a clear vision of each leader's hopes for and expectations of district colleagues, the school, or department—and regularly remind listeners or readers of the leader's vision for education and what he or she is committed to accomplish on behalf of young people entrusted to the local public schools.

Dreaming Dreams

(6) Every single leadership or instructional task should be focused upon, worked at, and completed as if it were the most important responsibility of a person's professional career. Educational leaders should concentrate on completing the school year as productively as it usually begins, on maintaining forward educational momentum, and on working with teachers to ensure they also finish each year's educational run well.

Finishing the Run

(7) Although choices sometimes must be made weighing factors peripheral to an issue's moral center, leadership instincts should recognize the essence of educational decisions, instead of focusing on extrinsic legal, political, or other considerations, which leads to pernicious personal at-

titudes and negative organizational effects. When leaders develop patterns that allow them to make even correct decisions for the wrong reasons, it becomes easier for them to make wrong decisions for the wrong reasons.

Puritans and Bears

(*8*) Leadership behaviors are infectious, and when superintendents, principals, or other school district leaders don't manage crises well, neither will colleagues. If, conversely, leaders exhibit a sense of ease and an ability to cope with any problem that may arise, that also is communicated to the staff. Effective leaders manage to "keep their heads when all about them are losing theirs and blaming it on them."

If You Can Keep Your Head When All About You . . .

(*9*) In most professions, each day is filled with choices between efficiency and effectiveness, and leadership requires balancing these two qualities. Endorsing the concept of the golden mean between extremes, leadership should take the long view, involve other people appropriately in major district educational decisions, and accept some inefficiency on behalf of long-range educational effectiveness—as long as vital educational services function acceptably.

Efficient or Effective—Choose Any Two

(*10*) School districts should lose the fancy names for simple notions, and administrative lives will be simpler and more productive.

Sit Down Turkey!—Or a Rose by Another Name Doesn't Smell as Good

(*11*) Whenever colleagues sense leadership despair, enthusiasm wanes; educators don't want leaders who feel their jobs are too hard for them. When leaders communicate enthusiasm for educational programs and activities and are confident about meeting leadership responsibilities, staff is much more likely to respond in kind. School leaders need to emulate the hardiness and the dogged persistence of aluminum siding salesmen.

I Always Knew This Would Happen Someday, and It Finally Did

(*12*) To prevent misunderstandings and their consequences, administrators should always call back and complete transactions definitively by reaffirming earlier directives as given, modifying them as needed, or canceling them. Confirming, follow-up telephone calls are easy, are a correct habit, and prevent serious staff embarrassment—and sometimes much more than that.

Telephone I—It's Not Alright Unless You Hear from Me

(*13*) School leaders should establish an obvious climate of openness and receptivity to personal visits and telephone calls and an open, receptive environment for staff, parent, and student constituents alike. Accessibility improves perceptions of school leaders, and it's a better way to treat people.

Say Hello to People at Least

(*14*) The best superintendents usually recognize daily staff leadership as their primary task—albeit followed closely by the need to work well with their boards of education.

The Lady or the Tiger?

(*15*) Leadership job changes present windows of opportunity for self-assessment of personal and professional strengths and shortcomings and for modification of attitudes and behaviors. In new positions, behavior modifications can be made without self-consciousness and with assurance they will be noticed instead of masked by long-standing perceptions of you.

Who Is This Person?—I

(*16*) Educational leaders need to cultivate important "closing out" skills in their sales of educational concepts to staff, boards of education, and communities and not continue talking until they lose what they've gained. We need to read our audiences and recognize signs, omens, and portents that point toward success; shut up; sit down; and "close out" the sale.

"Closers"

(*17*) Board of education meetings offer regular administrative opportunities for public administrative presentations for leadership to develop recurring themes on professional and personal leadership aspirations for local education. For important presentations, administrators should write what they plan to say and practice it so they won't appear to be reading it, even when they are. Extemporaneous speaking is also a major part of leadership life and requires practice, practice, practice. Our hours "on stage" are important moments in important professional lives.

"Strutting and Fretting Your Hours upon the Stage"

(*18*) As new superintendents or principals begin in new districts, they should never say, "Well, in my old district, we always. . . ." Nobody gives a damn about how it was done where you were before, and after about the third reference, they become increasingly hostile and don't want to hear another word about it. Your new colleagues will hate it when you do that and will dislike you personally as well.

We Never Did It That Way in My Old District

(*19*) Leaders need to maintain an appropriate balance between seriousness and enjoyment of life. A highly developed sense of the absurd should be considered a strong leadership attribute. Humorous situations are lying all around us like uncollected seashells to be gathered and treasured.

"The Emperor's New Clothes"

(20) Administrators should give paper shuffling a low priority, particularly during the school day so it won't keep leaders from more important student and staff interactions; should establish clear, fail-safe procedures to read anything that appears really important; should have clearly understood follow-up procedures to ensure appropriate and timely response and action; and follow such common advice from office manuals as "handle documents only once."

Thorns in Administrative Flesh

(21) District administrators occasionally receive unsigned letters and anonymous telephone calls. Whenever possible, anonymous communications should be ignored and callers told that's what will happen, but if a call involves possible injury to children, administrators don't have that luxury.

Whom Did You Say Is Calling?

(22) Educational leaders need to find the golden mean between covering up real problems and gratuitous revelations of minor issues to everyone who will listen. The golden mean is responsible acknowledgement of major issues and is somewhat closer to gratuitous revelations than to covering up.

There Aren't Any Cracks in My Facade

(23) Leaders must learn from mistakes.

This Isn't the First Time It's Happened to Me Either

(24) Educators need to strike a responsive balance between responsiveness to the will of the people and acting on personal principle contrary to strong public opinion. Deciding when to do what makes school leadership exciting, fascinating, and risky.

"Vox Populi, Vox Dei"–I

CHAPTER 4

Practice Makes Perfect—Summarizing Themes/Main Ideas

Summarize in three or four sentences the themes/main ideas of each of the following in Chapter 4:

Better Odds Are All You Can Expect–In Poker or Leadership Life in General

No matter what school districts do to improve student safety, risks can't be totally eliminated–good decisions reduce risks, but some danger always remains. No matter how good decisions are, the best they can do is improve the odds that what the board wants to happen will happen and what they don't want to happen won't happen. Public school leadership should be honest with boards of education and their various constituencies and promise them only greater chances for success—not unfounded guarantees of it.

But Sir, I'm Only a Poor Little Match Girl

Although some boards of education still perform well, too many others have abandoned responsibilities as child advocates and as supporters and defenders of district leadership and staff. From their cries of poverty, an onlooker might believe everyone in the school district sells penny boxes of matches on the streets of Victorian England or has joined a cloistered order, surrendering all worldly goods and comforts. Today, many boards of education enthusiastically defend the fiscal faith, while ignoring their irreplaceable roles as advocates for children and for budgets adequate for their support.

Dear God, He Chewed Off the Wrong Foot!

Public board member criticism of school district leadership erodes public support for budgets and thereby student programs. Although superintendents, other administrators, and staff usually survive their worst shots, it's often at significant educational costs. There are better ways to disagree with, and even kinder ways to remove educational leadership from office, at relatively little public relations cost to local school districts.

Don't You Pick on My Little Brother (or Sister)

When dissident board members publicly undercut majority board positions, the other board members typically act as if the naysayers were naughty children, instead of savaging them as they deserve. However, a superintendent's disagreements with board members should be temperate to avoid triggering the big brother/big sister defensive reflex of the board and having them turn on the superintendent for daring to criticize one of their own—forgetting entirely the original offense committed by the wicked board member. Even when dissident members of boards of education undercut majority board positions publicly, most board members only chide the bad guys instead of beheading them as they may well deserve. Board of education majorities don't have many legally effective ways of disciplining "rogue elephants," but the gentle finger shaking and "tsk tsking" do nothing to discourage repetitions of disloyal acts.

Educational Maritime Law

Many board of education members focus on perceived minor leadership flaws and ignore the preponderance of solid leadership performance. There's no immunity against this unfortunate practice; leaders can only prepare as well as possible and, when board members are distracted by an alleged personal, professional, or programmatic defect no matter how small, attempt to refocus them on personal, professional, or programmatic strengths.

How Much Is Board Harmony Worth?

There's a strong tendency among board members to bend on important issues to ensure every board member remains happy with all outcomes. Against logic, but in futile efforts to please all its members, boards often compromise, against their better judgments, instead of explaining clearly why the majority feels as it does, giving dissidents a final chance to elucidate a position, then voting the way the majority feels is appropriate and going on to the next piece of business.

How Much Information Is Enough?

Providing adequate data to boards is a moving target at which professional leaders often throw information futilely. A number of variables affect the degree to which the information target moves, and a half dozen of the most common include board member experience, board knowledge, overall superintendent relationships with boards, political climate, issue volatility, and a board of education's work ethic. All six board variables affect, in various ways, the amount of information boards require from superintendents. Experience, combined with careful reading and weighing of variables, help superintendents come closer to the optimum information flow a board desires, but they can't guarantee ultimate administrative success.

I Found These at the Dump

The bane of a superintendent's existence is "I gotcha"-playing board members whose lives are complete only when springing unholy surprises on superintendents at board of education meetings. Superintendents need board policy that clearly spells out requirements for board members to place items for discussion on agendas before meetings, and the chairperson must enforce these requirements by discouraging unscheduled items at meetings. School leaders need advance notification to research issues before being confronted publicly with them.

I've Had Many, Many Calls about That

There is a strong cause-and-effect relationship between (1) board members who claim to receive hundreds of telephone calls each week complaining about the schools and (2) board members who want to believe the worst about their own school system, who accept at face value all critical comments from callers about staff, who won't suspend judgment until after hearing staff perceptions, who never refer parents to teachers or administrators, and who don't alert the superintendent to alleged problems.

Henry M. Robert versus Common Sense

Parliamentary procedure, like other law, is a good servant but a poor master. Superintendents and board members are well advised to understand basic parliamentary procedures and to use them as the foundation of board meetings. A major caveat is that procedures shouldn't override common sense.

Pearls before Swine—Or Where Does It Say Precisely What I Said?

Board of education minutes should reflect what boards do, not what they say, but board members often expect that every remark they make will be recorded in meeting minutes so that, in the twenty-second century A.D., their great-grandchildren's great-grandchildren can read about their distinguished ancestor before the turn of the century.

Peter Pan Is Alive and Well on Your Board of Education

Lost innocence is inevitable if you want to grow up, and for every positive change in education, there is a cost to be paid for the gain to be made. Yet some board members have become adults without learning this lesson. Effective board members, as do effective leaders, understand this and, in considering changes, assess foreseeable negative effects, weigh them against anticipated positive outcomes, and when positives are significantly more important than negatives, proceed. Ineffective board members and ineffective leaders aren't prepared to pay any price and can't move forward with change, regardless of its benefits.

Questions That Don't Want Answers

Board members regularly ask questions not to learn, but with one of a number of irrelevant reason or reasons that nobody will ever understand. The best way for administrators to cope with these posturing interrogators is to treat them exactly as they would those who ask questions to learn—but always recognizing, and never losing sight of, what's really happening and why it's happening. Also, in answering questions from these people, school leadership should admit not having answers when good answers aren't readily available and be more than usually alert against careless or casual administrative responses that will certainly be used against them.

"Safe No's"

"Safe no's" are negative votes to please a dissident's like-minded constituency but are cast only when the "no" vote is safe and obviously won't affect the outcome. For example, when a negotiated contract is before the board of education for approval and the tenor of a long discussion indicates to the dissident or dissidents that approval is assured, he/she/or they can vote "no" without fear of negative consequences.

Smoking Guns—Or How Much Proof Do You Need Anyway?

Sometimes boards cling to forlorn hopes that sufficient data or information will make difficult decisions easy. Effective superintendents help boards distinguish between essential and superfluous information and lead them to timely decisions on important issues. Clearly, boards need databases for important judgments, but generating an endless flow of information, in futile attempts to make each decision easy, overloads decision-making circuitry.

The Old Rubber Stamp Gambit

Leadership frustration arises from board members becoming sensitive to public charges that they are "rubber stamps" for the superintendent when the board and superintendent share common educational goals for the district's schools and when, because of those common understandings, boards generally are supportive of and act favorably on leadership recommendations. Most of these accusations arise from public misunderstandings of the board's role as policymakers, and some of it also stems from the good working relationships that often exist between boards and superintendents. The stronger the accusation, the stronger the board member's natural desire to separate himself from the superintendent. The concept of an effective board and an effective superintendent working well together should be explored as often and in as many ways as possible without appearing obsessed by the issue.

"Vox Populi, Vox Dei"–II

New voices in front of boards of education are often listened to more seriously than people board members hear often—even when the board and superintendent work well together. In the order of their effectiveness with boards, the strongest and most persuasive voices are primary children, adolescents, town officials, custodians, parents, paraprofessionals, teachers, assistant principals, principals, central office administrators, talking mules, and superintendents of schools.

"And the Greatest of These Is . . ."–I

These three qualities of good board of education members remain: personal security, objectivity, and positive enthusiasm, and the greatest of these is that positive attitude toward public education generally; toward the school district's administrative leadership; toward teachers and other staff members; toward students and parents; toward the town and its leadership; toward being effective, constructive board members; and, of course, the one that gives rise to all the others—toward life and the living of it.

Brave, Loyal, Trustworthy . . .

For board chairmen, five qualities seem most important: knowledge, demonstrated personal leadership, personal security, objectivity, and constructive enthusiasm. Also, chairmen should guide the search for golden means between efficiency and effectiveness, data and intuition, objectivity and leadership responsibility, student needs and district ability to pay, public meetings and meetings held in public, and parliamentary procedure and common sense. Effective chairmen also resist inappropriate pressures; analyze issues thoroughly and request assistance from the staff as needed; really listen to and understand other views; guide the board to make timely decisions; relax about decisions once made, but remain open to changing positions; deal fairly with all factions on the board; act independently of partisan political interests; keep board meetings on track; establish and maintain a tone of courtesy and respect at meetings; understand parliamentary procedures; take the lead in public presentations before other town bodies; are instrumental in development, revision, and use of board of education policies; keep up with statewide educational issues and legislation; let the superintendent know of subterranean community and board currents and issues; publicly support the district's staff; and work effectively with representatives of the media.

Chinese Water Tortures

Superintendents and boards of education should review board committee structures, both the number of standing and ad hoc committees and their responsibilities and operations. Board committees, compared to their productivity, require significant amounts of superintendent time, and decisions made and actions taken by board committees are passed along to other central office staff, building administrators, and teachers. Many superintendents believe that the only standing board of education committee should be the policy committee; all others should be for specific purposes with specific tasks, and specific time schedules—and the fewer in number the better.

"Dammit, I Can So Accept Criticism!"

Although most of us can accept the general premise that we are imperfect human beings and even imperfect educational leaders, we have great difficulty acknowledging specific imperfections. There is no easy cure for this human frailty, nor is there any total immunity from its debilitating effects. Maybe the best psychic resistance to this disease is recognizing its epidemic nature, alertness to its symptoms, and remembering the line from Robert Burns, "Oh wad some Power the giftie gie us to see ourels as ithers see us!" [36].

Dress Rehearsals

Because a major part of superintendents' reputations are made or destroyed at board of education meetings, it's logical that they prepare themselves, their staffs, and board members prior to board meetings. The day of the board meeting, brief dress rehearsals are also good to review outcomes from more extensive earlier sessions, along with highlights of presentations and recommendations to be made at the board of education meeting. When leaders don't examine proposals or solutions thoroughly in rehearsal sessions, someone else will—to their embarrassment.

Let's Be Sure We're All on the Same Page Here

At times, superintendents may prefer to present specific information to all board members together at a meeting, then distribute supportive information and defer action until the subsequent meeting. Simultaneous presentations to board members keep them all on the same page, avoiding varied understandings of prepared material distributed before meetings and members locking themselves into intractable positions before fully understanding the issues.

Oh Yeah!—And You're Another!

A board considering board of education evaluation should discuss its own circumstances thoroughly, along with its readiness for the process. If, after careful consideration, there seems to be consensus supportive of the process, it should go ahead. The results might be painful, but board of education evaluation can also provide real benefits for district education and its students.

One Last Great Act of Defiance

Sometimes, when board of education members have histories of unfounded and unfair public attacks on individual staff members, superintendents may be obliged to take on publicly a few of the people controlling their professional destinies. Sometimes, the results approximate a moment in time after the eagle/mouse confrontation described, and the superintendent may fare no better than did the mouse.

The Parable of the Superintendent and the Duck

Not every fight is worth the pain—your pain or the pain you inflict on others. Superintendents don't need to run at every windmill or fight with boards of education over each issue; sometimes, it's smart to be a good neighbor and let the board keep the duck—unfortunately, occasions do arise when leaders must be prepared to stand up for issues, even at some risk to themselves and their professional careers and to some painful kicks. The trick is to recognize when the fight is worth the potential prize.

Ray Bolger and Other Straw Persons

The "straw man" gambit presents a sacrifical, weak argument contrary to your chosen position and then easily demolishes it; you then indicate that all other positions contrary to yours are equally fallible. Board of education members have refined the straw man into someone closer to Arnold Schwarzenegger. Superintendents of schools should resist using "straw persons" but, more importantly, should avoid placing themselves in vulnerable positions easily assaulted by straw men. School leaders should remain with their strongest positions and not offer weaker ones as easy targets. When they don't have sufficiently strong positions, they are better off waiting until they do.

Rotate the Dancers a Quarter Turn to the Left

Sometimes, it's a good strategy to give a board of education an easy kill on a recommendation you don't care much about anyway so they can subside, sated after showing the superintendent who's in charge here.

CHAPTER 5

Practice Makes Perfect—Summarizing Themes/Main Ideas

Summarize in three or four sentences the themes for each of the following from Chapter 5:

How Did We Get Here from Where?

American law grew from English common law. Federal, state, and local levels of government each have constitutions, judicial systems, and legislative and regulatory bodies.

Faxing Policy Manuals Is Expensive

School district counsel should have board of education policies and administrative regulations, copies of employee agreements, and other frequently used district information available in their offices to facilitate their assistance to the school district.

Fred and Ginger

Access to school district counsel should be limited to one or two people, usually the superintendent and board of education chairman, unless the superintendent approves direct contact by another administrator. This both saves money and facilitates legal business because the parties have built up a functional relationship from frequent work together.

It's the Kids, Stupid!

Decisions should be made on the basis of what is best for students, instead of extraneous reasons such as the possibility of a lawsuit; make correct decisions for the correct reasons, and it's less likely that incorrect decisions will be made for the wrong reasons at some future time.

Junkyard Dogs—I

Avoid nervous attorneys who sidle up to the law, watching it constantly out of the corners of their eyes; instead, seek educational counsel who will grab issues firmly the way junkyard dogs latch onto intruders' ankles.

Junkyard Dogs—II

Particular educational issues require legal review and advice: professional staff contract nonrenewals, terminations, and other significant personnel matters; collective bargaining issues; staff disputes or controversies with potential for grievance arbitrations; state labor relations board hearings; major special education issues; and board of education policies or administrative regulations with greater than usual potential for legal problems.

Legal Pen Pals

Put your queries to attorneys in writing when possible to sharpen the focus of your questions and for a written record of legal responses.

Legal Poultices, Potions, and Elixirs

Lawyers can't guarantee administrators immunity from leadership decisions or actions. When decisions and actions are logical, right for students and staff, and educationally sound, school leaders must accept a degree of legal uncertainty and do what they believe is right.

Lou Holtz, Esq.

School district lawyers will rarely be satisfied with administrative documentation and support of the case at hand, but as soon as they appear before a board or judge or jury, they will claim that this is one of the clearest cases they've ever tried. Nobody wants anybody to think his or her job is simple or easy.

Some of My Best Friends Graduated from Law School

Correspondence, telephone calls, or visits from attorneys should be referred to your counsel. That not only soothes your stomach and calms your disposition, it also lets the guys in the black hats know you're not someone who recently rode into town on a wagonload of wood, and it involves your attorneys early enough to deflect potential lawsuits or to prepare for trials if necessary.

Think First, Then Reach for the Telephone

An attorney's knowledge of case law is of great value, but it's important to understand when legal interpretations or previous judicial decisions should preempt use of common sense. Bad attorneys may claim that their legal dispensations, blessings, and wisdom are required for almost any decisions made in school districts. Although it is important to know what we don't know, it's also important to know what other people don't know any better than we don't know it.

Take Two of These and Call Me in the Morning

Attorneys on retainers may be habit forming, and a possible side effect is overdependence. Even the best attorneys can't see into the future, and a serious side effect of attorneys on call is administrative over-reliance on them to resolve problems that could and should be managed with board policy, administrative regulations, references to past practice, an administrators' own professional knowledge, and common sense.

Discussion Questions

(1) Distinguish common law from constitutional and statutory law.

Common law is case law based on decisions of courts; constitutional law is that governed by federal or state constitutions; statutory law is legislation by Congress and state legislatures.

(2) Summarize (key words as highlights are sufficient) major educational implications of

(a) Article 1, Section 10 of the U.S. Constitution—No State shall pass laws *impairing the Obligation of Contracts.* This article is the *contracts clause.*

(b) First amendment—Congress shall pass no laws that favor *establishment of religion* or *prohibiting the free exercise thereof* or *abridging the freedom of speech or of the press or the right of the people peaceably to assemble, and* the people's right *to petition the government for a redress of grievances.* Supreme Court interpretations of a fourteenth amendment provision make first amendment provisions applicable to states, as well as to the federal government.

(c) Fourth amendment—This provides the right of the people to be secure in their persons, houses, papers, and effects against unreasonable searches and seizures, and no warrants shall issue without probable cause. Court decisions allow school personnel greater latitude in searches of students and school property; *reasonable,* instead of *probable* cause is the usual standard to be met, and the difference is substantive, usually obviating the necessity of warrants prior to searches.

(d) Fifth amendment—This requires an indictment of a grand jury, except in the military or in the militia in time of war; it protects against self-incrimination, requires due process of law, and prohibits private property from being taken for public use without just compensation.

(e) Tenth amendment—Powers not delegated to the United States by the Constitution, nor prohibited by it to the states, are reserved to the states. It is from this "express powers" clause that states derive their control of public education.

(f) Fourteenth amendment—All persons born or naturalized in the United States are U.S. citizens and citizens of their state. No state shall abridge the privileges or immunities of citizens of the United States nor deprive any person of life, liberty, or property without *due process of law*, nor deny to any person within its jurisdiction the *equal protection of the laws*.

(3) Identify the two categories of school cases governed by the first amendment on religious freedoms.

(a) Federal funds used in private schools with religious affiliations

(b) Prohibitions on the free exercise of religion, which may be invoked against employers who act against persons because of any religious affiliations

(4) Distinguish between substantive and procedural due process.

Substantive due process involves insuring that legislative acts are within the legitimate authority of the legislative body, and procedural due process ensures that all legally required actions have been taken in administrative attempts to follow or enforce legitimate statutory intent.

(5) Identify types of education cases under the fourteenth amendment.

Cases involving state educational expenditure formulas for financial support of local school districts and cases of alleged de facto segregation, especially involving minority student concentrations in cities and larger school districts, are covered in this amendment.

(6) Explain briefly the relationship between the federal constitution and state constitutions.

The U.S. Constitution, as interpreted by the U.S. Supreme Court, establishes the framework within which Congressional acts, state constitutions, state legislation, local government ordinances and rules, and board of education policies must fall. Paralleling the U.S. Constitution, the fifty state constitutions provide frameworks for state legislation and have authority over it. State constitutions are interpreted by state judiciary systems and fall within the authority of the U.S. Constitution and federal Congressional legislation.

(7) What is the primary source of statutes affecting public schools?

State legislatures

(8) How do Constitutional limitations affect board of education policies, administrative regulations, and individual teacher regulations?

Board of education policies, administrative regulations, and individual teacher regulations must be consistent with the federal constitution.

(9) Identify the three levels of federal courts.

United States Supreme Court, Federal Circuit Courts of Appeal and United States District Courts throughout the nation and its commonwealths, territories, and the District of Columbia

(*10*) Discuss briefly precedential effect of higher court provisions on lower courts.

Higher court decisions are cited in lower court cases and are guides to lower court decisions.

CHAPTER 8

Practice Makes Perfect—Matching Themes/Main Ideas and Titles

Match the themes/main ideas with subhead titles:

A Chest Full of Ribbons	19
Beat It to Death with a Stick	16
Cause and Effect—A One-Item Intelligence Test	15
Consensus versus the Right to Differ and to Be Different	18
Divergence and Convergence	13
Frequently Understandable, Often Forgivable, Never Acceptable	11
"Fruere Die!"	17
It's What You Do That Gets Me in Trouble	14
I Went to College and You Didn't	7
If You Didn't Hear It Directly, You Didn't Hear It	12
Kitchen Cabinets and Associated Hardware	10
Let's Do It Again Soon	3
Managing Conflict	9
Telephone—II: One Ringy Dingy, Two Ringy Dingies . . .	20
The Captain Made Me Do It	8
The Strange Case of the Gigantic, Nearsighted, English Bulldog	2
Who Is This Person?—II	6
You Can't Tell Anybody Where You Heard This, But . . .	5
You People Aren't as Good as You Think You Are	1
You Are All Set to Retire—As Your Superintendent, I Guarantee It	4

Themes/Main Ideas

(*1*) Beginning a job in a positive manner is more productive than focusing on what is wrong in your new position.

You People Aren't as Good as You Think You Are

(2) People can control their choices of activities far beyond their willingness to admit that.

The Strange Case of the Gigantic, Nearsighted, English Bulldog

(*3*) School district leaders should use effectively the annual educational cycle of rebirth, growth and achievement, and rest and reflection.

Let's Do It Again Soon

(*4*) There are times when it's better not to give advice.

You Are All Set to Retire—As Your Superintendent, I Guarantee It

(*5*) Except in rare crises situations with legal implications, leadership shouldn't use information from staff or others who aren't willing to be identified as the source of the information.

You Can't Tell Anybody Where You Heard This, But . . .

(*6*) It's crucial for the superintendent of schools to be regularly visible in schools and at school and community events.

Who Is This Person?—II

(*7*) We need to remember who we are and from whence we cometh and, even if we come from the aristocracy, invest students with an equal potential to our own.

I Went to College and You Didn't

(*8*) If leaders disagree with directives from above, they should express that disagreement as articulately and forcefully as possible, but if they don't prevail, they should act as if they were their own ideas.

The Captain Made Me Do It

(*9*) Organizational conflict is inevitable, but effective educational leadership usually can make it productive instead of harmful to the school or school district.

Managing Conflict

(*10*) Advisory groups offer invaluable opportunities to school leaders for open communication and for establishing and cementing personal and professional relationships.

Kitchen Cabinets and Associated Hardware

(*11*) Mistakes of consequence should be examined and dissected in detail to find out exactly how they happened to keep them from happening again.

Frequently Understandable, Often Forgivable, Never Acceptable

(*12*) Don't react to individuals on the basis of something allegedly said about you.

If You Didn't Hear It Directly, You Didn't Hear It

(*13*) Leadership should accept the difference between diverging and converging views with objectivity and equanimity because they are inevitable.

Divergence and Convergence

(*14*) Among a school leader's greatest contributions to education is becoming as unnecessary as it's possible to become.

It's What You Do That Gets Me in Trouble

(*15*) Other people's problems with misunderstanding reasons for why events occur are the bane of leadership lives.

Cause and Effect—A One-Item Intelligence Test

(*16*) When issues fade, don't bring them back to be painted again.

Beat It to Death with a Stick

(*17*) Educators should recognize each moment of their lives as "quality time" and cherish each minute, day, and year we're given.

"Fruere Die!"

(*18*) Leadership should work toward group solidarity accompanied by understanding of individual freedom to disagree before decisions are final.

Consensus versus the Right to Differ and to Be Different

(*19*) Teachers do almost all of what the school district exists to do and should be recognized for it.

A Chest Full of Ribbons

(*20*) Office bureaucracies can do major damage to educational causes through cavalier treament of a school district's constituents.

Telephone—II: One Ringy Dingy, Two Ringy Dingies . . .

CHAPTER 9

Collective Bargaining and Contract Implementation Discussion Cases

In determining whether each situation described in Chapter 9 should be considered a prohibited practice, or in other ways illegal, by any of the parties involved in school district collective bargaining, responses should be based on the illustrative state collective bargaining statutes provided in Chapter 9 following the Discussion Cases for that chapter. (Statutes included don't always spell out exactly specific courses of action required, and responses may, in a few instances, need to be deduced from other sections of Chapter 9, from statutory context, and from as much professional experience as may be brought to bear on the case studies. In many of these real-life circumstances, administrative consultation with district counsel would be appropriate and often essential.) Suggested positions/responses/actions; citations (in italics) of specific statutes when possible; and reasons for recommended teacher, administrative, board of education, or other positions/responses/actions are given for the statements of FACTS previously provided in Chapter 9.

(*1*) SUGGESTED POSITION/RESPONSE/ACTION: There are possible legal consequences through an "unfair labor practice" or a "prohibited practice" complaint against the board of education for a unilateral change in administration of the contract—and, possibly, against the union for the same reason. Also, under most negotiated agreements, the union could grieve the superintendent's actions as an inequitable application of the contract. Although not specifically prohibited in statutes, this unilateral conferral of extra contractual benefits is barred by implication of law and through statutory interpretations that see these kinds of actions as *"interference, restraint, coercion . . . or discriminatory practices by an employing board of education or administrative agents or representatives thereof."* If there is a faction on the staff affiliated with a rival teacher association or union, its members may well object to the superintendent's conferring benefits on their competition's leadership.

Employers, or their agents, have no more right to add benefits unilaterally to a contract than they do to take them away unilaterally. The act described can also be viewed as a form of "union busting," wherein employers attempt to manipulate union or association leadership through paternalistic, or maternalistic, conferring of benefits on those who please them. If this is done successfully, it may cause employees to question the need for employee organizations because school district leadership appears so benign and benevolent.

(2) SUGGESTED POSITION/RESPONSE/ACTION: In this instance, the labor relations board probably could care less about your problem with the board of education on dental insurance. In defining good faith bargaining, the law is clear that neither party is required to accept the other's proposals.

> *"To negotiate in good faith" is the performance of the mutual obligation of the board of education or its representatives or agents and the organization designated or elected as the exclusive representative for the appropriate unit to meet at reasonable times, including meetings appropriately related to the budget-making process, and to participate actively so as to indicate a present intention to reach agreement with respect to salaries, hours and other conditions of employment, or the negotiation of an agreement, or any question arising thereunder and the execution of a written contract incorporating any agreement reached if requested by either party, but such obligation shall not compel either party to agree to a proposal or require the making of a concession.*

(3) SUGGESTED POSITION/RESPONSE/ACTION: This would likely be viewed as a prohibited practice through a transgression of state law, which states, "Members of the teaching profession shall have . . . the right to form, join or assist, or refuse to form, join or assist, any organization for professional or economic improvement . . . *free from interference, restraint, coercion or discriminatory practices by any employing board of education or administrative agents or representatives thereof."*

The legal remedy would be a prohibited practice or unfair labor practice complaint. The practical remedy would be for the superintendent to tell the building principal to stay out of the teachers' room and keep his mouth closed until the election is over—and afterwards, for that matter, unless his judgment improves dramatically.

(*4*) SUGGESTED POSITION/RESPONSE/ACTION: This is a very different situation from that described in #3 above where an agent of the board was behaving inappropriately. Laws can't, and don't try to, compel civility among employees, and in this instance, both the teacher and her organization just have to get over it.

(*5*) SUGGESTED POSITION/RESPONSE/ACTION: Yes, there are, under the section of state statutes that, in outlining eligibility for membership in certified bargaining groups, states, "*The superintendent of schools, assistant superintendents, <u>certified professional employees</u> who act for the board of education in negotiations with certified professional personnel or are <u>directly responsible to the board of education for personnel relations or budget preparation</u>, temporary substitutes, and all noncertified employees of the board of education are excluded from the purview of this section.*"

The reason for excluding these personnel is the belief they would have "insider trading information," which could place the employer at an unfair disadvantage (as opposed to a fair disadvantage) in negotiations with employees.

(*6*) SUGGESTED POSITION/RESPONSE/ACTION: This is one of those fact situations to which recommended positions/responses/actions must be inferred from a number of statutes, rather than being found in a single specific citation; however, the teachers' proposal is inappropriate because paraprofessionals have the same rights, although under municipal law rather than educational law, to form and join employee organizations for their own improvement. Although the flow of rivers, other fluids, and even noxious semifluids may be downhill, teachers have no greater right to negotiate working conditions for paraprofessionals than aides do for teachers in aides' collective bargaining agreements.

(*7*) SUGGESTED POSITION/RESPONSE/ACTION: This appears to be another example of administrative interference in the rights of employees to form and join, but good legal arguments can be made by school district counsel that a superintendent has the right to communicate factual information to employees at any time—and that such actions aren't interference with the "form and join" right under the law. In this instance, however, although some may empathize with the superintendent's good intentions, her/his assumptions that previous good working relationships are a fact and that a loss of good working relationships among the management team could result from formation of a bargaining unit are both questionable at best.

Had the superintendent's memorandum been abbreviated so s/he only cited current administrative association membership costs and asked each administrator to weigh carefully the relative advantages and disadvantages of forming an administrative bargaining unit, including financial advantages and disadvantages, the chances of a successful labor board action would have been reduced significantly. In either case, however, the decision could depend upon who investigates the complaint and his or her disposition that day.

In balance, the superintendent would be safer not writing the note or, if s/he feels compelled to share a point of view on the topic, to abbreviate it so there's no argument about it being factual — or better yet, don't write it, but say it personally and informally.

(8) SUGGESTED POSITION/RESPONSE/ACTION: You've been very patient in accepting the first two incidents without screaming to another authority. You probably have a successful labor relations board complaint that the board isn't bargaining in good faith. Sections 10-153a to 10-153c, inclusive, and Section 10-153g require the parties "to negotiate in good faith" and compel "the performance of the mutual obligation of the board of education or its representatives or agents and the organization . . . *to meet at reasonable times . . . and to participate actively so as to indicate a present intention to reach agreement.* Under these circumstances, your assertion would be a strong one that the board's behavior doesn't indicate active participation or an intention to reach agreement.

From your perspective, the probable labor board's order to the board of education to meet with you, as required by law, would be satisfying — but probably wouldn't change the outcome of collective bargaining. But making sloppy people look bad publicly may be a gratifying necessity once in a while, even with the attendant potential drawbacks of making an already surly group even surlier.

(9) SUGGESTED POSITION/RESPONSE/ACTION: This one's relatively easy because the laws specifically permit agency shops:

> *Nothing in this section . . . shall preclude a local or regional board of education from making an agreement with an exclusive bargaining representative to require as a condition of employment that all employees in a bargaining unit pay to the exclusive bargaining representative of such employees an annual service fee, not greater than the amount of dues uniformly required of members of the exclusive bargaining representative organization, which represents the costs of collective bargaining, contract administration and grievance adjustment; and that such service fee be collected by means of a payroll deduction from each employee in the bargaining unit.*

Also, the statutory provision that requires the parties *"to negotiate in good faith through representatives of their own choosing with respect to salaries, hours and other conditions of employment,"* absent a further provision excluding "agency shop" from among negotiations issues, as is done for school hours and school calendars in the same section of the law, requires board negotiations on the issue.

An important point to stress to the board chairperson is that negotiations don't compel agreement, although, in this instance, because such provisions are in the vast majority of negotiated agreements, the teachers' bargaining unit may well prevail if the issue were taken to arbitration.

(*10*) SUGGESTED POSITION/RESPONSE/ACTION: This is another situation where specific statutory authority doesn't exist to guide you. A practical argument can be made against a nontenured teacher's service as a negotiator, because it could add to his potential problems with the board through his active participation in an adversarial, although often civilized, role with board members—particularly the chairman.

However, from the perspective of a teacher organization, such service might be a partial immunity against his potential problems with the board; if, for whatever reason, the board moved to nonrenew or dismiss the nontenured teacher, he could cite his service as a negotiator and claim the board was committing a prohibited practice through illegal retaliation against him for the proper exercise of his rights under the statutes that prohibit boards from *"interfering, restraining or coercing certified professional employees in the exercise of the rights guaranteed . . . [by statute]."*

From the teacher's perspective, if the situation had already deteriorated to the point that the teacher and the organization were convinced that he was almost certain to be terminated or nonrenewed, the partial immunity theory might be worth testing.

(*11*) SUGGESTED POSITION/RESPONSE/ACTION: Class size is not excluded from the purview of collective bargaining, so the team member's rejection of the teacher's proposal on the grounds that class size is not negotiable is not legally sound. Yes, it's possible that running a bluff and taking an inappropriate position could work to the board's advantage if teachers were discouraged from pursuing a legitimate proposal; the worst legal outcome is that the labor board would order the board of education to negotiate in good faith on class size.

Taking an illegal position is clearly wrong on legal grounds, clearly wrong on ethical grounds (which often don't enter into negotiations but which should be part of the process), and of small consequence on practical grounds, but, as has been stated a number of times earlier in this exercise, negotiations don't compel agreements on specific proposals anyway, so why put yourself in a poor legal position? If the issue were later taken to arbitration, status quo usually prevails.

Boards have good practical arguments against these provisions, although many contracts contain them—fortunately for boards, the articles are often relatively innocuous such as, "Within budgetary constraints, the board will make reasonable efforts to maintain class sizes consistent with reasonable educational standards as defined by the superintendent of schools (or the board of education)." Within this wording, there's not much risk for a board of education.

(*12*) SUGGESTED POSITION/RESPONSE/ACTION: In last best offer arbitration, arbitrators must choose one of the parties' positions and may not award something between those positions. Although there are other relatively unpredictable factors, such as the financial resources of your district and its ability to pay for the eventual arbitration award, if prevailing area settlements are three percent, the board's zero percent offer is somewhat risky.

Statutes require arbitrators to give priority to "*. . . the public interest and the financial capability of the town or towns in the school district, including consideration of other demands on the financial capability of the town or towns in the school district.*" Also to be considered, in light of such financial capability, are the following:

> *(A) The negotiations between the parties prior to arbitration, including the offers and the range of discussion of the issues; (B) the interests and welfare of the employee group; (C) changes in the cost of living averaged over the preceding three years; (D) the existing conditions of employment of the employee group and those of similar groups; and (E) the salaries, fringe benefits, and other conditions of employment prevailing in the state labor market, including the terms of recent contract settlements or awards in collective bargaining for other municipal employee organizations and developments in private sector wages and benefits.*

If teachers come into arbitration at three, or even four percent, their position would be closer to the area norm and could become the arbitrator's position. Two percent might be a reasonable board offer on the expectation teachers will come in at four—at which point it becomes a toss-up, and the other factors arbitrators must consider weigh more heavily. If the other side's last offer is five or more, the board's two percent offer is closer to the norm.

Although it's always a gamble considering all the variables in the statute's provisions, *two percent* seems to be a reasonably safe board position with the smallest risk of major loss. However, an equivocation may be in order; if the board can prove the town is on the brink of financial ruin, arbitrators could choose the zero percent offer—that has happened a few times.

(*13*) SUGGESTED POSITION/RESPONSE/ACTION: The law is clear that a board of finance, or other fiscal authority, has the right to be represented at negotiation sessions following the requisite performance of the ritual minuet between the board of education and the board of finance—in which the board of finance pleads town poverty and the board of education argues it must keep up with other district Joneses.

> ***Meeting between board of education and fiscal authority required. Duty to negotiate. Procedure if legislative body rejects contract.*** . . . *Within thirty days prior to the date on which the* . . . *board of education is to commence negotiations* . . . *such board of education shall meet and confer with the board of finance in each town or city having a board of finance, with the board of selectmen in each town having no board of finance and otherwise with the authority making appropriations therein.* <u>*A member of such board of finance, such board of selectmen, or such other authority making appropriations, shall be permitted to be present during negotiations pursuant to this section and shall provide such fiscal information as may be requested by the board of education.*</u>

For practical and tactical reasons, many school attorneys do not advise this course of action, but argue that the board of finance's right to be present during negotiations is qualified and doesn't require a board of education to allow fiscal authority representatives' participation in, or even attendance at, board negotiating team caucuses during bargaining sessions. Most lawyers assert that the board of finance representative has no right to speak at negotiating sessions and is in attendance only as an observer and to help the board of education with necessary fiscal information to its negotiating team.

(*14*) SUGGESTED POSITION/RESPONSE/ACTION: Legally, you have every right to be a hard-nosed "whatever" and stonewall the union representative's request. The contract is negotiated. That's it. Case closed. But what's the big deal here; be a nice person, or a soft-nosed negotiator, and draw up a sidebar agreement, or memorandum of understanding, and take care of the union's request for dues deductions. With everything computerized these days, it's no problem for the school district administration to be reasonable in this instance, especially considering how the dues deduction appears to have been omitted from the current contract. Dues deductions are the lifeblood of the union, and if there's a reasonable "quid pro quo" you want, this may be a good opportunity to get it.

(*15*) SUGGESTED POSITION/RESPONSE/ACTION: Unless you want the state's human rights commission on your case or, even worse, the EEOC, you'd better persuade your team member to forget about it. His position is clearly discriminatory against women and inappropriate in all respects. *"Discrimination on account of marital status. No local or regional board of education shall discriminate on the basis of sex or marital status in the employment of teachers in the public schools or in the determination of the compensation to be paid to such teachers."*

(*16*) SUGGESTED POSITION/RESPONSE/ACTION: Tell your fellow negotiators to rest easy, because the board has negotiated the issue in good faith on three occasions but just didn't agree with your position. If the issue is important enough to your union, it will be heard again in mediation and arbitration.

(*17*) SUGGESTED POSITION/RESPONSE/ACTION: You do, indeed, have effective recourse in the form of a prohibited labor practice charge against either or both parties, probably more effectively against the teacher organization.

Statutory provisions on this subject are clear that the annual service fee shall not be greater *"than the amount of dues uniformly required of members of the exclusive bargaining representative organization, which represents the costs of collective bargaining, contract administration and grievance adjustment; and that such service fee be collected by means of a payroll deduction from each employee in the bargaining unit."* This provision usually means a fee of somewhere between sixty percent and ninety percent of regular membership, depending upon what claims the union or association makes about costs of collective bargaining, contract administration, and grievance adjustment. The union or association must be able to prove, if challenged, how much it spends for ". . . the costs of collective bargaining, contract administration and grievance adjustment." They would have a hell of a time proving they spend more than a hundred percent of dues collected this way—or any way.

Also "an organization of certified professional employees . . . is prohibited from . . . interfering, restraining or coercing . . . certified professional employees in the exercise of the rights guaranteed . . . providing that this shall not impair the right of an employees' bargaining agent or representative to prescribe its own rules with respect to acquisition or retention of membership *provided such rules are not discriminatory."* These rules are discriminatory against nonmembers.

(*18*) SUGGESTED POSITION/RESPONSE/ACTION: A couple of small points are noted, such as (1) an assistant superintendent who didn't think it important to discuss with you in advance his appearance as a spokesperson for the administrative bargaining unit and (2) an assistant superintendent who has little or no knowledge of collective bargaining laws: *"The superintendent of schools, assistant superintendents, certified professional employees who act for the board of education in negotiations with certified professional personnel or are directly responsible to the board* of education for personnel relations or budget preparation, temporary substitutes, and all noncertified employees of the board of education are excluded from the purview of this section. . . ."

(*19*) SUGGESTED POSITION/RESPONSE/ACTION: The board has every right to choose "Vlad the Impaler" as its spokesman if he again becomes available, and the concern that he's the "worst, most arbitrary, least respectful . . ." is just something the teachers must learn to live with. This isn't to say a board should choose an obnoxious spokesman, but only that the law allows this choice. *"An organization of certified professional employees or its agents is prohibited from . . . interfering, restraining or coercing . . . a board of education in the selection of its representatives or agents."*

(*20*) SUGGESTED POSITION/RESPONSE/ACTION: Don't just do something, sit there! You will have your chances later, on the board of education budget.[209]

(*21*) SUGGESTED POSITION/RESPONSE/ACTION: Yes, it's legally appropriate, even if maybe tactically unsound, because statutes only authorize the board of finance to be present during negotiations, usually defined by attorneys as "actual negotiations exclusive of caucuses."[209]

(*22*) SUGGESTED POSITION/RESPONSE/ACTION: The statute requires a certified employee bargaining unit to prepare *"a written response to such rejection and shall submit it to the legislative body or legislative bodies, as appropriate, and the commissioner"* which will be considered by the second arbitration panel, but *allows* the board of education to make a choice about whether or not to submit a written response.

In this instance, both factions on the board are legally correct, and you should tell them that. However, the board of education shouldn't take the decision of the second arbitration panel for granted; if its members want the original arbitration upheld, a written response to the legislative body's contract rejection should be prepared and sent, stating that position and the board's reasons for it.

> *Mediation and arbitration of disagreements. (c) (7) . . . Within ten days after receipt of such notice [legislative body rejection of an initial arbitration award] the exclusive representative of the teachers' or administrators' unit shall prepare, and the board of education may prepare, a written response to such rejection and shall submit it to the legislative body or legislative bodies, as appropriate, and the commissioner. . . . The review conducted [of the legislative body's rejection of the initial arbitration award] pursuant to this subdivision shall be limited to the record and briefs of the hearing pursuant to subdivision (2) of this subsection, the written explanation of the reasons for the vote, and a written response by either party. . . .*

[209]See also, this appendix, Case #13.

(*23*) SUGGESTED POSITION/RESPONSE/ACTION: Zero recourse because the statute excludes this issue from its list of mandatory collective bargaining issues:

> *The local or regional board of education and the . . . exclusive representative for the appropriate unit . . . shall have the duty to negotiate with respect to salaries, hours and other conditions of employment about which either party wishes to negotiate. For purposes of this subsection . . . (1) "hours" shall not include the length of the student school year;* the scheduling of the student school year; *the length of the student school day; the length and number of parent teacher conferences; and the scheduling of the student school day, except for the length and the scheduling of teacher lunch periods and teacher preparation periods. . . .*

(*24*) SUGGESTED POSITION/RESPONSE/ACTION: Don't do it! It's illegal. *"**Residency requirement prohibited.** No municipality or school district shall require that an individual reside within the municipality or school district as a condition for appointment or continued employment as a school teacher."*

(*25*) SUGGESTED POSITION/RESPONSE/ACTION: How about "Move to another state until all this blows over." Absent that unlikely eventuality, the board's attorney should (1) immediately obtain an injunction from superior court for the union's deliberate violation of statute and (2) file a prohibited practice complaint with the state labor relations board against the union for the actions of their president and against any teachers who followed his requests. The fact that the board of education spokesperson acted inappropriately doesn't excuse the union's "sick-in."

The board must also signal its willingness to negotiate, although not required to agree, on the teacher proposal as soon as the major battle is resolved.

Attendance records should be used to deduct salary amounts for each day teachers were absent during this period of work stoppage and the burden placed on the union to justify teacher absences during the "sick-in" on any legitimate grounds that might exist in individual cases. In obvious circumstances, such as a teacher's having been confined in a medical facility for two weeks prior to the illegal action, the superintendent may grant a dispensation for the absence.

> *No certified professional employee shall, in an effort to effect a settlement of any disagreement with the employing board of education, engage in any strike or concerted refusal to render services. This provision may be enforced in the superior court for any judicial district in which said board of education is located by an injunction issued by said court or a judge thereof. . . . A prohibited practice committed by a board of education, its representatives or agents shall not be a defense to an illegal strike or concerted refusal to render services.*

Grievance Simulations

Using the teacher contract (WFCT) or the administrator contract (WASA) in Appendix A, provide written administrative decisions on the Grievance Simulations provided in Chapter 9. Suggested administrative responses are provided in this appendix. For purposes of these exercises, unless otherwise stated, you are a building principal who has held the informal discussion required in Step 1 of the grievance procedure and could not resolve the issue at that point. Reading grievance procedures in each contract before beginning the exercise is recommended. *(In the WFCT contract, although the contract wording isn't as clear as it should be, Step 1 is the informal discussion with the teacher's immediate supervisor, and Step 2 is the formal meeting with the supervisor.)*

THE ADMINISTRATIVE HEARING OFFICER

Your choices as the administrator hearing the grievances are either to grant the redress sought by the grievant, at which point the grievance ends, or you may reject the grievance, and the grievant must then make a decision whether or not to proceed formally to the next step of the grievance procedure. It's good procedure for administrators faced with a grievance to have discussed it with their superintendent prior to making a decision at their level—this is neither inappropriate nor prejudicial to a later decision when grievances reach a higher level. It's a normal and expected part of the grievance process.

Examples of various grievance froms are given in Chapter 9, and the suggested grievance responses for the simulated grievances, with reasons therefor, follow:

(1) RECOMMENDED ADMINISTRATIVE RESPONSE: Reject the grievance, because a grievance can only be brought successfully under this contract for an alleged violation of his/her rights under the specific language of the contract or that for him/her there has been a misapplication or misinterpretation of the specific provisions of the agreement. The grievance is defective because it cites no contract article alleged to have been violated, misinterpreted, or misapplied.

There is, however, a significant problem with past practice here, and a labor relations board complaint charging the board of education with violation of past practice could well ensue if an improper labor practice charge were to be filed with that body. The board then would be ordered to negotiate such assignments with the union, rather than imposing them unilaterally.

(2) RECOMMENDED ADMINISTRATIVE RESPONSE: Although this grievance might be rejected on the grounds that assigning paraprofessionals is not practicable, if that is his or her decision, the principal should be sure

that he or she truly had no "practicable" alternatives. This decision should be checked with the superintendent first to see how he or she feels about defending this possible grievance rejection.

(*3*) RECOMMENDED ADMINISTRATIVE RESPONSE: Accept the grievance as substantive and review possible corrective measures with the superintendent. Although twenty-five is the contractual "desirable maximum" class size for grade five, and the district has not exceeded the "maximum established" by more than five students, the contract further states

> *that if class size enrollment exceeds the maximum established, the Board should endeavor to correct the situation by the employment of one of the following, whichever is most practicable: 1) hiring a new teacher, 2) hiring a paraprofessional, 3) reassignment of students, or 4) transfer of students. The use of classroom paraprofessionals should be a measure only for the remainder of any one (1) school year.*

It seems clear that the principal, or the superintendent if the grievance were to be rejected by the principal because he or she feels unable to solve the problem at the building level, is obliged to use the most "practicable" of the four options listed in the agreement for at least the remainder of the current school year. It's also important for the superintendent to review other district class sizes to be sure he or she understands the potential scope of the union issue at this time.

The statement in the agreement that *"the following school year a balance should be reached by the opening of a new class at the appropriate grade level or by one of the alternatives stated above"* is ambiguous and easily circumvented by Machiavellian administrators (some would argue that "Machiavellian" is a redundant description of administrators) by regrouping students and leaving one of the sixth-grade classes at twenty-seven – at which point, one of the less expensive solutions could be used again for the remainder of that school year, and so on, until the students reached middle school and other kinds of classroom arrangements from the often self-contained elementary patterns.

(*4*) RECOMMENDED ADMINISTRATIVE RESPONSE: Reject the grievance; contract wording in Article 37, Class Size, allows unlimited class sizes in the class size article, which states: *"Exceptions to the above desirable maximums shall be acceptable in music 7–8, physical education, chorus, band, study halls and library classes."* This isn't to say you may not want to alleviate class sizes of 45 per period in physical education, but it is to say you should do so outside of the grievance process.

(*5*) RECOMMENDED ADMINISTRATIVE RESPONSE: Reject the grievance only if you are prepared to defend your judgment that transferring each of the people with less seniority than the transferred teacher would have been "detrimental to the best interests of students." You might deal with a rejection of the grievance more positively through argument that the transferred teacher is so qualified for the particular position that anyone else in that assignment would have been detrimental to students' best interests—rather than trying to prove the relative incompetence of all junior teachers.

If the transfer were done without thought of a potential grievance, which shouldn't be the case but sometimes is, your best position might be to work out the best deal possible, depending upon the time of year the grievance is brought and the complexities of backing off an earlier imperfect decision.

This might be a difficult case before the board of education and especially in arbitration unless your reasons for transferring a more senior teacher are sound.

(6) RECOMMENDED ADMINISTRATIVE RESPONSE: Accept the grievance, and turn over all materials to the superintendent in the central office; you are probably in violation of Article 42, Personnel Files, part of which states: *"There shall be only one official personnel file per teacher to be kept in the central office. Information not contained in the above official file shall not be used in any way against the teacher at any hearing, disciplinary action or meeting concerning the teacher."*

(7) RECOMMENDED ADMINISTRATIVE RESPONSE: Reject the grievance unless you want to open the proverbial can of wrigglers and review all administrative personnel files for similarly unnecessary concessions. The contract requires that administrators *"shall be placed on a step equivalent to years of experience <u>as a public school administrator</u> in the position, or a substantially equivalent position, for which the administrator is hired."*

(8) RECOMMENDED ADMINISTRATIVE RESPONSE: Give her the money, because there has been a district error. The grievance was also filed in a timely way, only a day after the period ended in which she could have been, and should have been, paid.

(9) RECOMMENDED ADMINISTRATIVE RESPONSE: Article 8 changes the amount paid from $400 annually to $1,400, commencing with the twentieth year of teaching. Unfortunately, the grievance was filed late—sixty days after the teacher "knew or should have known" of the mistake, and the contract only allows thirty days from the time she knew or should have known of the error. Although the grievance could be rejected on a technicality, only a bureaucratic misanthrope would do so, even at the risk of having to live with similarly untimely grievances in the future. When responsible district administrators err this egregiously, they should make good on the contract intent, even when it might be possible to weasel out of it. Others may disagree and insist on rejection because of untimeliness—different strokes . . .

(10) RECOMMENDED ADMINISTRATIVE RESPONSE: You may need to call your attorney on this one unless the association cooperates fully with you in this instance. Although the Association *"agrees to indemnify and save the Board harmless from all claims, demands, lawsuits or other forms of liability arising from the Board's fulfillment of its obligations under this Article,"* the deduction is incorrect under the contract provision, which also states, *"All members of the bargaining unit employed by the Board shall, as a condition of continued employment, join WASA or pay WASA a service fee. Said service fee shall be equal to the proportion of WASA dues uniformly required of members to underwrite the costs of collective bargaining, contract administration and grievance adjustment."*

Either the Association didn't supply the figures to the business office as required, in which case the business manager should have gone after them—or they did, and the business office made another mistake. In either case, the superintendent should involve the Association immediately, before the grievance hearing is held, and try to resolve the issue before the hearing under the auspices of the contract provision that says, *"WASA shall have the right to compromise or settle any claim or lawsuit against the Board under this Article, but shall not do so without Board approval, such approval not to be unreasonably withheld."* Somehow, the principal should have some money returned, but granting this particular redress will require Association cooperation.

(11) RECOMMENDED ADMINISTRATIVE RESPONSE: Give her the money and in the same year it was requested. The contract says only that such payment will be made after ten years of service in the district—not ten consecutive years.

> *Salary Adjustment. Teachers shall receive during the last year prior to retirement, after ten (10) years or more service in the district, an increase in pay of Eight Hundred Twenty-Five Dollars ($825) for that year. Application for such increase in pay must be made to the superintendent of schools by September 15 of the year prior to the school year in which retirement is planned for the increase to be paid in that final year of teaching—otherwise, the increase shall be paid in the school year following retirement."*

(12) RECOMMENDED ADMINISTRATIVE RESPONSE: Take two aspirin, fire the business manager, call your attorney, ask him or her to intercede with the insurance company, dust off your resume, call your friends who do superintendent searches, notify the board of education of the screw-up, take your phone off the hook, and read a good book until an angry board chairman appears at your door.

If your insurance company is within its rights not to pay under the terms of its contract with the district, and it's also clear major medical claims would have been paid absent the business manager's horrendous error, the district will inevitably be required to come up with the funds.

(13) RECOMMENDED ADMINISTRATIVE RESPONSE: Pay the principal her money and call the director of personnel into your office for an attention-getting chat—a two-by-four is optional. The contract makes no distinction between preapproved courses taken while on sabbatical leave and those taken while not on sabbatical leave, and because you had approved the course, the personnel director should certainly have been bright enough to touch base with you prior to his denial of course reimbursement.

(14) RECOMMENDED ADMINISTRATIVE RESPONSE: Possibly, this is a new personnel director, but he or she managed to get this one right. First, the teacher doesn't claim to have taught over half the school year, which is the wording in Article 20, Leave of Absence, but even if he so claimed, he didn't. Although the article would be improved through requiring a specific number of days, the minimum the teacher would be required to teach to earn credit for the year would be ninety-one days in a 180-day school year. With school years growing slightly longer because of negotiated agreements adding a few professional days to a teacher's obligation, changing "over half a school year" to the correct number of days that must be taught and spelling out whether days without students count as days taught would clarify the issue—even though it's not bad with the present words.
Reject the grievance.

(15) RECOMMENDED ADMINISTRATIVE RESPONSE: Reject the grievance; she doesn't have a case; Article 25, Sabbatical Leave, says the board *may*, not *shall*, grant sabbatical leaves under the conditions specified.

(16) RECOMMENDED ADMINISTRATIVE RESPONSE: Reject the grievance. The contract doesn't say every teacher must play a role in curriculum development, just that teachers shall be actively involved as a group.

(17) RECOMMENDED ADMINISTRATIVE RESPONSE: Another puny grievance that should be rejected as insubstantial and not a contract violation. Article 32 states only that, *"Upon request, a teacher shall be informed at which level a budget item has been cut,"* and provides no guidance on specific amounts of teaching supplies to be provided by the district. Again, a look at this outside the grievance process is certainly in order.

(18) RECOMMENDED ADMINISTRATIVE RESPONSE: Article 33, Meetings and Extra Work Scheduled by Administration, states only:

> *Attendance at parent-teacher association/organization meetings is considered to be a professional obligation for all teachers for the back-to-*

school night and any night the teacher is part of the program. In the event of a time conflict between a parent-teacher association/organization meeting and a college or university course, the teacher shall be excused by the immediate supervisor at his/her discretion from the parent-teacher association/organization meeting.

Assuming from data presented in this simulation that the teacher didn't skip any parent-teacher meetings when he was on the program, he met his specific obligation under Article 33, and the principal can't cite the teacher for any contractual violations. However, there's nothing in the contract either that protects a teacher against hearing the principal's point of view about what a teacher's professional obligation should be.

Reject the grievance, but suggest to the principal that, although you may agree with his point of view, he be more careful with his comments when he has no contractual justification for his teacher critiques.

(*19*) RECOMMENDED ADMINISTRATIVE RESPONSE: Let's hope it's not the same principal. One of the requirements of effective grievance procedures is that the grievant indicate a specific redress sought if his or her grievance is upheld. In this instance, if the grievant asked that the principal butt out of their meetings called within the authority of Article 34, you should grant his wish, remind the principal of the provisions of the contract, and inform the principal that similar errors in judgment may be dealt with more harshly.

(*20*) RECOMMENDED ADMINISTRATIVE RESPONSE: Phrased as nicely as possible, tell her to get lost also because she has no grievance. Reject the grievance, but indicate your willingness to discuss your reasons for particular discipline, or the lack thereof, with her or other teachers at any time as a normal part of your day as principal.

(*21*) RECOMMENDED ADMINISTRATIVE RESPONSE: Reject the grievance because there has been no contract violation. The only prohibitions under terms of Article 38, Classroom Collections, are collections for "school pictures, lunch, dental, or pupil insurance programs." The contract says teachers are responsible for other collections assigned by the principal other than those specifically barred.

(*22*) RECOMMENDED ADMINISTRATIVE RESPONSE: Reject the grievance. Your case is strong, and you have minimum to nonexistent vulnerability in arbitration under Article 18e. Following the general prohibition *"Personal leave shall not be used to extend holidays or vacation periods,"* the article continues, *"The Superintendent may waive requirements in this article if in his or her judgment there are extenuating circumstances that justify such action."* Implicit in these words under paragraph e is the superintendent's clear right *not to waive* requirements in this article if in his or her judgment there are *no* extenuating circumstances that justify such action.

(23) RECOMMENDED ADMINISTRATIVE RESPONSE: Reject the grievance. The teacher missed the deadline to be paid in June, which requires him to notify the superintendent during the first pay period in June. But he can relax, because he will receive payment under Article 22 within a few days, since the new fiscal year begins July 1—possibly by the time his grievance is heard by the superintendent.

> *Teachers, upon retirement in accordance with the State Teacher Retirement Act or death, after ten (10) years of serivce in the district, the last five (5) of which must be consecutive, shall receive payment of up to forty-three (43) school days of unused sick leave. The payment shall be made in the first pay period of June of the year of retirement. If notification is not given by that date, sick pay shall be made payable in the first pay period in the fiscal year following retirement.*

(24) RECOMMENDED ADMINISTRATIVE RESPONSE: The business manager's information is crucial—reject the grievance. Specific provisions of Section VI include: *"Those employees not contributing to the sick leave bank may not participate in it."*

(25) RECOMMENDED ADMINISTRATIVE RESPONSE: Reject the grievance. The relevant words in Article 28 are that, *"Five (5) preparation periods per week are regarded as desirable for teachers,"* not that they *must be provided.* But a contract article that can only be met to forty percent of its stated intent isn't a good situation for superintendents to live with, and it would be much better to either negotiate a change providing a more realistic target or move closer to compliance with current wording.

CHAPTER 11

Practice Makes Perfect—Excerpts

Match the following titles with the correct extract(s); some titles will have more than one excerpt.

A Confederacy of Dunces	6, 14
Could Socrates Survive the Superintendency?	11, 16
"Dead before Takeoff"	3
Don't You Realize How Dangerous It Is Out There?	9
Holiday Nuts to Staff	5
Just a Red Ant in the Noonday Sun	8, 15
Lanterns in the Window	10
May I Have the Envelope Please?	24
Old Dogs, New Tricks	7

Excerpts

(1) Although I'm sure you already have, take a close look at the crowd at your next budget or town meeting when an issue has heated up the political climate. Too many of those present are wild-eyed, foam-flecked angries living lives of "noisy desperation"; too many of the town or district's comparatively well-adjusted people are at home watching a TV ball game with a beer or a sherry in one hand, patting their spouse on his or her backside with the other. An Irish poet, who undoubtedly had attended many such meetings, captured this school district dilemma when he wrote, "The best lack all conviction while the worst are full of passionate intensity" [14].

The Best Lack All Conviction . . .

(2) Therefore, it's important for educators to be poised, enthusiastic, willing, and able to impart 180 days of wisdom, knowledge, attitudes, facts, and skills on Tuesdays and Thursdays during those two available April weeks.

School Calendars—I

(3) But before superintendents accept new positions, they should understand the choices they are making before they no longer have any choices to make.

"Dead before Takeoff"

(4) Interviewers often ask administrative aspirants, whether for the superintendency or a principalship or a director's position, what qualities they have admired in those for whom they have worked and what qualities those same people exhibited that the candidate would not want to emulate. It's a revealing question, not only of the strengths and weaknesses of the applicant's former bosses, but of the candidate him or herself and of his or her professional and personal insights and values.

Rabbis—II

(5) When John Milton wrote, "When I consider how my light is spent . . ."

[72] he was, among other things, reminding some of us to keep our eyeglasses close by.

Holiday Nuts to Staff

(6) Nobody ever said public life was devoid of frustrations—or that every member of the general public, all staff, each board of education member, every parent, all town officials, all students, and every other person and groups of persons with whom school leadership is in professional contact will always be intelligent, insightful, open, empathetic, tolerant, emotionally secure, flexible, well motivated, or any other way you'd prefer them to be.

A Confederacy of Dunces

(7) One significant administrative opportunity to adjust or modify personal and professional behaviors occurs when superintendents, principals, assistant superintendents, and other administrators change positions—from one superintendency to another; from one principalship to another; from a principalship to an assistant superintendency, a superintendency, or some other central office position; from an assistant superintendency to a superintendency; or from any administrative position to another administrative position. At these special times, the leader isn't working against strong, preconceived perceptions of him or her, and all personal and professional leadership changes have a much better chance of being recognized and appreciated. Also, there is a lack of self-consciousness when leaders work with new colleagues who accept their new and possibly improved behaviors without puzzling over them because they are new.

Old Dogs New Tricks

(8) The superintendent didn't fully empathize with ants until he became a superintendent of schools and had to endure state education department bureaucracies with their circles of heat generated by too many dangerously enthusiastic middle management chiefs. Many of these energetic men and women, unforunately, have nothing better to do than crisp superintendents the way he did his boyhood ant victims. Experiences with state education department functionaries made him further regret the way he had treated his little red ant buddies.

Just a Red Ant in the Noonday Sun

(9) The year's first snowfall of any consequence is the most dangerous of the season. Over the spring, summer, and early fall months, automobiles and buses somehow forget how to climb slippery hills and how to stop at intersections; vehicles require a period of retraining for the long winter ahead.

Don't You Realize How Dangerous It Is Out There?

(*10*) The ensuing ambush and massacre have already been best described in English verse.

Lanterns in the Window

(*11*) Regardless of any unfair disqualifications of these well-known historical personages, it remains true that public positions today are not for everyone—only a select few measure up to their rigors and demands. Unlike the superintendent's or other official's divergent view of the world looking outward at hundreds and even thousands of people, he or she is the focus of intensely convergent views from staff, parents and the general public, board members, town officials, and others. Every personal and professional flaw is magnified by this close scrutiny, and only the strong and the lucky can survive it forever.

Could Socrates Survive the Superintendency?

(*12*) One sunny afternoon years ago, as a number of visitors to "The Point" lazed cozily in post-martini euphorias, enjoying the outstanding view from their automobiles over Stonington Harbor, a pair of carrier-based seagulls swooped low out of the sun, searching for targets of opportunity—they found some beauties.

The wingman did what many superintendents would like to do, but that few can afford to do; he made a sizable deposit on a new Mercedes. The flight leader simultaneously devastated the monument, thereby accomplishing what few superintendents intend to do, but which many do well even if accidentally—he obfuscated the message.

"This Is to Remember . . .

(*13*) Ah, well . . .

The Conscience of a Shellfish

(*14*) It's counterproductve to indulge yourself this way. It comes across clearly to others, even to dunces, and this makes working with them constructively and productively almost impossible.

A Confederacy of Dunces

(*15*) He'd cast a quarter-sized circle of light and heat over the ants, and they'd begin to sweat, stagger, and give out little ant screams. He would narrow the circle, and they'd fall over with their tiny little tongues hanging out. Then he'd focus the light to a pinpoint and crisp them—snap, crackle, and pop. In retrospect, he feels bad about that practice, but then it was fun; if reincarnation exists, he suspects he already knows in which insect form he will return, and it's probably only fair.

Just a Red Ant in the Noonday Sun

(*16*) . . . public leadership positions today are more difficult than ever before because of inflated public expectations, an abundance of only semi-solvable problems, and the gaggle of single-issue constituencies infesting all levels of government. With the . . . evaluation as a guide, it may be instructive to examine other important historical figures to determine whether or not they could be effective as a nineties kind of school superintendent guy or gal—as well as having been successful, or at least well known, in their own special fields and in their own eras. Identified eccentricities, peccadilloes, or other shortcomings would, in most cases, equally lessen their effectiveness today as a school principal, or town manager, or any other appointed public leadership post; for elective positions, interestingly enough, aberrant behaviors almost seem to be prerequisites.

Could Socrates Survive the Superintendency?

(*17*) "We don't need to subsidize ski bums at the expense of our children's future economic success—and the kids have the presidents' birthdays off anyway."

School Calendars—II

(*18*) Often, at these high-level affairs, airplanes fly overhead, and Madeline Hunter or Lamar Alexander or Public Education's Savior du Jour parachutes down to tell superintendents more things they should do to teachers, or have teachers do for them.

A Vast Armada of Small Boats

(*19*) . . . believed that people are moved chiefly by desire for power and by fear of others and that "without common power to keep them in awe" (read superintendent of schools), human life is "solitary, poor, nasty, brutish, and short" [73]. If you think those views shocked his contemporaries, contemplate for a moment the reaction those words would generate today from avid proponents of total quality management.

Some Days You Might Think Tom Hobbes Had It Right

(*20*) This phenomenon can also be identified frequently among faculties, teachers' unions or associations, board of education candidates, and boards of education. Empirically, it appears emotionally easier and more satisfying to fight against causes perceived to be evil than to fight in support of those believed good. Nut cases remain eternally poised to leap out against something—anything—while rational people take forever to become excited enough to involve themselves in the fray.

The Best Lack All Conviction . . .

(*21*) Demonstrating the proper leadership ethics and behavior may be far more important than teaching the techniques of leadership, and even with the best of mentors, it's also true that those with whom we work often learn much of what they shouldn't do, as well as what they should, by observing our peculiar frailties and imperfections.

Rabbis—II

(22) *A grain of sand,*
the conscience of a shellfish,
though irritating to the oyster
is responsible for the pearl.
If men were like mollusks
and mollusks like men,
we'd have some damn small pearls
and a whole lot of oysters fooling around with other oysters' girls!
The Conscience of a Shellfish

(23) After spending a major part of your professional life in the precarious, challenging, frustrating, enervating, and sometimes exhilarating role of educational leadership shared by superintendents of schools and other school leaders, your "own ones," the teachers, principals, superintendents, and others with whom you have striven toward worthwhile causes, will mean a great deal to you. And opportunities to "talk awhile with your own ones" will always remain among life's great pleasures.
Educational Colleagues and Friends

(24) Superintendent and other administrative groups may present these awards at meetings, conferences, workshops, or major awards assemblies — similar to those award presentations for graduating high school seniors or the annual "Oscar" ceremonies in Hollywood. They or variations thereon are joys to give, and recipients will treasure them forever — or at least a few weeks.
May I Have the Envelope Please?

(25) In a perfect microcosm of administrative life, the seagulls also brought reality back into a previously idyllic day. One minute you're watching a gorgeous sunset or rocking along enjoying an unusually peaceful board of education meeting. The next thing you know, you're covered with seagull splatter — it's important to remember always the vagaries of public school leadership and how you earn your living.
"This Is to Remember . . ."

Staffing Plan

INTRODUCTION AND ANALYSIS

Adequate school district staffing is crucial to successful educational programs, and long-range staff planning is essential to providing and maintaining adequate staffing. It's surprising how few school districts have a single document that lays out precisely their current district staffing. All districts can go to their payroll records to count names and, through other methods, determine the number of current employees, but each district needs one official record of staffing. When school districts must cut certified staff through reduction in force procedures, there should be a baseline established from which the reduction takes place. Conversely, to justify added staff, there should be a staffing plan based upon individual school enrollments and specific district educational programs.

CERTIFIED STAFF

Certified staffing plans may be divided into elementary, secondary (which is further subdivided into middle school/junior high and senior high), special education, and administration. Other groupings may be preferred, for example, combining special education with the regular education levels of elementary, middle school/junior high, and high school, or as required by districts' particular grade groupings.

An example of a certified staff plan is given on succeeding pages; staff and student numbers are actual numbers from a school district moved forward to the years shown for the plan.

SUPPORT STAFF

Although support staff positions can be affected by declining student enrollments, the major effects of smaller student numbers are not felt until declining enrollment requires closing a school or schools because support staff positions are more facility- or function-related than enrollment-related.

503

An example of a support staff plan is given following the sample certified staff plan; positions are actual positions from a Connecticut shoreline school district moved forward to the current and sequential years shown for the plan. It's important to note that positions listed range from full-time, full year to part-time, part-year—or from eight hours each work day all year to two hours a day for 180 days. Additional detail is provided, on each support staff position, indicating hours and days worked. (Full-time is forty hours per week for fifty-two weeks (or 2,080 hours), including paid holidays and vacation days.)

CERTIFIED STAFF PLAN

Elementary

	History			Planned					
	92/93	93/94	94/95	95/96	96/97	97/98	98/99	99/00	00/01
Enrollments	1,184	1,179	1,198	1,221	1,325	1,362	1,362	1,365	1,425
(Percentage of Persistence Method)									
Classroom	61.0	59.0	61.0	60.0	61.5	63.0	64.0	65.0	66.0
Librarian	0.0	0.0	0.0	0.0	0.0	0.0	1.0	1.0	1.0
Computer	1.0	1.0	1.0	1.0	1.0	1.0	1.0	1.0	1.0
PE and Health	2.3	2.3	2.3	2.8	3.5	3.5	4.0	4.0	4.0
Music	4.8	4.8	5.0	5.0	5.0	5.0	5.0	5.0	5.0
Art	3.0	3.0	3.0	3.0	3.0	3.0	2.5	2.5	2.5
Reading	5.0	5.0	5.0	5.0	5.0	5.0	5.0	5.0	5.0
Remedial Rdng	0.0	0.0	0.0	0.0	0.0	0.0	1.0	0.0	0.0
Totals	78.1	76.1	78.3	77.8	80.0	81.5	83.5	83.5	84.5

Secondary—Middle School

	History			Planned					
	92/93	93/94	94/95	95/96	96/97	97/98	98/99	99/00	00/01
Enrollments	462	436	394	352	365	354	339	367	389
(Percentage of Persistence Method)									
PE and Health	2.4	2.4	2.4	2.2	2.0	2.0	2.0	2.0	2.0
Guidance	2.0	2.0	2.0	2.0	2.0	2.0	2.0	2.0	2.0
Library	1.0	1.0	1.0	1.0	1.0	1.0	1.0	1.0	1.0

Secondary—Middle School *(continued)*

	History			Planned					
	92/93	93/94	94/95	95/96	96/97	97/98	98/99	99/00	00/01
Enrollments	462	436	394	352	365	354	339	367	389
(Percentage of Persistence Method)									
English, etc.	9.6	9.6	9.0	8.0	8.0	7.0	7.0	7.0	7.0
Math	5.0	5.0	5.0	4.0	4.0	4.0	4.0	4.0	4.0
History and Social Studies	5.0	5.0	4.0	4.0	4.0	4.0	4.0	4.0	4.0
Home Economics	2.0	2.0	2.0	2.0	2.0	2.0	2.0	2.0	2.0
Industrial Arts	3.0	3.0	3.0	3.0	3.0	3.0	2.0	2.0	2.0
Business	0.0	0.0	0.0	0.0	0.0	0.0	0.0	0.0	0.0
Dist. Ed & CWE	0.0	0.0	0.0	0.0	0.0	0.0	0.0	0.0	0.0
Computer	1.0	1.0	1.0	1.0	1.0	1.0	1.0	1.0	1.0
Content Area etc.	0.0	0.0	0.0	0.0	0.0	0.0	0.0	0.0	0.0
Science	5.0	5.0	5.0	5.0	4.0	4.0	4.0	4.0	4.0
Foreign Language	2.4	2.4	2.0	2.0	2.0	2.0	2.0	2.0	2.0
Career Education	0.5	0.5	0.5	0.5	0.5	0.5	0.5	0.5	0.5
Music	2.2	2.2	2.2	2.2	2.2	2.2	2.2	2.2	2.2
Art	1.0	1.0	1.0	1.0	1.0	1.0	1.0	1.0	1.0
Reading	1.0	1.0	1.0	1.0	1.0	1.0	1.0	1.0	1.0
Total	43.1	43.1	41.1	38.9	37.7	36.7	35.7	35.7	35.7

Secondary—High School

	History			Planned					
	92/93	93/94	94/95	95/96	96/97	97/98	98/99	99/00	00/01
Enrollments	929	906	854	838	781	703	673	642	644
(Percentage of Persistence Method)									
PE and Health	7.3	7.3	7.3	7.0	5.5	5.5	5.0	5.0	5.0

Secondary–High School *(continued)*

	History			Planned					
	92/93	93/94	94/95	95/96	96/97	97/98	98/99	99/00	00/01
Enrollments	929	906	854	838	781	703	673	642	644
(Percentage of Persistence Method)									
Guidance	4.0	4.0	4.0	4.0	4.0	4.0	4.0	4.0	4.0
Library	1.0	1.0	1.0	1.0	1.0	1.0	1.0	1.5	1.5
English, etc.	13.0	13.0	12.0	12.0	10.0	10.0	9.5	9.5	9.0
Math	10.0	10.0	10.0	9.0	8.5	7.5	7.5	7.5	7.0
History and Social Studies	9.0	9.0	9.0	8.0	8.0	8.0	7.0	7.0	7.0
Home Economics	2.0	2.0	2.0	2.0	1.5	2.0	2.0	2.0	2.0
Industrial Arts	5.0	5.0	5.0	5.0	5.0	5.0	5.0	5.0	5.0
Business	5.0	5.0	4.0	4.0	4.0	4.0	4.0	4.0	4.0
Dist. Ed & CWE	2.0	2.0	2.0	2.0	1.0	1.0	1.0	1.0	1.0
Audio Visual	0.0	0.0	0.5	0.0	0.0	0.0	0.0	0.0	0.0
Content Area etc.	1.0	1.0	1.0	1.0	1.0	1.0	1.0	1.0	1.0
Science	9.0	9.0	9.0	9.0	8.0	8.0	7.5	7.5	7.0
Foreign Language	6.0	6.0	6.0	6.0	6.0	6.0	6.0	6.0	6.0
Career Education	0.5	0.5	0.5	0.5	0.5	0.5	0.5	0.5	0.5
Music	2.0	2.0	2.3	2.3	1.8	1.3	1.3	1.3	1.3
Art	2.0	2.0	2.0	2.0	2.0	2.0	2.0	2.0	2.0
Reading	1.0	1.0	1.0	1.0	1.0	1.0	1.0	1.0	1.0
Totals	79.8	79.8	78.6	75.8	68.8	67.8	65.3	65.8	64.3

Special Education

	History			Planned					
	92/93	93/94	94/95	95/96	96/97	97/98	98/99	99/00	00/01
ELEMENTARY									
Classroom	14.5	14.5	14.5	14.5	15.5	15.5	15.5	15.5	15.5
TAG	2.0	2.0	2.0	2.0	2.0	2.0	2.0	2.0	2.0
Psychologist	3.0	3.0	3.0	3.0	3.0	3.0	3.0	3.0	3.0

Special Education *(continued)*

	History			Planned					
	92/93	93/94	94/95	95/96	96/97	97/98	98/99	99/00	00/01
Speech	5.3	5.3	5.3	5.6	5.2	5.2	5.2	5.2	5.2
Social Worker	1.0	1.0	1.0	1.0	1.0	1.0	1.0	1.2	1.2
	25.8	25.8	25.8	26.1	26.7	26.7	26.7	26.9	26.9
MIDDLE SCHOOL									
Classroom	7.0	6.0	5.0	4.0	4.0	4.0	4.0	5.0	4.0
TAG	1.0	1.0	1.0	1.0	1.0	1.0	1.0	1.0	1.0
Psychologist	0.5	0.5	0.5	0.5	0.5	0.5	0.5	0.5	0.5
Speech	0.6	0.6	0.6	0.3	0.2	0.2	0.2	0.2	0.2
Social Worker	1.0	1.0	1.0	1.0	1.0	1.0	1.0	1.0	1.0
	10.1	9.1	8.1	6.8	6.7	6.7	6.7	7.7	6.7
HIGH SCHOOL									
Classroom	7.0	7.0	7.0	6.0	6.0	6.0	6.0	5.5	5.0
Psychologist	0.5	0.5	0.5	0.5	0.5	0.5	0.5	0.5	0.5
Speech	0.1	0.1	0.1	0.1	0.1	0.1	0.1	0.1	0.1
Social Worker	1.0	1.0	1.0	1.0	1.0	1.0	1.0	0.8	0.8
	8.6	8.6	8.6	7.6	7.6	7.6	7.6	6.9	6.4
Totals	44.5	43.5	42.5	40.5	41.0	41.0	41.0	41.5	40.0

Administration

	History			Planned					
	92/93	93/94	94/95	95/96	96/97	97/98	98/99	99/00	00/01
Central Office	3.0	3.0	3.0	3.0	3.0	3.0	3.0	3.0	3.0
High School	3.0	3.0	3.0	3.0	3.0	3.0	3.0	3.0	3.0
Junior High	2.0	2.0	2.0	2.0	2.0	2.0	2.0	2.0	2.0
Elementary	5.0	5.0	5.0	5.0	5.0	5.0	5.0	5.0	5.0
Special Education	2.0	2.0	2.0	2.0	2.0	2.0	2.0	2.0	2.0
Totals	15.0	15.0	15.0	15.0	15.0	15.0	15.0	15.0	15.0
Total Crtfd	260.5	257.5	255.5	248.0	242.5	242.0	240.5	241.5	239.5

Special Education *(continued)*

	History			Planned					
	92/93	93/94	94/95	95/96	96/97	97/98	98/99	99/00	00/01
	Enrollment Totals								
Elem	1,184	1,179	1,198	1,221	1,325	1,362	1,363	1,365	1,425
Mdl Schl/ Jr Hi	462	436	394	352	365	354	339	367	389
High Schl	929	906	854	838	781	703	673	642	644
Grand Totals	2,575	2,521	2,446	2,411	2,471	2,419	2,375	2,374	2,458

SUPPORT STAFF PLAN

Elementary

	History			Planned					
	92/93	93/94	94/95	95/96	96/97	97/98	98/99	99/00	00/01
Secretaries (two – 8 hours/199 days) (three – 7 hours/199 days)	5	5	5	5	5	5	5	5	5
Teacher Aides (three – 4 hours/188 days) (three – 5.5 hours/188 days) (one – 3.0 hours/188 days)	2	3	4	4	7	7	7	7	7
Playground/ Cafeteria Monitors (one – 1 hour/180 days) (five – 1.5 hours/180 days) (ten – 2 hours/180 days)	16	16	16	16	16	16	16	16	16
Library Assistants (6.33 hours/190 days)	5	5	5	5	5	5	5	5	5
Custodians (ten – full-time) (two – 4 hours/194 days)	12	12	12	12	12	12	12	12	12
Cafeteria Employees (two – 4 hours/191 days) (one – 4.5 hours/191 days)	10	10	10	10	10	10	10	10	10

Elementary *(continued)*

	History			Planned					
	92/93	93/94	94/95	95/96	96/97	97/98	98/99	99/00	00/01
Cafeteria *(continued)*									
(one—5 hours/191 days)									
(one—5.5 hours/191 days)									
(five—6 hours/191 days)									
Crossing									
Guards	7	7	7	7	8	8	8	8	8
(three—1 hour/180 days)									
(five—2 hours/180 days)									
Totals	57	58	59	59	63	63	63	63	63

Secondary—Middle School

	History			Planned					
	92/93	93/94	94/95	95/96	96/97	97/98	98/99	99/00	00/01
Secretaries	4	4	4	4	4	4	4	4	4
(one—full-time)									
(one—7.5 hours/220 days)									
(two—7.0 hours/199 days)									
Playground/									
Cafeteria									
Monitors	2	2	2	2	2	2	2	2	2
(2 hours/180 days)									
Library									
Assistants	1	1	2	2	2	2	2	2	2
(7 hours/199 days)									
(5 hours/189 days)									
Teacher									
Aides	1	1	0	0	0	0	0	0	0
Custodians	5	5	5	5	5	5	5	5	5
(five—full-time)									
Matron	1	1	1	1	1	1	1	1	1
(5 hours/180 days)									
Crossing									
Guard	1	1	1	1	1	1	1	1	1
(2 hours/180 days)									
Security									
Guard	0	0	1	1	1	1	1	1	1
(2 hours/180 days)									

Secondary – Middle School *(continued)*

	History			Planned					
	92/93	93/94	94/95	95/96	96/97	97/98	98/99	99/00	00/01
Cafeteria									
Employees (two – 6 hours/191 days) (one – 5 hours/191 days)	4	4	3	3	3	3	3	3	3
Totals	19	19	19	19	19	19	19	19	19

Secondary – High School

	History			Planned					
	92/93	93/94	94/95	95/96	96/97	97/98	98/99	99/00	00/01
Secretaries (two – full-time) (three – 8 hours/199 days) (one – 6 hours/189 days)	6	6	6	6	6	6	6	6	6
Teacher Aides (one – 6 hours/188 days) (one – 6.5 hours/188 days)	0	2	2	2	2	2	2	2	2
Playground/ Cafeteria Monitors	0	0	0	0	0	0	0	0	0
Library Assistants (one – 7 hours/199 days) (one – 6.5 hours/189 days)	2	2	2	2	2	2	1	2	2
Custodians (twelve – full-time)	13	11	13	13	13	12	12	12	12
Matrons (one – 6 hours/180 days) (one – 4.5 hours/180 days)	2	2	2	2	2	2	2	2	2
Crossing Guards (1.5 hours/180 days)	2	2	2	2	2	2	2	2	2
Security Guard (5.75 hours/180 days)	1	1	1	1	1	1	1	1	1

Secondary—High School *(continued)*

	History			Planned					
	92/93	93/94	94/95	95/96	96/97	97/98	98/99	99/00	00/01
Cafeteria									
Employees	9	9	9	8	8	8	8	8	8
(three—4 hours/191 days) (one—5 hours/191 days)									
(two—6 hours/191 days)									
(two—7 hours/191 days)									
Totals	35	35	37	36	36	35	34	35	35
Totals Mdl Sch/Jr Hi Support									
Staff	19	19	19	19	19	19	19	19	19
Total Secondary									
Staffing	54	54	56	55	55	54	53	54	54

Special Education

	History			Planned					
	92/93	93/94	94/95	95/96	96/97	97/98	98/99	99/00	00/01
Secretaries	3	3	3	3	3	3	3	3	3
(one—8 hours/254 days)									
(one—8 hours/210 days)									
(one—7 hours/210 days)									
Clerk	1	1	1	1	1	1	1	1	1
(6 hours/120 days)									
Teacher									
Aides	24	22	20	20	20	20	20	20	20
(one—4 hours/188 days)									
(eight—5.5 hours/188 days)									
(eight—6 hours/188 days)									
(two—6.5 hours/188 days)									
(one—6.67 hours/188 days)									
R.I.S.E. Registered									
Nurse	0	0	0	0	1	1	1	1	1
(7 hours/211 days)									
R.I.S.E.									
Licensed									
Practical									

Special Education *(continued)*

	History			Planned					
	92/93	93/94	94/95	95/96	96/97	97/98	98/99	99/00	00/01
R.I.S.E. *(continued)*									
Nurse	0	0	0	0	1	1	1	1	1
(7 hours/211 days)									
Dental									
Hygienist	1	1	1	1	1	1	1	1	1
(6 hours/181 days)									
Occupational									
Therapist	1	1	1	1	1	1	1	1	1
(6.5 hours/198 days)									
Physical									
Therapist	1	1	1	1	1	1	1	1	1
(7.5 hours/206 days)									
Bus Driver	1	1	0	0	0	0	0	0	0
(6.5 hours/180 days)									
Totals	32	30	27	27	29	29	29	29	29

Administration – Central Office

	History			Planned					
	92/93	93/94	94/95	95/96	96/97	97/98	98/99	99/00	00/01
Administrative Assistant to the Super-intendent (full-time)	1	1	1	1	1	1	1	1	1
Accounts Supervisor/Computer Systems Manager (full-time)	1	1	1	1	1	1	1	1	1
Payroll & Benefits Supervisor (full-time)	1	1	1	1	1	1	1	1	1
Director of Buildings and Grounds (full-time)	1	1	1	1	1	1	1	1	1
Food Services Director (5.5 hours/214 days)	1	1	1	1	1	1	1	1	1
Secretaries	6	7	7	7	7	7	7	7	7
Executive Sec – Director of Inst and Pers Services									
Executive Sec – Business Mngr									

(continued)

Administration – Central Office (*continued*)

	History			Planned					
	92/93	93/94	94/95	95/96	96/97	97/98	98/99	99/00	00/01
Administrative Secretary I– Dir Bldgs & Grnds	1	1	1	1	1	1	1	1	1
Word Processor									
Commun Assist (full-time)									
Business Office Assistant (8 hours/244 days)	1	1	1	1	1	1	1	1	1
Payroll Secretary (6 hours/254 days)	1	1	1	1	1	1	1	1	1
Enumerator									
Substitute Caller (4 hours/180 days)	1	1	1	1	1	1	1	1	1
Custodian (full-time)	1	1	1	1	1	1	1	1	1
Totals	15	16	16	16	16	16	16	16	16

Districtwide Administration

	History				Planned				
	92/93	93/94	94/95	95/96	96/97	97/98	98/99	99/00	00/01
Maintenance (full-time)	10	12	10	10	10	10	10	10	10
Media Specialist (full-time)	0	0	0	0	1	1	1	1	1
Messenger (full-time)	1	1	1	1	1	1	1	1	1
Totals	11	13	11	11	12	12	12	12	12
Total Admin Support Staff	26	29	27	27	28	28	28	28	28
Total Elem Support Staff	57	58	59	59	63	63	63	63	63
Total Secon Support Staff	54	54	56	55	55	54	53	54	54
Total Sp Ed Support Staff	32	30	27	27	29	29	29	29	29
Grand Totals	169	171	169	168	175	174	173	174	174

515

REFERENCES

1. Churchill, W. S. L., October 1, 1939. "The First Month of War," Radio Broadcast.

2. Colyar, A. S., 1904. *Life and Times of Andrew Jackson.* Nashville, TN: Press of Marshall & Bruce Co.

3. Crockett, D., 1834. *A Narrative of the Life of David Crockett, of the State of Tennessee.* Philadelphia, PA: E. L. Carey and A. Hart.

4. Pascal, B., 1910 (First Published 1670). *Blaise Pascal—Thoughts.* Section II, No. 162, Translated by W. F. Trotter, New York, NY: P. F. Collier & Son Company.

5. Aristotle, 384–322 B.C. *The Nichomachean Ethics* (II, ix, 4).

6. Brathwaite, R., 1640. *Art Asleep, Husband?* London, England: R. Bishop.

7. Herbert, G., 1640. *Jacula Prudentum* (Book of Proverbial Sayings). Number 711.

8. Ovid, c. A.D. 8. *The Metamorphoses.* Book II, 137, Translated by A. E. Watts.

9. Theognis, c. 500 B.C. *The Elegies of Theognis.*

10. Horace, c. 23–13 B.C. *Odes.* Book II, Ode X, "The Golden Mean," Line 5, Translated by C. E. Bennett.

11. Rickover, H. G., 1981. Presentation before the Columbia University School of Engineering and Applied Science.

12. Carlyle, T., 1900. *History of Friedrich II of Prussia, Called Frederick the Great.* Book IV, Chapter 3, New York, NY: C. Scribner's Sons.

13. Orwell, G. (Eric Blair), 1946. *Animal Farm.* New York, NY: Harcourt, Brace and World Inc.

14. Yeats, W. B. 1963 (First Published 1903). "The Second Coming," *Immortal Poems of the English Language,* Edited by Oscar Williams, New York, NY: Washington Square Press.

15. Emerson, R. W., 1909 (First Published 1841). "Self-Reliance," *Essays and English Traits,* New York, NY: P. F. Collier & Son Company.

16. Milton, J. 1645. "Il Penseroso," Line 32.

17. Shakespeare, W., 1643. *Twelfth Night.* Act II, sc. v, 1, 158.

18. Henly, L. and Bell, K., "Is It Still Over," Performed by Randy Travis on Album, *Old Eight × Ten.* 1988. Burbank, CA: Warner Brothers Records.

19. Percy, W., 1966. *The Last Gentleman.* New York, NY: Farrar, Straus, and Giroux.

20. Job 16:3, *The Holy Bible.* New Revised Standard Version. Nashville, TN: Thomas Nelson Publishers.

21. Kipling, R., "If," *The Home Book of Verse,* Ninth Edition, Volume II, Selected and Arranged by Burton Egbert Stevenson, New York, NY: Holt, Rinehart and Winston.

22. Macaulay, T. B. 1959. *History of England.* Volume 1, Chapter 2, London: Dent.

517

23. Tennyson, A. L. 1900. "Morte D'Arthur," Line 172.

24. von Schiller, J. C. F., 1801. *Die Jungfrau von Orleans or The Maid of Orleans*. III, vi, Translated by Anna Swanwick, London, England: G. Bell and Sons.

25. Shakespeare, W., 1603. *Macbeth*. Act V, scene v.

26. Andersen, H. C., 1959. *The Emperor's New Clothes*. New York, NY: Harcourt, Brace, and World.

27. Lovelace, R., 1649. "To Lucasta on Going to the Wars," Stanza I.

28. 2 Corinthians 12:7, *The Holy Bible*. New Revised Standard Version, Nashville, TN: Thomas Nelson Publishers.

29. Farmer, P., 1872. *The Serpent's Teeth: The Story of Cadmus*. New York, NY: Harcourt, Brace, Jovanovich.

30. Alcuin of York, 797. "Letter to Charlemagne."

31. Frost, R., 1963 (First Published 1930). "The Road Not Taken," *Immortal Poems of the English Language,* Edited by Oscar Williams, New York, NY: Washington Square Press.

32. Connecticut General Statutes. January 1, 1993. Section 17a-101.

33. Job 16:2, *The Holy Bible*. New Revised Standard Version, Nashville, TN: Thomas Nelson Publishers.

34. Milton, J., 1667. *Paradise Lost*. Book II, I. 185.

35. Shakespeare, W., 1598. *King Henry the Fourth*. Part One, Act III, sc. i, I 140.

36. Burns, R., 1947 (First Published 1786). "To a Louse," *Seven Centuries of Verse,* Edited by A. J. M. Smith, New York, NY: Charles Scribner's Sons.

37. Paley, W., 1785. "Philosophical Treatise," *Principles of Moral and Political Philosophy,* Volume I, Book V, Chapter 9.

38. Tennyson, A. L., 1859. *Idylls of the King*. Line 1082.

39. Dickens, C., 1907 (First Published 1849). *David Copperfield*. New York, NY: Dodd, Mead & Co.

40. Merideth, G., 1947 (First Published 1883). "Lucifer in Starlight," Line 6. *Seven Centuries of Verse,* Edited by A. J. M. Smith, New York, NY: Charles Scribner's Sons.

41. Jonson, B., 1598. *Every Man in His Humor*. Act II, sc. i, 1. 151.

42. Proverbs 11:14, *The Holy Bible*. New Revised Standard Version, Nashville, TN: Thomas Nelson Publishers. "Where there is no guidance a nation falls, but in an abundance of counselors there is safety."

43. Psalm 139:14, *The Holy Bible*. New Revised Standard Version, Nashville, TN: Thomas Nelson Publishers.

44. Mitchell, J., 1943. *McSorley's Wonderful Saloon*. New York, NY: Duell, Sloan, and Pearce.

45. Gilbert, W. S., 1878. *H.M.S. Pinafore*. Act I.

46. Connecticut General Statutes. January 1, 1993, Sec. 10-220, paragraph (a).

47. Connecticut General Statutes. January 1, 1993. Sec. 10-221, paragraph (a).

48. Wouk, H., 1962. *Youngblood Hawke*. Garden City, NY: Doubleday and Company, Inc.

49. Lewis, C. S., 1962. *The Screwtape Letters and Screwtape Proposes a Toast*. New York, NY: Macmillan.

50. Ross, E. A., 1907. *Sin and Society: An Analysis of Latter Day Iniquity*. Boston, MA: Houghton, Mifflin.

51. News Story, 1968. "Death under Tractor Cancels Retirement Plans of Man, 64," Utica, NY: The Utica Press.

52. National Commission on Excellence in Education, 1983. *A Nation at Risk: The Imperative for Educational Reform.* A Report to the Nation and the Secretary of Education, United States Department of Education. Washington, D.C.: United States Government Printing Office.

53. Goodman, E., April 2, 1984. Hartford, CT: *The Hartford Courant.*

54. Carroll, L., 1983. (First published 1871). *Lewis Carroll's Through the Looking Glass.* Chapter 5, Berkeley, CA: The University of California Press.

55. Shakespeare, W., 1600. *Much Ado about Nothing.* Act V, sc. iii, 1. 3.

56. Swift, J., 1711. *Thoughts of Various Subjects Moral and Diverting* (Collection of Epigrams). London, England: Barton & Harvey.

57. Read, T. B., 1867. *Poetical Works of Thomas Buchanan Read* (Complete in 3 volumes). "What a Word May Do," Stanza I. Philadelphia, PA: J. B. Lippincott.

58. Horace. c. 23–13 B.C. *Odes.* Book I, Ode XI, "Enjoy the Passing Hour," Last Line, Translated by C. E. Bennett.

59. Moore, J., c. 1970. "John Moore's Place – Justice Was Quick Back in Judge Frisby's Day," in Houston, TX: *The Houston Post.*

60. Shakespeare, W., 1600. *Henry V.* Act III, sc. i, 1. 1.

61. Ideas on managing conflict are from a series of seminars for superintendents of schools and state education department bureau chiefs arranged and sponsored by Connecticut's Commissioner of Education Mark Shedd in the late seventies. Crosby Deaton, managing partner of the Athyn Group of Philadelphia, led discussions on conflict management with assistance from Rod Napier – also from the Athyn Group who was the group leader for other topics.

62. Churchill, W. S. L., 1940. "First Speech to the House of Commons."

63. Addison, J., 1711. *The Spectator.* Volume I, number 122.

64. Connecticut General Statutes. January 1, 1993. Sec. 10-153.

65. Connecticut General Statutes. January 1, 1993. Sec. 10-153a.

66. Connecticut General Statutes. January 1, 1993. Sec. 10-153b.

67. Connecticut General Statutes. January 1, 1993. Sec. 10-153d.

68. Connecticut General Statutes. January 1, 1993. Sec. 10-153e.

69. Connecticut General Statutes. January 1, 1993. Sec. 10-153f.

70. Connecticut General Statutes. January 1, 1993. Sec. 10-155f.

71. Gauss, J., January 1962. "Evaluation of Socrates as a Teacher," in *Phi Delta Kappan,* 43:Cover IV.

72. Milton, J., 1655. "On His Blindness."

73. Hobbes, T., 1910. *French and English Philosophers.* Edited by Charles W. Eliot LL.D., New York, NY: P. F. Collier and Son Co.

74. Hruska, J., 1990. Speech at the October Conference for the Exchange of Educational Opinion. North Conway, New Hampshire.

75. Morrison, V., 1945. *Irish Heartbeat.* Recorded 1987. Dublin, Ireland: Windmill Lane Studios.

CONTRACT ADMINISTRATION

AFTER ATTENDING PUBLIC schools in Houston, Texas, David L. Cattanach received a Bachelor of Science Degree in 1953 from the University of Houston and began four years as a commissioned officer in the U.S. Navy, where he served aboard minesweepers and submarines.

After leaving regular naval service, he began his teaching career, from 1957–1960, in Houston, Texas, teaching grades four, five, and Spanish at Oak Forest School. He remained an active naval reserve officer and, for six consecutive summers, directed the Reserve Training Division of the U.S. Naval Submarine School in Groton, Connecticut. After his third tour at the base, he and his family moved to Connecticut where, from 1960–1963, he taught grades four, five, six, physical education, and Spanish in Chester, Connecticut. From 1963–1966, he was principal of the elementary and middle school in Bozrah, Connecticut.

His graduate study began at the University of Houston and was continued at the University of Hartford, where in June 1963, he received a Master's in Education. That fall, he began a Ph.D. program at the University of Connecticut in Storrs. During 1966–1967, he served as a research assistant at the university while fulfilling doctoral residency requirements and, in June 1967, was awarded a Ph.D. in Educational Administration.

Upon receiving his doctorate, he became superintendent of schools in Westmoreland, New York, remaining in that post from 1967–1972. Dr. Cattanach's next superintendency was in Regional District #8 Hebron, Andover, Marlborough, Connecticut from 1972–1983. In 1983, he was elected superintendent of schools in Waterford, Connecticut, where he served until his retirement in 1992 after twenty-five years as a superintendent of schools in five communities.

As a superintendent of schools, he was active with area superintendents' organizations; the Connecticut Association of Public School

527

Superintendents, serving as its president in 1982–1983; and the American Association of School Administrators.

Dr. Cattanach has taught graduate courses at the University of Connecticut, Connecticut College, Sacred Heart University, Eastern Connecticut State University, and Southern Connecticut State University. He began and directed a new program at Southern Connecticut State University preparing experienced educators to be school superintendents. In addition to his continued teaching at Connecticut College and Sacred Heart University, he also has been a student teacher supervisor at Sacred Heart.

Since retirement, he has been an active consultant in a dozen Connecticut school districts for superintendent searches, board of education policy development and revision, and with a variety of other school district topics and issues such as interdistrict cooperation, facilities studies, and administrative reorganizations.

From August 1992 to January 1993, he served as interim principal at Lyme Consolidated School in Lyme, Connecticut. Thirty years previously, in his initial administrative application in 1963, he had applied unsuccessfully to be that school's principal. It is his contention that acceptance of the interim principalship in Lyme was to be able to say that he finally got the job he originally wanted—even if thirty years late and even if it's a step over the line from stubborn to obsessive.

Recently, he served as interim superintendent of schools of Canterbury, Connecticut, while conducting the search for his replacement there, and in Eastford, Connecticut.